PLAINS INDIAN BUFFALO CULTURES

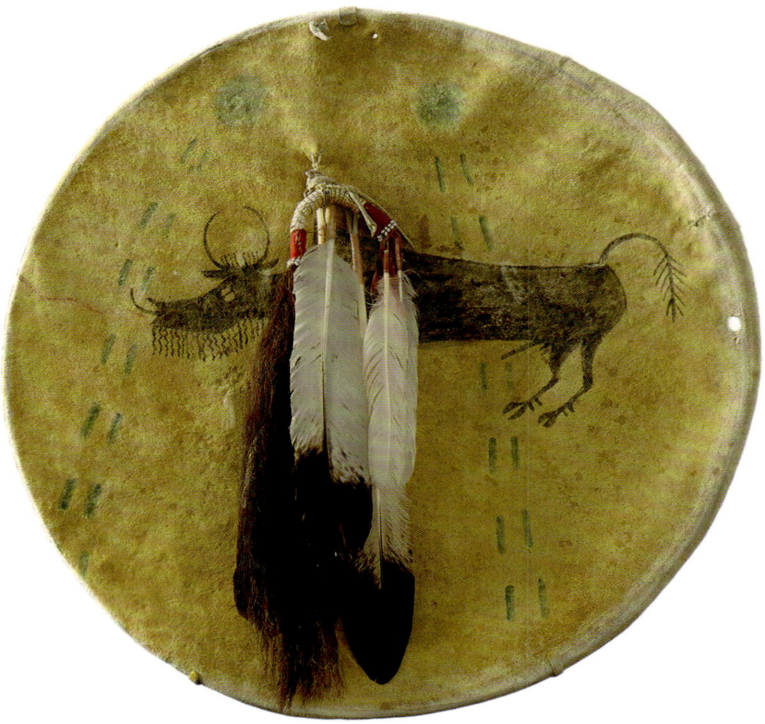

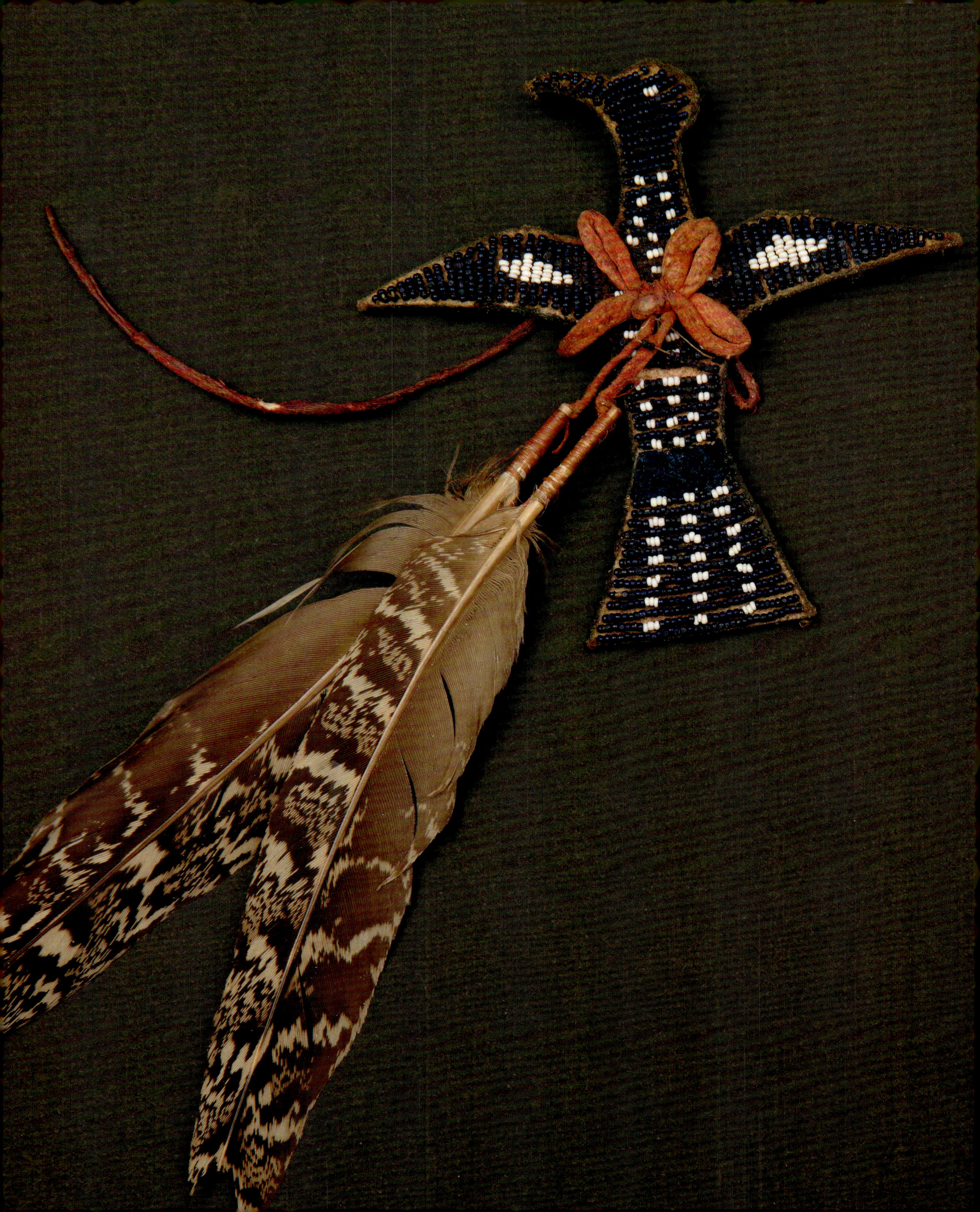

Plains Indian Buffalo Cultures

ART FROM THE PAUL DYCK COLLECTION

EMMA I. HANSEN

Foreword by ARTHUR AMIOTTE

UNIVERSITY OF OKLAHOMA PRESS : NORMAN

In cooperation with the
BUFFALO BILL CENTER OF THE WEST, CODY, WYOMING

Library of Congress Cataloging-in-Publication Data
Names: Hansen, Emma I., author. | Amiotte, Arthur, writer of foreword.
Title: Plains Indian buffalo cultures : art from the Paul Dyck collection / Emma I. Hansen ; foreword by Arthur Amiotte.
Description: Norman : University of Oklahoma Press, 2018. | Includes bibliographical references and index.
Identifiers: LCCN 2017037668| ISBN 978-0-8061-6011-5 (hardcover : alk. paper) | ISBN 978-0-8061-6012-2 (pbk. : alk. paper)
Subjects: LCSH: Indian art—Great Plains—Catalogs. | Dyck, Paul, 1917–2006—Art collections—Catalogs. | Art—Private collections—Wyoming—Cody—Catalogs. | Dyck, Paul, 1917–2006—Ethnological collections—Catalogs. | Indians of North America—Material culture—Great Plains—Catalogs. | Buffalo Bill Center of the West—Catalogs.
Classification: LCC E78.G73 H347 2018 | DDC 978.004/97—dc23
LC record available at https://lccn.loc.gov/2017037668

The paper in this book meets the guidelines for permanence and durability of the Committee on Production Guidelines for Book Longevity of the Council on Library Resources, Inc. ∞

1 2 3 4 5 6 7 8 9 10

The following works appear uncaptioned on the pages noted:

PAGE i:
Shield and cover
Apsáalooke (Crow), Northern Plains, ca. 1850
Plains Indian Museum, NA.108.152.1-.2
(See figure 1.17, page 31)

PAGE ii:
Charm
Apsáalooke (Crow), Northern Plains, ca. 1890
Tanned hide, glass beads, pigments, sage grouse feathers; 8½ x 4 inches
Plains Indian Museum, NA.502.345

This charm carries with it the power of the thunderbird that has the ability to create thunder and lightning.

PAGE vi:
Charm
Northern Plains, ca. 1870
Rawhide, eagle feathers, tanned hide, pigments; 16 × 8½ inches
Plains Indian Museum, NA.502.344

PAGE 1:
Shield cover
Kaigwa (Kiowa), Southern Plains, ca. 1890
Plains Indian Museum, NA.108.154
(See figure 2.22, page 52)

Dedicated to the Native artists and culture bearers
of the North American Great Plains

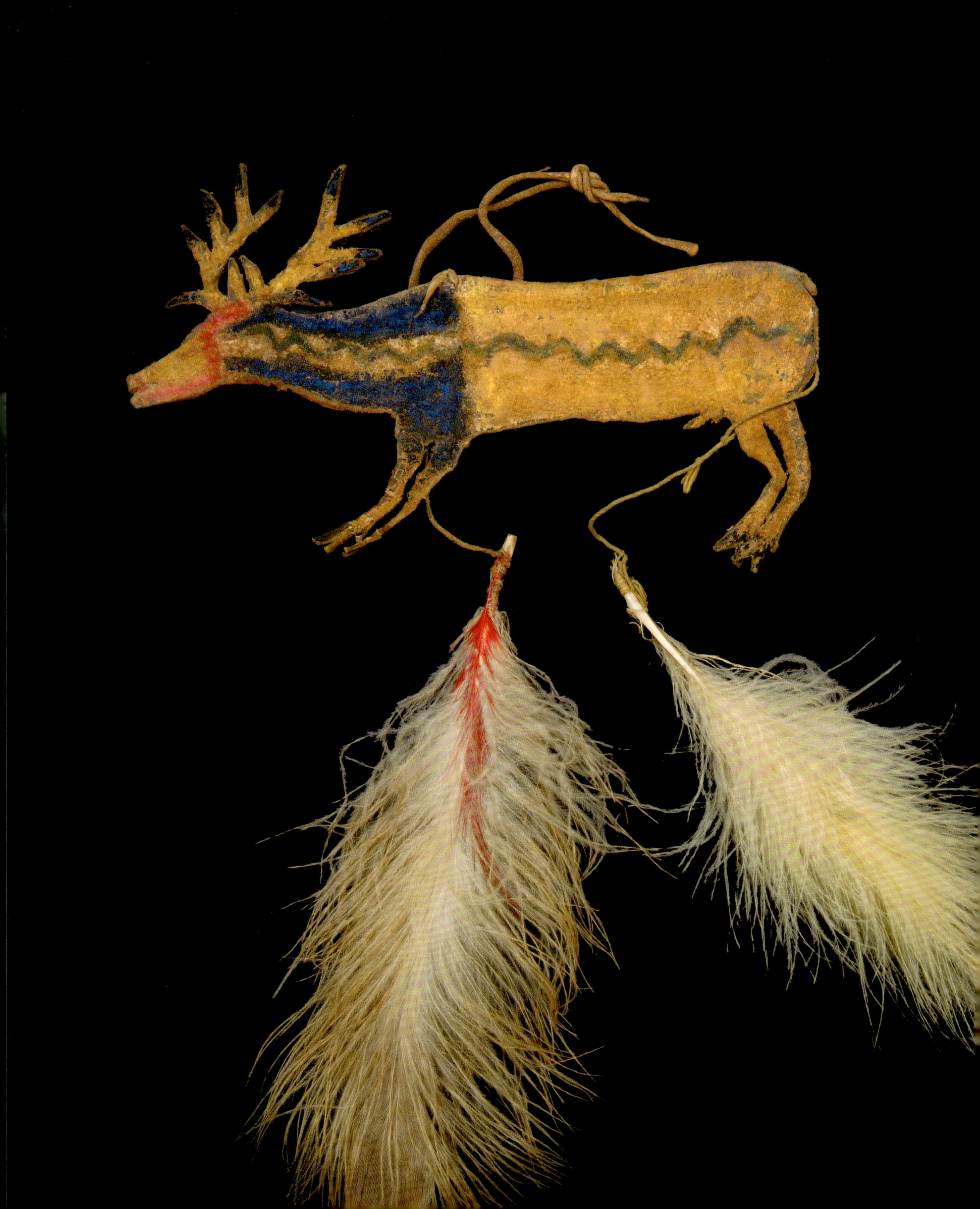

CONTENTS

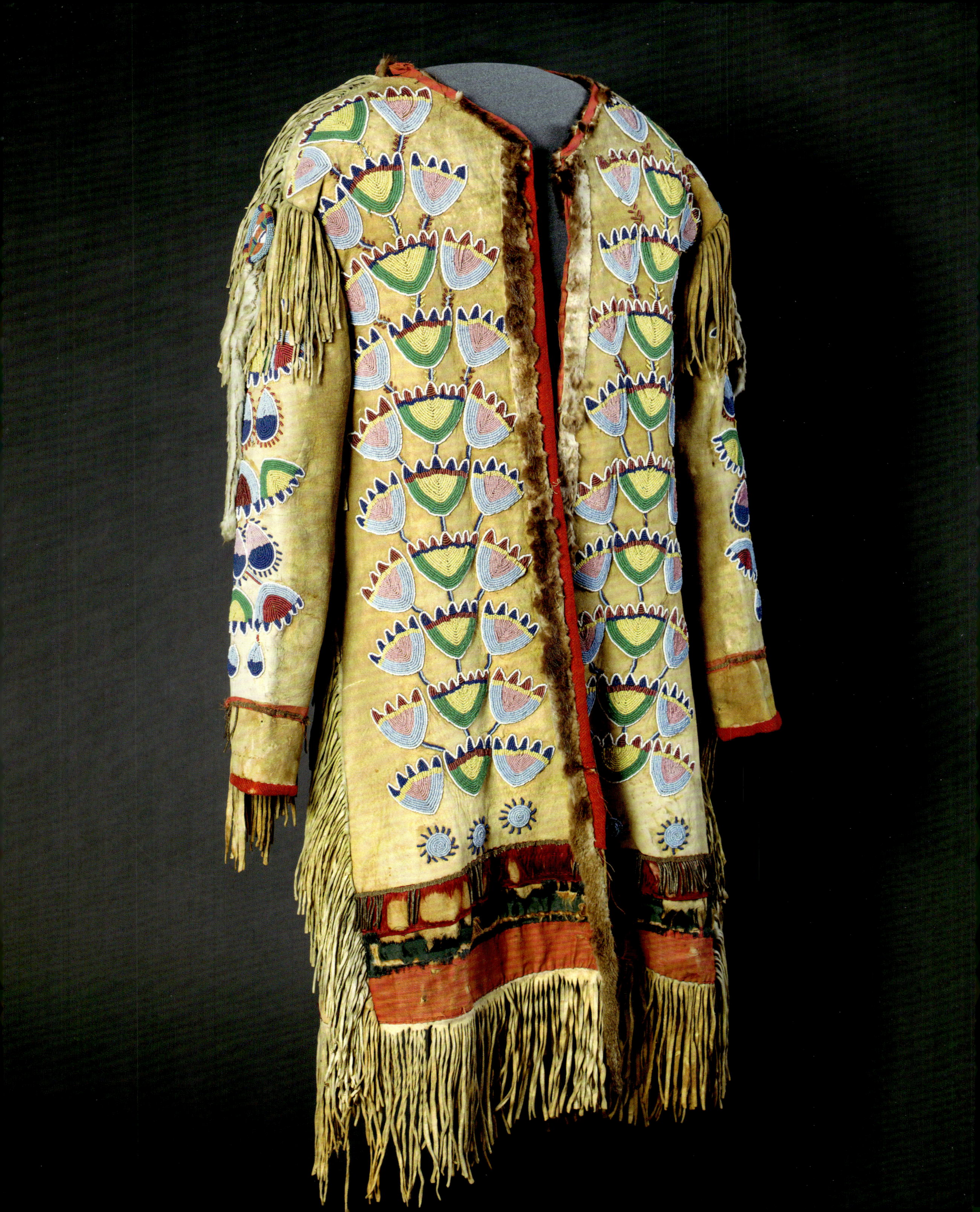

FOREWORD
Paul Dyck as Collector

ARTHUR AMIOTTE

The Paul Dyck Collection is a prime and comprehensive body of culturally iconic forms from a period in Northern Plains history—from 1800 to 1870—thought of as the apex of classical Plains Indian cultures. It is exhibited and stored in its new home since September 21, 2007, at the Plains Indian Museum of the Buffalo Bill Center of the West in Cody, Wyoming. As avid museum visitors and those with a passion for history and art can attest, an actual museum viewing experience sometimes is just not enough, even with printed panel texts and sophisticated audio guides. One may think of a museum installation as the body or face of a collection. The didactics and printed catalogue discourse are thus its voice. Together they enrich and help fulfill the mission of a museum to educate, enlighten, and inspire.

The significance of this book as a companion to the Paul Dyck Collection is manifold. Its components present a wealth of visual and narrative messages to be quietly and individually pondered by readers at their convenience after or before viewing the actual collection. For some, this book may be inspiration and impetus to want the actual museum experience. For others, it will serve as research as they continue their journey toward understanding the history and art of the indigenous tribal people of this country.

The collection speaks to us of the appreciative and intellectual character of the artist-collector Paul Dyck (1917–2006). The collection came about during his lifetime because Dyck sincerely believed in the value of the historical, cultural, and aesthetic messages encrypted within these art objects as expressed through media, composition, and creative processes. Early in his life, his mission to collect arose from fascination with the lives and cultures of Plains Indians. He was further encouraged by his father, Anton Cifka, who began the collection. His father, and later Dyck himself, visited descendants who still owned these treasured heirlooms in their homes on reservations. Several generations of Native Americans still practiced traditional techniques and styles of pre-reservation art forms. Paul Dyck sought personal contact with these descendants of historical heroes and heroines on numerous reservations of the Great Plains during the first half of the twentieth century. He also sought out and maintained associations with other non-Indian collectors, dealers, and auction houses. From all these sources, he garnered the treasures featured in this exhibition.

Dyck preferred objects made during the earlier decades of the nineteenth century (1800–1850), but he augmented these with items created through the 1870s, the beginning of the reservation period, and thereafter throughout the twentieth century. When a particular,

Coat
Dakota (Eastern Sioux), ca. 1850
Tanned hide, glass beads, metal chain, silk ribbon, silk cloth, cotton cloth, wool cloth, tanned otter hide, brass buttons; 43 × 24 inches
Plains Indian Museum, NA.202.1476

irresistible older item became available on the market, he would trade objects. Thus, his collection was always evolving.

Paul Dyck, in the tradition of his own Dutch ancestors, was also a gifted fine artist in oil painting. He chose as the subjects of his expressive paintings Native-made objects inspired by intrinsic aesthetic qualities of the historic objects themselves. With highly plastic and masterful brush strokes, he captured the essence of the texture, chroma, and light of the Native materials. Because of his passion for collecting, and the results of this devotion, we are able to view and contemplate these masterpieces that so captivated Paul Dyck.

THE PAUL DYCK COLLECTION: HISTORICAL PERSPECTIVES

The main message of this collection is the worldview of the Plains Indian cultures as represented by the art itself. These indigenous masterpieces made and used by the ancestors speak to us as predecessors of contemporary forms still made and used during tribal ceremonies and celebrations. The historical pieces reveal to us how a people processed the vegetal, animal, and mineral resources of the Great Plains to meet their survival needs. These artisans, however, went beyond mere function and utility and expressed their spiritual and aesthetic sensibilities by meticulously embellishing their garments, household goods, and implements; riding gear; and the interiors and exteriors of their lodges and tipis. Special attention was given to those implements, clothing, and accessories used and worn during rituals, ceremonies, and celebrations.

Even under the stress of surviving the life-threatening activities of the hunt and intertribal rivalry, these remarkable people simultaneously recognized the need for adornment. Their worldview regarded spiritual power as a necessity that could be gained by adorning one's body, implements, and materials with cosmic, animal, and visionary images and symbols. In the Native worldview, this expression did not represent a dichotomy but rather a synthesis declaring the interrelationship of essential powers in a world that demanded extraordinary endurance. When confronted with new solutions, techniques, and technologies, the people adapted that which proved to be useful. Their identity as tribal beings depended on their tenacity and ability to survive and to protect themselves and their relatives.

THE EFFECT OF TRADE

Westward expansion of Euro-Americans introduced new trade items, some of which proved to be beneficial and were welcomed by indigenous people; other items proved to be destructive of Native lives and cultures. Traders introduced the horse, metal tools, knives, axes, sewing awls, kettles, firearms, and lead for making shot. The Natives embraced these new elements and technologies that enhanced their ability to survive. Goods of cloth, blankets, bright manufactured dyes and pigments, metal buttons, decorative metal accessories, glass beads, and objects made of shell and bone explicitly for the Indian trade were equally welcomed.

Women quickly adapted to metal awls and needles in place of bone awls, as well as cotton and linen thread alongside animal sinew. While some manufactured clothes were available through trade, they were not readily adapted as acceptable tribal dress. Instead, the women disassembled the clothes and used them as patterns for making garments of native tanned leather. Odd pieces of cloth also served as decorative elements in designs on traditional clothing. Ever creative in their aesthetic endeavors, the makers created a synthesis of new and indigenous materials. The bright dyes and pigments intensified the hues of painted surfaces and dyed porcupine quills. Women combined the initially rare seed beads with the older media of newly dyed brilliant porcupine quillwork embroidery. Different sizes and shapes of larger glass and bone beads were combined to form new embellishment for headdresses, garments, and status objects such as pectorals, necklaces, and bandoliers for both men and women. Many pieces in the Dyck collection are examples of this early creative melding of media.

As contact with non-Indians increased through the latter years of the nineteenth century so did the availability of trade goods. More varieties of glass seed beads in smaller sizes and qualities resulted in a proliferation of beaded surfaces on clothing, household storage bags, horse gear, and items previously undecorated. As Euro-Americans began to dominate the West, with the simultaneous decimation of the vast bison herds and other game animals, trade blankets and cloth replaced bison robes as well as items previously made of tanned deer, elk, and antelope hides. Women, though, continued to decorate these trade items with beads and quillwork in appropriate tribal styles.

THE WARRIOR SOCIETIES

As increasing numbers of non-Indians populated the West, the wild game of the Great Plains diminished. Reduction of the traditional hunting territories led to greater intertribal competition and warfare among Native tribes. Later, as the tribes were pushed farther west, they retaliated against the Euro-American invaders. The Plains Indian warrior societies became formalized in response to non-Indian settlements and their protection by the U.S. military. Fraternities of warriors within particular tribes were integral to the social, political, and governance structures. As organizers, the warrior societies were responsible for maintaining a rotating schedule of guarding, policing, and enforcing order in a tribal camp. They also organized hunts and military actions against enemies.

Warriors were honored on public occasions for their distinction in combat. Each warrior society owned specially embellished clothing, regalia, weapons, and implements that symbolically represented esoteric vows and obligations of membership. When worn on public occasions of ceremony and celebration, these accoutrements honored the accomplishments not only of the individual but also of the warrior society's qualities because of the man's membership in that society. The warrior's exploits, along with vision-inspired protective images, were narratives illustrated by drawings and paintings in semirealistic style. According to tradition, only men created in this style and paint-media art form. The men applied painted images to the surfaces of shields, robes, male attire, tipi liners, and exterior tipi surfaces. Later on, the men painted on cotton muslin cloth and paper ledger books obtained from military and trading posts.

At the same time, women continued to make porcupine quill and bead embroidery. Unlike the male painting of images and events, women painted geometric designs on rawhide and soft tanned leather and only approached imagery of life-forms as semiabstractions in beads and quills.

Men and women collaborated by combining their traditionally defined techniques on warrior society paraphernalia, personal dress of both men and women, and household items. This collaboration of artistic expression was a public declaration not only of warrior achievement but also of the industriousness, craftsmanship, and artistic accomplishment of women. Many of the objects in the Paul Dyck Collection are examples of the female traditions of expertly tanned leather, porcupine quillwork, and beadwork. We are compelled to pay homage to Native women for their artistic accomplishments in the promulgation of historical Plains tribal art.

By 1881, the free-roaming days of bison hunting had come to an end. However, it did not mean the end of Plains tribal culture, their worldview, or their arts. The early reservation period of the northern plains (1870–1889) was a time of desperation and false starts on the path to adjustment. It was a time of ending and a time of beginning. Plains tribes had to make radical changes in order to survive. Despite the hardships and pressures to abandon their lifeways and beliefs, these tribes called forth their intrinsic strengths of resilience, courage, and creativity and proceeded to adapt. Tribal artistic traditions continued through the late nineteenth, twentieth, and into the twenty-first centuries. The Plains Indian art from the Paul Dyck Collection presents us with fine examples of this dynamic collaboration of artistic endeavors by tribal men and women. Their art exemplifies a culture in which aesthetic principles were as important as utilitarian craftsmanship for sustaining life.

SHARED SIGNIFICANCE OF THE COLLECTION

The acquisition and incorporation of the Paul Dyck Collection into the Plains Indian Museum's exhibition programming and halls has made a replete chronology of Plains Indian art from the earliest times of collecting to the present time. As such, the Plains Indian Museum's entire collection has now become a premium repository with the added quality of being a unique resource for research and augmentation of ongoing cultural revitalization by the tribes represented in it. Tribal academic scholars and Native schools and colleges now increasingly turn to museums, as anticipated by the Plains Indian Museum's original Plains Indian Museum Advisory Board, established in 1976, and encoded in that board's mission statement. Since the founding of the advisory board, the trustees of the Buffalo Bill Center of the West have recognized this interaction as well as the goal to foster education of the non-Native public.

The Plains Indian Museum is one of four museums and a research library that make up the Buffalo Bill Center of the West. The center was founded in 1917 to pay homage to William F. Cody, a dynamic and colorful promoter, performer, and entrepreneur who lived in the late nineteenth century. Because Cody included Plains Indians in his Wild West Show, Indian-made objects were a part of his memorabilia that form the core of the museum's Indian collection. Items in this collection date from the 1880s to 1914. The Indian collection was composed of randomly collected Indian items that had been featured in the Wild West Shows. The originators of this collection added items from Buffalo Bill's homes and ranches. They also collected items from ranch homes of the same period.

As the Buffalo Bill Center of the West expanded into a modern museum complex, in 1979 the Plains Indian Museum was added to showcase, preserve, and conserve the growing collection of historic and contemporary Native art. Generous donors and patrons contributed funds and objects toward building a premier collection. As an integral part of planning for the new Plains Indian Museum, in 1976 the board of trustees established a Plains Indian Museum Advisory Board to maintain the spirit of William Cody, who had a special regard for Plains Indian people and their history. This advisory board, composed of scholars, educators, leaders, and practitioners of sacred and artistic traditions, became an integral part of the Plains Indian Museum functions. The board is the link between contemporary artists and the historic makers of collection items. The advice, expertise, and scholarship of board members have been incorporated into the vision and mission statements that have guided the museum for forty years. Because the mission of the Plains Indian Museum is to go beyond educating only the general public, contemporary Native people are included in its many dimensions. Curators, advisory board members, research scholars, interns, visiting program presenters and artists—all have been Native people—descendants of the originators of the historical collection. Furthermore, outreach programs include Native people as viewers of the permanent and contemporary exhibitions. Educational programs have always been available to regional Native students and national Native scholars and educational institutions.

The trustees, patrons, and administrators of the Plains Indian Museum provide recognition that the historic and contemporary collections are great American art treasures. Some collection pieces are ethnological in nature; but others are examples of artistic achievement equal to historical masterpieces from ancient cultures of the Western Hemisphere and the world. Some collection pieces transcend the context of the past and generate their own aesthetic aura as fine art. All these collection items deserve exposition, contemplation, wonder, speculation, and appreciation. Recognized as fine art, these Native art forms mitigate the historical contexts and consequences of their origins and journey to their present exposition. They are monuments to the ancestral creators and to the continuing lives of the descendants.

Contemporary Native artisans of traditional techniques, as well as fine artists, are awed and influenced by researching the Plains Indian Museum collection. The historic masterpieces inspire Native people and, in a sense, fulfill a dynamic legacy that all people viewing this collection can share in appreciating the greatness of these treasures.

PREFACE

A highlight of my experiences as Curator, and later, Senior Curator, of the Plains Indian Museum of the Buffalo Bill Center of the West was the acquisition of and opportunity to research and interpret the renowned Paul Dyck Plains Indian Buffalo Culture Collection. The Paul Dyck Collection had been characterized by Native American art specialists as one of the most comprehensive privately held assemblages of Plains Indian artistry and related historical materials documenting the lives and cultures of the Native people of the Great Plains. Beginning in 2002 with my first visit with center administrators and members of the board of trustees to Paul Dyck's picturesque yet isolated ranch near Rimrock, Arizona; to the acquisition of the collection in 2007; to the opening of the Paul Dyck Plains Indian Buffalo Culture Gallery in 2013; and, finally, to the completion of this publication, the Plains Indian Museum has devoted fifteen years to the acquisition, preservation, research, and documentation of this unique and irreplaceable collection for current and future generations of scholars, tribal communities, and the American public.

Paul Dyck aspired to build his own museum within the Northern Plains that would provide a bridge between Native and non-Native cultures and promote a greater understanding of the heritages and contributions of Indian people to the story of the American West. Although Dyck was unable to achieve this personal aspiration, the unique and exceptional works of the collection he built have been returned to the Great Plains, where they are accessible to the descendants of the original nineteenth-century artists and others with interest in Plains Indian arts and cultures. There remain countless opportunities for research and interpretation of this collection beyond this introductory publication of many of the significant works.

Several individuals and organizations contributed to the realization of the museum's long efforts with regard to the Paul Dyck Collection. The Plains Indian Museum incorporates the guidance and advice of tribal scholars, artists, educators, leaders, and other community members as it acquires and manages collections and plans exhibitions and other programming. Since 1976, such involvement has been formalized through the guidance and support of the Plains Indian Museum Advisory Board, whose members have contributed their knowledge, experiences, and creativity toward developing accurate representations of Plains Indian arts, cultures, and histories from the buffalo-hunting past to the present.

The Plains Indian Museum has been extremely fortunate to have nationally recognized scholars, writers, artists, and community leaders and supporters as members of the advisory board. Over many years, Oglala Lakota artist and scholar Arthur Amiotte, a founding member of the advisory board, has contributed countless hours and his learned expertise to the work of the Plains Indian Museum. For this book, he generously wrote the excellent foreword that addresses the artistic and cultural significance of the Paul Dyck Collection. Joe Medicine Crow, who passed away in 2016 at the age of one hundred and two, was another original member of the Plains Indian Museum Advisory Board. A recognized scholar in Crow and Northern Plains history, Joe personally was acquainted with many of the old warriors and leaders who lived into the twentieth century. Because of his firsthand knowledge, scholarship, and unique perspectives, it seemed fitting that his reminiscences guide the narrative of the book. Joe was a constant respected, distinguished, and gracious participant at Plains Indian Museum events, particularly our annual powwow, where he presided over the opening ceremony and danced every summer. It was a unique privilege and pleasure to know Joe and be able to experience his knowledge and seek his guidance about the museum's projects and programs.

Other past and present advisory board members supported and provided wise counsel that guided the acquisition of the Paul Dyck Collection, its exhibition, and this publication. These individuals include Mary Gooch Armour, Robert D. Coe II, David L. Ferris Sr. (Eastern Shoshone), Adeline C. Fox (Northern Cheyenne), Garrett E. Goggles (Northern Arapaho), Marilyn C. Hudson (Hidatsa/Mandan), Billie Joe Kipp (Blackfeet), Jay F. Nielson, Harold Ramser Jr., Birdie Real Bird (Crow), Rusty R. Rokita, Mitchell S. Rouse, Betty Lou Sheerin, Gordon D. Smith, Margo Grant Walsh (Turtle Mountain Chippewa), the late Mrs. Margaret S. Coe, Dilworth P. "Buz" Sellers, M.D., Harriet Stuart Spencer, and Curly Bear Wagner (Blackfeet). The Center of the West's Board of Trustees, under the leadership of past chair Alan K. Simpson and current chair Barron G. Collier II, supported and guided the acquisition and subsequent work in preservation and interpretation.

A Save America's Treasures Grant provided funding for the cataloguing and storage of the Paul Dyck Collection. The museum also received generous contributions for this work from the William H. Donner Foundation, Dan and Mary Armour, Marilyn and Kent Hudson, Dr. and Mrs. Van Kirke Nelson, the Nielson family, Mr. and Mrs. J. Laurence Sheerin, Harriet and Ed Spencer, and Margo Grant Walsh.

Generous donations from Rusty and Deborah Rokita and the Honorable Robert D. Stuart, in honor of Harriet Stuart Spencer, and a grant from the Wyoming Humanities Council supported the creation of the Paul Dyck Plains Indian Buffalo Culture Gallery, which is a permanent exhibition space in the museum for this collection. I also greatly appreciate the support of the following individuals and agencies for the planning of a special exhibition on the Paul Dyck Collection as well as the publication of this book: Dan and Mary Armour, Bob and Angela Coe, Mr. and Mrs. John Dyck, Marilyn and Kent Hudson, Jim Nielson and Anne Young, Rusty and Deborah Rokita, Mitch and Alice Rouse, Buz and Judy Sellers, Robert L. Snyder, Bob and Lillian Stuart, Naoma Tate and the family of Hal Tate, the National Endowment for the Arts, and the National Endowment for the Humanities.

Plains Indian Museum Curator Rebecca S. West, who competently and dutifully served in the role of Assistant Curator for nineteen years, was instrumental in the research, cataloguing and storage, and exhibition of the Paul Dyck Collection since its initial acquisition. She has managed many of the details related to this publication, including photography of the objects, retrieval and organizing other images, and review of the manuscript and captions. As former Intern and current Curatorial Assistant, Hunter Old Elk has assisted Rebecca in these activities and offered her own valuable perspectives. Anne Marie Shriver, as Research Associate for the Dyck Collection, had the enviable position of unpacking, handling, and cataloguing all of the almost two thousand objects in the collection over a three-year period. The contributions of her work to the preservation and interpretation of the collection have been tremendous. Other Center of the West staff members who assisted in myriad aspects of cataloguing, exhibition, and conservation of the Paul Dyck Collection as well as this publication include Registrar Ann Marie Donoghue, Exhibition Manager Gary Miller, Conservator Beverly Perkins, Grants Manager Lynn Pitet, and Housel Director of the McCracken Research Library Mary Robinson. I am also grateful to friends and family of Paul Dyck who related their experiences, knowledge, and insights about this unique artist, collector, researcher, and writer. These individuals include Rusty Rokita of Hardin, Montana; Heywood Big Day of Pryor, Montana; and Peter J. Welsh of the University of Kansas. John Dyck and his wife, Cindy, as well as Paul Dyck's grandchildren, John Paul and Jeffrey James Dyck, have offered welcomed support and assistance throughout the acquisition and interpretation of the collection.

Sean Campbell, William J. O'Connor, and Kim Zierlein are responsible for all of the marvelous images of Dyck collection objects in this book. I also appreciate the professionalism and assistance of University of Oklahoma Press staff in this publication, including B. Byron Price, Alessandra Jacobi-Tamulevich, Stephanie Evans, Julie Rushing, and freelance copyeditor Nancy Warrington. The comments and recommendations of James Nottage from the Eiteljorg Museum and an anonymous reader who reviewed the manuscript provided insights that assisted in the refinement of the manuscript.

Finally, it is appropriate to recognize the passion and foresight of Paul Dyck, who devoted his entire adult life—over seventy years—to fostering an appreciation and understanding of Plains Indian people, their cultures, and histories, and building this magnificent collection. In doing so, we also must honor the memories of the Plains Indian men and women who created the objects of superb artistry and spiritual resonance represented in the Paul Dyck Plains Indian Buffalo Culture Collection.

The Paul Dyck Plains Indian Buffalo Culture Collection was acquired through the generosity of the Dyck family and additional gifts of the Nielson family and the estate of Margaret S. Coe. Unless otherwise noted, all of the works featured in this book are from the Paul Dyck Plains Indian Buffalo Culture Collection at the Plains Indian Museum of the Buffalo Bill Center of the West, Cody, Wyoming.

PLAINS INDIAN BUFFALO CULTURES

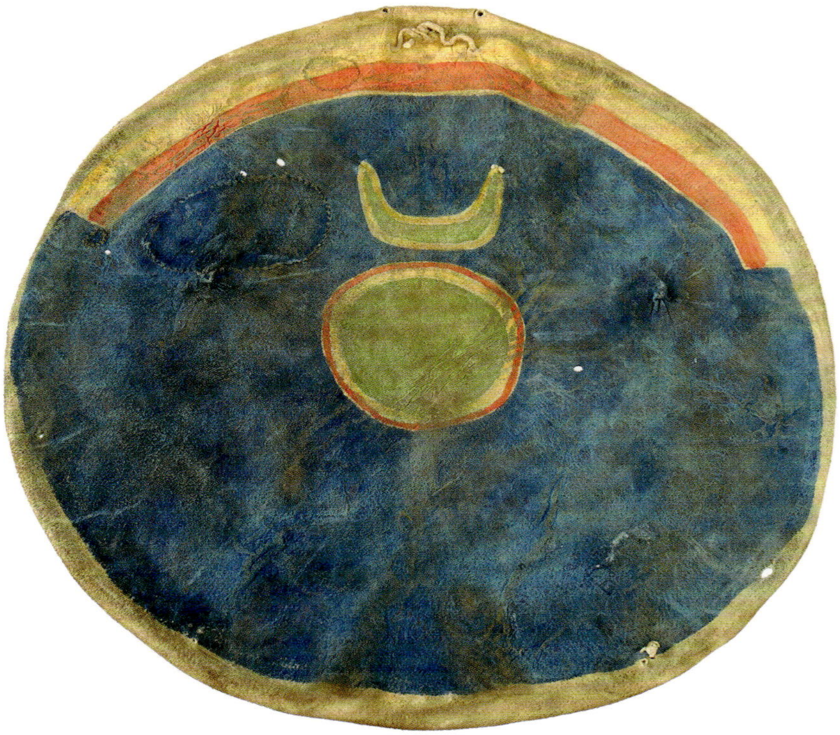

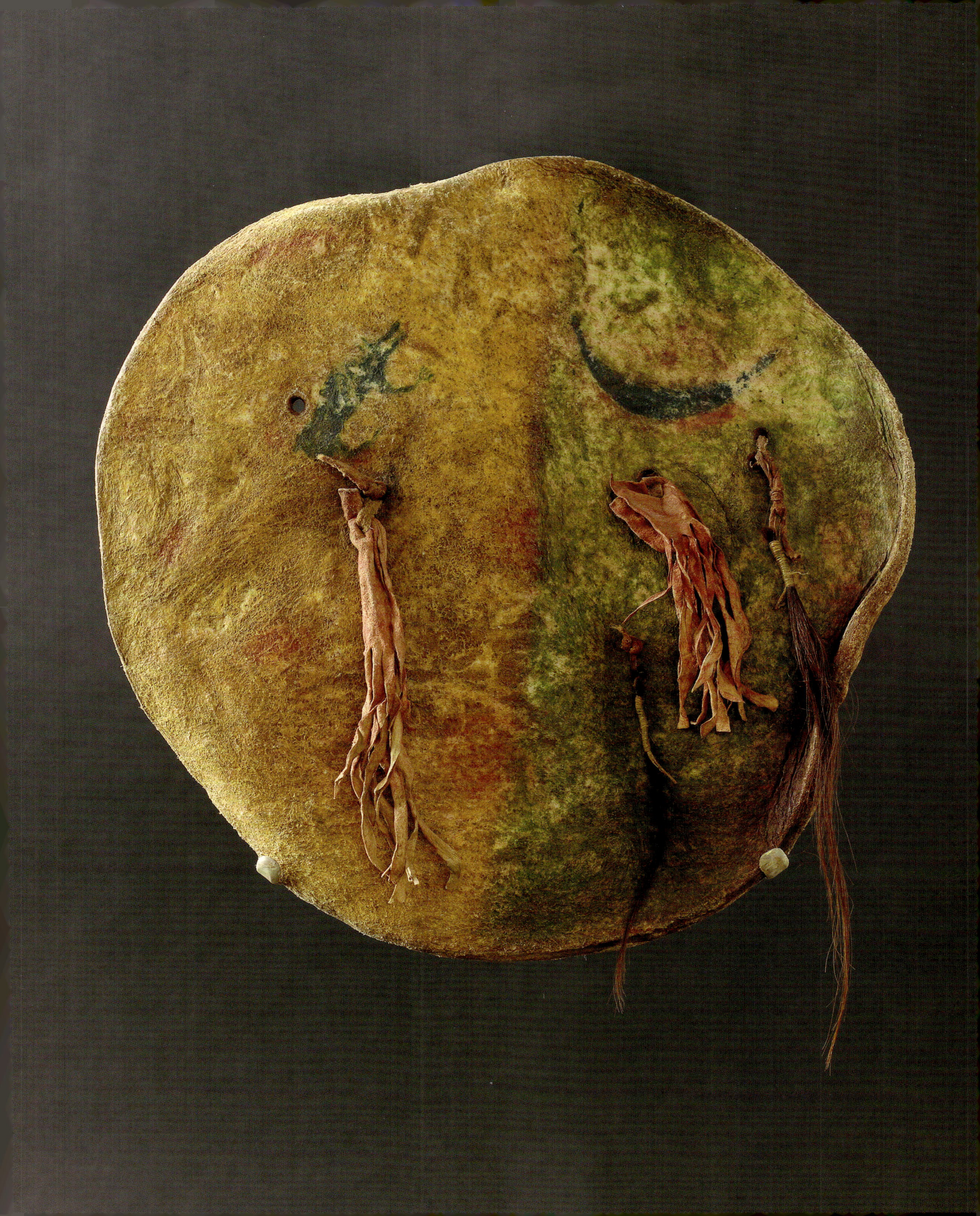

Introduction

Beginning in 1991, when I became Curator of the Plains Indian Museum at the Buffalo Bill Historical Center (now Buffalo Bill Center of the West), I often heard the name of the artist Paul Dyck of Rimrock, Arizona, who was said to have built a legendary collection of art and artifacts representing the buffalo-hunting people of the Great Plains. During the late 1970s, Paul Dyck consulted with Historical Center staff and trustees as they developed plans for the Plains Indian Museum, scheduled to open in 1979 as a new addition to the museum complex located in Cody, Wyoming. Since its founding in 1917, the center has served as an interpretive resource for the presentation and understanding of the history and art of the American West. Dyck discussed with the center's representatives the possibility of bringing his collection to Cody to be a part of the planned Plains Indian Museum exhibitions. Dyck took part in many similar discussions and negotiations with other regional and national museum boards, government officials, and elders and leaders representing Plains nations for over thirty years. However, Dyck had other ideas for his treasured collection that he passionately and single-mindedly pursued throughout his long and distinctive life.

PAUL DYCK: ARTIST AND COLLECTOR

Paul Dyck was born August 17, 1917, in Chicago, Illinois. His family was originally from Czechoslovakia but had immigrated to North America in the 1880s and lived in Alberta, Canada; Chicago, Illinois; and St. Paul, Minnesota, before returning to Europe in 1921. There, he lived with his family in the former Czechoslovakia (now Czech Republic and Slovakia) and in Germany. Dyck attended an English-speaking school in Prague before moving at eight years of age to Florence, Italy, where he served an artistic apprenticeship under Johannes Ritter von Skramlik (1860–1936), his uncle and a recognized portrait artist at the time. He also worked at his uncle's studios in Rome, Prague, and Paris.[1] At the age of fifteen, Dyck became a student at the Academy of Fine Arts in Munich, Germany.[2]

Dyck's father, Anton Cifka, known to the family as Tony, had lived near the Blackfoot Reserves in southern Alberta beginning in 1886. Following his interest in Blackfoot[3] and other Native people, he began building the collection that would eventually become the Buffalo Culture Collection. Cifka's interest in Plains Indians in time became Paul Dyck's own lifelong pursuit as he began to research and collect Native art and became friends with tribal members who would inspire his own artistic pursuits.

0.1. **Shield**
Apsáalooke (Crow), Northern Plains, ca. 1870
Pigment, human hair, sinew, tanned hide, buffalo rawhide; 15 inches (diameter)
Plains Indian Museum, NA.108.137

Paul Dyck collected, researched, and wrote about Plains Indian shields as a part of his lifelong interest in warrior history and traditions. This shield, painted in red, green, and blue pigments, features prominent elements of the earth and sky with an image of a bear on the left and a crescent moon on the right.

Actually I had been painting Indians all the way back to 1933. You see, I had been born with an attraction for the Indians. My father had pioneered among the Blackfeet in the late 1880s and I grew up hearing their stories. My father had fallen in love with those people when he was fairly young. Even the short time I spent as practically an infant at Calgary has a lot to do with it. My father had collected many Indian artifacts and since my brother never had those interests they automatically came to me. In fact, when I came back from Europe to New York in '34 I had two huge steamer trunks full of Indian stuff and one suit of my own clothes and five dollars of borrowed money in my pocket.[4]

While living in Germany, Dyck was attracted to the writings of Karl May (1842–1912). Although May only traveled to the United States in 1908, four years before his death, he was known for writing a series of fanciful and adventurous novels about cowboys and Indians of the American Old West. Adding to Dyck's literary interests in works about Native Americans was a chance meeting in 1932 in Dresden with One Elk and his family, Lakota performers from Standing Rock Reservation in the Carl Hagenbeck Circus. As Dyck recalled, "Well, when we were in Dresden the famous Hagenbeck Circus came to the city and they had some American Indians riding in a big, open bus. They were parading through the city, so I pushed my way through to get close to the Indian chief. Behind the chief sat some Sudanese camel drivers."[5] Dyck reported that he invited One Elk and his family home for dinner that evening.

In 1934, Dyck returned to the United States and made his way by bus to the Standing Rock Reservation in North and South Dakota to see the One Elk family.

I was seventeen when I came home. You see, I was born in '17 and I came home in 1934. Well, I worked around Chicago for about three weeks doing odd jobs. You see, there was no way that I could get into art at that time. When I managed to scrape up thirty-five dollars I took the Greyhound bus to Dakota, got to Cannonball and from there I hitched a ride to where One Elk lived. He lived a mile from where old Sitting Bull was killed. . . . One Elk at that time was close to eighty, but in fine shape. I married his girl who was about sixteen and that's how I got involved with the Indians.[6]

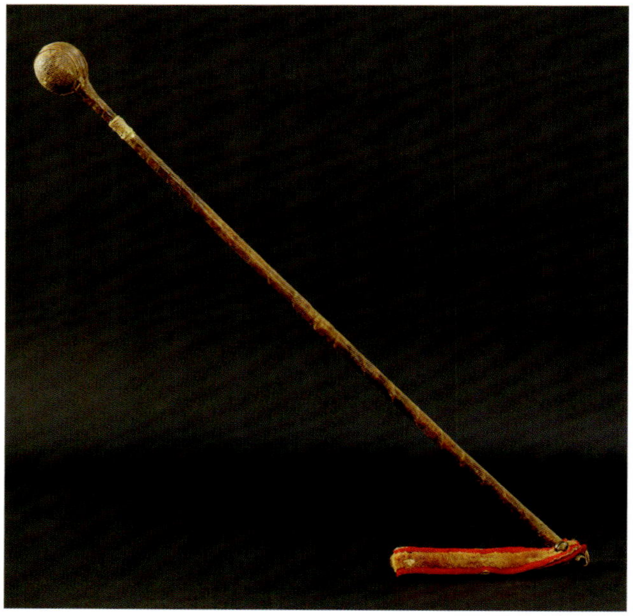

0.2. War club
Hunkpapa Lakota (Sioux), Grand River, South Dakota, ca. 1870
Wood, stone, rawhide, otter hide, cotton and wool cloth, brass bells, cotton thread; 8½ × 38 inches
Plains Indian Museum, NA.108.183

According to a tag attached to the club, Paul Dyck acquired this war club from One Elk during his first visit to the Standing Rock Reservation in 1934. Dyck's writings indicate that One Elk fought at Little Bighorn, and the tag indicates that the club was used during the battle.

During his visit to Standing Rock, Dyck met Old Elk and several other old warriors who had fought at the Battle of the Little Bighorn. While at Standing Rock, he also acquired a war club from One Elk that he said he had used at the battle (fig. 0.2). Unfortunately, Dyck's wife, Fawn, died while giving birth in 1935. He left Standing Rock soon after and traveled by motorcycle throughout the West for the next few years, returning during winters to Chicago, where he worked as a freelance commercial artist. He financed his travels by making small watercolor sketches of Indians and other subjects that he sold for twenty-five to fifty cents. He also worked odd jobs such as chopping wood. In 1938, he settled in the Verde Valley near Rimrock, Arizona,

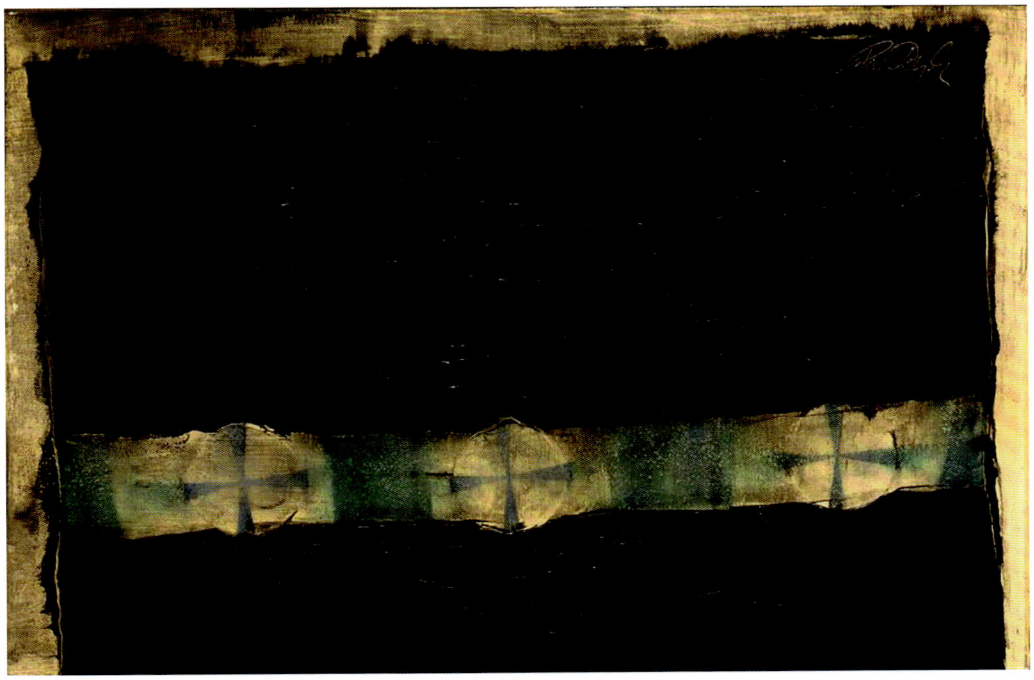

0.3. **Paul Dyck** (1917–2006),
Blanket of Hope, 1964
Oil on board; 23½ × 35½ inches
Whitney Western Art Museum, Gift of Alan and Cindy Horn, 14.96

Paul Dyck found artistic inspiration in his study of Plains Indian histories, cultures, and arts, including many objects in his own collection. This painting depicts a beaded or quillwork blanket strip. Women created such blanket strips to embellish and cover center seams of buffalo robes and, later, wool blankets acquired through trade beginning in the mid-nineteenth century.

on a 312-acre ranch, earning just enough income from his commercial work in Chicago for the purchase price. Until 1942, when he entered the United States Navy, Dyck continued to follow a cycle of traveling to Chicago for work as a commercial illustrator and to reservations and tribal communities in the Great Plains and the Southwest, where he met Indian people and often attended their ceremonies before returning to the ranch in Arizona.[7]

After World War II and his honorable discharge from the navy, Dyck returned to his Arizona ranch, where he spent the remainder of his life raising horses, cattle, and buffalo; growing crops; and painting in his home studio. During summers, he continued to travel to reservations for visits with Plains Indian people, where he found inspiration for his art and found exquisite examples of American Indian art to add to his growing collection. Dyck developed a strong relationship with the Blackfeet artist Lone Wolf (Hart Merriam Schultz, 1882–1970), who took him as a son and added to his knowledge of Northern Plains people during the transitions of the late nineteenth and early twentieth centuries.

By the 1960s, Dyck had become a recognized artist of Native American subjects and during his artistic career, had had sixty-five solo exhibitions in New York, Chicago, Los Angeles, Tucson, and other cities. His paintings are in collections of the Phoenix Art Museum, the Museum of Northern Arizona, the Tucson Museum of Art, and the Whitney Western Art Museum of the Buffalo Bill Center of the West (fig. 0.3), in addition to many private collections. Dyck was known by his Lakota friends and relatives as Wi-'hun'ke E'ta'pa (Rainbow Hand) for his paintings characterized by sweeping abstract lines and bold use of color executed in egg tempera with "old master" oil glazes, watercolor, and Sumiye ink using Japanese brushes.[8]

On the ranch, Dyck also continued to research Plains Indian arts, cultures, and histories and was also an author of articles and books about Northern Plains cultures and arts. His best known work, *Brulé: The Sioux People of the Rosebud,* was published in 1971.[9] He lectured and worked as an appraiser and consultant for museums and private collectors in the United States and Canada as he built the Buffalo Culture Collection. In 1989, the University of Montana awarded Paul Dyck an honorary Doctorate of Humane Letters in recognition of his efforts to collect, protect, and preserve Plains Indian cultures. Until his passing in 2006 at the age of eighty-eight, Paul Dyck continued to study, experience, and find inspiration in the lands of the West and the arts and cultures of the Native people who live there. In 1994, he wrote:

> Of course, One Elk left a fantastic impression on me, an impression on the spiritual side of life. My father's values, too, as hard a man as he was, were very straight. So I found out very early that what he said was quite valid, as tough as it was. For an artist to survive in America you had to be on something solid. If you had money, maybe, you could call that something solid. If you didn't have money, you had better be somewhere where you could eat.
>
> And you have to preserve your freedom. Without that, there is nothing. For myself, I have to be on Mother Earth to be able to have sincerity in my art. If I can't touch earth with my hands, I'm nothing.[10]

PAUL DYCK PLAINS INDIAN BUFFALO CULTURE COLLECTION

My first visit to Paul Dyck's ranch located near Rimrock, Arizona, and introduction to his treasured collection occurred in October 2002 as part of a delegation of Historical Center trustees, administrators, and staff. In 1959, he had designed and built (assisted by Apache workers) the home located on the scenic ranch in the Verde Valley, with its diverse landscapes ranging from desert grasslands to ponderosa pine forests and highlighted by the meandering Wet Beaver Creek, a swinging bridge, and caves and rock shelters containing archaeological remnants of past generations of Native inhabitants.[11]

Artistic expressions of life on the Great Plains representing all of the Native nations—the Lakota, Crow, Pawnee, Arapaho, Cheyenne, Dakota, Nakota, Mandan, Hidatsa, Arikara, Kiowa, Comanche, Assiniboine, Gros Ventre, Blackfoot, Otoe, Plains Cree, Ponca, and other peoples—filled his home. These included hide clothing: men's war shirts, women's dresses, children's clothing, moccasins, and leggings; cradles decorated in beads and porcupine quillwork in culturally distinctive designs; buffalo hide tipis and furnishings; painted buffalo robes; saddles, horse masks, and other riding equipment; drums, shields, and weapons; pipes, pipe bags, and other ceremonial items; bear claw necklaces; eagle feather bonnets; a pictographic painting on muslin of scenes of warfare by the Crow warrior White Swan, who served as a U.S. Army Scout as a young man; and peace medals manufactured for presentation to Indian leaders. Every item was created, worn, and used by Native American men, women, and children who had lived as buffalo hunters of the Great Plains. Dyck referred to the period exemplified by the collection as the "Buffalo Culture Era." According to Dyck, this era occurred from the late 1700s until about 1890. During this period, the Plains Indian buffalo-hunting way of life, with the freedom to hunt, gather

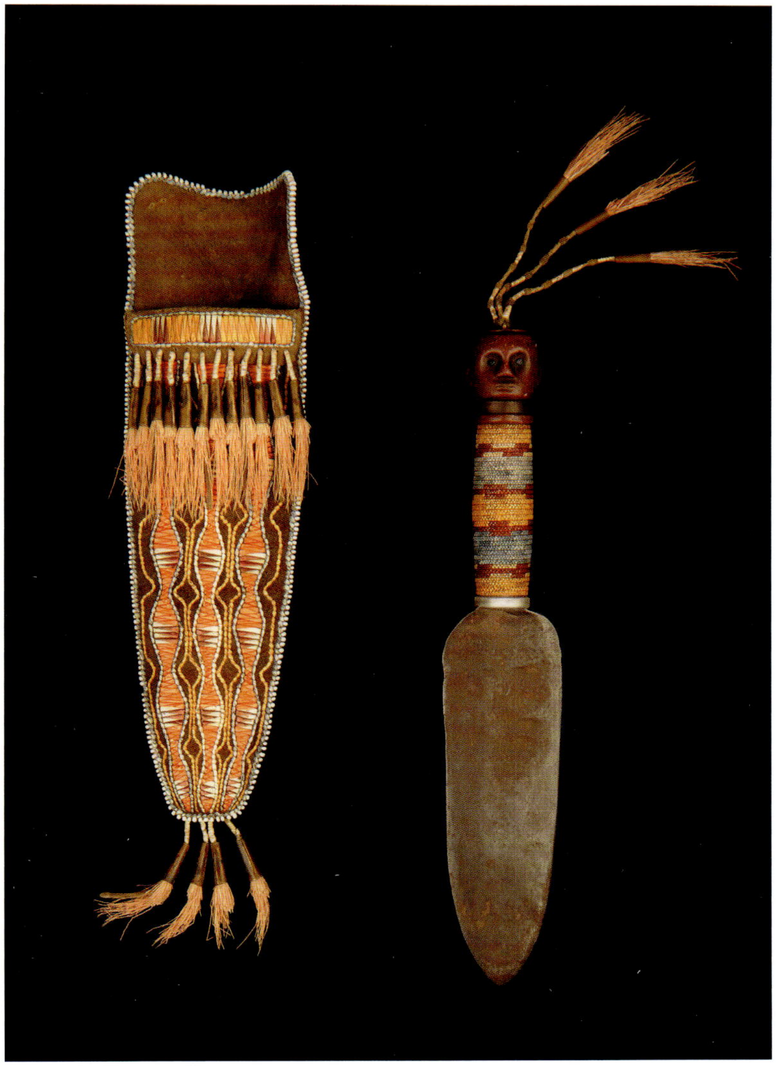

0.4. **Knife and sheath**
Menominee, Great Lakes, ca. 1830
Steel, pipestone, tanned and dyed deer hide, glass beads, porcupine quills, tin cones, metal, vegetal fibers; knife: 14 × 2 inches; sheath: 12 × 3 inches
Plains Indian Museum, NA.102.210

Although Paul Dyck specialized in researching and collecting artistry from the Great Plains, he also appreciated the creative works of peoples of the Southwest, Plateau, Great Lakes, and Eastern Woodlands regions. This knife and sheath are from the Menominee of the Great Lakes. The distinctive carving in pipestone that tops the knife's handle is the image of a man with his hair in a scalp lock.

wild plants, cultivate their traditional gardens, and follow a yearly ceremonial cycle, flourished. By the 1880s, the destruction of the once-great buffalo herds, disease, warfare, starvation, and government policies forced the tribes into the confinement of reservations. A decisive end to this era came with the Wounded Knee Massacre that occurred on December 29, 1890.

Dyck also held collections representing other cultures and historical periods, including Navajo, Apache, Hopi, Zuni, Eastern Woodlands and Great Lakes peoples, Salish, Kootenai, and Nez Perce of the Plateau, and Spanish colonial objects (fig. 0.4). On the walls of the large central room were Dyck's portraits of Plains leaders that he entitled the *Overland Trail Series,* many of which referenced the designs of clothing, regalia, weapons, shields, and accoutrements in the collection (fig. 0.5). His studio was in the center, with natural light emanating from a window—a long floor-to-ceiling expanse with a canvas tipi serving as a curtain. Dyck's ongoing study and research of Plains Indian people and cultures were evidenced by his library containing historical photographs and books, including recent publications and museum catalogues.

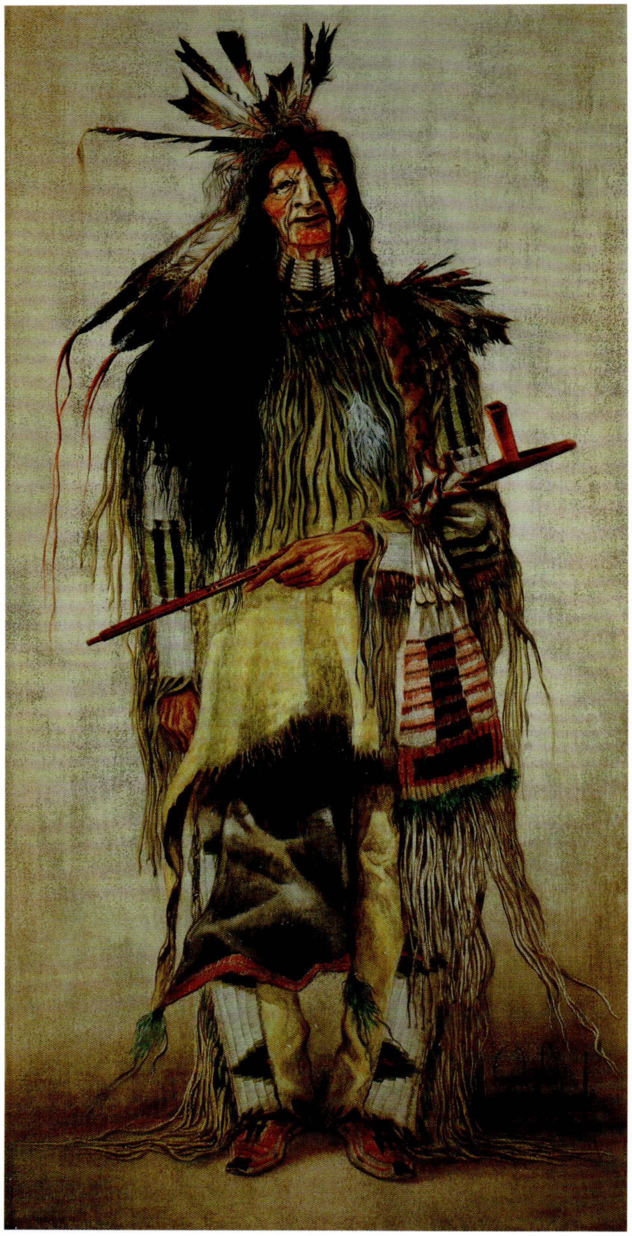

0.5. **Paul Dyck** (1917–2006)
Shahi'yena—Cheyenne Warrior, ca. 1958
Oil on board; 49 × 124½ inches
Whitney Western Art Museum, Loan from the Paul Dyck Foundation, L.312.2010.1

Paul Dyck was a student of history as well as an artist. He found ideas for his art in his research and study of objects in his collection of Plains Indian materials. This painting is one of his depictions of Plains and Plateau warriors in the Overland Trail Series.

During the daylong visit in 2002, Dyck talked about his collection and the Lakota, Crow, Pawnee, and other tribal elders he had known. His passion for Plains Native arts and cultures, as well as the people, became clear as he expressed his deeply felt aspirations, visions, and plans for preserving and interpreting the collection he had worked essentially his entire life to build. The collection constituted Dyck's life's work based on his mission: to assemble the finest examples of Plains Indian arts available to him and build a museum to exhibit the collection. The interpretation of the museum would be based on his study of Native cultures and history and would include input from tribal members. He had designed a model for a museum building that incorporated ceremonies and symbolism from Plains Native traditions. The model was prominently displayed on the dining room table in his home. He hoped to build the museum in the Northern Plains and staff it with professionals dedicated to a culturally sensitive preservation of the collection, research, and a knowledgeable and sympathetic interpretation of Plains Native cultures and histories.

Paul Dyck researched, visited, and served as a consultant to museums with Native American exhibitions throughout the United States. He was critical of museums primarily located in large metropolitan areas that exhibited indigenous art and artifacts as separate and apart from the contexts of the cultures and people who created them. A feasibility study for the proposed museum quotes Austrian ethnologist Christian Feest, who defined museum collecting as "a process by which samples of a complex whole are removed from their meaningful and functional context in order to be preserved under artificial conditions and within a new framework."[12]

Dyck's writings and interviews demonstrate his respect for Plains Native cultures and deplore the historical treatment of indigenous people. In a 1975 interview for the Tucson, Arizona, *Daily Star,* he described the "fantastic beauty" of the cultures. However, he questioned the ability of non-Native people to understand or respect such American Indian traditions and beliefs, particularly in light of contemporary political issues such as the Wounded Knee Occupation on the Pine Ridge Reservation that occurred in 1973 and ongoing struggles concerning tribal water rights in the Southwest.[13]

Dyck aspired to build a museum that would stand as a memorial to Plains Indian people and, through innovative exhibitions and programs, fully integrate the artistry revealed through the collection within traditional cultures, values, knowledge, and spirituality. He asserted that a museum informed and developed through such a respectful and knowledgeable approach would serve to strengthen contemporary Plains tribal cultures and communities and educate the general public to foster an appreciation and understanding of the lives of Indian people. In a 1987 statement about his proposed museum, Dyck wrote:

> The beauty and truth of the Buffalo Culture, their love of this land as home and their inborn respect for Mother Earth are more valid today than ever before. The Plains Indians believed an indifference to "the environment" would banish man from life altogether. When you look at what we are doing to this planet, you realize how prophetic the wisdom of our Indian ancestors is. . . . We need to know the facts about the accomplishments of America's original people—their love of beauty, their love of this land, their worthiness of life. This museum will be a memorial to the freest man in the history of the world, one who in his lifestyle was the true ancestor of the Constitutional American. . . . The Indian people have a lot to be proud of. They have contributed a great deal to this country's heritage. Perhaps, an acknowledgement of these contributions will be a bridge of understanding between our cultures.[14]

Dyck owned forty acres near the site of the Battle of the Little Bighorn in Montana on which he planned to work with the Crow Nation in building a museum. He considered the 1876 conflict to be a pivotal event in the history of Northern Plains tribes. Although the outcome of the battle was decisive and the assembled Lakota, Cheyenne, and Arapaho warriors were victorious, afterward U.S. officials and the military strengthened their resolution to defeat the Plains tribes. The devastating results were near annihilation of the once-vast buffalo herds, increased warfare resulting in many deaths, intense assaults on traditional cultures, and eventual confinement of surviving tribal peoples to reservations. According to Dyck, "The defensive victory over Custer and his men united this nation's political forces to destroy the Buffalo Culture. In doing so, the nation lost the greatest cultural treasure this continent has produced. To this day, this loss has been ignored and minimized."[15] His lifelong fascination with the Little Bighorn battle, war, and leadership also shaped Dyck's collecting priorities as he strove to assemble magnificent examples of weapons, shields, and military-society clothing used and worn by nineteenth-century Plains Indian warriors.

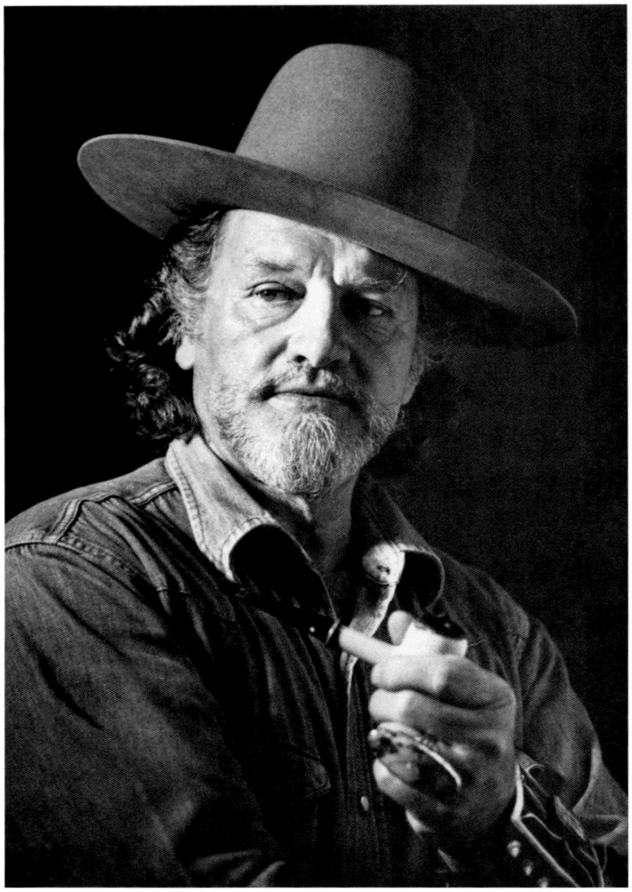

0.6. **Paul Dyck**
Dyck Ranch, Rimrock, Arizona, ca. 1975
Photograph by Peter Balestrero, Western Ways Photography
Wolheims' Rosequist Galleries, Tucson, Arizona

Dyck established the Paul Dyck Foundation to preserve and manage the Buffalo Culture Collection and establish a museum for its interpretation. He met and collaborated with Crow Nation officials, private and public museums, state and county agencies, and private organizations during the 1980s–2000s. However, because of financial, organizational, and other reasons, Dyck was never able to realize his goal of developing his own museum located within the Northern Plains region where Native and non-Native scholars and visitors could research, experience, and learn to appreciate Plains Native arts, cultures, and histories.

After the initial visit to the Dyck Ranch in 2002, Historical Center staff and trustees continued to communicate with Paul Dyck regarding a long-range objective of bringing these symbols of tribal cultures and heritages back to the Northern Plains, to Cody, Wyoming, near the traditional lands and contemporary homes of Plains Indian people. Dyck fell ill during the fall of 2005. In February 2006, he agreed to loan the Buffalo Culture Collection to the Plains Indian Museum for its ongoing protection and preservation.

After his passing on February 14, 2006, the center began working with the Paul Dyck Foundation to ensure the preservation of this magnificent assemblage of Plains Indian artistry and cultures. Members of the Plains Indian Museum Advisory Board, consisting of Plains Native scholars, artists, and community leaders, supported the acquisition of the collection. The Oglala Lakota artist Arthur Amiotte stated that the objects in the Paul Dyck Collection could be considered the "grandparents" or even "great-grandparents" of the existing Plains Indian Museum materials dated primarily from the late nineteenth century to today.[16] "This is a beautiful, one-of-a-kind collection," said Marilyn Hudson, director of the Mandan, Hidatsa, and Arikara Three Affiliated Tribes Museum. "It's most important that something of such beauty be cared for properly and preserved for many future generations."[17]

In September 2007, the Paul Dyck Plains Indian Buffalo Culture Collection, consisting of approximately two thousand pieces, joined other superb works of art in the Plains Indian Museum documenting the cultures and lives of the Native people of the Great Plains. The Paul Dyck Plains Indian Buffalo Culture Gallery, a permanent feature of the Plains Indian Museum, opened to the public on June 15, 2013. Though not his own museum of Plains Native arts and cultures that he had hoped to establish near the site of Little Bighorn, the gallery is a beginning toward fulfilling Paul Dyck's lifelong aspiration of finding a home for the Buffalo Culture Collection. Here, tribal artists, teachers, scholars, spiritual leaders, community members, and schoolchildren visit to study the magnificent art of the collection. Perhaps, as Paul Dyck had hoped, other national and international museum visitors will also develop a better understanding and appreciation of Plains Indian cultures and lives through viewing the Buffalo Culture Collection.

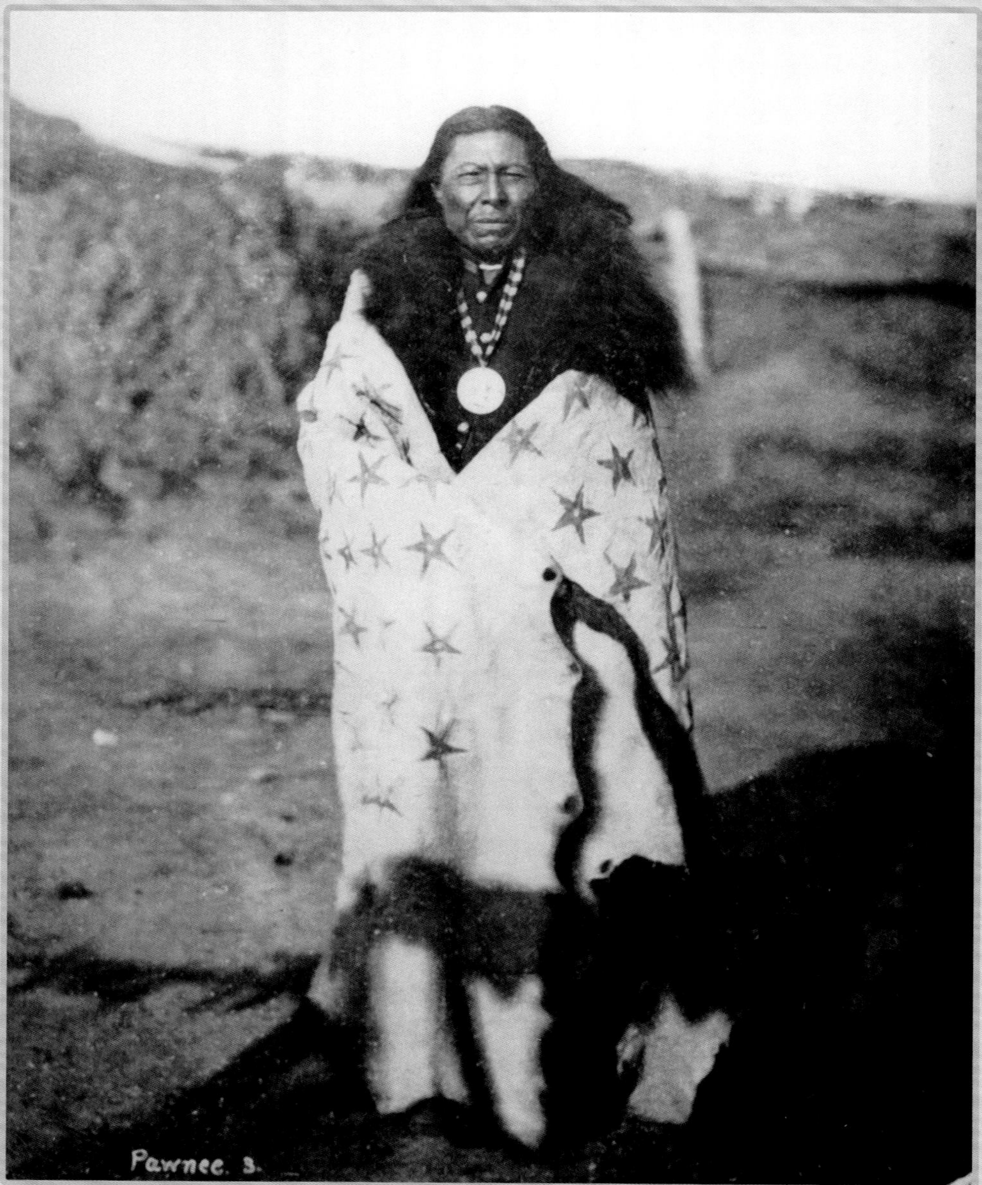
Pawnee. 3.

1 Buffalo Culture Era

In 2003, in his characteristically direct and vibrant manner, ninety-year-old Joseph Medicine Crow described the Buffalo Culture Era when his Crow ancestors lived as buffalo hunters of the Great Plains with all the attendant beliefs, philosophies, and cultural traditions that defined and supported this way of life.

> Before the government established the Crow Reservation in 1884, the Crows had lived as nomads, traveling here and there, hunting buffalo, going on the warpath, capturing enemy horses, counting coup, enjoying their particular way of life. It was a good life, I think. But when the reservations were established, they were required to forget about their old ways and live like white people. They had to start farming, learn English, and become Christians.
>
> It wasn't easy. In their minds, in their hearts, they were still living in the past, still cherishing their traditional religion, philosophy, and way of life. So when the United States Government forbade them to dance, sing, speak their language, or carry on their cultural traditions, the old people would just hide and continue to do things the way they used to do them. For that reason, all the boys of my age on the Crow Reservation were brought up in two ways at the same time. We were raised to be warriors but we were also expected to succeed in the white man's world. In a way, then, I have walked in two worlds my entire life.[1]

1.1. Sun Chief
Chaticks si Chaticks (Pawnee), ca. 1868
Photograph by William Henry Jackson
Nebraska State Historical Society, 1667

Sun Chief was a Pawnee leader who died on August 5, 1873, at Massacre Canyon after a group of Lakota attacked Pawnee men, women, and children as they traveled on their summer buffalo hunt. Here, Sun Chief wears a peace medal and a buffalo robe painted with many images of stars as he stands in his earth lodge village located on the Loup River in present-day Nebraska.

Medicine Crow himself was born in October 1913 and lived with his mother and father, Amy Yellowtail and Leo Medicine Crow, until his father's death in 1915. After that, he often stayed in the home of his grandfather Chief Medicine Crow, but primarily lived with his mother's family, the Yellowtails.

In the Yellowtail home, Medicine Crow was introduced to the stories of the old chiefs, warriors, and other elders who lived nearby. These elders included renowned leaders such as White Man Runs Him, One Star, Arm Around His Neck, Flathead Woman, Old Crow, and Not Afraid. White Man Runs Him, Medicine Crow's great-uncle—in Crow kinship terms, his grandfather—had served as a U.S. Army Scout in the Seventh Cavalry under Lieutenant Colonel George Armstrong Custer. He told Medicine Crow about his experiences during the 1876 campaign leading up to the Battle of the Little Bighorn. White Man Runs Him and the other elders had participated in the Plains buffalo-hunting way of life at its zenith. As the nineteenth century came to an end, the elders also experienced the near destruction of the Crow and their way of life that occurred with the devastation of the buffalo herds, confinement to the reservation, and prohibition by government officials and Christian missionaries of long-standing cultural traditions.[2]

Many of the elders' reminiscences recounted battles and the acts of bravery of individual warriors. Others described the Great Plains as it had been in the mid-1800s, with herds of buffalo, deer, elk, and other game to hunt; wild plants to gather for food and medicines; and the accompanying knowledge, beliefs, and ceremonies that sustained, as Medicine Crow described, "a good life."

> During the sweat bath seasons in the fall and early spring, Grandfather Yellowtail would invite these old warriors to our house. I heard legends, myths, and regular stories from plenty of other people, but the war stories, the important stories, I learned from those old chiefs. Often they would correct each other. Sometimes one would say, "That's not the way I heard it." He would then tell his version. That way I sometimes learned several versions of the same story.
>
> Telling stories was important to those old people because everything they valued from the pre-reservation days was gone except their memories. They loved talking about the good old days when there were buffalo to hunt and they could enjoy the traditional life of the Plains Indians. Back then, of course, the chiefs had been the big shots, the leaders. But all of a sudden, when the reservation was set up, everything had come to a halt. Now a white Indian agent was boss. Chiefs were no longer chiefs. They were nothing. I think that's why they were always talking about the past, reliving it.[3]

CREATING "A GOOD LIFE" IN THE GREAT PLAINS

As Arthur Amiotte summarizes below, particular themes recur in the ongoing narratives that delineate the tribal histories of Plains Indian people, such as survival during challenging, seemingly overwhelming conditions; resilience in the face of adversity; and endurance of significant cultural beliefs and identities that supported them through difficult times.

> Over thousands of years, Plains tribes survived the many forces of pre-contact history. Then in less than three hundred years, they endured and survived the perpetrations of American western expansion and domination. . . . Today descendants of these ancient peoples still stand, some on the very ground of their ancestral homelands, testimony to their extraordinary resilience and enduring faith in Native beliefs and identity.[4]

Over generations, Plains Indian people had created distinct cultures with diverse languages, philosophies, spiritual beliefs, and arts that defined tribal identities. The cultures were centered on long-standing knowledge that guided hunting, plant gathering, and farming practices adapted to the diverse and sometimes demanding Great Plains environments.

The vast expanse of the Great Plains region stretches from the foothills of the Rocky

Mountains in the west, to the Mississippi River basin in the east, and from the Upper Saskatchewan River in central Alberta, Canada, in the north, to the Rio Grande in South Texas. The region can sometimes be a severe and unforgiving land with variable climates that range from hot summer days to cold, dry winter nights, with periodic droughts, sudden spring thunderstorms, and blinding snowstorms. Today, when crossing the plains, a traveler experiences subtle variations in landscapes with flat to rolling grasslands, terraced stream valleys, isolated mountain areas, and intermountain basins. For Native people living in the Great Plains in the eighteenth and nineteenth centuries, the land also harbored many resources that provided physical sustenance and cultural and spiritual inspiration. Tallgrass prairies had abundant herds of buffalo and other grazing animals that could be hunted. River valleys provided rich and fertile land where gardens of corn, beans, and squash flourished. Prairies and adjoining mountain foothills produced wild plants, including berries, nuts, seeds, and tubers, that could be seasonally gathered for food and medicines.

Through writings and illustrations, some nineteenth-century Euro-American travelers to the region described the unfamiliar landscapes and Native inhabitants of the Plains as foreign, exotic, and, perhaps, dangerous. Major Stephen H. Long and other early-nineteenth-century expedition leaders described the western Plains as the "Great American Desert," and considered the region unfit for cultivation and, because of a scarcity of water and wood, unsuitable for Euro-American settlement.[5]

Despite this characterization, Thomas Jefferson viewed the American West, including the Great Plains, as an "agrarian Eden," a chosen country suitable for territorial expansion and colonization by Euro-Americans. As president, he ordered the Lewis and Clark (Corps of Discovery) Expedition of 1804–1806 to explore the West from St. Louis to the Pacific coast.[6] Underlying the early explorations and expeditions to the Great Plains was the national objective of domination of the land and its Native inhabitants to make way for territorial expansion and establishment of Euro-American settlements. By the middle of the nineteenth century, this objective, conceived under the term "Manifest Destiny," led to inevitable conflicts between indigenous peoples and the U.S. military and to the ultimate conclusion of the Buffalo Culture Era.

Native American people of the Great Plains, however, perceived the land through significantly different cultural, historical, and spiritual perspectives. What Euro-American explorers, writers, and artists regarded as wilderness, Native people recognized as their traditional homelands. For centuries they had traveled, explored, studied, and cherished the distinctive plains landscapes, the source of waters, plants, animals, and sacred sites that underpinned their cultural knowledge, beliefs, traditions, and values. Curly Bear Wagner of the Blackfeet often spoke of the enduring reverence of Plains Indian people for the land. This reverence expanded beyond the physical environment and its earthly elements to its associated spiritual relationship to the universe as a whole.

> Everything is important to our people. We respect everything that the Creator has given to us. We respect it because everything out there is living—the sun, the moon, the stars, the clouds, the sky, the mountains, the trees, the rocks, the grass, the water—all those

> things are living. They are all related and we are part of that relationship. The Creator gave us these things for our survival. So, therefore, we respect these things he has given to us. We honor these things. He has given us the roots, the herbs, the plants, the trees for healing purposes. He has taught us how to go up into the mountains and fast, to call upon him to show us how to use these different things he has given to us for our survival. Everything out there was important for our survival as a people. This is what we call our way of life. And even today these things are important for our survival, not only the Indians', but all people's survival.[7]

Anthropologist Keith Basso characterized indigenous peoples' knowledge as well as their close cultural and spiritual connections to their homelands as "senses of place." In writing of the Western Apaches' deep knowledge of their homelands, he wrote that one of the most basic dimensions of human experience is "that close connection of heart and mind, often subdued, yet potentially overwhelming, that is known as sense of place."[8]

Through songs, stories, reminiscences, and oral traditions, Plains Indian people articulate their senses of place and reinforce their connections to their traditional homelands. Hidatsa tribal member Marilyn Hudson has expressed her understanding and reverence for her people's homelands where the Hidatsa people originated based upon oral tradition. The oral traditions describe village sites along the Missouri River, on the Fort Berthold Reservation in northern North Dakota, prior to their destruction by the river's flooding after the construction of Garrison Dam beginning in 1947.[9] She described this place as "land which no longer exists, but a place in time to which I, and others of my generation, am irrevocably tied spiritually and physically."[10]

> It is the land of our birth and the land of our fathers and their fathers before them. It is the land which nourished and sustained the Mandan, Hidatsa and Arikara people from time well before Columbus to the twentieth century.
>
> The Mandan origin story of the universe describes quite well the land on which we lived. A ball of mud is divided between Lone Man and First Creator. They first created a river as a dividing point. First Creator took the west side and Lone Man took the east side. First Creator made the mountains, hills, coulees, running streams on the west side of the river. Lone Man made mostly flat land with lakes and ponds on the east side. Then they created the four-leggeds, the swimmers of the waters, and those that crawl over the creation, the winged beings of the skies, and finally the two-leggeds. The west side of the Missouri River is rugged and hilly with badlands suited to cattle ranching. The east side has rich, level soil well suited to fields and farming.[11]

The economic essentials of Plains Indian life—hunting, gathering, and farming—are ancient traditions. Francisco Vázquez de Coronado described his encounters with Apache buffalo hunters as he and his Spanish army crossed the Southern Plains in 1541. The small family groups lived in buffalo-hide tipis and traveled with their dogs dragging tipi poles and travois loaded with belongings.[12] The expedition journeyed on to present central Kansas to a place the Spanish called Quivira. The people here—ancestors of the Wichita—lived in villages and followed an ancient way of life based on both farming and hunting.[13] Over a thousand years ago, Plains farmers established such villages along the Missouri, Platte, Republican, and Arkansas Rivers. By the eighteenth century, these farmers were known as the Mandan, Hidatsa, and Arikara of the Missouri River region of present North Dakota; the Pawnee, Omaha, Ponca, Kansa (Kaw), and Otoe of the Central Plains region of present Nebraska and northern Kansas; and the Osage and the Wichita of the Southern Plains, including what is now southern Kansas, Oklahoma, Missouri, and Texas.

Living in large villages of grass houses in the Southern Plains, or mat-covered lodges and earth lodges in the Central and Northern Plains, the women of these tribes tilled gardens along the fertile river bottoms, raising several varieties of corn, beans, squash, and sometimes, melons and sunflowers.[14] Once or twice a year in the summer and sometimes the winter, the people traveled into the prairies where men hunted buffalo. Like other buffalo hunters, they lived in buffalo-hide tipis and used dogs to carry belongings. Men also hunted deer, elk, mountain sheep, and antelope. Seasonally, the bands collected berries, nuts, and seeds and dug tubers for food and medicines.

There were other buffalo-hunting tribes in the Northern Plains of present Wyoming, Montana, and Alberta and Saskatchewan, Canada, including the Blackfoot, Crow, Assiniboine, and Gros Ventre. As the tribes gradually acquired horses after the Pueblo Revolt of 1680, Plains buffalo hunters began traveling greater distances to hunt and trade. The hunters carried with them larger lodges and more belongings. Through trade, Natives began to acquire European goods, including firearms, metal knives, kettles, glass beads, cloth, and needles. The advantages of buffalo hunting assisted by horses and firearms attracted tribes from the Great Lakes and other regions. By the beginning of the 1800s, the historical tribal territories of the Cheyenne, Arapaho, Shoshone, and Sioux in the Northern Plains and the Kiowa and Comanche in the Southern Plains were firmly established.

Once on the Plains, tribes from diverse cultural traditions, though differentiated by languages and other characteristics, developed similar economic strategies for meeting the environmental challenges of the region. The Buffalo Culture Era, made possible by the introduction of the horse, was dramatic in both its rise and its decline. Despite the timeless popular image of the Plains Indian warrior on horseback, often used to represent all Native American people, this era lasted less than two hundred years. The cultural and spiritual significance of the buffalo that sustained Plains Native people, however, continues symbolically to this day.

THE BUFFALO—OUR BROTHER

The following Chaticks si Chaticks (Pawnee) song, recorded by the ethnomusicologist Alice Fletcher and translated by the Pawnee scholar James R. Murie during research in 1898–1901 on Pawnee music and ceremonies, is a part of the Hako or Calumet ceremony. The song spoke to the promise of the buffalo to Pawnee people. The ceremony was a prayer for children that was conducted to ensure that the Pawnee would increase in numbers, be strong, have long lives, and be at peace.[15]

Clouds of dust arise, rolling up from the earth,
Spreading onward; herds are there,
Speeding on before,
Going straight where we must journey.
What are those we see moving in the dust?
This way coming from the herd;
Buffalo and calf!
Food they promise for the Children.[16]

The song refers to the great billowing clouds of dust stirred up by running buffalo that Pawnee bands might see as they journeyed across the Plains. At times, a cow and her calf would separate from the herd and approach the travelers. Pawnee people were taught to be observant when they traveled because such sights signified the promise of abundant buffalo for the hunters to pursue to provide meat for Pawnee families. Because of the centrality of the buffalo to Plains Indian cultures, the buffalo and calf symbolized the survival of the people. When this song was recorded at the beginning of the 1900s, vast herds of buffalo could no longer be found on the Plains, and the hunting way of life had ended. Yet the song continued to be a part of the ceremony so that the people, especially the children, would remember the importance of the buffalo to the Pawnee.

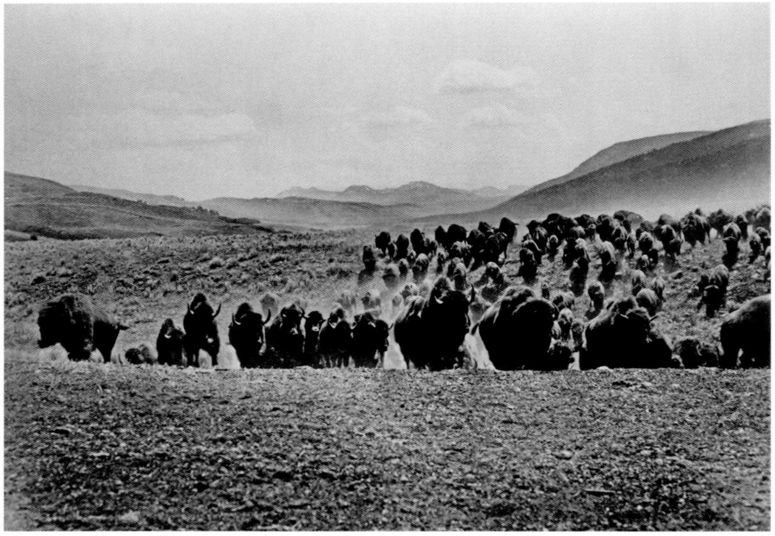

1.2. **A herd of running buffalo**
Yellowstone Park, ca. 1881
Photograph by Frank Jay Haines
University of Oklahoma Western History Collection, PG2065.PH:1–16

For generations on the Great Plains, Native people celebrated successful hunts with feasts and ceremonies that reinforced their reverence and gratitude for the buffalo and its significant role in their economic, cultural, and spiritual lives. They understood that when the buffalo were treated with honor and respect, they allowed themselves to be killed for food, shelter, clothing, robes, and other necessities. Buffalo communicated with the people through dreams and visions and were called upon for help during the hunt, war, hunger, illness, and other times of need. To Plains Indians, the buffalo symbolized sustenance, power, courage, strength, honor, and protection. The relationship of the buffalo to Plains Indian people has been and continues to be commemorated and celebrated in songs, stories, and ceremonies passed from one generation to the next. In an interview, Joseph Medicine Crow recounted:

> The old storytellers of the tribe used to tell us buffalo stories. They would say that long, long time ago that the buffalo were just like human beings, that they had their own chants, their own dances and songs, and they just lived like human beings. They were brothers to the human beings of all the tribes. So the animals and the human beings were always here together and associated together and considered themselves brothers.
>
> The buffalo, our brother, always here with us, furnishing us food, hides for our clothes, robes for our beds, sinew, bones, everything that they provided for our

> livelihood. So, we have a special relationship historically and religiously with the *bishée* (we call it *bishée*), bison, or buffalo that is still strong to this very day.[17]

Stories of the Hidatsa, from whom the Crow had separated in their early history, also emphasized the kinship and similarities between people and the buffalo. Elders often told stories about the buffalo as a means of instructing young people about tribal beliefs and values, as described by Gerard Baker: "As all tribes, we believed that the buffalo had a spirit and at one time in our early creation, we learned that like all of the animals that the Creator made, the buffalo could talk. The stories that are still passed down to younger generations were meant as teaching stories and there was always a lesson in each story, even the humorous ones."[18]

The central role of the buffalo in Lakota spiritual beliefs is personified in the White Buffalo Calf Woman, a messenger from the buffalo nation. She brought the ceremonial pipe to the Lakota during a desperate time of starvation. She asked that the people be brought together, and then taught them in the ways of the pipe and its ceremonies that were to be used in making peace with other peoples.

White Buffalo Calf Woman spoke to the women, children, and men, instructing each in their respective roles and responsibilities. She reminded the women of their importance to their families and that they have been given the knowledge to clothe and feed their family members. She talked with the children about their futures and admonished that they should always lead pure lives. She told the men that the pipe was to be used for nothing but good purposes, because the tribe as a whole depended upon it for the necessities derived from elements of the earth and sky. White Buffalo Calf Woman told the men that they should revere these elements and, when in need of buffalo meat, smoke the pipe and pray for what was needed. According to tradition as narrated by Lakota elder Lone Man to Frances Densmore, "Then, rising, she started, leaving the pipe with the chief who ordered that the people be quiet until their sister was out of sight. She came out of the tent (tipi) on the left side, walking very slowly; as soon as she was outside the entrance she turned into a white buffalo calf."[19] The buffalo and White Buffalo Calf Woman are of continuing spiritual significance to Lakota people as expressed by John Fire Lame Deer:

> According to our belief, the Buffalo Woman who brought us the peace pipe, which is at the center of our religion, was a beautiful maiden, and after she had taught our tribes how to worship with the pipe, she changed herself into a white buffalo calf. So the buffalo is very sacred to us. You can't understand about nature, about the feeling we have toward it, unless you understand how close we were to the buffalo. That animal was almost like a part of ourselves, part of our souls.[20]

For all Plains Indian people, the buffalo was the center of their economic, cultural, and spiritual practices. They understood that by honoring and showing reverence for the buffalo through ceremonies, the herds increased in number and came closer to the tribes so buffalo could be hunted. When buffalo herds were abundant and within reach and hunters were successful, the people celebrated and gave thanks for this magnificent gift that provided nourishment and the raw materials from which the necessities of life were created.

Tribes preserved their spiritual connections to the buffalo through prayers, rituals, and ceremonies considered essential for their physical and cultural survival. Ceremonial leaders communicated with the buffalo and had special powers related to the animal that had been given to them through visions or dreams. Among the Blackfoot people, an *iniskin,* or small segment of an ammonite fossil resembling a buffalo, was used in special ceremonies to call buffalo to jumps and places where they could be surrounded and killed.[21] Among the Mandan and Hidatsa, according to Gerard Baker, "The buffalo played a role in the older men's Buffalo Bull society which had many responsibilities, including teaching young boys to be adults through learning the prayers, hunting skills, and the making of implements used in the hunt and for warfare."[22]

The Mandan and Hidatsa held a series of buffalo-calling ceremonies sponsored by men's and women's societies to increase the herds and draw the buffalo closer to their villages.[23] A major ritual of the Mandan people, the Okipa (O-Kee-Pa) ceremony dramatized tribal origins and the creation of the earth, its plants, animals, and people. The Okipa emphasized the importance of the buffalo to the people and served as an initiation ceremony for young men. The four-day ceremony took place each summer after the corn was planted and before the tribal buffalo hunt. A part of the ceremony was the Buffalo Dance in which men wearing masks of tanned buffalo hide and horns, hide breechcloths, and wrist and ankle decorations of buffalo hair impersonated buffalo bulls (fig. 1.4). The Okipa ceremony ensured an abundance of buffalo and brought the herds closer to the villages.[24]

Plains Indian women's societies also conducted ceremonies associated with the power of buffalo to sustain the people and their way of life. The Motoki Society was an exclusive women's society among the Kainai (Blood) people of present Alberta, Canada. This society was considered a companion to the men's Horn Society. Once a year, the societies held their own four-day ceremony during the Sun Dance. During the ceremony, the women wearing distinctive buffalo horn and feathered headdresses held dances during which

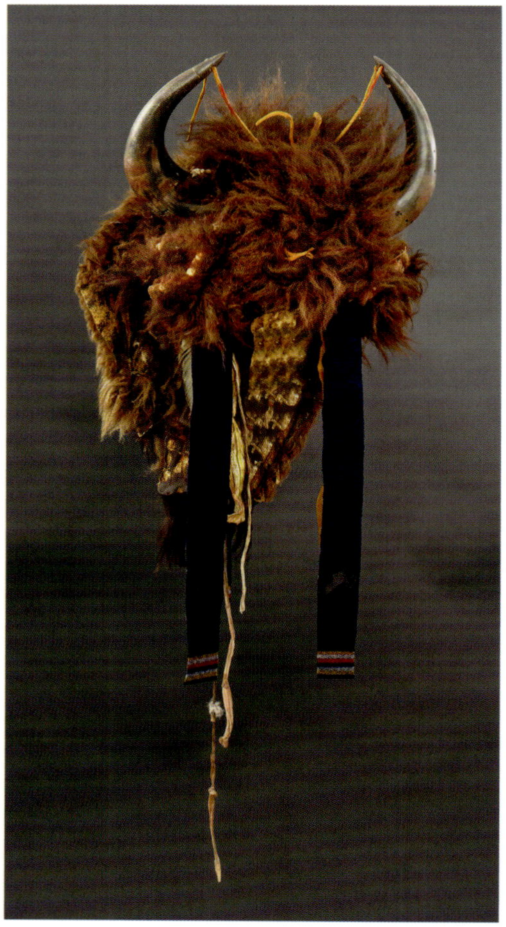

1.3. **Buffalo horn bonnet**
Northern Plains, ca. 1840
Buffalo hide and horns, cotton cloth, tanned hide, cotton twine, wool cloth, turkey feathers; 11 × 20 × 39 inches
Plains Indian Museum, NA.203.1467

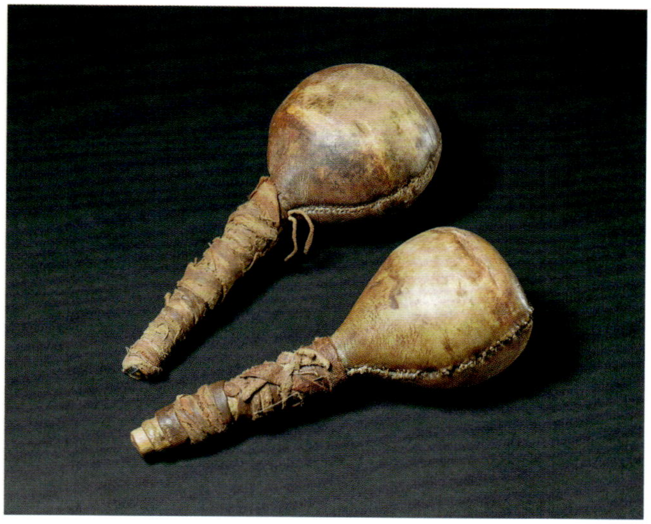

1.4. **Rattles**
Nueta (Mandan), Upper Missouri River Region, ca. 1840
Buffalo rawhide (scrotum skin), sinew, wood, stones, tanned hide, cotton cloth; 9½ × 6 inches
Plains Indian Museum, NA.502.268

Men carried these rattles in the Bull Dance, the second phase of the Mandan's annual Okipa ceremony. The four-day-long Okipa dramatized the Mandan story of creation and their historical traditions.

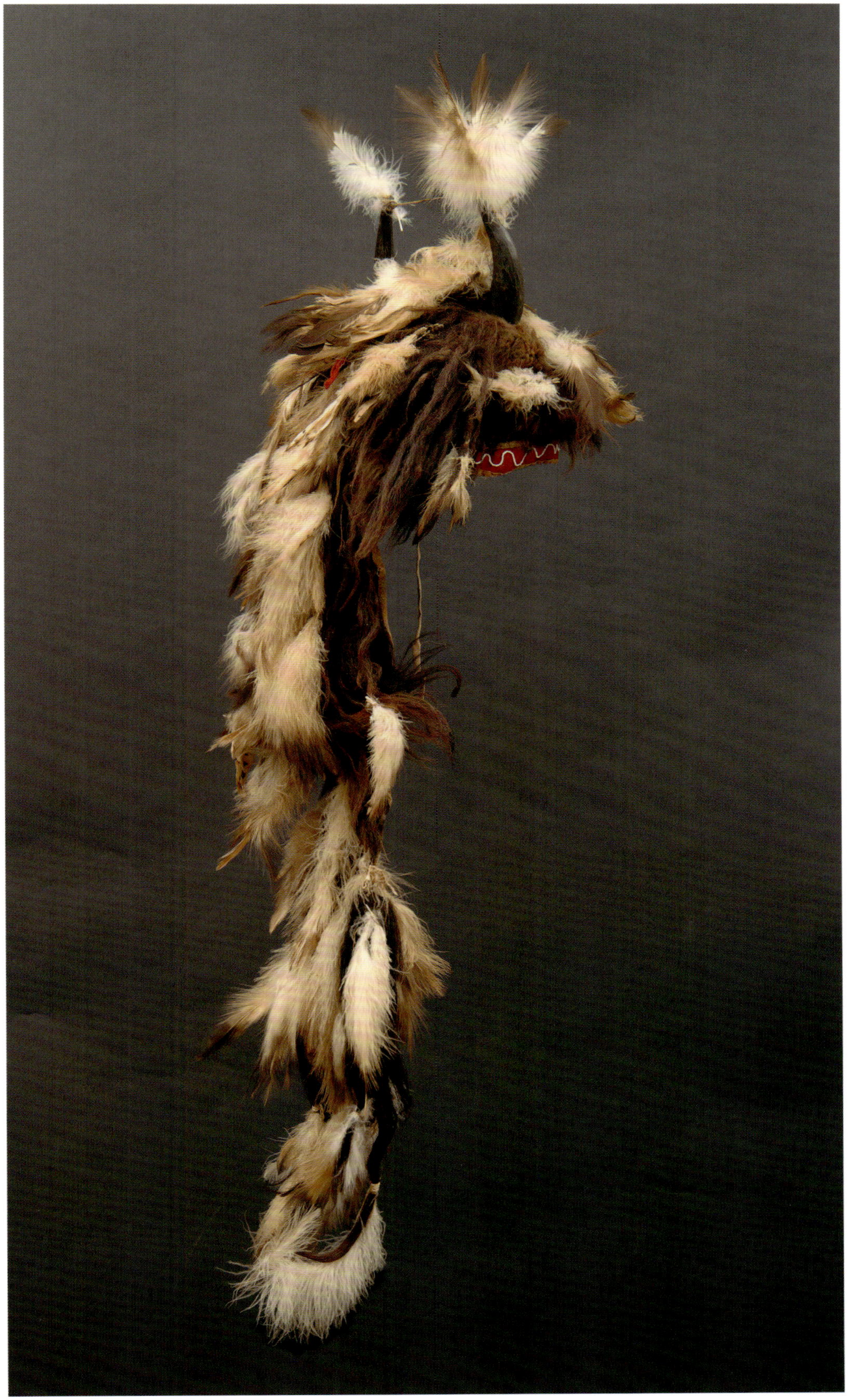

1.5. **Motoki Society buffalo horn bonnet**
Kainai (Blood), Northern Plains, ca. 1860
Buffalo hair, buffalo hide, buffalo horns, golden eagle feathers, hawk feathers, wool, cotton cloth, glass beads, sinew; 44 × 11½ inches
Plains Indian Museum, NA.205.109

The Motoki was an exclusive women's society among the Kainai (Blood) people of present-day Alberta, Canada. Members wore distinctive buffalo horn and feathered bonnets during their ceremonies, which took place during the annual Sun Dance. A Bird member of the society owned this bonnet.

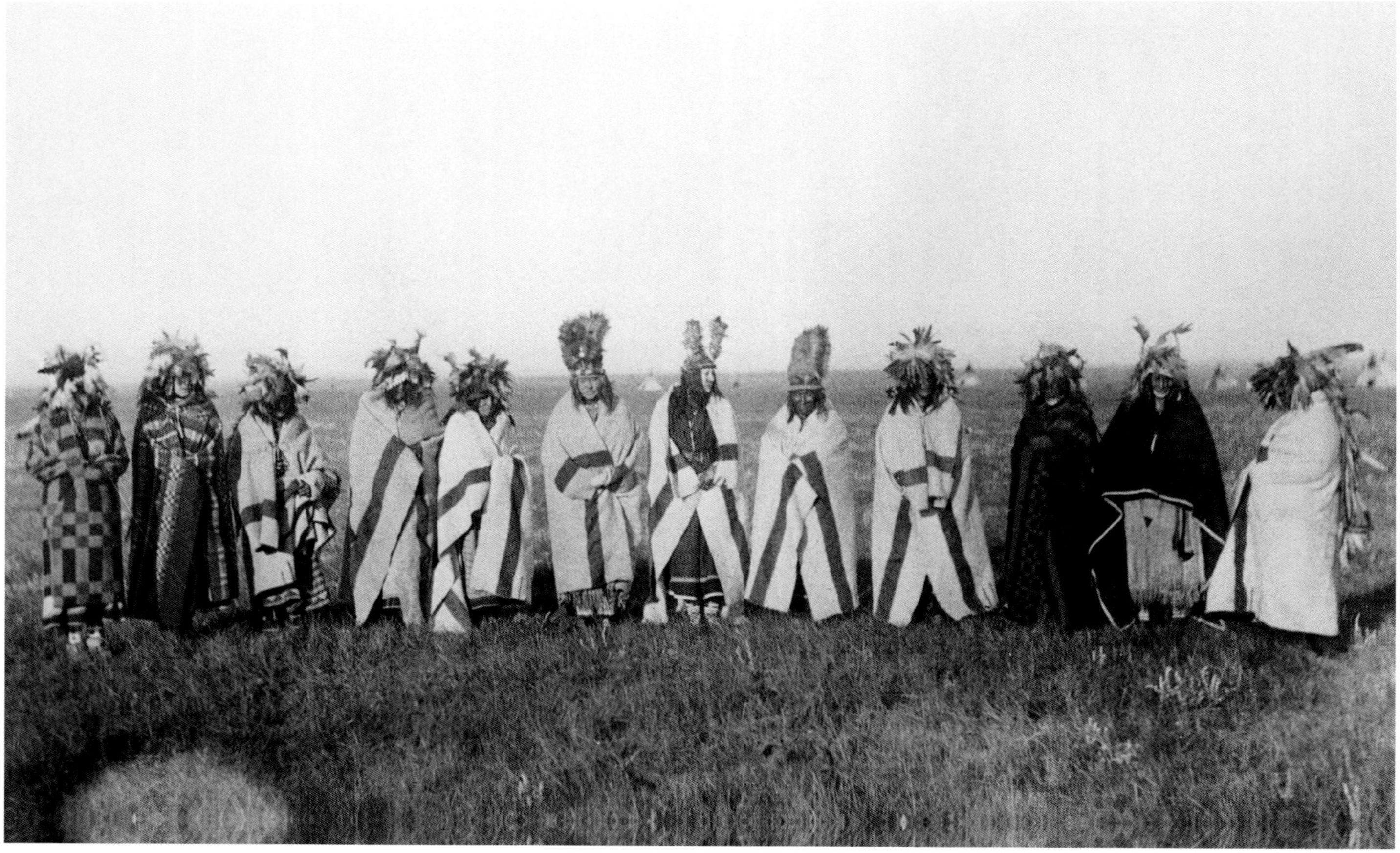

1.6. **Motoki Women's Society**
Kainai (Blood), Blood Reserve, Alberta, Canada, 1892
Photograph by R. N. Wilson
Glenbow Museum Archives, NA.688–27

they impersonated buffalo. Through the ceremony, the Motoki Society acknowledged the importance of the buffalo and ensured successful hunts. The Motoki Society headdress (fig. 1.5) in the Dyck collection, consisting of a buffalo hide cap with horns, hair, and golden eagle and hawk feathers, belonged to a Bird member.[25]

Arapaho women participated in a similar women's society dedicated to the significance and power of the buffalo. During their ceremony, like the Kainai women, Arapaho women imitated the movements of a buffalo herd. Women held ranks within the Arapaho society that were signified by the design of the bonnets and the belts. The belt in the Dyck collection from the Southern Arapaho (fig. 1.7) people of present Oklahoma is made of tanned buffalo hide and decorated with buffalo tails and hair, porcupine quills, and hawk feathers.[26]

Plains Indian members of some warrior societies acknowledged the spiritual power of the buffalo through the wearing of eagle feather bonnets with split buffalo horns (fig. 1.8). The maker of the Shoshone example in the Dyck collection (fig. 1.9) painted the split horns, made from a single buffalo horn, and trimmed the tips with dyed horsehair and strips of glass beadwork. Twenty-four golden eagle feathers, porcupine quillwork, and beadwork embellish the bonnet's cap and brow band, and thirty-eight golden eagle feathers trim the long red wool trailer. Three ermines, or winter weasels, hang from each side of the bonnet. The addition of the weasels—small but ferocious animals admired for their courage and fierce fighting ability—also provided powerful war medicine for the wearer of the bonnet.

OPPOSITE:
1.7. **Buffalo Dance belt**
Hinono'ei (Southern Arapaho), Indian Territory, Oklahoma, ca. 1890
Tanned buffalo hide, buffalo tail, porcupine quills, buffalo dewclaws, buffalo hair, hawk feathers, sinew;
28 × 7¾ inches
Plains Indian Museum, NA.203.1564

This belt was part of the regalia of the Arapaho Women's Buffalo Lodge worn during their Buffalo Dance. A woman wore the belt over her dress along with a bonnet, which, together, represented her membership level within the lodge.

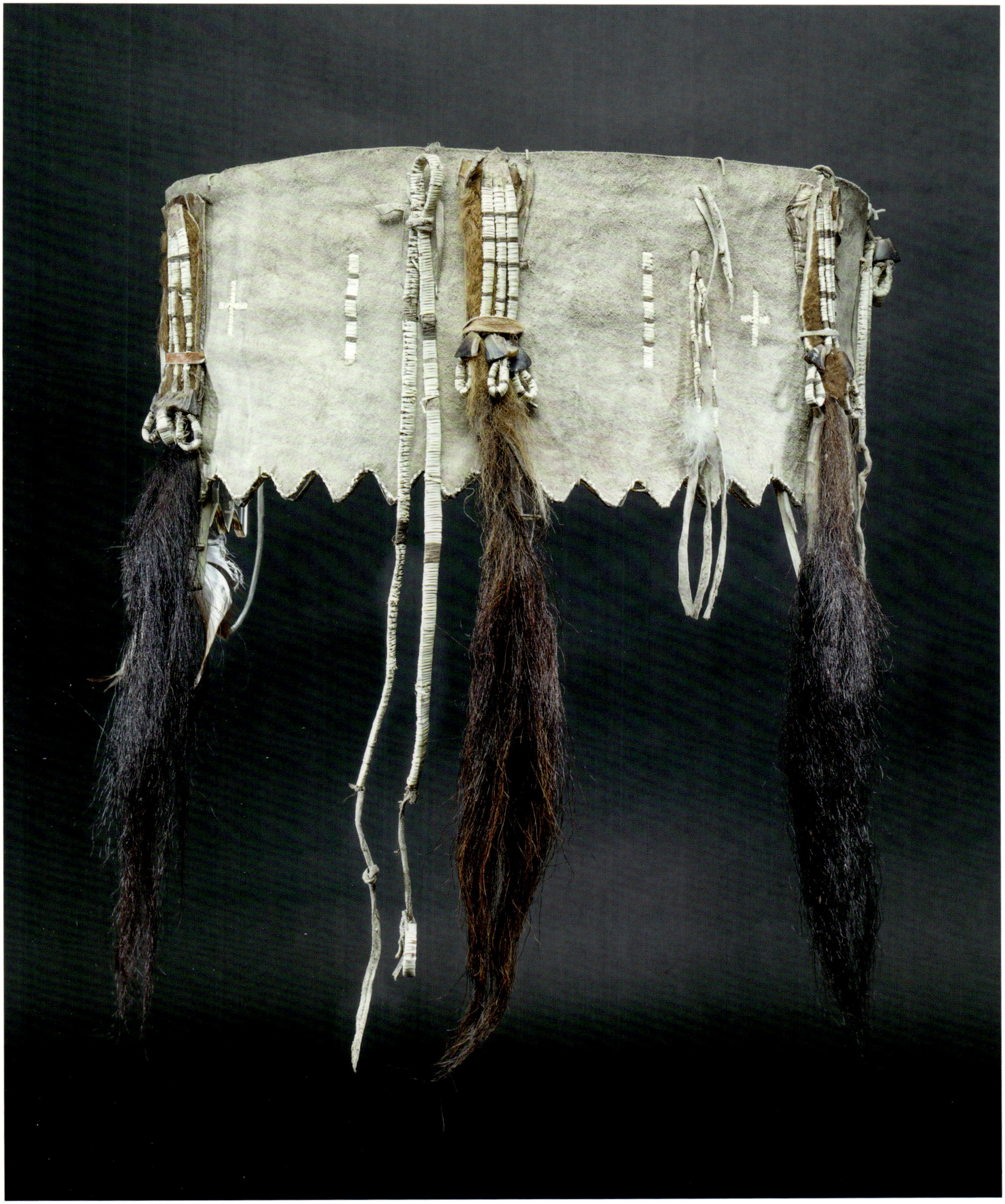

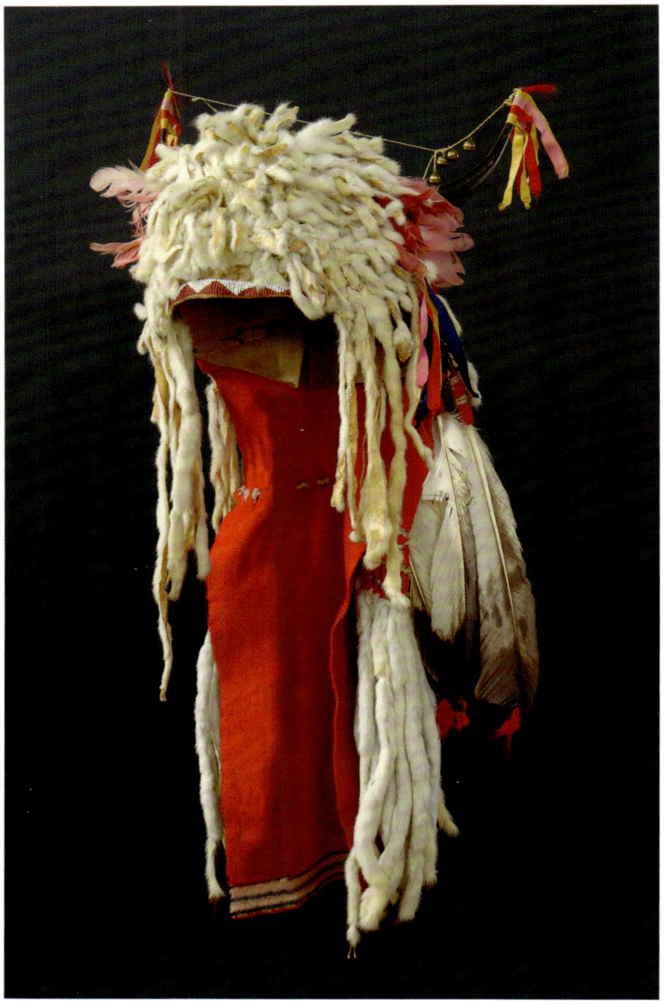

1.8. **Buffalo horn bonnet**
Niitsitapi (Blackfoot), Northern Plains, 1870–1890
Buffalo horn, feather fluffs, golden eagle feathers, pigment, ermine, satin ribbon, cotton cloth, glass beads, tanned hide, brass bells, wool cloth, cotton thread, dyed horse hair, commercial felt, dyed feathers; 17½ x 24 inches
Plains Indian Museum, NA.203.1603

Men created strong shields from the thick rawhide taken from the necks of buffalo bulls, thickening the pieces even more by heating them. Painted with images that would provide spiritual protection for owners, the shields were essential elements of warriors' equipment (fig. 1.10). In keeping with Paul Dyck's interest in the roles of warriors and the conflicts of the late nineteenth century, he collected several shields from the Northern and Southern Plains.[27] He identified one example as a dance shield of the Buffalo Bull Society, a Kainai man's society, that belonged to Water Chief who lived on the Blood Reserve in Alberta, Canada. Made of cowhide, the shield has a painted central image of a buffalo head under a curtain of eagle feathers (fig. 1.11).

From the buffalo, including meat, hide, horns, bones, hooves, hair, and organs, Native people of the Plains produced food, shelter, clothing, and other necessities of life. The meat itself was eaten fresh or preserved by cutting it in strips that were dried in the sun. Stored in hide bags, the preserved meat could be combined with prairie turnips, corn, squash, or other vegetables for a nutritious soup. Dried meat was also pounded and mixed with buffalo fat and chokecherries to make pemmican, which could be kept for several months.

Women worked long hours with implements of sharpened bone and horn to scrape hair from, soften, and tan hides from which they produced tipi covers, clothing, robes, moccasins,

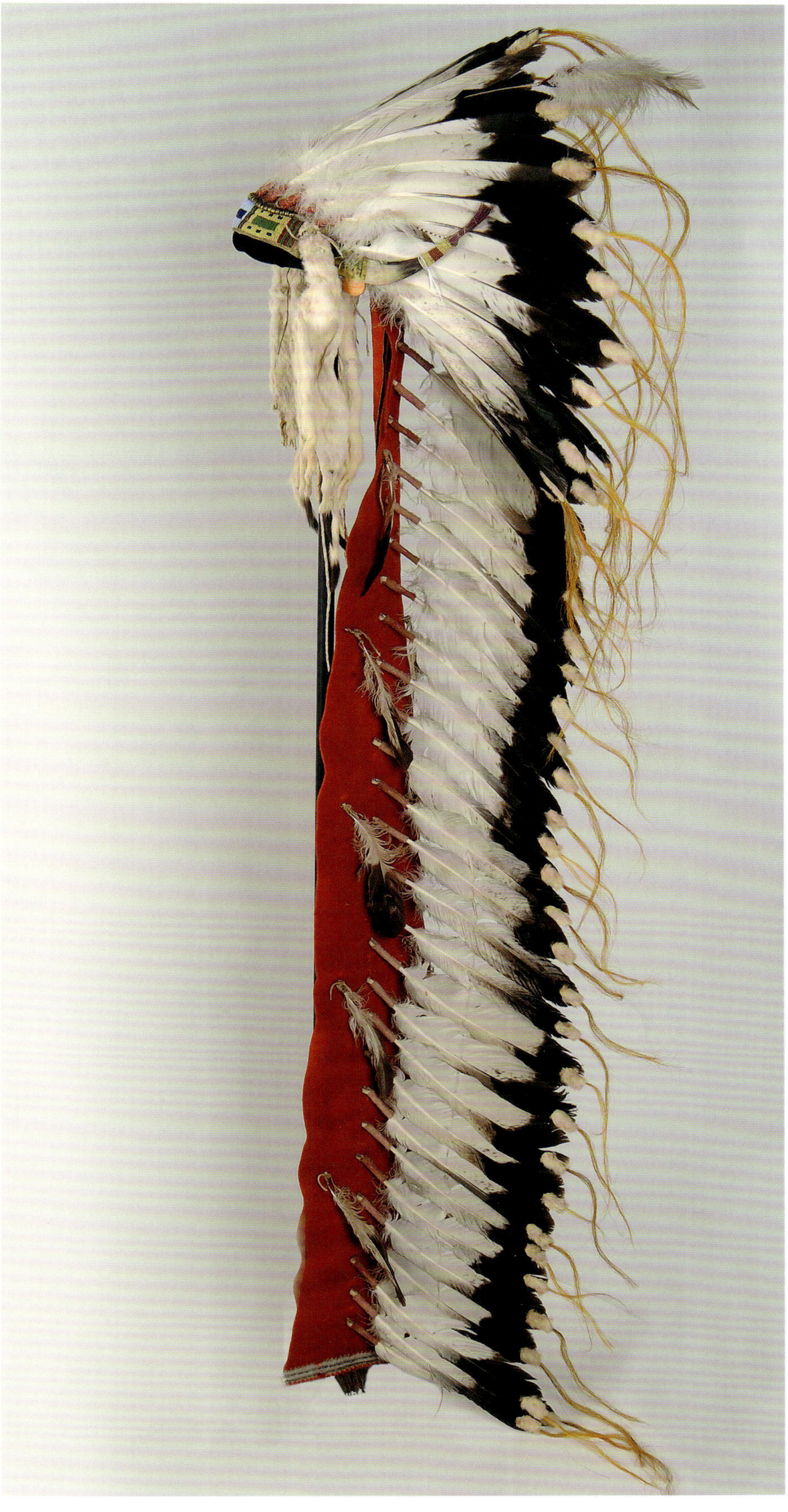

1.9. **Bonnet and trailer**
So-soreh (Shoshone), Northern Plains, ca. 1880
Buffalo horns, golden eagle feathers, wool cloth, ermine, porcupine quills, glass and brass beads, tanned elk and deer hide, pigment, horsehair; 54 × 20 inches
Plains Indian Museum, NA.203.1498

The man who wore this bonnet and trailer carried with him the spiritual powers of the buffalo and the eagle. The winter weasels (ermine), known to be fierce and courageous fighters, also provided powerful war medicine for the wearer.

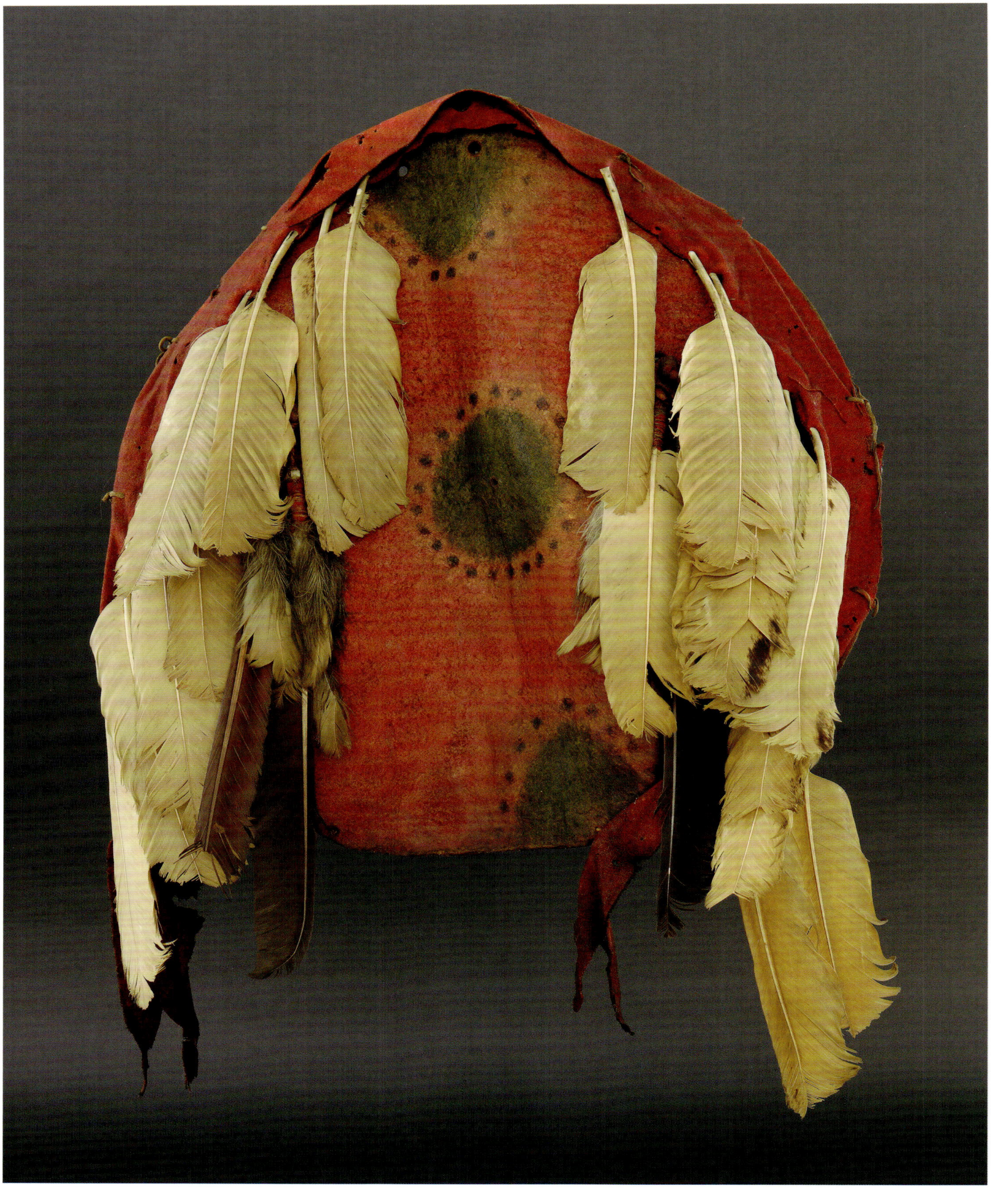

OPPOSITE:

1.10. **Shield**
Kaigwa (Kiowa), Southern Plains, ca. 1830
Buffalo rawhide, pigment, bald eagle feathers, sinew, tanned hide, wool cloth; 20¼ × 21 inches
Plains Indian Museum, NA.108.131

According to Dyck, the painting on the shield represents four sacred mountains and the Kiowa camp circle.

1.11. **Dance shield**
Kainai (Blood), Alberta, Canada, ca. 1880
Domestic cow rawhide, wool cloth, sinew, pigment, brass bells, cotton cloth, cotton thread, feather fluffs, tanned hide; 16¾ inches (diameter)
Plains Indian Museum, NA.108.139

This is a dance shield of the Buffalo Bull Society, which was a Kainai man's society. Water Chief, of the Blood Reserve in Alberta, Canada, owned the shield. Made of lightweight cow rawhide, the shield features the painted image of a buffalo head in the center under a cover of eagle feathers.

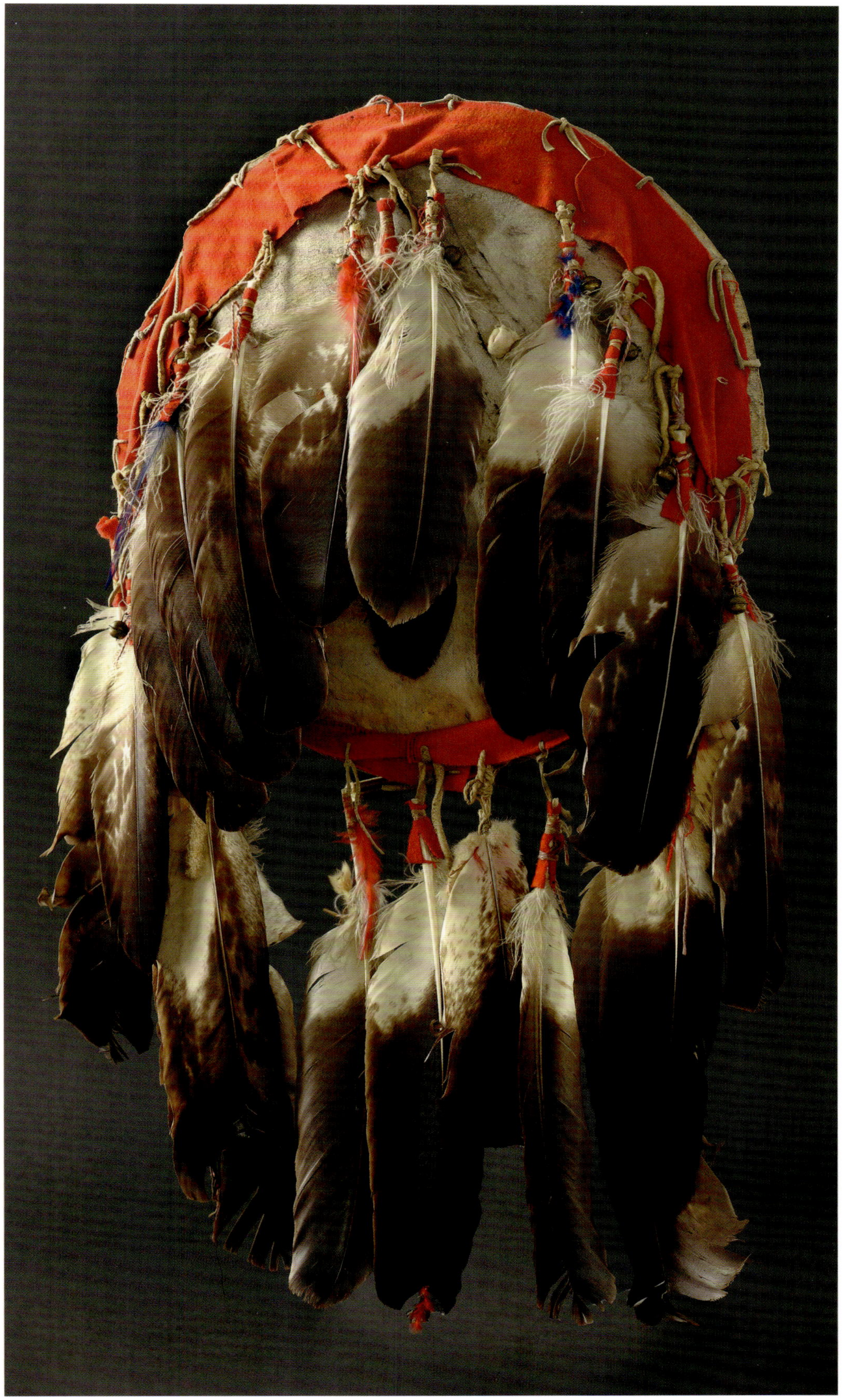

bags, and warm bedding. Women made parfleches from buffalo rawhide decorated with incised or painted designs to carry and store foods and family belongings. Buffalo bones were made into hoes, digging sticks, and painting and hide-working tools, and horns were used for cups and spoons. The paunch and bladder served as containers that were suspended over cooking fires or filled with hot stones to boil meat. Sinew served as thread and bowstrings, and hair was braided into ropes.

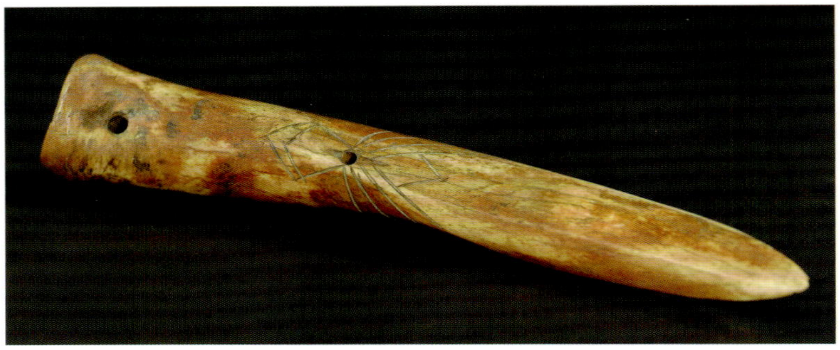

1.12. **Bone knife**
Plains, ca. 1880
Animal bone; 10½ × 2 inches
Plains Indian Museum, NA.102.244

Made from an animal's leg bone, the knife is decorated with a carved geometric design.

Crow elder Alma Snell remembered how her grandmother Pretty Shield, living on the reservation, continued to tan hides that she used for warm covers in her small home. Often, Pretty Shield involved all of her granddaughters in the process, each pulling and stretching the hide to make it soft. Other times she worked the hide by herself until it was soft. Alma Snell recounted, "I have seen her take that robe and go against her knee in a fold and roll that fold and keep rolling it until it got soft. Then, she'd go to another spot. That robe I know very well because I slept in it. I slept in the robe with her."[28]

After tanning, women could paint the buffalo robes using natural pigments made from the minerals, clays, and plants they had gathered or decorate them with porcupine quillwork

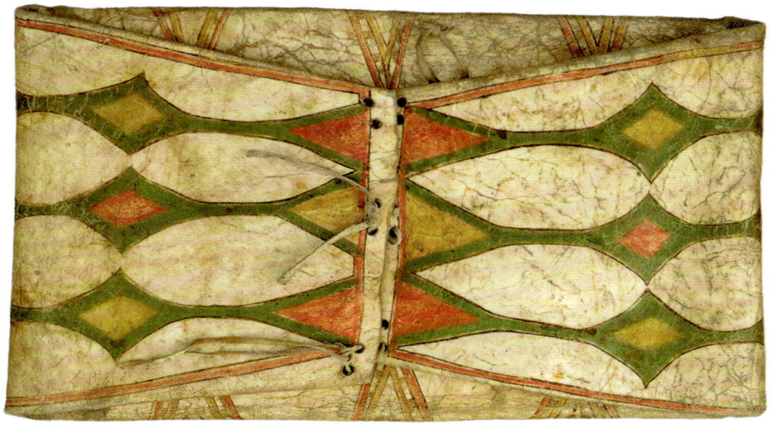

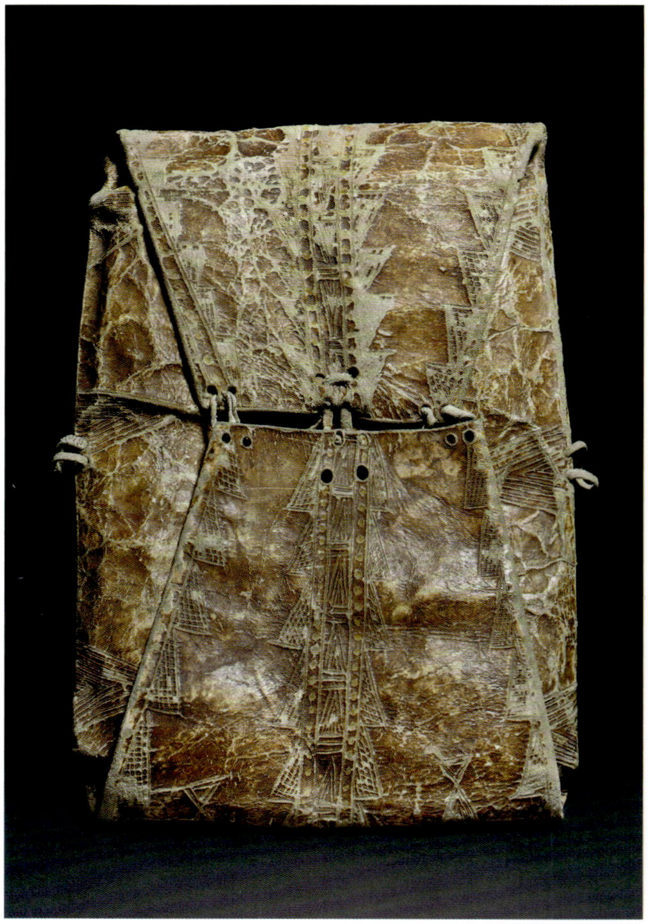

ABOVE:
1.13. **Parfleche**
Tsitsistas (Cheyenne), Northern Plains, ca. 1850
Buffalo rawhide, pigments, tanned hide; 29 × 16½ inches
Plains Indian Museum, NA.106.906

The envelope-shaped parfleche is the most recognizable type of container among Plains peoples. The tradition of parfleche painting developed tribally and regionally, defined by specific techniques of construction, color, and design.

RIGHT:
1.14. **Parfleche**
Niitsitapi (Blackfoot), Northern Plains, ca. 1840
Buffalo rawhide, tanned hide; 12½ × 20½ inches
Plains Indian Museum, NA.106.934

Incising, created by cutting and scraping designs in the wet upper layers of buffalo rawhide, is an older technique for decorating parfleches. Examples of fully incised bison parfleches from the Blackfeet are very rare, with only a few known in museum collections.

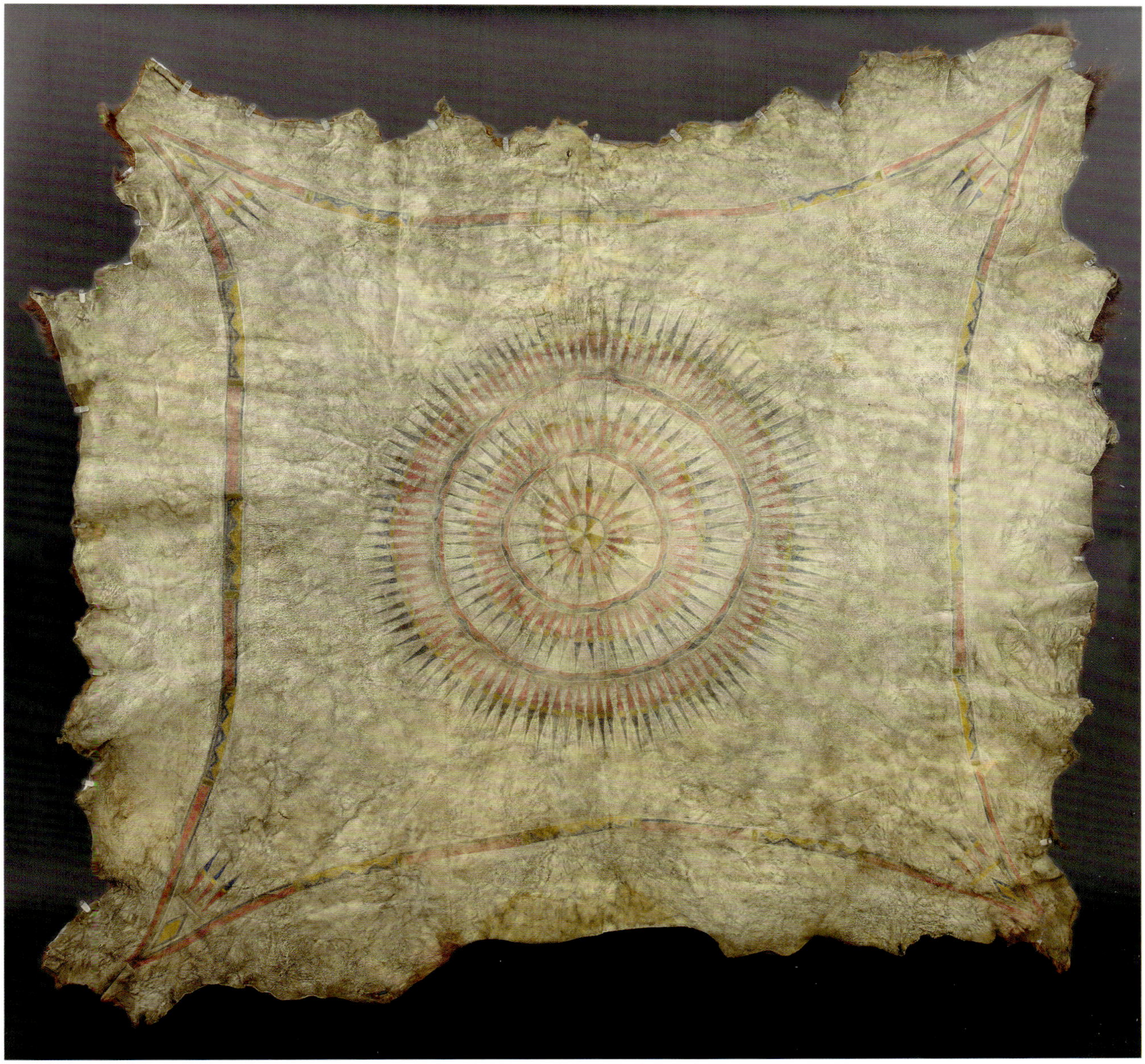

1.15. **Buffalo robe**
Northern Plains, ca. 1870
Tanned buffalo hide, pigment, sinew;
79½ × 68½ inches
Plains Indian Museum, NA.203.1511

The painted design on this robe, called the feathered circle, consists of circles of feathers radiating from the central figure representing the sun.

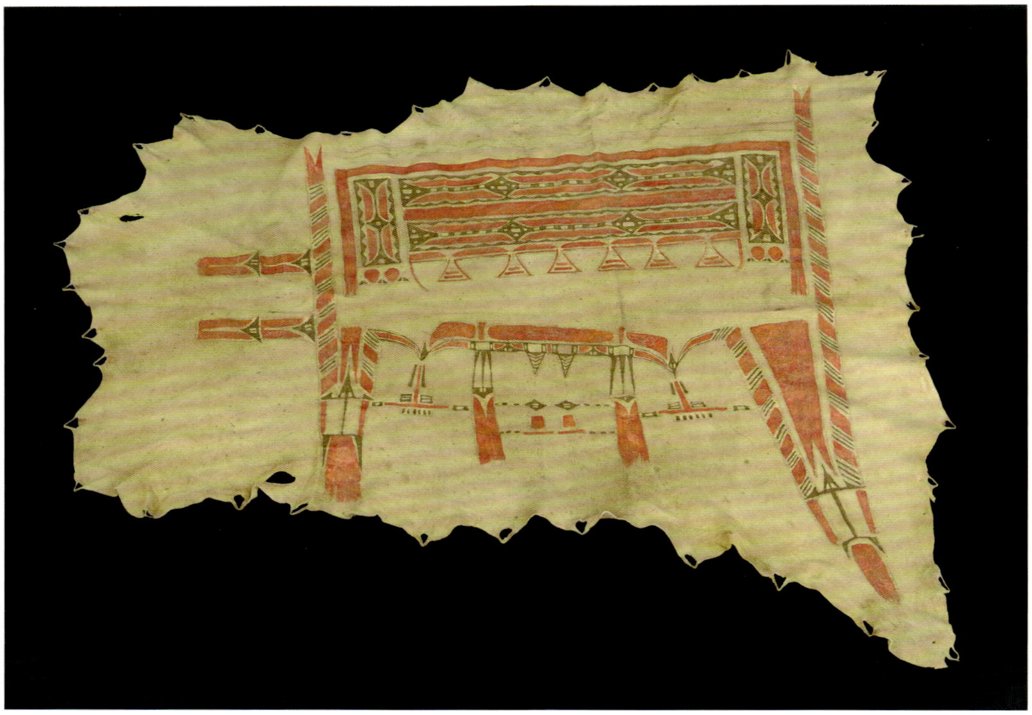

1.16. **Painted hide**
Northern Plains, ca. 1880
Tanned deer hide, pigment;
46 × 44¼ inches
Plains Indian Museum, NA.702.39

This painted deer hide features the box-and-border design, a motif commonly used on buffalo robes. The design is said to represent the internal organs of the animal.

or glass-beaded designs. During the 1800s, women also used commercial pigments as colors became available through Euro-American traders. For women, the painted robe designs were primarily geometric using colors and patterns sometimes revealed to them in dreams and passed on as gifts to daughters and granddaughters.

A frequently used design called the feathered circle consists of circles of abstract forms representing eagle feathers radiating out from a central figure representing the sun (fig. 1.15). The circles of eagle feathers symbolize an eagle feather bonnet, although they can also be seen as the rays of the sun. The design combines two powerful images in Plains Indian symbolism: the eagle, represented by the feather bonnet, and the life-giving sun. Plains Indian women frequently used this design when painting robes to be worn by their male relatives.

For many generations, Plains Indian women painted another common pattern known as the box-and-border design on buffalo robes. An example in the Dyck collection is actually a small tanned deer hide featuring the design (fig. 1.16). The box-and-border design has been interpreted as an abstract representation of the internal structure or organs of the animal. The border of the painting tends to follow the deer hide's shape. The box-and-border design was used by several tribes of the Central and Northern Plains but seemed most prominent among the Lakota.

Traditional arts of Plains Indian people reflected the economic and spiritual significance of the buffalo. Men painted images of buffalo as whole figures in profile or represented by head and horns, hooves, and tracks on rawhide shields and shield covers made of tanned hide (figs. 1.17 and 1.18). They carved depictions of the buffalo on pipe bowls and stems, bone whistles, and wood and bone quirts representing its significance as an intermediary between humans and the spirit world (fig. 1.19). Women of the early reservation period (1870–1910) also used similar

OPPOSITE:
1.17. **Shield and cover**
Apsáalooke (Crow), Northern Plains, ca. 1850
Buffalo rawhide and tail, golden eagle feathers, pigment, snow goose feather, glass beads, porcupine quills, sinew, tanned hide, wool cloth;
shield: 20½ × 20¾ inches; cover: 20¾ × 21 inches
Plains Indian Museum, NA.108.152.1-.2

The buffalo is a symbol used on Plains shields and covers to represent its protective power. This shield cover features a bull with shaggy hair, curved horns, and a protruding tongue.

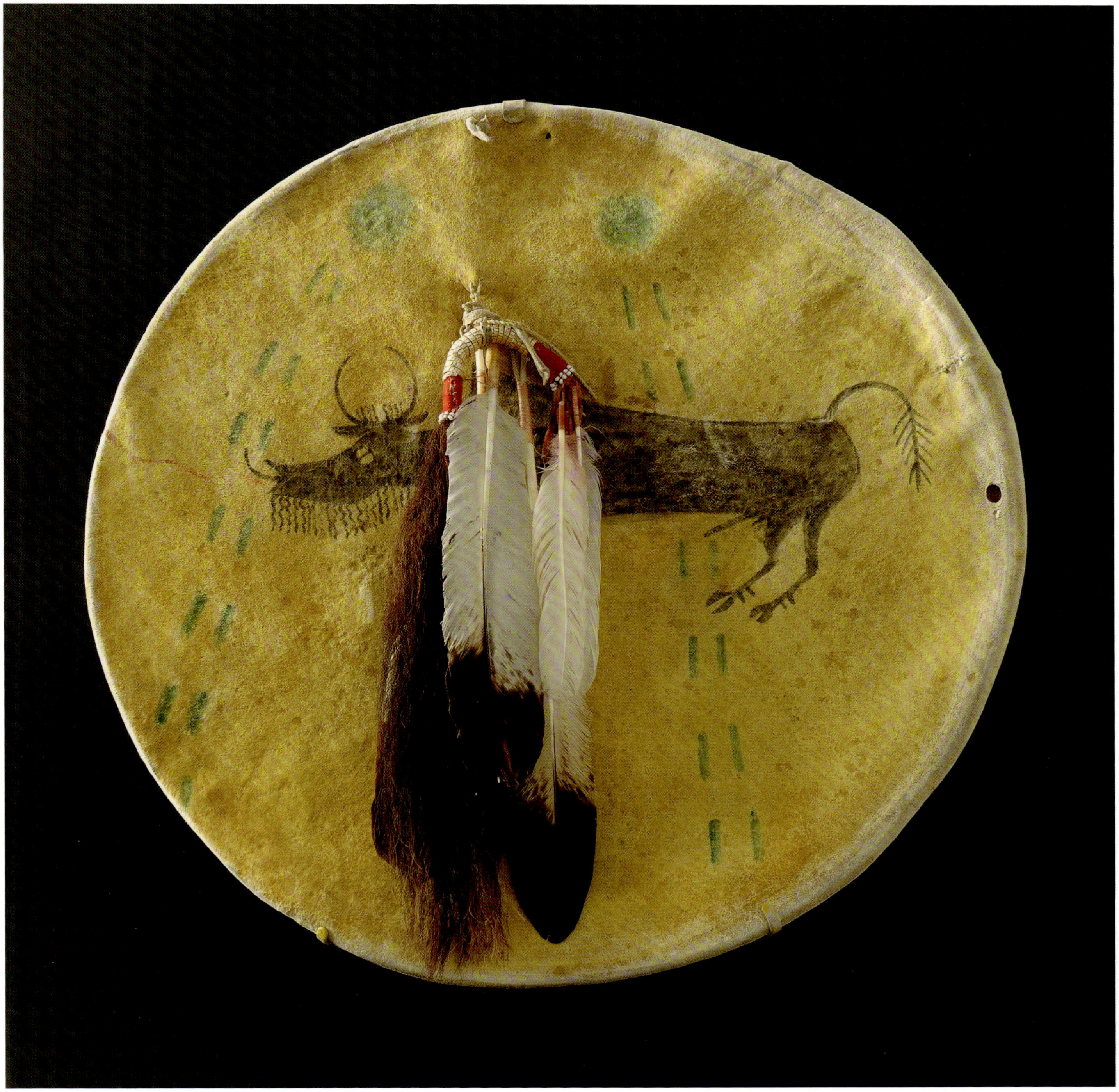

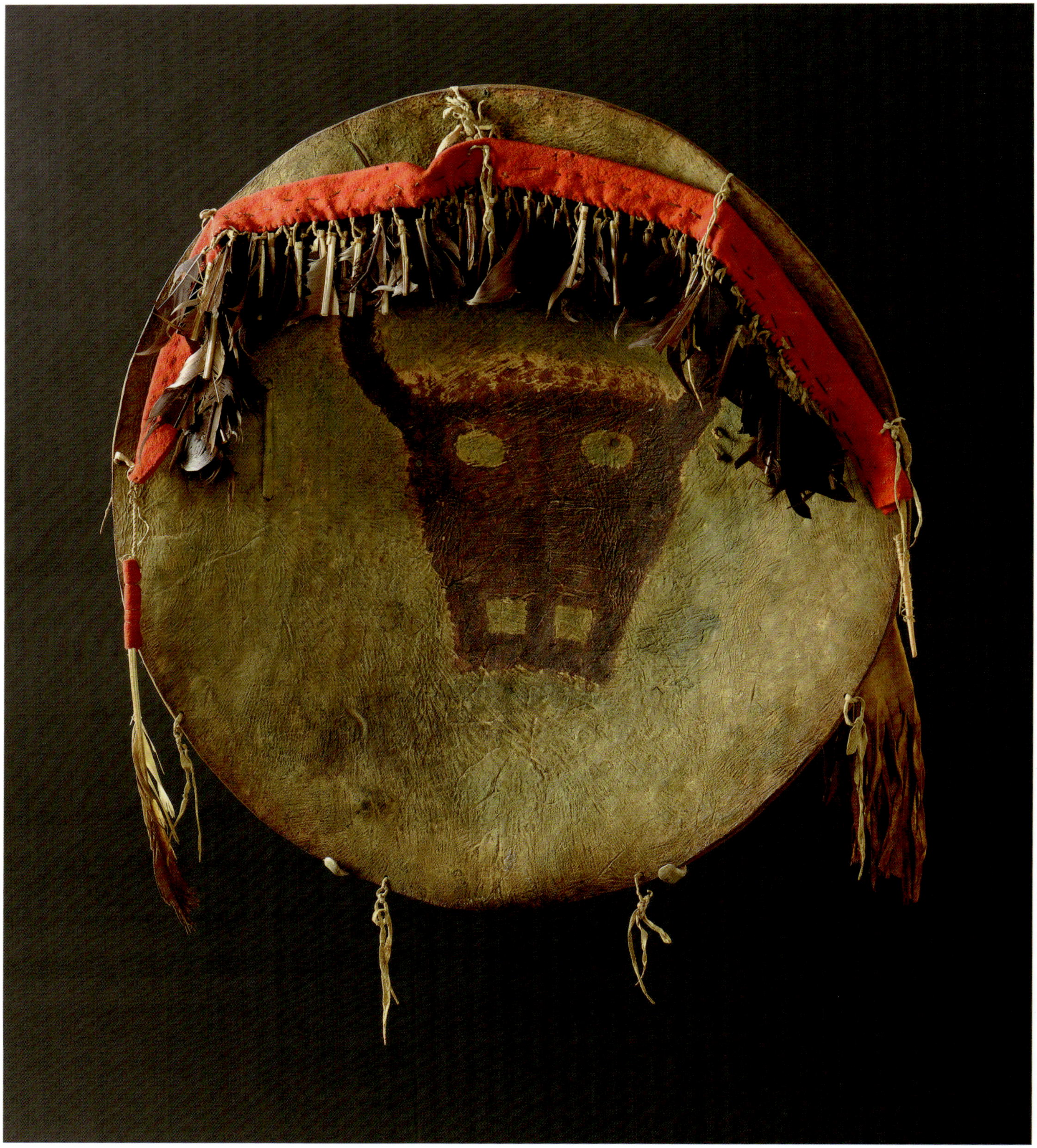

images of the buffalo, beaded or embroidered, in porcupine quillwork on moccasins and other articles of clothing.

By the 1880s, the once-vast herds of buffalo that had served to define the North American Plains had been almost totally eradicated. The loss of the buffalo, along with widespread depopulation due to disease and warfare and taking of traditional homelands, brought the free lives of Native warriors, hunters, and their families—so intertwined with that of the buffalo—to an end. Yet descendants of the people who lived through that period known as the Buffalo Culture Era continue to honor the strength and creativity of their antecedents. Gerard Baker recounted:

> Many tribes, including the Mandan, Hidatsa and Arikara of the Fort Berthold Reservation, now have a very healthy herd of buffalo that once again roam parts of our homeland and reservation. We utilize and sell the meat and bi-products [*sic*], and also use the buffalo for tourism activities. The buffalo and the spirit of the buffalo are still very important.
>
> The buffalo is making a comeback. The elders in my family have told me, "The buffalo is like us Indians. The white man put us on reservation, like the buffalo in a zoo, they also killed our game and degraded our ceremonies and our way of life." But they add that we will never go away, and neither will the buffalo. We still need them and we still need to recognize the spirits through ceremony.[29]

OPPOSITE:
1.18. **Shield**
Lakota (Sioux), Northern Plains, ca. 1860
Buffalo rawhide, golden eagle feathers, raven feathers, pigment, sinew, tanned hide, wool cloth, cotton thread; 21 inches (diameter)
Plains Indian Museum, NA.108.146

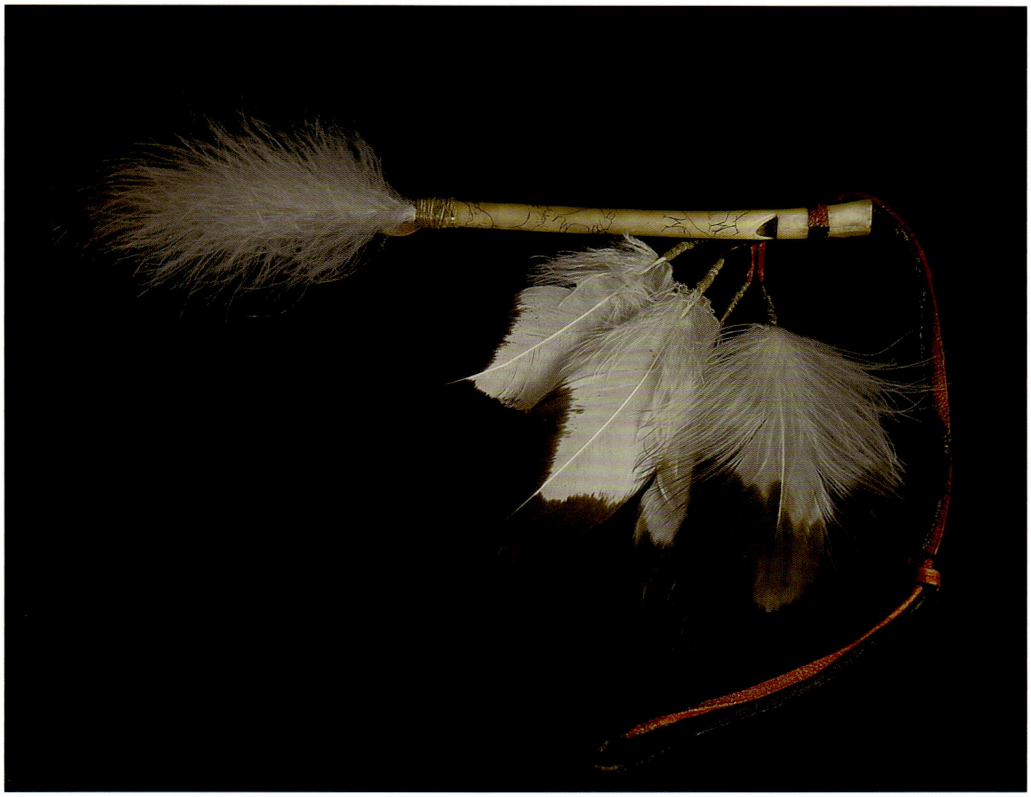

1.19. **Eagle bone whistle**
Northern Plains, ca. 1890
Eagle bone, pigment, eagle feathers, sinew, tanned hide, eagle down; 7½ × 8½ inches
Plains Indian Museum, NA.502.278

Six carved images of buffalo are etched into the length of this ceremonial whistle.

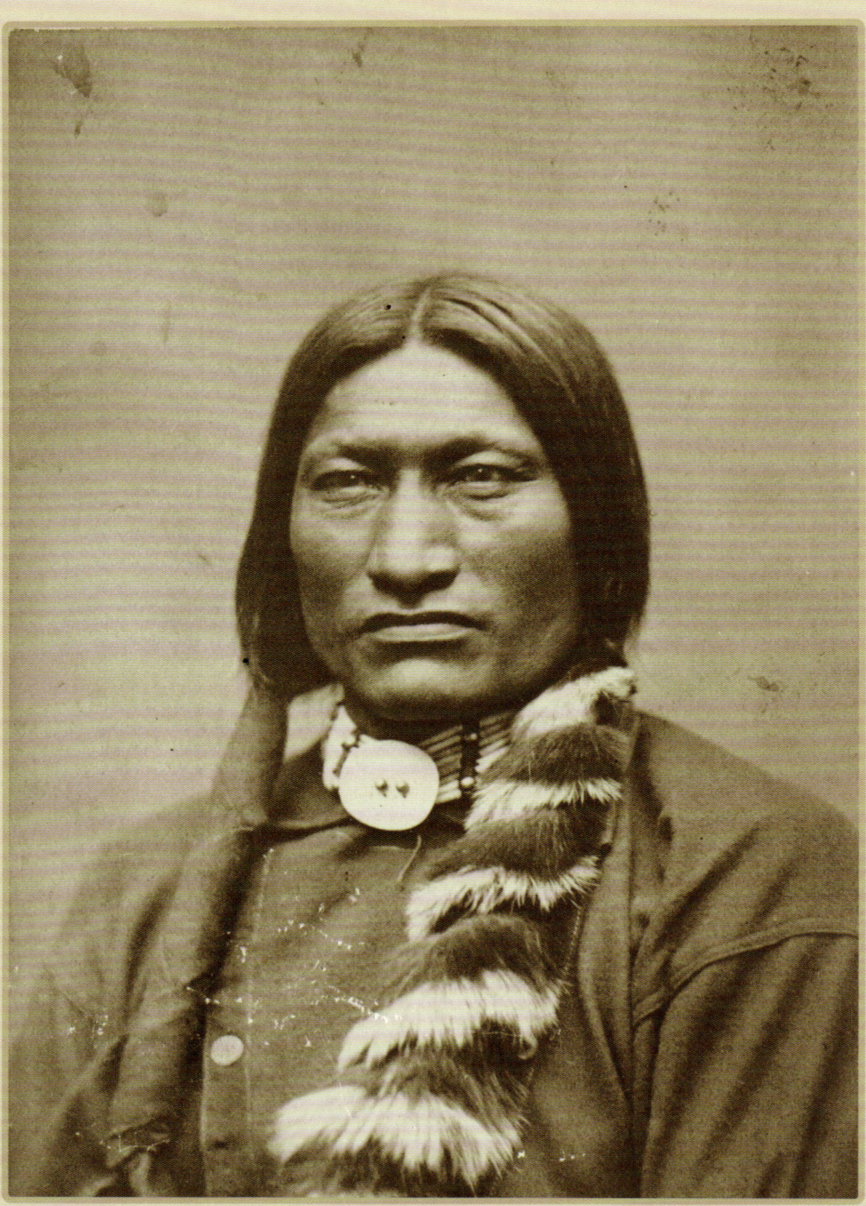

2 Protecting the Land and the People

Plains cultures encouraged and fostered idealized roles and responsibilities for men, women, elders, and children. These roles were exhibited through individual actions and supported by inherent beliefs that emphasized courage, fortitude, and physical and mental endurance. Such characteristics were considered essential for a successful life in the Plains and, in difficult times, actual survival. As Arthur Amiotte describes it,

> An economy based on hunting required protection from enemies, and courage was essential to confront natural and man-made threats. As the herds of bison diminished, intertribal warfare increased in the conflict over the valuable assets. At this time, warrior societies formalized their codes of behavior and membership expectations, including the prescribed decoration of objects worn for bravery in enemy confrontations. Fortitude in men, women, and children stressed endurance of physical and mental hardships, as in long periods of food scarcity or during recovery from wounds or accidents. The ideal was courage without complaint, as one endured the vigorous labors of a hunting-warrior society in an unforgiving climate of extreme weather.[1]

Men's roles centered on hunting and warfare, and they were honored and celebrated for their achievements in these spheres as providers and protectors of their families and

OPPOSITE:
2.1. High Bear
Lakota (Sioux), Standing Rock Reservation, ca. 1890
Photograph by L. A. Huffman
McCracken Research Library, P.100.3119

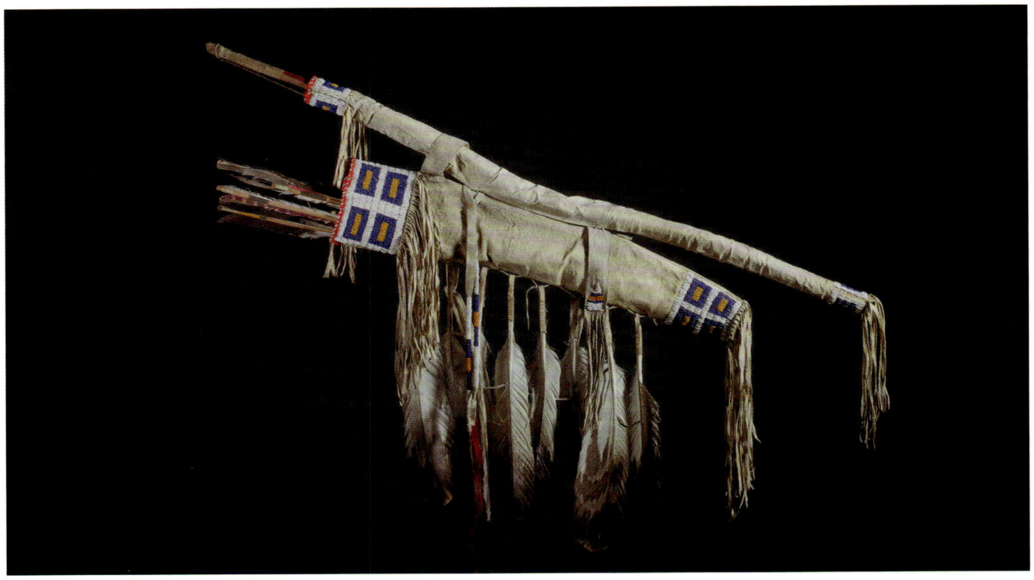

2.2. Bow case and quiver, bow, and arrows
Northern Plains, ca. 1890
Metal, wood, eagle feathers, glass beads, sinew, tanned hide, wool cloth, pigments, dyed horsehair; bow case and quiver: 33 × 6½ inches; arrow: 25 × ¼ inches; bow: 40 × 1¼ inches
Plains Indian Museum, NA.102.209

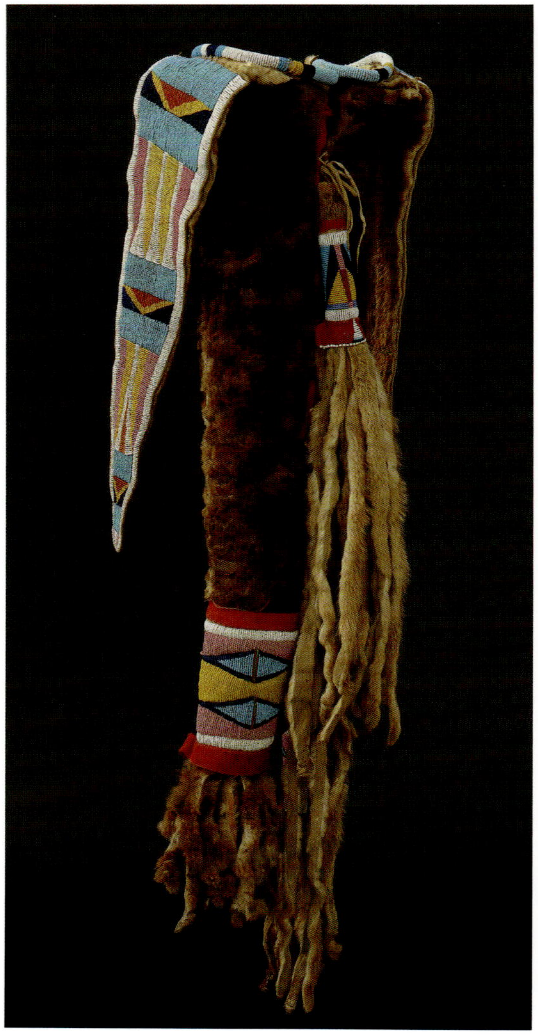

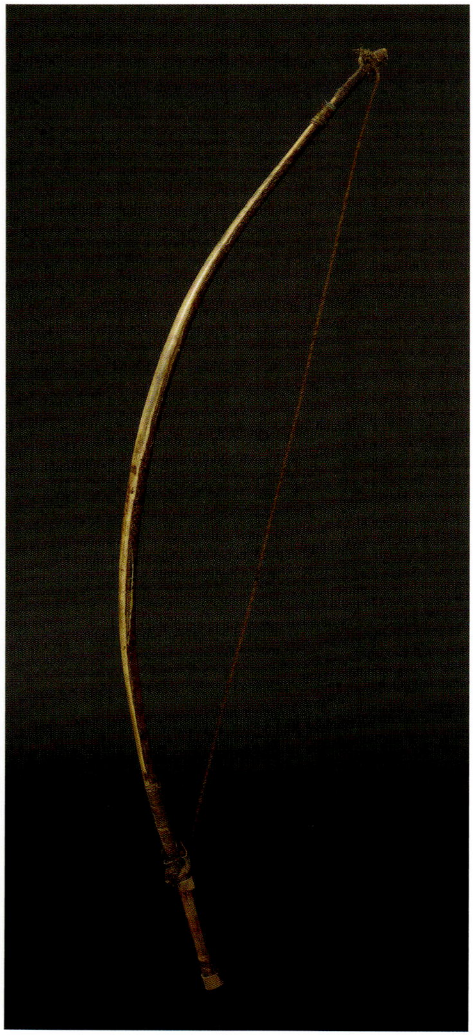

2.3 and 2.4. **Bow case and quiver and bow**
Nimi'ipuu (Nez Perce), Plateau, ca. 1875
Bow case and quiver: otter hide, wool cloth, glass beads, tanned hide; 56 × 8½ inches;
arrow: 26¼ × ⅜ inches;
bow: bone, snakeskin, sinew, wood, feathers; 40 × 1¼ inches
Plains Indian Museum, NA.203.1424.1–2

This bow case and quiver made from tanned otter hide, with broad straps and distinctive beadwork, is similar to those of the Crow of the late nineteenth century. Men carried beautifully beaded bow cases and quivers like this one in early reservation parades and other formal occasions.

their homelands. When not away from camp actively hunting or engaging in raiding and warfare, men invested much time in fashioning and maintaining weapons and refining skills indispensable to effectively meeting their economic and cultural responsibilities. Reflecting Paul Dyck's ongoing fascination with Plains Indian warfare and the roles of warriors, the Buffalo Culture Collection includes rare examples of bows, arrows, clubs, lances, and clothing and regalia used and worn by nineteenth-century Plains Indian hunters and protectors.

GREAT PLAINS HUNTERS

From an early age, women and men were taught the essential skills and knowledge needed to fulfill their roles. Girls learned from their mothers, aunts, grandmothers, and other adult females; and boys found role models in their fathers, uncles, and other male relatives and men of high prestige. As boys grew up, they often admired and emulated successful hunters, warriors, and leaders as they sought individual honors while remembering that their actions were done for the benefit of all.

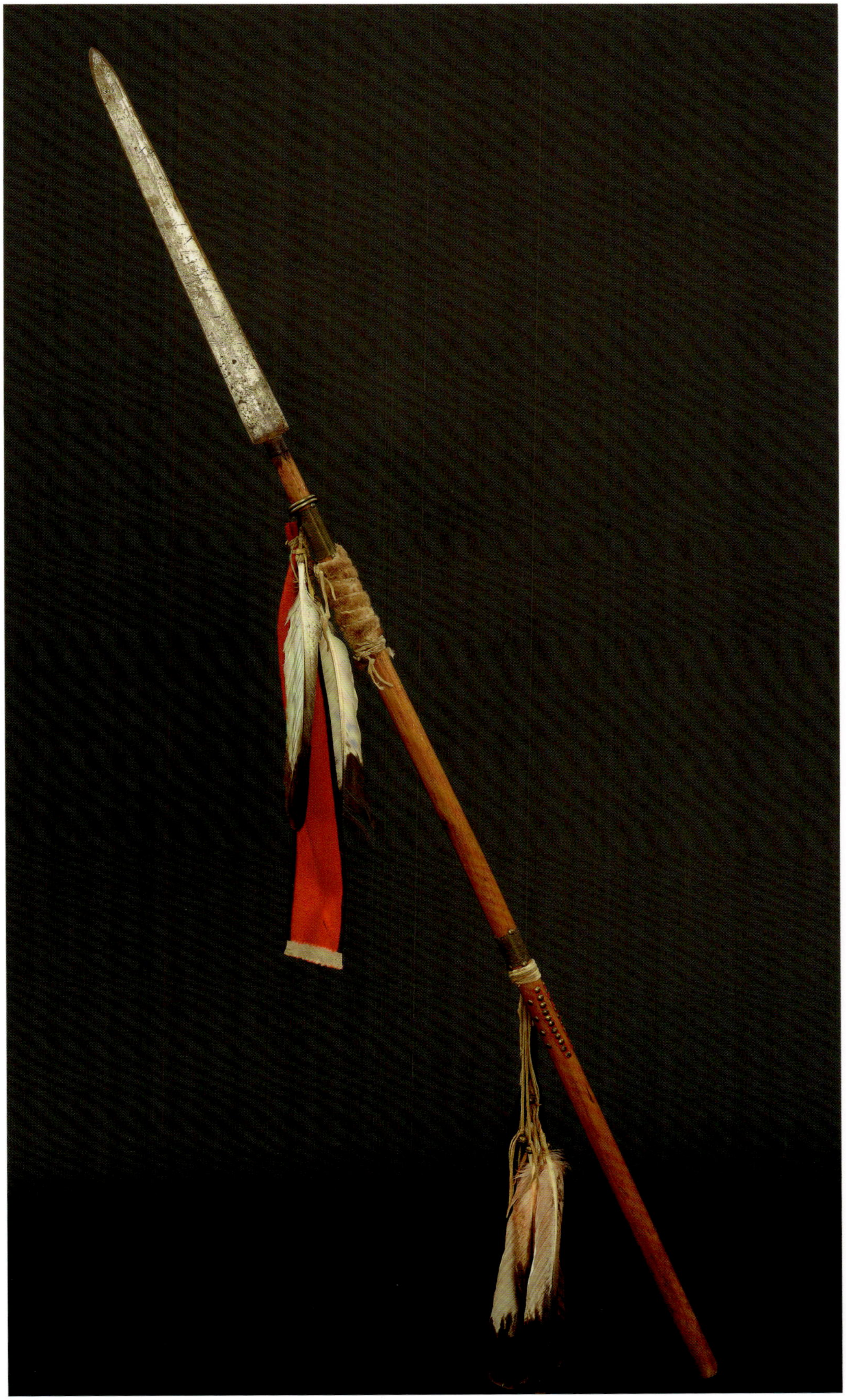

2.5. **Lance**
Northern Plains, ca. 1870
Metal, wood, otter hide, wool cloth, golden eagle feathers, tanned deer hide, wire, brass tacks, cotton twine; 69½ × 4 inches
Plains Indian Museum, NA.108.159

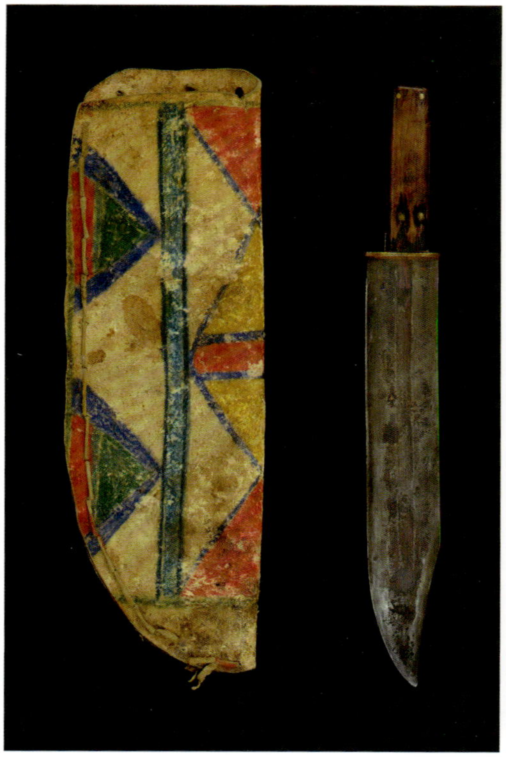

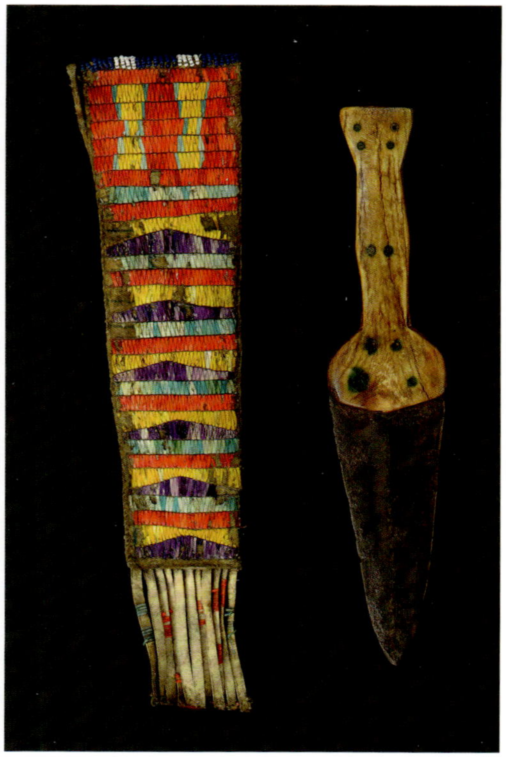

FAR LEFT:

2.6. **Knife and case**
Lakota (Sioux), Northern Plains, ca. 1890
Metal, wood, rawhide, brass, pigment, tanned hide;
knife: 17¼ × 2 inches;
case: 17½ × 5½ inches
Plains Indian Museum, NA.102.245

LEFT:

2.7 **Knife and sheath**
Northern Plains, ca. 1870
Rawhide, brass, steel, bone, lacquer, glass beads, tanned hide, cotton thread, dyed porcupine quills;
knife: 10⅞ × 2¼ inches;
sheath: 12¾ × 3 inches
Plains Indian Museum, NA.102.232

Men carried knives obtained through trade, such as this one, on war expeditions for use in hand-to-hand combat. Women often made beautiful knife sheaths decorated with porcupine quills or glass beads such as this one covered in quillwork.

Although individual men hunted elk, deer, antelope, and mountain sheep, Plains Indian hunting traditions focused on the buffalo, which because of its size provided abundant meat, hides, and other essentials to support families for a period of time. Like warfare, buffalo hunting required cooperation, organization, leadership, policing and restrictions, and spiritual assistance as well as individual endurance and courage.

Before horses became widely used in the eighteenth century, groups of men on foot pursued buffalo in seasonal hunts using buffalo jumps, pounds or corrals, and other resourceful means to gain advantages over the herds. These methods required knowledge of the migration patterns and habits of the buffalo, skills, and collaboration. Hunting required special preparations accompanied by ceremonies and prayers for the success of the hunt and safety of the hunters. These ceremonies also thanked the buffalo for their sacrifices.[2]

Hunting buffalo on foot was a dangerous, arduous, and time-consuming process, sometimes lasting several days. The acquisition of horses made the process more efficient but by no means less challenging or dangerous. When great numbers of buffalo came together in vast herds, Native bands conducted organized communal hunts. Leaders selected scouts to go ahead and locate the herds, and warrior societies—known as Akicita among the Lakota—policed all movements to prevent individual hunters from striking out on their own, thereby panicking and scattering the buffalo.[3]

After the hunt, men did the preliminary butchering of the buffalo, removing the hide in one piece by cutting along the stomach rather than the back if it was to be used in making a tipi cover. The hunters wrapped the meat in hides and packed it on the backs of their horses to transport it back to camp. Women then finished cutting and preparing the meat for drying and preservation. Women who were good riders sometimes accompanied men on the hunt to help with butchering and to tend the horses as they were loaded with meat and other animal parts.

Spiritual leaders and those with special powers guided the buffalo hunt from beginning to end. They were charged with knowing the locations, assisting the scouts in finding buffalo, or calling the buffalo closer to the camps. Spiritual leaders provided prayers and ceremonies to ensure success in the hunt, that is, that the men would return with sufficient meat, plenty for their families and for those in need, and that they would not be injured. Finally, as the feasts of fresh meat took place, the people gave thanks for gifts provided by the buffalo.

For Plains Indian people, hunting was essential for survival, not a sport or amusement as early Euro-American travelers to the Plains sometimes described. Men, who were assisted by female family members in preparing for and conducting the seasonal hunts, considered themselves fortunate when they were successful, and they and their families were thankful for the buffalo meat, hides, and other materials they had procured.[4]

WARRIOR TRADITIONS: DEFENSE AND PROTECTION

The role of men as warriors was idealized with specific attributes necessary for success and recognition—physical strength and abilities such as endurance, horsemanship, skill with weaponry, and bravery. In addition to the willingness to defend themselves and others, warriors were admired for kindness and generosity to the poor and needy, as described to Frances Densmore by a Lakota man named Shooter.

> The best part of a man's life is between the ages of 18 and 33. Then he is at his best. He has the strength and ability to accomplish his aims. He is brave to defend himself and others and is free to do much good. He is kind to all, especially to the poor and needy. The tribe looks to him as a defender, and he is expected to shield the women. His physical strength is at its best. He is light on his feet and can reduce long distances to short ones. He is taught true politeness and is very gallant.[5]

Northern Cheyenne warrior Wooden Leg also spoke to the preeminent role of warriors among Plains tribes.

> The regular rule was, every man was classed as a warrior and expected to serve as such until he had a son old enough to take his place. Then the father retired from aggressive fighting and the son took up the weapons for that family. If a man came into early middle age without any son, he adopted one. If he had more than one son, he might allow the additional one or more to be adopted by another man who had none. By following this system, all of the offensive fighting was done by young men, mostly the unmarried young men. The fathers and the older men ordinarily stayed in the background, to help or to shield the women and children.[6]

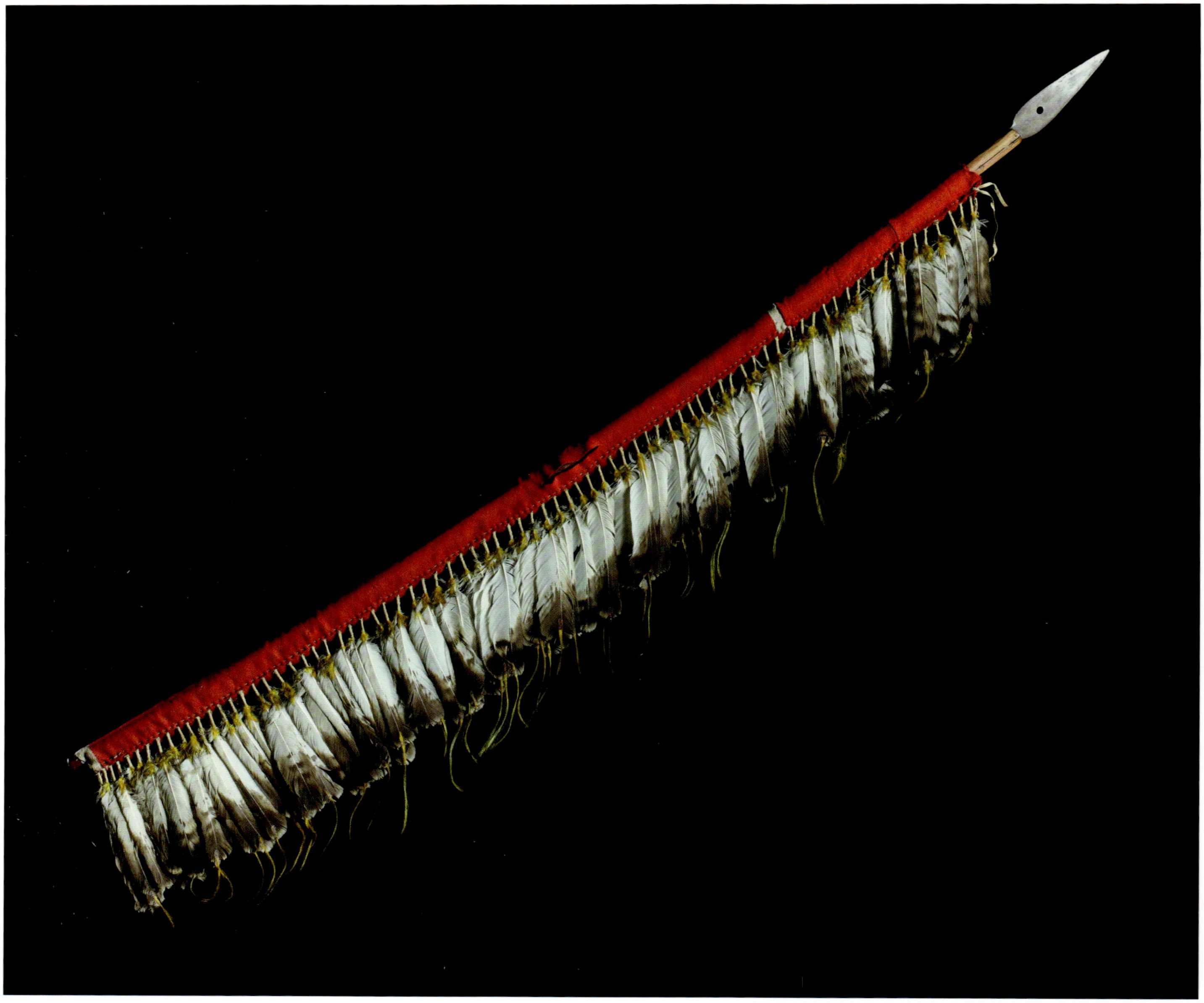

2.8. **Lance with banner**
Lakota (Sioux), Northern Plains, ca. 1840
Wood, golden eagle feathers, pigment, steel, glue, cotton cloth, tanned hide, cotton twine, wool cloth, cotton thread, dyed horse hair, dyed feather fluffs; 80 × 10 inches, with 3-inch diameter
Plains Indian Museum, NA.502.265

During the eighteenth and nineteenth centuries, up until reservations were established, warfare and its associated preparations—making and maintaining weapons, planning and leadership, military society ceremonies, and other traditions—were aspects of the daily life of Plains Indian men. Warfare among competing tribes and with the U.S. military intensified as the Euro-American frontier moved west, bringing forts, railroads, and settlements into tribal territories. The greater availability of horses and firearms and the increasing scarcity of buffalo and other game also were conditions leading to warfare. Much fighting occurred during raiding for horses or retaliations for such raids among tribes. Bands and individuals increased their wealth through accumulation of increasingly essential horses. Iron Teeth recollected the experiences and thoughts of Northern Cheyenne women when male family members went on horse-raiding expeditions.

> I remember when parties of our men used to go afoot from the Black Hills far southward to get horses. Each man took along only his lariat rope, his bows and arrows, his sheath-knife, a little package of dried meat, and two or three extra pairs of moccasins tucked into his belt. Their women were sad in heart as they made these moccasins, for sometimes, the travelers were gone a whole year, or sometimes they were killed.[7]

It is difficult to estimate the level of warfare that occurred among Plains Indians prior to the eighteenth and nineteenth centuries. The Euro-American presence on the continent began to influence life on the Plains in the seventeenth century, at first indirectly through the introduction of horses and displacement of Native peoples in the east. Throughout the eighteenth century, the new waves of Native emigrants onto the Plains were accelerated by population pressures in the east and by the availability of horses, which made the buffalo-hunting way of life more attractive. With the accessibility of firearms acquired at Euro-American trading posts, buffalo hunting became more efficient, and competition for hunting territories intensified. As emigrant trails, military forts, and then railroads and Euro-American homesteads and towns advanced on the Plains during the nineteenth century, intertribal rivalries increased as tribes struggled to protect their homelands. Plains Indians and Euro-Americans competed for buffalo and other food, resources tribes had always depended on. Many tribes also fought against the Euro-American military and colonizers, while others allied with them against traditional tribal enemies. Contributing to the hostilities in the last half of the nineteenth century was the dwindling number of buffalo, which were almost totally annihilated by commercial hide hunters. Native hunters had to travel farther from their home territories to find remnants of the scarce herds, bringing them into conflict with other competing tribes.

Men achieved glory in war through counting coup, a deed acted out by striking or touching an enemy with their hands, quirts, clubs, coup sticks, or other weapons (figs. 2.9, 2.10, 2.11, and 2.12). Almost any heroic deed in battle could count as a coup, but those that occurred within an enemy camp were considered most important. Among the Cheyenne, examples of coups include being the first to locate an enemy, saving a wounded tribesman, having a horse shot out from under a rider, and charging a group of enemies alone. The actual killing and scalping of enemies were also considered coups, although they were not as highly ranked as touching an

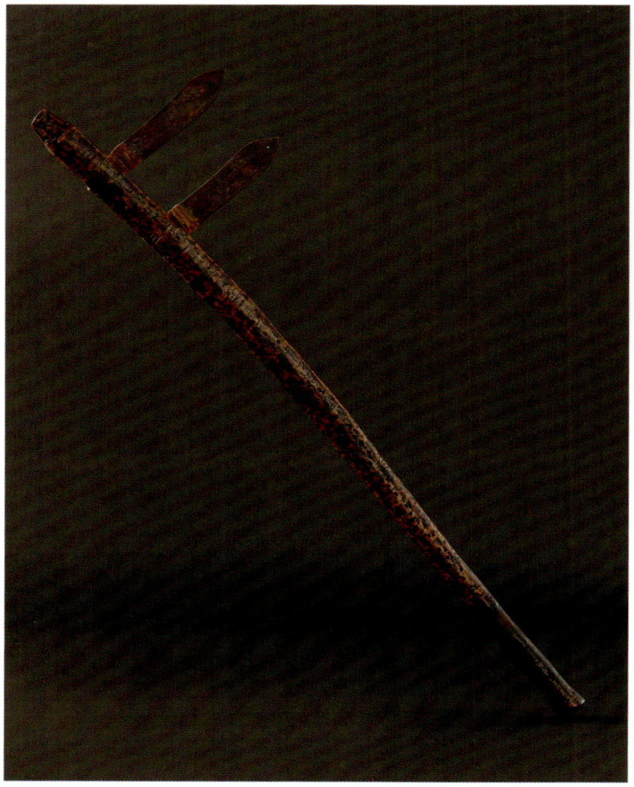

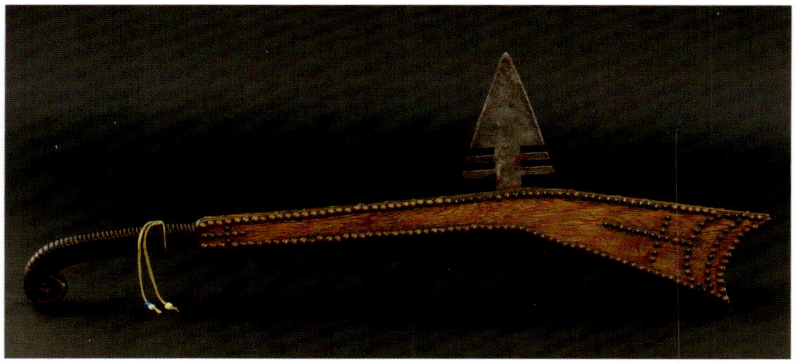

LEFT:

2.9. War club
Lakota (Sioux), Northern Plains, 1860–1880
Metal, wood, rawhide; 3½ × 32¾ inches
Plains Indian Museum, NA.108.175

Plains warriors used war clubs for close fighting. After acquiring firearms and metal tomahawks in the early nineteenth century, Lakota men continued to carry the clubs in military society dances or as symbols of prestige. This war club belonged to One Elk, who introduced Paul Dyck to Plains Indian cultures and people.

ABOVE:

2.10. Gunstock war club
Plains, 1850–1870
Wood, metal, brass tacks, glass beads, pigments; 4 × 33¼ inches
Plains Indian Museum, NA.108.186

Plains warriors carved gunstock clubs to resemble the stocks on European muskets and rifles. Men used clubs in hand-to-hand fighting and carried them in warrior society dances and ceremonies.

enemy without harming him. Men were ranked according to their total number of coups and their abilities to successfully lead war parties.[8]

Plenty Coups recounted that for a Crow warrior to count coup he had to "strike an armed and fighting enemy with his coup-stick, quirt, or bow before otherwise harming him, or take his weapons while he was yet alive, or strike the first enemy falling in battle, no matter who killed him, or strike the enemy's breastworks while under fire, or steal a horse tied to a lodge in an enemy's camp."[9] Plenty Coups also said that the first warrior named was the most honorable and that achieving such coups was an indication of bravery A warrior who had counted coup would wear an eagle feather in his hair as a mark of distinction, perhaps one for each coup he counted. If a warrior was wounded while counting coup, he wore an eagle feather painted red to show that he had bled.[10]

In writing about the Crow warrior tradition of counting coup, Joseph Medicine Crow said, "It was the object of every man to win as many coups as possible, for all social privileges and perquisites depended on this achievement."[11] His grandfather Medicine Crow, whose name is more accurately translated "Sacred Raven," had counted many coups and achieved the traditional ranking of chief at the age of twenty-two through the completion of all Crow military requirements. These requirements included touching or striking the first enemy fallen, whether alive or dead; taking a weapon away from an enemy warrior; entering an enemy

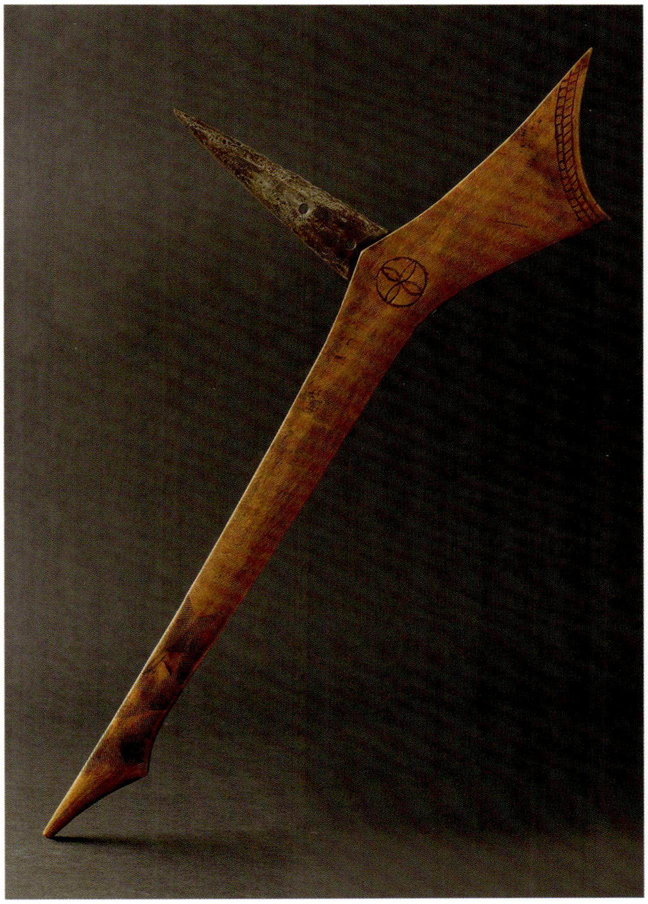

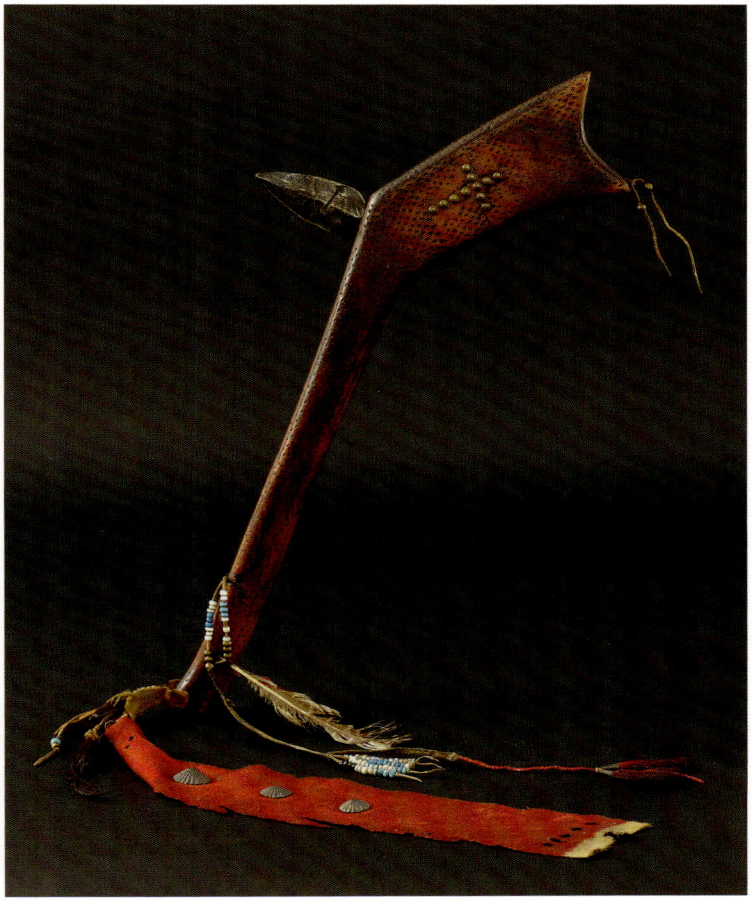

LEFT:
2.11. Gunstock war club
Plains, 1870–1880
Wood, metal; 13 × 18 inches
Plains Indian Museum, NA.108.187

RIGHT:
2.12. Gunstock war club
Lakota (Sioux), 1850–1870
Wood, metal, wool cloth, tanned hide, brass tacks, glass and brass beads, dyed horse hair, porcupine quills, silver conchos; 25 × 3½ inches
Plains Indian Museum, NA.108.184

camp at night and stealing a horse; successfully leading a war party. Medicine Crow was also a visionary and in later years, he was an effective reservation leader who traveled frequently to Washington, D.C., as a diplomat on behalf of the Crow people.[12]

WARRIOR SOCIETIES AND THEIR REGALIA

Men's warrior or military societies were essential in the organization and functioning of most tribal activities. In addition to leading and participating in warfare, men's societies policed buffalo hunts, organized horse-raiding expeditions, guarded horse herds, and directed camp movements.[13] According to Wooden Leg, warrior societies were the foundation of tribal government among the Cheyenne and had significant roles in the selection of tribal leaders.[14] He described his own initiation into the Elk Warriors Society.

> I joined the Elk warriors when I was fourteen years old. We were camped then at Antelope creek, near the Black Hills. Their herald chiefs were going about the camp circle calling, "All Elk warriors come for a dance and a feast." They were gathering at a large tipi made of two family lodges combined into one. Left Handed Shooter, at that time leading chief of the Elks, came to my father's lodge and said to me: "We want you to join the Elk warriors."

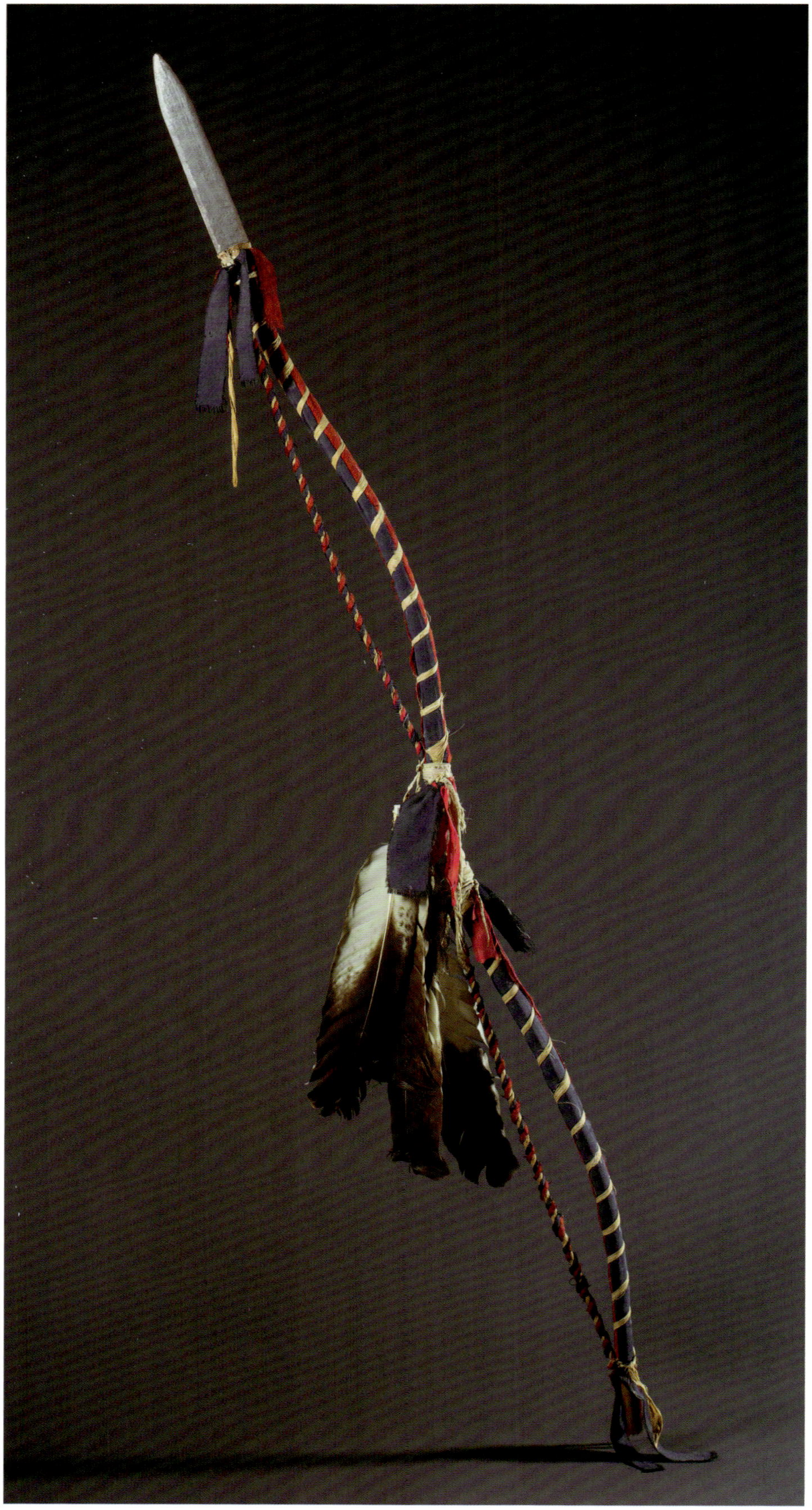

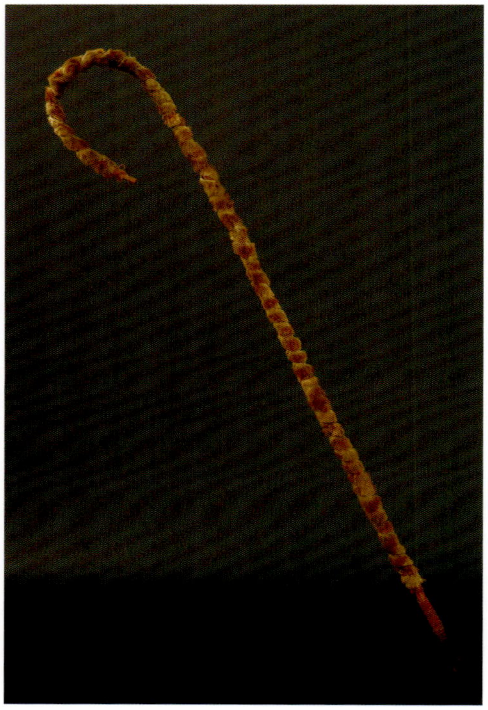

LEFT:

2.13. **Bow lance**
Lakota (Sioux), North Dakota, ca. 1875
Tanned hide, metal, wood, silk ribbon, eagle feathers, cotton cloth, wool cloth, cotton thread; 58¾ inches
Plains Indian Museum, NA.102.223

High-ranking members of a Lakota warrior society carried bow lances as they led warriors into battle. The bow lance is designed as a bow, but it was never strung. Attached to one end is a spear point that served as a weapon. Among the Lakota, the bow lance symbolized the courage of the warrior.

RIGHT:

2.14. **Staff**
Northern Plains, ca. 1880
Wood, pigment, steel, sinew, otter hide; 74¾ × 10½ inches
Plains Indian Museum, NA.502.267

Seventy or more Elks were dancing. Occasionally one fired a gunshot into the air. As they danced they were scraping their rattlesnake sticks, the special emblem of Elk membership. Each of these sticks was made of hard wood, in the form of a stubby rattlesnake seven or eight inches long. On each stick was cut forty notches. Another stick was used for scraping back and forth along the notches. The combined operation of many instruments made a noise resembling the rattlesnake's warning hum.[15]

Through military societies and lodges, Plains men trained, prepared for, and celebrated their victories in battle with special ceremonies, dances, and songs. Plains warrior societies had special songs, dances, traditions, initiations, and regalia symbolic of membership (figs. 2.13 and 2.14). In addition to the Elk Warriors described by Wooden Leg, Cheyenne political structure included the following military societies: Fox or Kit Fox Men, Bowstrings, Red Shields, Crazy Dogs, and the Dog Soldiers.[16] As Plains Indian warfare increased during the last half of the nineteenth century, the Dog Soldiers evolved into a separate militaristic band that led the Cheyenne resistance against Euro-American expansion. In the 1860s–1870s, they often camped, allied, and intermarried with the Lakota in warfare against the U.S. military, raids on Euro-American settlers, and engaging enemy tribes.[17]

A Dog Soldier bonnet in the Dyck collection (fig. 2.15) was acquired at Grand River on the Standing Rock Reservation in South Dakota. Identified by Dyck as Hunkpapa Lakota, the

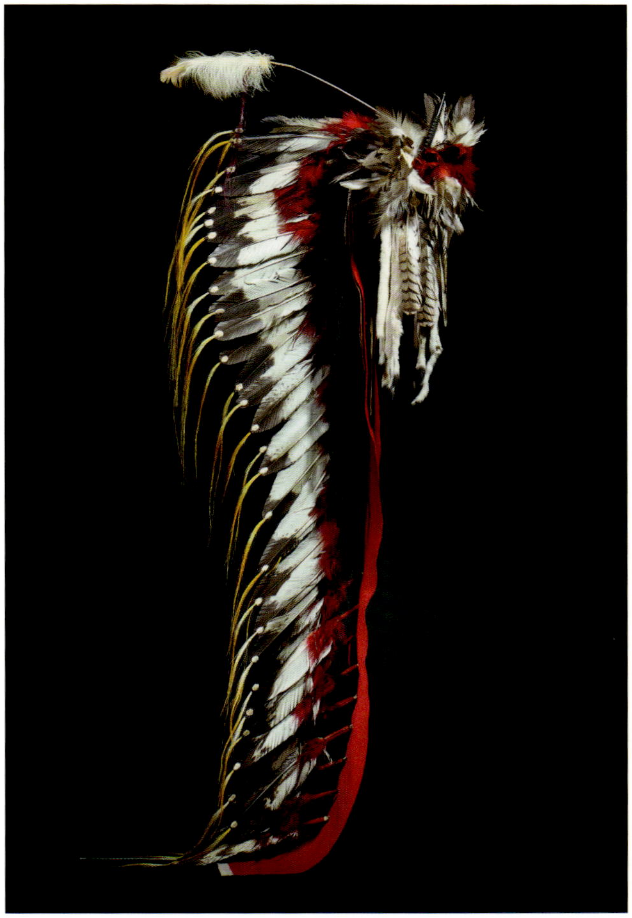

2.15. **Dog Soldier feather bonnet and trailer**
Hunkpapa Lakota (Sioux), Grand River, Standing Rock Reservation, South Dakota, ca. 1850
Rawhide, golden eagle feathers, canvas, ermine, adhesive, cotton cloth, glass beads, horse hair, sinew, tanned hide, brass bells, wool cloth, pigments, dyed horse hair, bison horn, hawk feathers, dyed feather fluffs, dyed porcupine quills, eagle down fluff; 72 × 8½ inches (trailer width) and 10½ inches (bonnet width)
Plains Indian Museum, NA.205.110

Members of military societies and lodges prepared for battle and celebrated victories with special ceremonies and dances. Their regalia, such as this Dog Soldier bonnet, symbolize their membership in a military society.

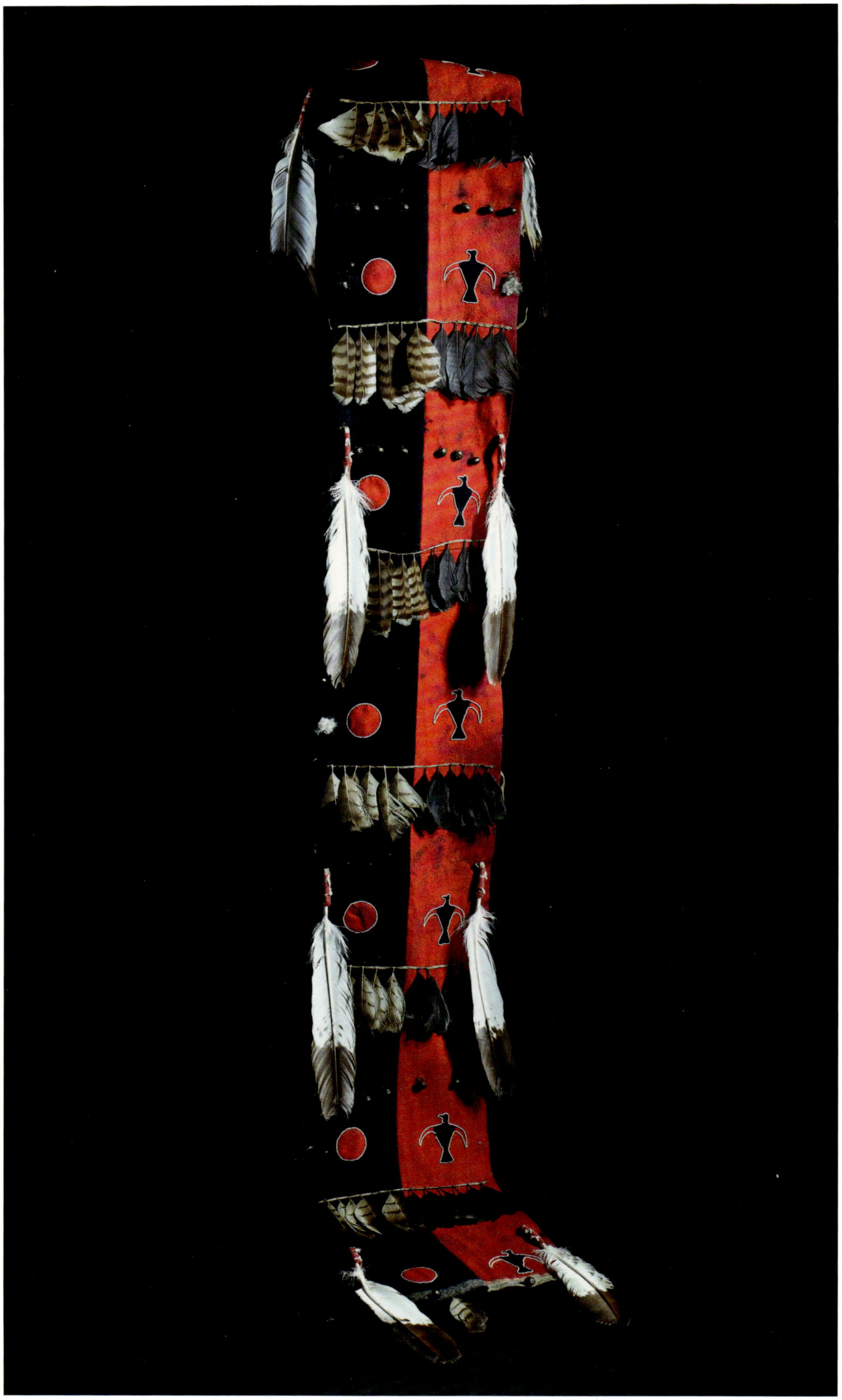

2.16. **Sash**
Oglala Lakota (Sioux), Northern Plains, ca. 1850
Golden eagle feathers, cotton cloth, glass beads, sinew, tanned hide, cotton twine, brass bells, wool cloth, cotton thread, owl feathers, raven feathers; 95 × 11 inches
Plains Indian Museum, NA.203.1594

Members of the Miwatani warrior society pledged to sacrifice their own lives in war to defend their comrades. Their long sash, owl, and eagle feather bonnets characterized this group.

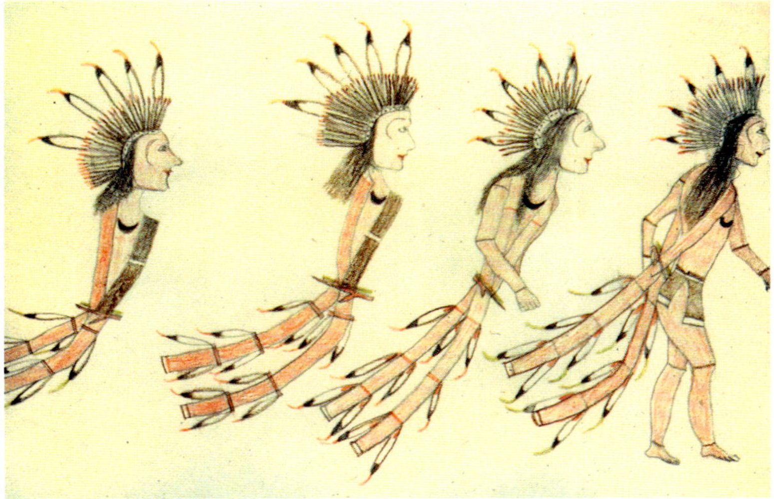

2.17. **Standing Bear**
Oglala Lakota, Pine Ridge Reservation, South Dakota, 1920–1930
Drawing, from a series of 33 drawings
Image courtesy of Buechel Memorial Lakota Museum Photo Archives

bonnet consists of a cap topped with split and carved buffalo horns. The bonnet is covered with bundles of eagle and hawk feathers with a red wool trailer decorated with thirty-two golden eagle feathers.

Arthur Amiotte provided information on the Miwatani (Owl Headdress) Society sash from the Oglala Lakota in the Dyck collection (fig. 2.16). The sash is made of blue wool trade cloth and decorated with golden eagle, raven, and owl feathers and beaded thunderbird designs. In a drawing now in the collection of the Buechel Memorial Lakota Museum, Amiotte's great-grandfather Standing Bear depicted a warrior wearing a similar sash during a warrior society dance (fig. 2.17). The Miwatani Society was an ancient and important military society among the Lakota whose members were exempt from Akicita duty. Through the society, members pledged to sacrifice their own lives in battle in defense of their comrades.[18]

According to Charging Thunder, a Lakota society member, the Miwatani originated through a man's vision in which an owl and a buffalo appeared to him. During the vision, the owl and buffalo brought the distinctive regalia worn by society members in ceremonial dances. The regalia consisted of the sashes and society bonnets made of owl feathers, with those of the leaders also having eagle feathers. Dancers carried rattles of deer dewclaws and wore eagle-bone whistles decorated with beads or porcupine quillwork on thongs around their necks. Members used owl feathers on their arrows.[19]

In addition to the Miwatani Society sash, another military society sash in the collection is from the Arapaho Dog Lodge (fig. 2.18). Made of a thin tanned piece of hide and painted in red pigment, the sash is decorated in feathers of hawks, owls, and golden and bald eagles; glass beads; and sections of embroidered grass or other plant fibers. This sash is associated with Little Left Hand of the Southern Arapaho and was collected in Oklahoma. For the Arapaho, a man's life followed a journey through four significant stages, or hills, of life: childhood, youth, mature adult, and old age. Beginning in adolescence, Arapaho males organized into age sets of peer groups and progressively passed through a series of seven ceremonial lodges, including two for youth, four for adult men, and one for elders. These ceremonial lodges in the order in which they were entered were the Kit Fox, Star, Tomahawk, Spear, Crazy, Dog, and Old Men.[20]

Elders who entered the Old Men's lodge, the seventh grade composed of men who no longer went to war, were considered the definitive authorities in ceremonial and spiritual matters. Elder men were instructed by a group known as "Water-Pouring Old Men," who held a status above all other Arapaho based on their experience and knowledge of sacred matters. This group of seven elderly spiritual leaders, who had earned honors through personal ordeals and sacrifices, were keepers of the seven tribally owned men's medicine bundles. The seven elderly spiritual leaders were ultimately responsible for directing all tribal ceremonies. Such elders also had other influences because Arapaho chiefs consulted with them and relied on them for public support.[21]

As men progressed through each of the lodges, they accumulated increasing sacred knowledge. As a result, older men were responsible for teaching younger men at the levels below their own. They also had responsibilities such as police duties, organizing camp movements, and making political decisions. Arapaho men had to be members of a lodge in order to participate in warfare, and leadership came from those who had achieved war honors and led expeditions.[22]

Each of the lodges had its own regalia, dances, and songs. The Dog Lodge consisted of mature men of about fifty years or older who were experienced warriors. Their distinctive sash worn in ceremonial dances was also worn in battle. According to Alfred Kroeber, "In battle the men wearing them fasten the ends to the ground with an arrow or stick. When they are thus fastened, they do not flee, however great the danger, until a companion releases them and orders them away."[23] In 1899, Kroeber collected two similar sashes, identified as Dog Society Second Degree sashes. These sashes, from the Southern Arapaho in Oklahoma, are currently in the collections of the American Museum of Natural History.

In the late 1800s, as tribes were confined to reservations, the functions and significance of Plains warrior societies transitioned among many Plains tribes. As buffalo herds diminished, hunters were no longer able to participate in the large communal hunts that required the structure and organization provided by warrior societies. However, warfare against the U.S. military intensified as tribes resisted the final losses of their lands and freedoms. Warriors continued to celebrate their victories and successes against Euro-American forces through their old warrior societies as well as the new Grass Dance. One account states that this dance originated with the Omaha. The Grass Dance spread across the Plains before 1860 and developed into a society that celebrated and honored the role of men as warriors among several tribes in many variations. By 1880, tribes from the Southern Plains to as far as the Northern Plains had adopted the Grass Dance.[24]

Like the traditional warrior societies, each of the Grass Dance Societies had its own songs, dances, specialized clothing, regalia, and accessories. Men carried dance shields painted with images imparting spiritual power and protection and dance sticks decorated and carved with images of vanquished enemies or horses taken in raids. Members carved dance sticks in the images of favorite horses that had carried them into battle and had perhaps suffered wounds or death. Society members also carried dance mirrors, reminiscent of the mirrors they had used as warriors to signal to other members of a war party, as a way to reflect light as they danced.

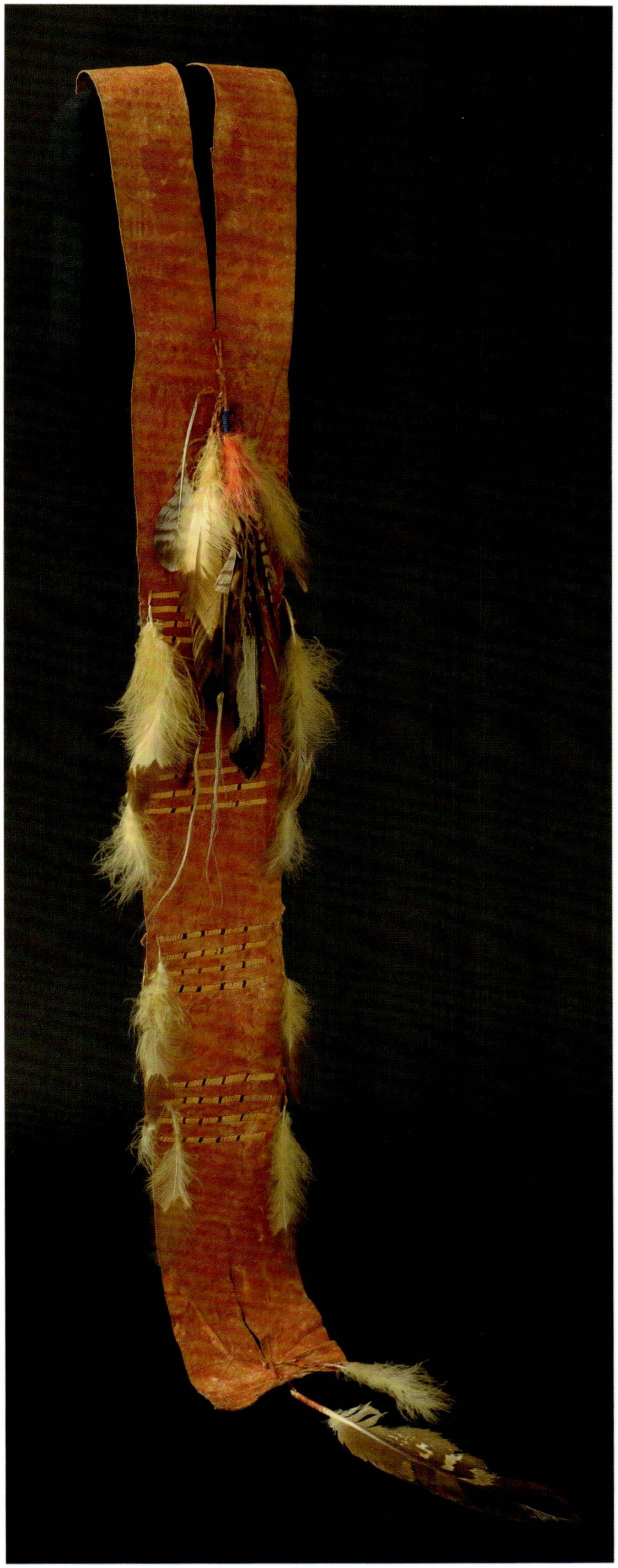

2.18. **Dog Lodge sash**
Hinono'ei (Southern Arapaho), Oklahoma, ca. 1880
Tanned hide, golden eagle feathers and fluffs, bald eagle feathers, owl feathers, hawk feathers, metal, pigment, horse hair, turquoise, glass beads, sinew, plant fibers; 70 × 6¾ inches
Plains Indian Museum, NA.205.118

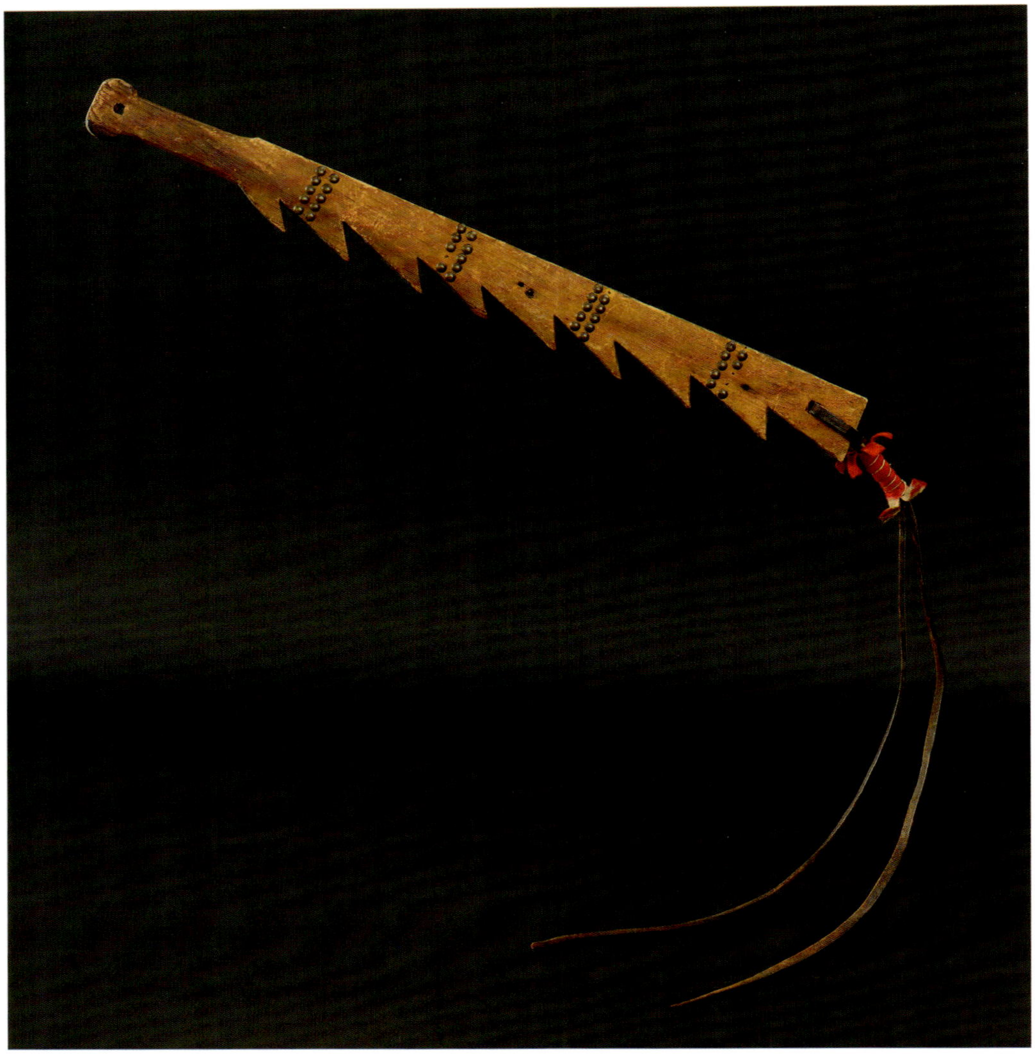

2.19. Warrior or Grass Dance Society whip
Plains, ca. 1870
Wood, brass tacks, wool cloth, commercially tanned leather, cotton thread; 51 × 2½ inches
Plains Indian Museum, NA.502.328

Some leaders carried whips to provide order and encourage dancers to participate (fig. 2.19). Forms of the Grass Dance, each with elements of earlier warrior society traditions, continued into the twentieth century as Plains Indian warriors returning from World War I and II were honored and celebrated by their grateful families and tribal communities for their roles as protectors of the land and the people.

MEN'S ARTISTRY: BIOGRAPHY AND SACRED VISIONS

Rooted in centuries-old petroglyphs and pictographs still preserved in caves and on rock formations throughout the Plains, warriors illustrated and recorded their hunting and war experiences—including coups and acts of valor—in representational drawings on tipi covers and liners, buffalo robes, shirts, and leggings. Paintings on buffalo robes and elk and deer hides with natural pigments emphasized the action of the story with figures engaged in battle, chasing and killing buffalo, and other action scenes. The paintings depicted individuals and tribes with specific clothing, moccasins, hairstyles, shields, weapons, and warrior society insignia providing identification. Since the artistic focus was on the narrative action, backgrounds and landscapes were largely omitted.

The paintings, accompanied by oral recitations of events, validated warriors' heroic deeds and courageous acts in battle. Individually, such artistic expressions through paintings and oral narrations provided autobiographies of individual warriors. Taken as a whole, these paintings expanded and enhanced the understanding of tribal histories. As described by a traditional Lakota historian, "The picture is the rope that ties memory solidly to the stake of truth."[25]

As buffalo hides became scarce, men began using cow hides and new materials available through trade to record their biographical experiences. Pencils, ink pens, watercolors, crayons, and commercial paints were added to the natural pigments. Stick and bone brushes formerly used in hide painting allowed men to draw their accomplishments in scenes on canvas, muslin, and paper. Painted and decorated canvas and muslin were sometimes used as tipi liners, and as tribes settled on reservations in log houses, muslin paintings also served as wall liners. In the 1860s, Plains warriors began to illustrate their battle exploits in ledger books and sketchbooks obtained through traders, military posts, and other government agencies. The ledger art tradition continued through the 1930s, with anthropologists and historians sometimes commissioning pieces directly from the artists as a part of their research.

One example in the Dyck collection of a biographical painting on hide dates from the early-twentieth-century reservation period (fig. 2.20). The animal hide used was cow rather than buffalo, which was no longer available. The painting, likely Lakota in origin, features sixteen different vignettes of a man on horseback encountering standing men and women figures. The mounted horsemen wear single eagle feathers in some scenes, and eagle feather bonnets

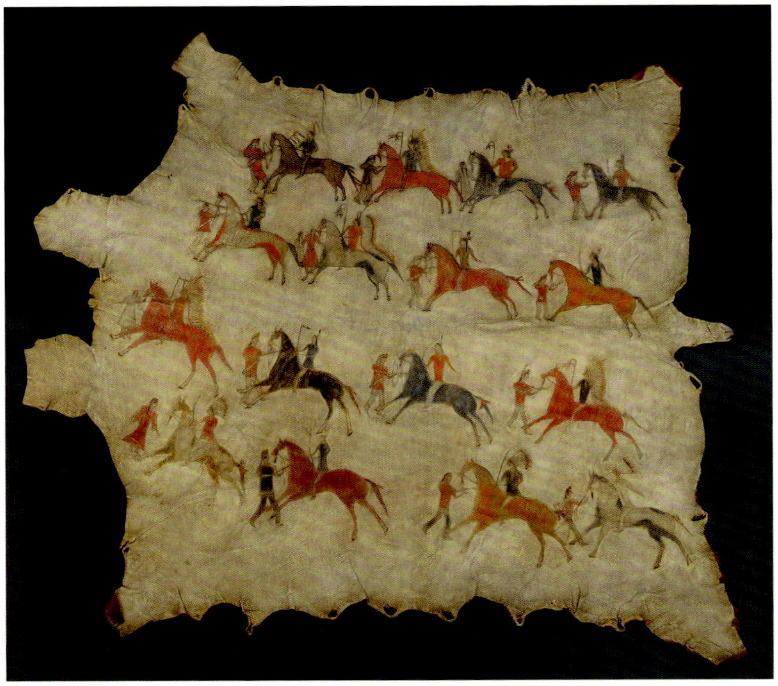

2.20. **Painted hide**
Lakota (Sioux), Northern Plains, ca. 1900
Tanned domestic cow hide, ink, cotton thread, pigments; 71 × 81 inches
Plains Indian Museum, NA.702.41

with trailers or buffalo horn and eagle feather bonnets in others. Horsemen also carry various weapons, including firearms, bows, and coup sticks. Four of the scenes feature women. In many of the scenes, horses are depicted as ready for battle, with feathers or medicine bags hanging from their bridles and with their tails tied with red wool. The painting may represent warfare experiences of a single individual or of several against various enemies, many of which appear to be Crow.

In addition, Plains Indian men produced other types of art derived from dreams and visions. Such visionary art was often drawn on tipi covers, drums, and rawhide shields and hide shield covers. Men sought spiritual guidance from individuals with special medicine and powers in interpreting dreams and visions and in illustrating the events. For tipi covers, they also sought help from family members who would produce the drawings under their direction. Men created powerful images on shields and shield covers to provide spiritual as well as physical protection in battle. George Bird Grinnell described the shield as the most important part of a Cheyenne warrior's equipment. For many warriors, the shields possessed strong spiritual powers, and the painted images of mammals, birds, and other figures of the earth and sky provided sacred protection for the owners (figs. 2.21, 2.22, and 2.23). Some shields were associated with the weather and could provide protection from severe storms, thunder, and lightning or be used to create weather barriers between the shield owners and their enemies (figs. 2.24 and 2.25). A shield adorned with the image or feathers of the eagle was believed to give its owner the swiftness and spiritual power of that bird (fig. 2.26). If the feathers of the owl were tied on it, the man perhaps shared the owl's power to see in the dark and to move silently and unnoticed. The figure of a bear painted on the shield, or with its claws attached, gave him the bear's toughness and strength (fig. 2.27). An image of a buffalo symbolized its inherent power and courage (fig. 2.28).[26]

According to Paul Dyck, "To the Plains Indian the shield was a personal flag, a testimonial to his own religious experience—a vision sought by every young warrior upon reaching manhood. The shield's magic, in reality, the medicine power, protected its owner, who was a believer in the power against all the encounters which filled his life both in war and peace

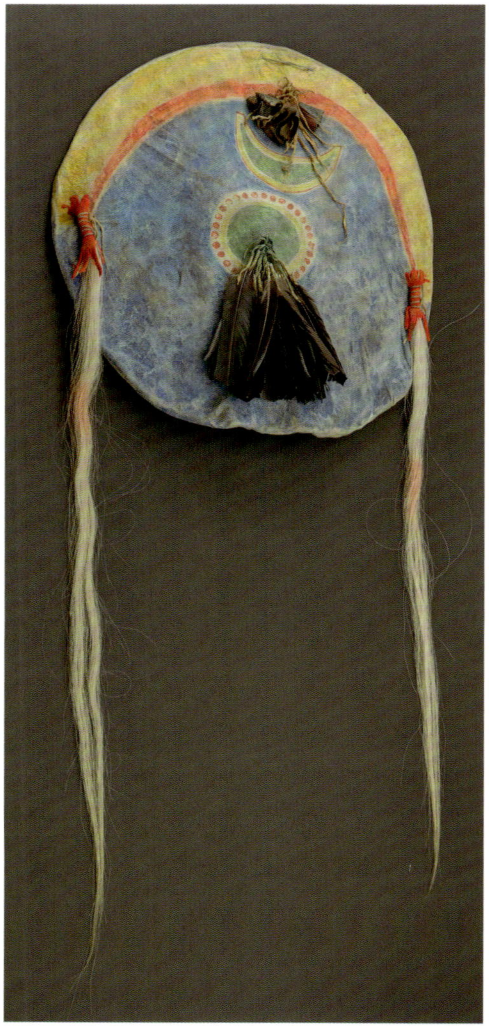

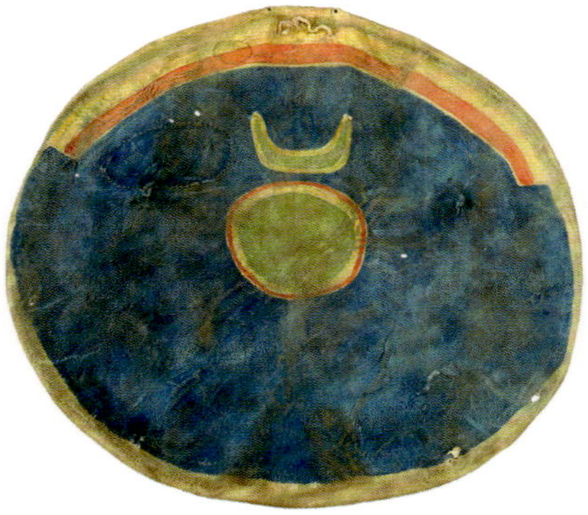

2.21 and 2.22. **Shield and shield cover**
Kaigwa (Kiowa), Southern Plains, ca. 1890
Buffalo rawhide, tanned hide, pigments, bald eagle feathers, sinew, wool cloth, horse hair; shield: 18¾ inches (diameter); shield cover: 20¼ × 21 inches
Plains Indian Museum, NA.108.130 and NA.108.154

Plains Indian men painted their shields and shield covers with powerful designs derived from dreams and visions. The designs on this shield and cover include painted images of a crescent moon and, perhaps, the sun or Kiowa camp circle. Bald eagle feathers are tied in the center of the shield. Shield covers provide both physical and spiritual protection for the shields.

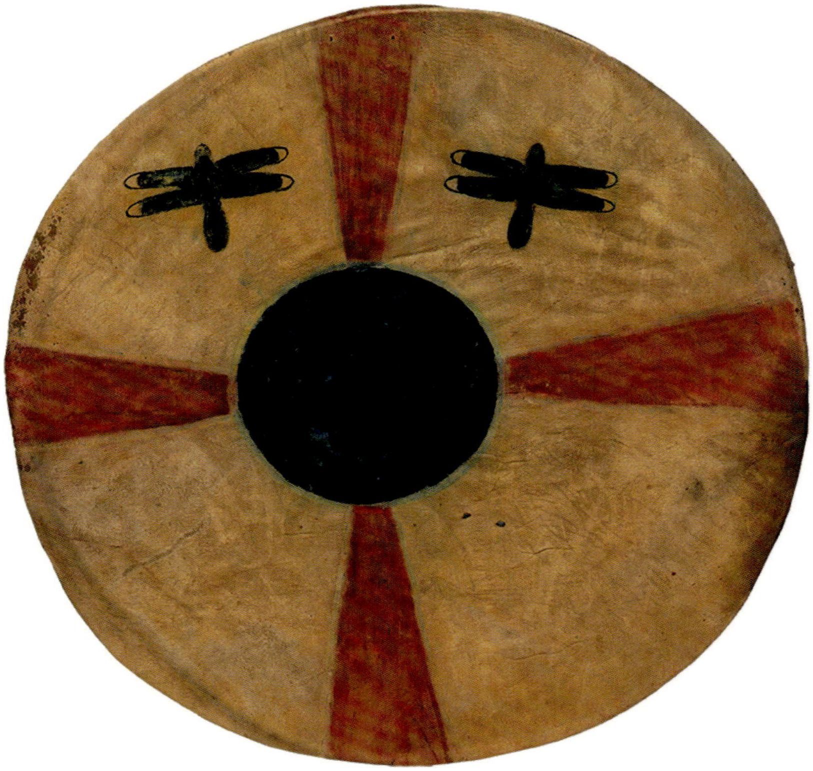

2.23. **Shield cover**
Hinono'ei (Arapaho), Southern Plains, ca. 1880
Pigment, tanned hide;
17½ inches (diameter)
Plains Indian Museum, NA.108.126

On this shield are painted images of the sun and two dragonflies. Men often painted the figures of dragonflies on their bodies before going to battle and on shields and other items associated with war. They admired the dragonfly for its swiftness in flight and sought its protective powers that assisted warriors in escaping the arrows and bullets of the enemy.

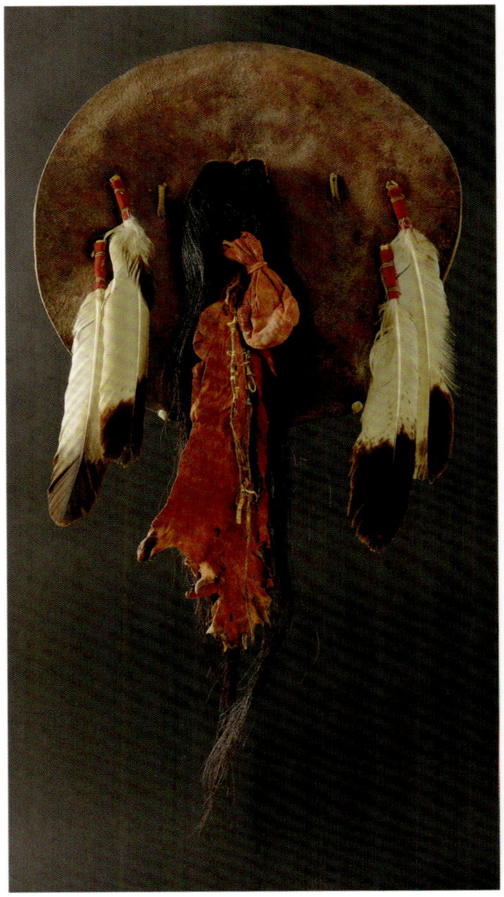

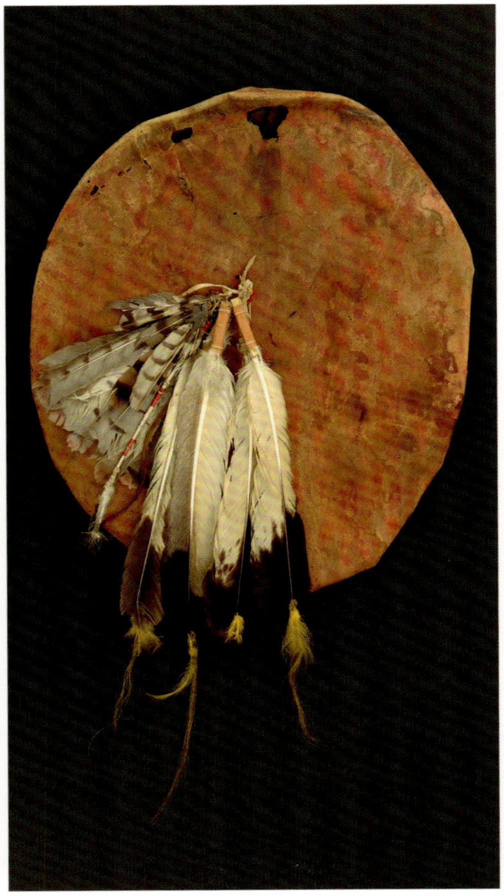

2.24 and 2.25. **Shield and shield cover**
Hidatsa, Upper Missouri Region, ca. 1820
Metal, feather fluffs, pigment, yarn, cotton cloth, porcupine quills, horse hair and hide, mountain lion feet, tanned hide, cotton thread, owl feathers;
shield: 20¾ inches (diameter);
shield cover: 20½ inches (diameter)
Plains Indian Museum, NA.108.138 and NA.108.155

According to Dyck, in 1907, Wolf Chief was the last recorded keeper of this shield. The shield possesses the power to protect the Hidatsa from enemies through the use of weather. The shield is painted red with two mountain lion feet and horse hide and hair attached to it. Eagle feathers are also attached. The cover is painted with symbols of rain and hail.

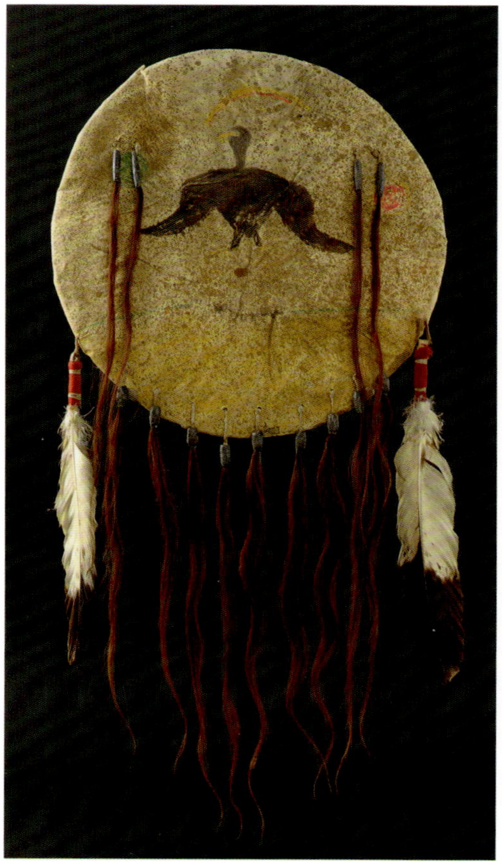

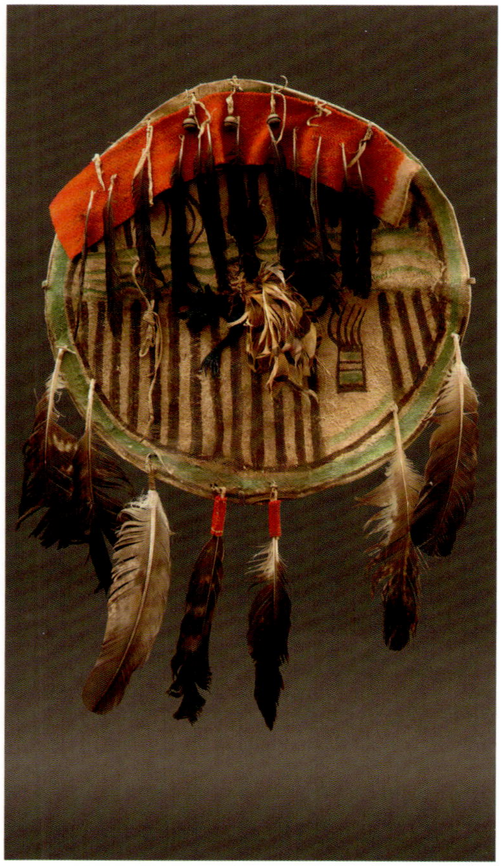

LEFT:

2.26. Shield and cover
Hunkpapa Lakota (Sioux), Grand River, Standing Rock Reservation, ca. 1860
Buffalo rawhide, tanned hide, eagle feathers, pigments, human hair, metal sinew, wool cloth, cotton thread; 18¼ inches (diameter)
Plains Indian Museum, NA.108.142

With its painted image of an eagle against a yellow background, this shield and cover are endowed with the protective power of the courageous bird. Flattened lead bullets serve as the mounts for hair decorations. Running Hawk, who fought at Little Bighorn, owned this shield.

RIGHT:

2.27. Shield and cover
Apsáalooke (Crow), Northern Plains, ca. 1870
Rawhide, tanned hide, golden eagle feathers, owl feathers, magpie feathers, ochre, pigments, brass bells, wool cloth; 19 inches (diameter)
Plains Indian Museum, NA.108.160

Two stylized images of bear paws with long claws dominate the design of this shield. The grizzly bear was respected by Plains Indian warriors for its power and strength.

time."[27] When men received revelations through dreams and visions, they often sought spiritual guidance from individuals who had special medicines and powers to assist them in understanding, interpreting, and illustrating their visions. Men also sought direction from these individuals in every step of the process of constructing the shields and covers—heating the circular piece of rawhide from a buffalo bull to shrink and thicken it; creating the tanned deer hide cover; painting the symbols and other images; and attaching feathers, bear claws, small bundles of dried medicinal plants, or fur—accompanied by prayers, smudging with herbs, and ceremonial singing.

Spiritual leaders also taught the men how they should provide the special care that such powerful shields required. According to Dyck, Plains warriors had strict rules concerning the handling of their shields. Dyck said, "Some concerned women; some warned against the presence of certain animals; others prevented specific actions, such as the shield touching the ground or the use of the white man's trade goods, such as steel. The restrictions were limitless; the older the shield, the more restrictions there were. Each successive generation, should the shield be passed from relative to relative, added their own vision-inspired limitations."[28]

The anthropologist Robert Lowie recorded the story, as told by Yellow Brow, of the origin of a shield in the Dyck collection that belonged to a Crow warrior named Humped Wolf (fig. 2.29). According to the story, when Humped Wolf (Hump) was about eighteen years old, he went on

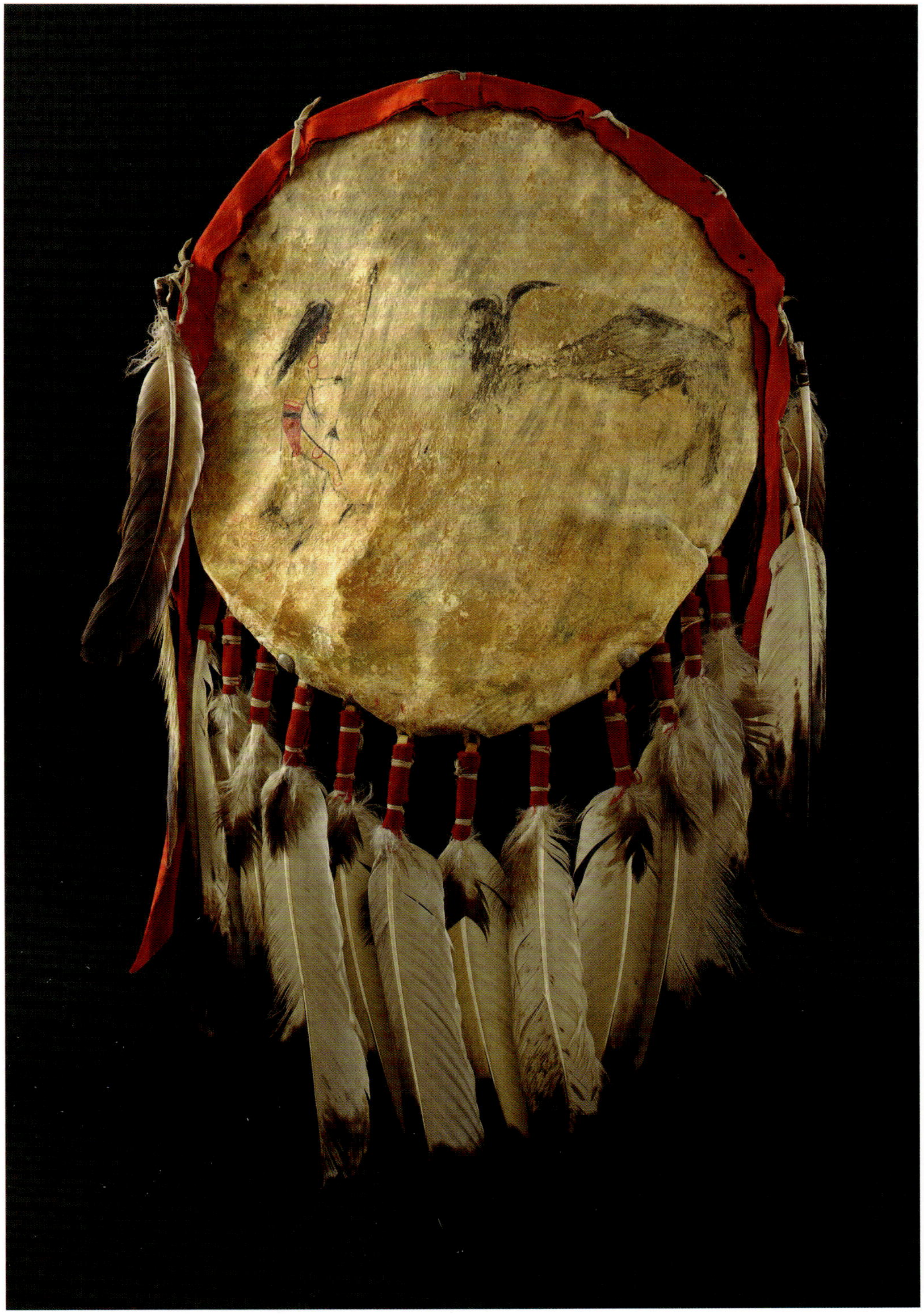

2.28. **Shield and cover**
Brulé Lakota (Sioux), Northern Plains, ca. 1870
Buffalo rawhide, golden eagle feathers, pigment, sinew, tanned hide, wool cloth, cotton thread; 18¼ × 17¾ inches
Plains Indian Museum, NA.108.141

On the cover is a man wearing a buffalo horn bonnet and carrying a lance as he faces a buffalo. According to Dyck, the shield inside the cover has paintings of two bears painted in blue. Dyck referred to this shield and cover as a "Medicine Shield," used to search out buffalo.

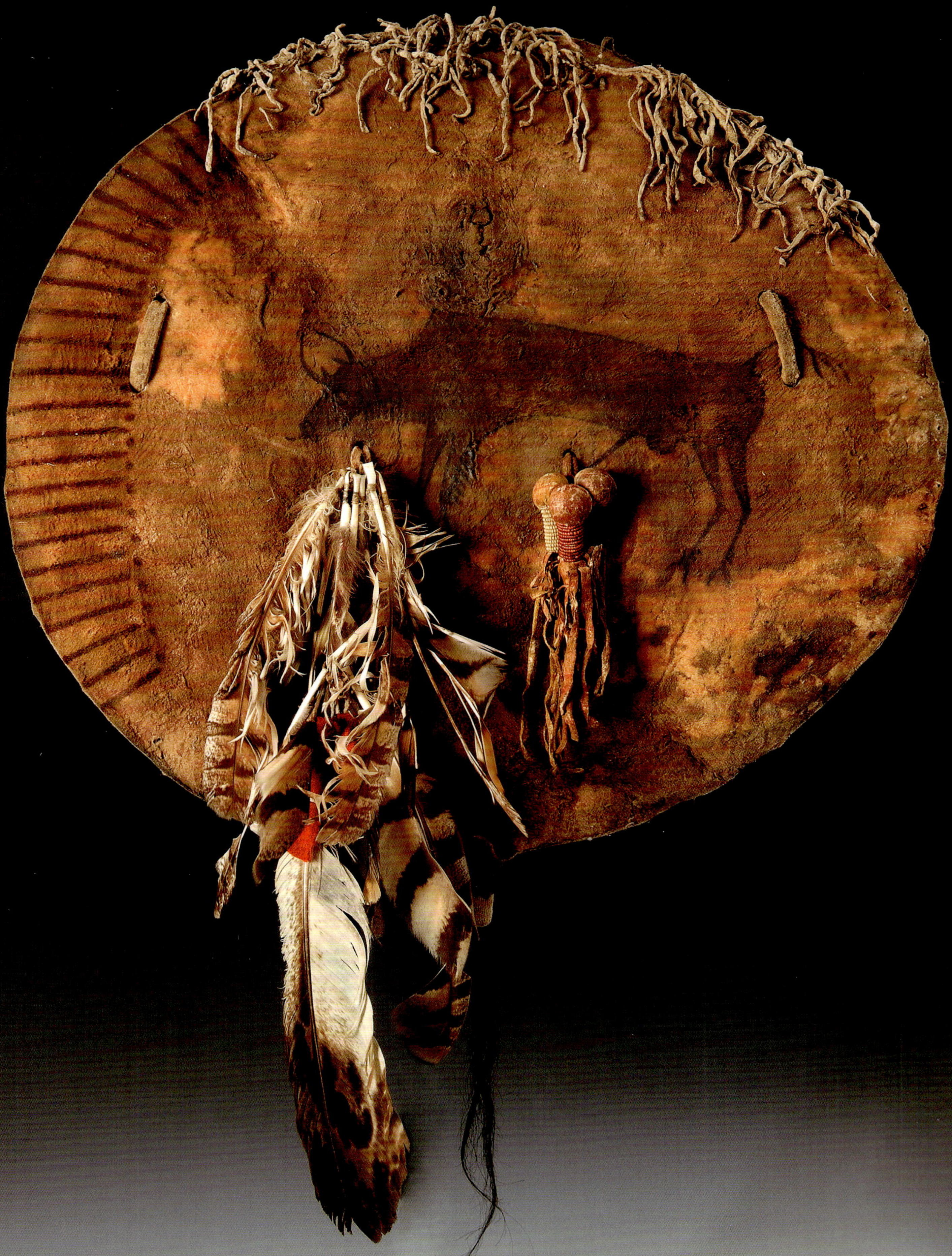

a war expedition against the Lakota. After traveling a great distance, a group of Lakota attacked and killed several of the Crow. Humped Wolf, who had been shot through both legs above his knees, traveled with other survivors before becoming separated in a blizzard. Fearing he would die, he came across a freshly killed buffalo. Taking shelter within the buffalo as he was falling asleep, he heard the snorting of the buffalo. Then he had a dream in which a buffalo came to him.

> It was a buffalo bull with another behind him; the first changed into a man, the second into a bay horse. Humped Wolf noticed what the buffalo-man was wearing. He wore a horned bonnet with a short streamer decorated with eagle feathers, a calfskin shirt with the hair on it, sleeve-holders of buffalo tail, a necklace of buffalo horns between dewclaws. In his hand he held a buffalo tail mounted on a pointed stick and he was carrying the shield. He was painted white from his nose downward and all over his body. His horse was also painted white below the eyes, from the knees down, and to about the middle of his tail; a plume was tied to the horse's forehead. The man came up to Humped-wolf and said, "I have made you go on the warpath and come where you were and go inside the buffalo . . . I have given you this medicine. That plume is the body of your horse (meaning that it could not be shot). When a person is shot, he is considered a man. I have placed you among the Crow. Henceforth you shall not be driven back by the enemy. I have given you everything that makes a man."[29]

When Humped Wolf returned to the Crow camp, he learned that the people, thinking he had died, were in mourning. He summoned all of the older men to his tipi and told them of his vision. "Make it," they said. One of them asked if he had any songs, and he sang the following:

> Whenever there is any trouble, I shall not die but get through.
> Arrows many though there be, I shall arrive. My heart is manly.[30]

According to Lowie, Crow ceremonial objects were sometimes made in as many as four versions.[31] In addition to the shield in the Dyck collection, Crow shields of similar designs are in the collections of the National Museum of the American Indian and the Minneapolis Institute of Art. The shield's design draws from the power and courage of the buffalo with its central image of the buffalo bull. The buffalo appears to be urinating, or marking its territory, a behavior that is associated with mating. On the upper left of the shield are brown wavy lines representing bullets and arrows glancing off the shield. The owl feathers tied beneath the painted buffalo bull symbolize the sacred vision of the bird at night, a power that transferred to the owner of the shield.[32] A small beaded medicine pouch is also tied to the shield. Located above the painted design is the scar of an old wound suffered by the buffalo, which was later killed and its hide used to make the shield. To Humped Wolf, perhaps, the scar represented the strength and endurance of the buffalo that had once survived its wounds, qualities for which the warrior also strove.

As the dramatic era of communal buffalo hunting and Plains Indian warfare ended with the destruction of the herds, establishment of reservations, and associated maladies of the late nineteenth century, the deep-seated ethos related to warrior traditions survived. In the

2.29. **Shield and cover**
Apsáalooke (Crow), Northern Plains, ca. 1870
Buffalo rawhide and tanned hide, great horned owl feathers, immature golden eagle feathers, pigments, glass beads, human hair, sinew, wool cloth; 20½ inches (diameter)
Plains Indian Museum, NA.108.136

Crow men sometimes made up to four versions of shields to give to relatives. Other versions of this shield reside at the Minneapolis Institute of Art and the National Museum of the American Indian. Note the old wound in the buffalo's hide above the painted figure.

early 1900s, on the Crow Reservation near Lodge Grass, Montana, Joseph Medicine Crow's grandfather Yellowtail instructed him in the fortitude and skills of a warrior. Medicine Crow said: "Although my grandfather Yellowtail had not been a warrior, he raised me to be one, to be tough and strong like the old-time warriors. When I was about six or seven, he started my physical-education regimen."[33] This regimen included exposure to cold winter elements like running shoeless through the snow and swimming in the near-frozen Little Bighorn River. According to Medicine Crow, "I had to go through that kind of training every winter while I lived with the Yellowtails. I've always been able to withstand cold weather, and I've never been sick."[34] Like his grandfather Medicine Crow, Joseph Medicine Crow did go on to achieve all the requirements of a chief during his military service in Germany during World War II. For his service in the U.S. Army during 1943–45, he earned a Bronze Star. During his later years, he was awarded the French Legion of Honor Chevalier medal in 2008 and the Presidential Medal of Freedom in 2009 in recognition of his military service, scholarship, and contributions to the Crow Nation.

Throughout their histories, Plains Indian people have honored their warriors—both men and women—for defending their homelands and protecting their people. Welcome ceremonies and celebratory dances for returning veterans of World Wars I and II and those who served in conflicts in Korea, Vietnam, and the Middle East have taken place across the Great Plains.[35]

Today, recognition of such service often takes place at powwows, parades, and welcoming-home and other ceremonies.[36] At powwows, a color guard of military veterans carrying eagle-feather staffs, the American flag, and tribal nation flags leads the dancers into the circle during the Grand Entry or Parade In that begins each powwow. The color guard stands at attention during the singing of the Flag Song and posts the colors before the Victory Dance (fig. 2.30). Families often honor with songs and giveaways men and women entering or returning from military service and those scheduled to be posted to overseas duties. When eagle feathers fall from dancers' regalia during the powwow program, the veterans lead rituals to retrieve the feathers. Often, a fallen feather in the dance arena represents a fallen veteran in combat. These ceremonies are culturally specific and in some cases involve dancing, "counting coups" upon the feathers by veterans, and the recitation of war experiences. According to Curly Bear Wagner:

> We always honored our veterans. This is one of the most important things in our society because they put their lives on the line for us. We always honored them, just as a long time ago when they'd come home we always did an honor dance for our veterans, or, for our warriors. . . . Today, it's the same thing. The first thing they start talking about is the importance of the veterans, putting their lives on the line for their loved ones, for their families, for their nations, for all Indian people. So, therefore, we always look at it in a good way, that these guys come home and we'll honor them.[37]

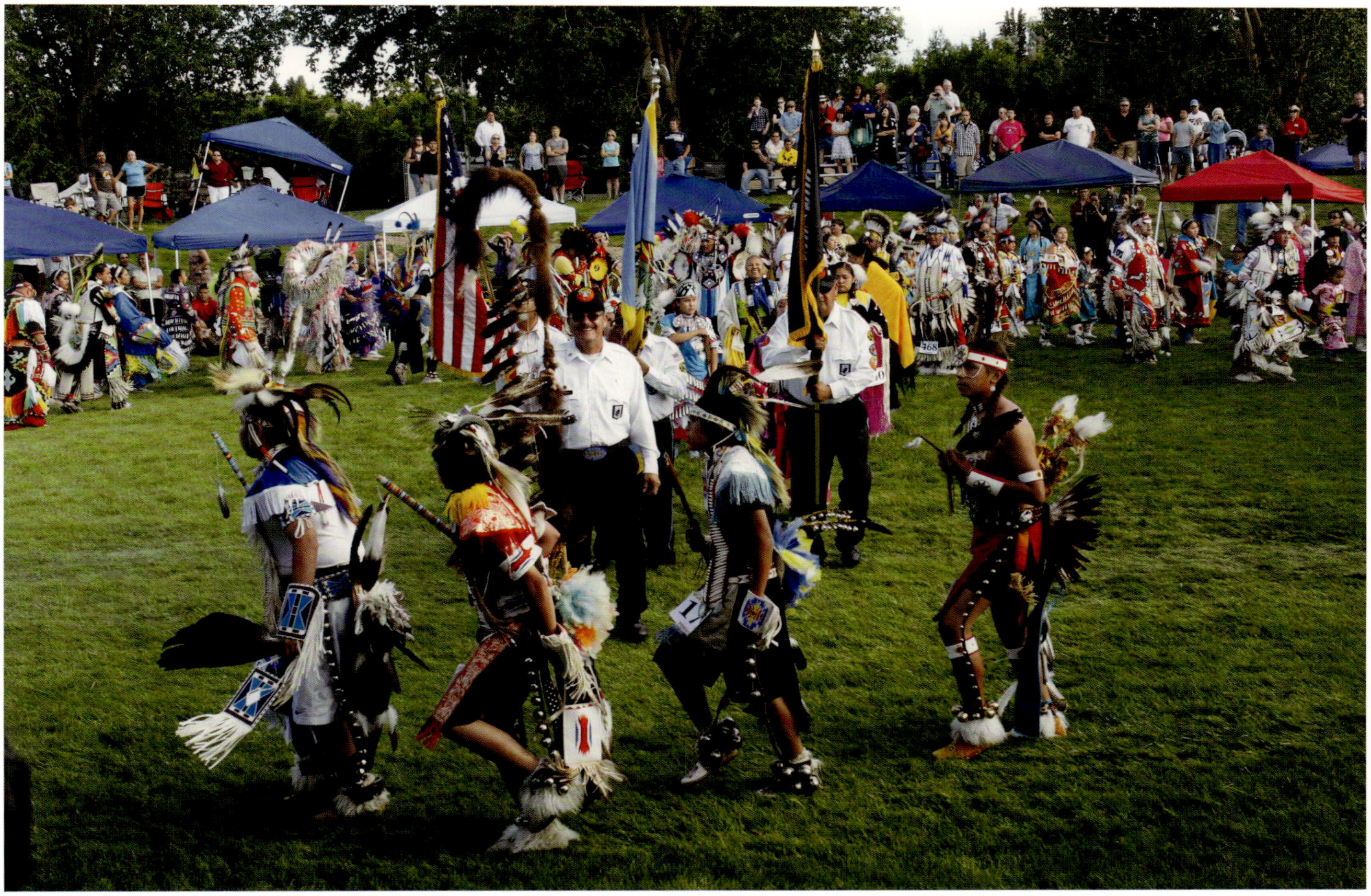

2.30. **Apsáalooke Nation Color Guard and dancers**
Plains Indian Museum Powwow, June 16, 2012
Photograph by Ken Blackbird

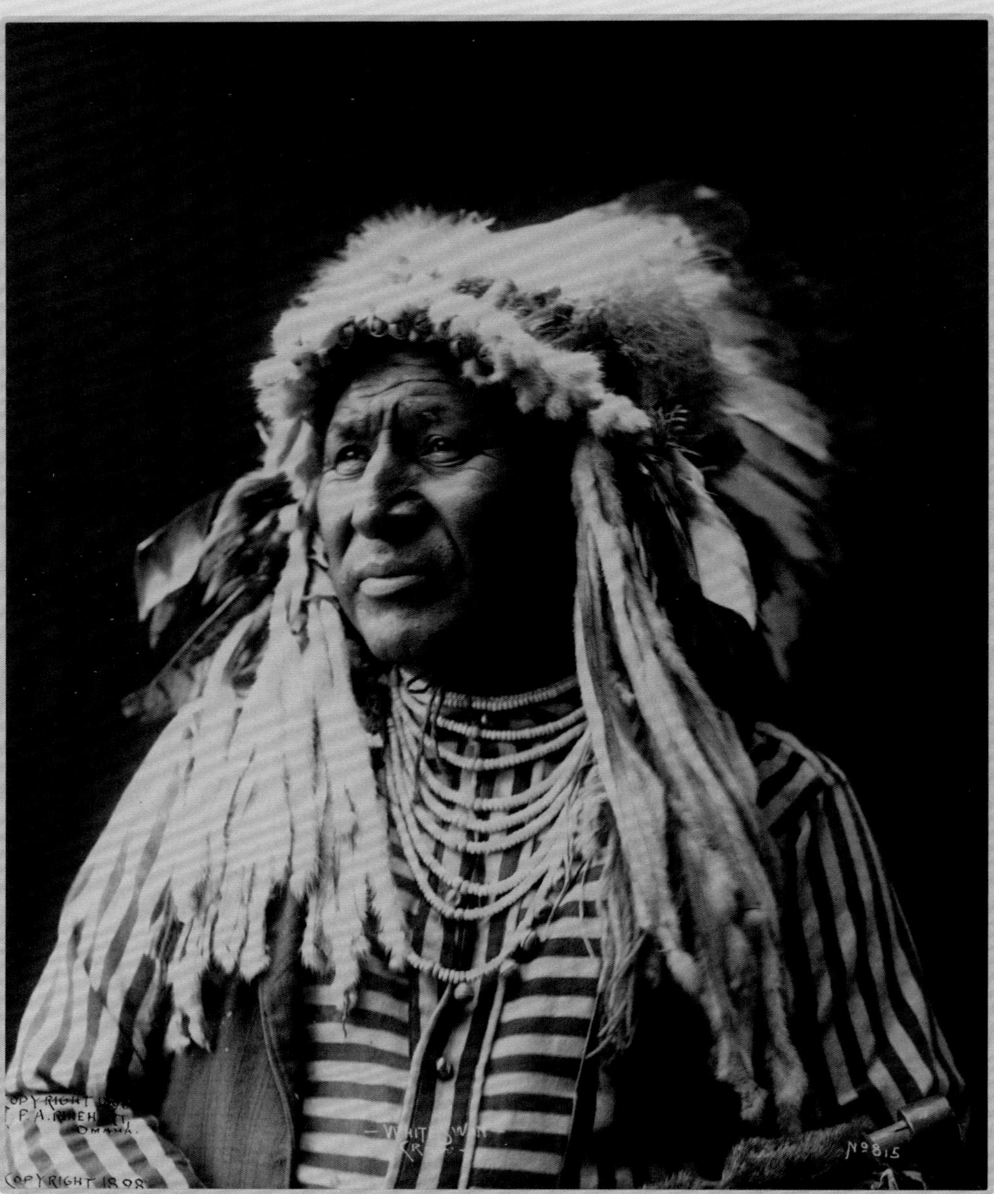
OMAHA.
COPYRIGHT 1898
Nº815

3 White Swan

CROW WARRIOR AND ARTIST

When asked about his experiences and actions leading up to and during the Battle of the Little Bighorn, former Crow warrior and U.S. Army Scout White Man Runs Him reportedly responded to the Western movie actor Tim McCoy:. "I am an old man, and soon my spirit must leave this earth to join the spirits of my fathers. Therefore, I shall speak only the truth in telling what I know of the fight on the Little Bighorn where General Custer was killed. Curley, who was with us, will tell you I do not lie."[1] White Man Runs Him was one of the six Crow scouts, and one of the youngest when he enlisted and served under the command of Lieutenant Colonel George Armstrong Custer. However, he lived the longest of the six scouts, his death occurring in 1929 at about seventy-three years of age. Joseph Medicine Crow personally knew most of the old warriors who had made up the scout unit.

> Six of the twenty-nine Crow warriors who volunteered for scout duty with the combined forces of Generals Terry and Gibbon were assigned to Custer as scouts. These young men, aged sixteen to twenty-five, were Goes Ahead, Hairy Moccasin, Curley, Half Yellow Face, White Swan, and White Man Runs Him, my grandfather. I knew all of these men well except White Swan, who died about 1904 before I was born, and Hairy Moccasin (1854–1822), who I think was married to the mother-in-law of Moccasin, a half brother of my grandfather Yellow Tail. They would take sweat baths together and tell stories.[2]

In the aftermath of the legendary battle on June 25 and 26, 1876, historians, writers, newspaper reporters, and other individuals with interests in the conflict sought out surviving eyewitnesses and participants from both sides, including the Cheyenne and Lakota combatants and the Arikara and Crow army scouts who had located the enemy camps and fought alongside the Seventh Cavalry soldiers. Researchers and curious inquirers continued to interview the warriors as they aged and as the country moved into the twentieth century, in an attempt to understand how the Lakota, Cheyenne, and Arapaho forces had so soundly defeated the large and well-equipped military contingent, resulting in the deaths of Custer and all of his command of two hundred and sixty-three men.

3.1. White Swan, Apsáalooke (Crow)
Photograph by Frank Rinehart, 1898
Omaha Public Library Collections, TM100467

In 1898, White Swan traveled as a part of a Crow delegation to appear at the Trans-Mississippi and International Exposition held in Omaha, Nebraska. Frank Rinehart photographed White Swan, as well as other participating Native Americans.

James Welch, a Gros Ventre and Blackfeet writer, explored the national significance of Little Bighorn in American history and the disastrous aftermath for the Lakota and Cheyenne victors. He also wrote about the ongoing fascination with the Little Bighorn Battle and Custer on the part of many Euro-American writers and scholars as well as the general public. Welch observed that the commemoration and glorification of Lieutenant Colonel Custer's and the Seventh Cavalry's defeat began immediately after the event and continues today. Upon reflection, Welch speculated that people often seem to dwell on their defeats rather than their victories, resulting in the continuing research and interest in one of the largest military defeats in American history.[3]

Among early-twentieth-century writers who traveled to the Crow Reservation in Montana to photograph and interview the Crow scouts was Edward Curtis. In 1907, Curtis visited Crow Agency, Montana, and three of the former scouts, White Man Runs Him, Hairy Moccasin, and Goes Ahead, who accompanied him as he rode Custer's route into battle. He persuaded the men to describe the events as they witnessed them along the way. White Man Runs Him, Hairy Moccasin, and Goes Ahead reenacted their actions during the battle on June 25 before they departed upon dismissal after locating the main contingent of Lakota and Cheyenne warriors for the soldiers. White Man Runs Him was the spokesman for the group.[4]

By the time of Curtis's visit, the Crow scout White Swan (1851–1904) had died. Like the other scouts, he also had been sought out by renowned visitors to the Crow Reservation, including artists and writers such as Elbridge A. Burbank, Ernest Thompson Seton, Charles Schreyvogel, and Joseph Henry Sharp.[5] Unlike the other scouts, White Swan, who was deaf and mute due to his battle injuries, was unable to orally recount his war exploits. Instead, he communicated through sign language and through a remarkable series of paintings and drawings on hide, muslin, and paper. Through his art, White Swan documented his war record, including his exploits and experiences as a Crow warrior and U.S. Army Scout at Little Bighorn and other conflicts in which he had engaged. According to Joseph Medicine Crow, "White Swan, at twenty-five, was the oldest of the six. He was also the first of the scouts to die. Although no interviews with White Swan are known to be extant, he did leave a pictorial record of his activities in the battle. These and a drawing by Curley at the Karl May Museum in Radebeul, Germany, are the only drawings of the Custer fight known from the Crow and Arikara scouts."[6]

A CROW WARRIOR'S LIFE

Mee-nah-tsee-us, also known as White Swan, was born in about 1851 and grew up in the traditional manner of young Crow males, maturing into a warrior probably by the age of thirteen.[7] By this time, Crow warfare with their surrounding enemies, including the Cheyenne, Arapaho, and Lakota, had intensified as tribes increasingly competed for scarce resources. With the incursions of Euro-American settlements, railroads, and emigration trails, hunting territories in present-day Montana, Wyoming, and the Dakotas had declined along with the buffalo herds and other game. During the 1860s–1870s, the U.S. Army established a series of military posts throughout the region to provide protection for travelers, miners, and increasing settlements in the area. Unlike tribes such as the Cheyenne and Lakota, who chose to directly engage with Euro-American invaders, the Crow chose to ally with the American military against their traditional enemies. Following a vision he had had as a young man, the great leader Plenty Coups believed the Crow, as a small nation surrounded by enemies, could only survive through seeking peace and cooperation with the whites.[8]

Led by Plenty Coups, many Crow warriors volunteered to serve as U.S. Army Scouts in the conflicts leading up to Little Bighorn. For the Crows, scouting was a viable role that allowed them to use their skills as warriors and horsemen while also earning income that helped their families to survive as buffalo hunting became decreasingly viable. The warriors and their families considered scout service to be an honorable pursuit and means of protecting their people from the threat of enemy attacks. For ambitious young warriors, it also provided opportunities for the young men to count coup and earn distinction and respect for their accomplishments on the battlefield.[9]

White Swan, at the age of twenty-five, enlisted at the Crow Agency as a scout serving with the Seventh Infantry in April 1876.[10] In June of that year, he was reassigned to the Seventh Cavalry under Custer just a few days before the Little Bighorn battle. Fighting alongside troops and Arikara scouts under Major Marcus Reno, the Crows attacked the south end of the Lakota, Cheyenne, and Arapaho encampment. White Swan was seriously wounded in this engagement. Joseph Medicine Crow explained,

> White Swan and Half Yellow Face had retreated with Reno back across the Little Bighorn River in a defensive position in a depression atop a hill overlooking the river. Later, in that day, Reno's forces were bolstered by those of Lieutenant Frederick Benteen, whom Custer had sent on a scouting expedition to the south. During the action with Reno in the valley, White Swan had been severely wounded by bullets that had ripped through his right hand and into his right knee and thigh.[11]

As the fighting continued, Half Yellow Face managed to get the wounded White Swan on a horse and led the horse across the river and up to the bluffs where Reno's troops had gathered. Although severely wounded, White Swan reportedly tried to continue to fight. The following day, Half Yellow Face made a horse travois and, assisted by the Arikara scouts Young Hawk and Goose, transported White Swan approximately twelve miles from the site of the battle to the steamer *Far West* on the Bighorn River.[12] Then, he was carried to a temporary hospital facility for the wounded on the Yellowstone River. Meanwhile, White Man Runs Him, Goes Ahead, and Hairy Moccasin traveled to the Crow village on Pryor Creek and mistakenly reported that both White Swan and Half Yellow Face had been killed. According to Goes Ahead's wife, Pretty Shield, the Crow were in mourning. Pretty Shield recounted, "When Half-yellow-face and White-Swan got back we heard their story, and it was like hearing the dead speak, because we thought they had been killed.[13]

After treatment and partial recovery from his wounds, although seriously disabled, White Swan reenlisted for scout duty periodically over about a five-year period. In 1897, he applied to the War Department and was awarded a small pension for his disabilities, as described by Joseph Medicine Crow. "Indeed, there is no doubt White Swan was in the thick of the fighting. During the Reno phase of the Battle, a bullet tore his right hand apart. He was also shot in the right thigh and knee and whacked in the head by a Sioux war club. Although he eventually returned to active duty as a scout, the injuries caused him serious difficulty in his declining years."[14]

In later years, White Swan lived at Crow Agency, which had been established in 1884 on the Little Bighorn River and the battlefield of the same name. Following warrior traditions, he began to illustrate his battle exploits and experiences through drawings on paper and paintings on muslin using pencil, ink, and watercolors. White Swan offered his art for sale to interested visitors to the Crow reservation and the battlefield. His customers included other artists, military personnel, scholars, and missionaries. White Swan earned a small income by selling these illustrated accounts of his war experiences. At the time of purchase, the buyers likely considered the paintings and drawings as souvenirs and nostalgic reminders of their western travels. Elbridge A. Burbank, who visited the reservation in 1894 and painted White Swan's portrait, described White Swan's art as "rude pictures." Not understanding the Crow warrior tradition of documenting coups and deeds in battle, Burbank erroneously concluded that White Swan was bragging about his part in the Little Bighorn battle.[15] For White Swan, however, in addition to being a source of income, the paintings were an authentic record of his experiences as a warrior, scout, protector, and defender of the Crow people. Through his paintings, he asserted and reinforced the respected role of the Plains warrior and served as a chronicler of the history of the Crow people. In addition to Burbank, other visiting artists painted White Swan's portrait, including Ernest Thompson Seton, Charles Schreyvogel, and Joseph Henry Sharp (fig. 3.2). White Swan died in 1904 and was buried with military honors in the national cemetery at the Little Bighorn Battlefield National Monument.

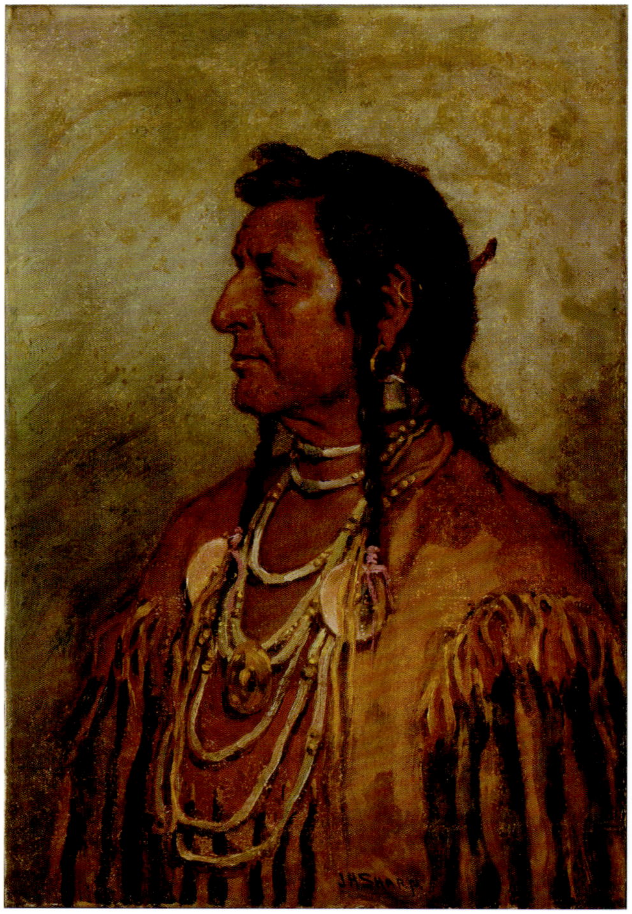

3.2. Joseph Henry Sharp (1859–1953)
White Swan, ca. 1904
Oil on canvas; 17⅝ × 11¾ inches
Whitney Western Art Museum, Whitney Fund Purchase 18.61

DOCUMENTING HISTORY: WHITE SWAN'S WAR RECORDS

Over three dozen pictographic drawings and paintings on paper, muslin, and hide are attributed to White Swan. The muslin paintings can be found in the collections of the Heard Museum, Denver Art Museum, Gilcrease Museum, Autry Museum of the American West, Snite Museum of Art at the University of Notre Dame, the University of Arkansas Museum, and in the homes of private collectors.[16]

The White Swan painting in the Dyck collection is on a single piece of muslin measuring 37¼ × 70½ inches and covered with figures outlined in pencil or ink and filled in with vibrant watercolors (fig. 3.3). The muslin, pencil, ink, and watercolors were available through purchase or trade at a reservation trading post or store. The painting consists of thirteen vignettes—scenes of White Swan's war deeds and experiences—featuring figures of White Swan, adversaries, military men, and horses.

The vignettes do not correspond to a sequence of episodes through time or several events of a single battle, but rather represent thirteen individual and meaningful encounters experienced by White Swan as a Crow warrior. Much of the scholarly interest in White Swan's paintings relates to his association with Little Bighorn, and three of the scenes in this painting, indicated by the presence of the Seventh Cavalry guidon, definitely depict actions taken during that conflict. Other vignettes represent events of the battle that have been documented through historical accounts.

Following the conventions of nineteenth-century warrior art, each vignette focuses on the narrative actions of a specific event depicted through figures alone, without backgrounds or landscapes. Men with limited or no facial details and horses are shown primarily in profile. Specific warriors or their cultures can be identified through tribally distinctive clothing, hairstyles, shields, and weapons.

In Plains Indian men's representational art, artists often created rich self-portraits with precise depictions of their own clothing, accoutrements, shields, weapons, warrior society regalia, and horses. With these details, other members of their small community identified the subjects of the drawings, reinforcing the honors and respect they had achieved. Adversaries were usually shown in far less detail. White Swan, however, represented himself in a relatively simple fashion, while reserving more details for the images of his enemies. He consistently is shown with a traditional Crow men's hairstyle with the front cut short and stiffened to stand upright. In some drawings, he wears a single eagle feather wrapped in red cloth that billows from his hair. In other images, White Swan has painted his forehead and lower face in red. He wears a simple fringed shirt, a striped breechcloth, moccasins, and sometimes leggings. In still other scenes, he wears a red blanket tied around his shoulders like a cape, but he is never shown with a shield or an eagle feather bonnet. In contrast, many of White Swan's adversaries are painted wearing warrior society shirts, beaded leggings, and eagle feather bonnets with long trailers and carrying painted shields decorated with eagle feathers.

Plains Indian warriors had special relationships with their horses. Men depended on horses to maneuver swiftly and carry them safely when chasing buffalo herds or engaged in combat. Warriors trained their favorite horses to perform well in battle, that is, to resist shying under gunfire and to protect their riders when in combat with enemies. For this reason, Plains Indian army scouts provided their own horses upon enlisting, for which they were paid a stipend. In the Dyck collection muslin painting and others White Swan produced, he rides either a yellow (perhaps buckskin) or red (bay or sorrel) horse. He rode the yellow horse at Little Bighorn, where it was wounded and died.

The composition of the muslin painting is roughly three tiers of separate vignettes, each representing a particular deed performed by White Swan in battle. Going from left to right, in the first vignette there is a tipi camp represented by twenty tipis, each painted in a variety of designs (fig. 3.3). To the right of the camp is the first scene featuring White Swan engaging with an enemy in pursuit. In this scene, White Swan, mounted on his yellow horse, carries his coup stick with an attached eagle feather upright. He leans back on his horse as he turns to fire three shots at the enemy. The enemy, using a quirt, urges on his red (bay) horse, who wears a silver

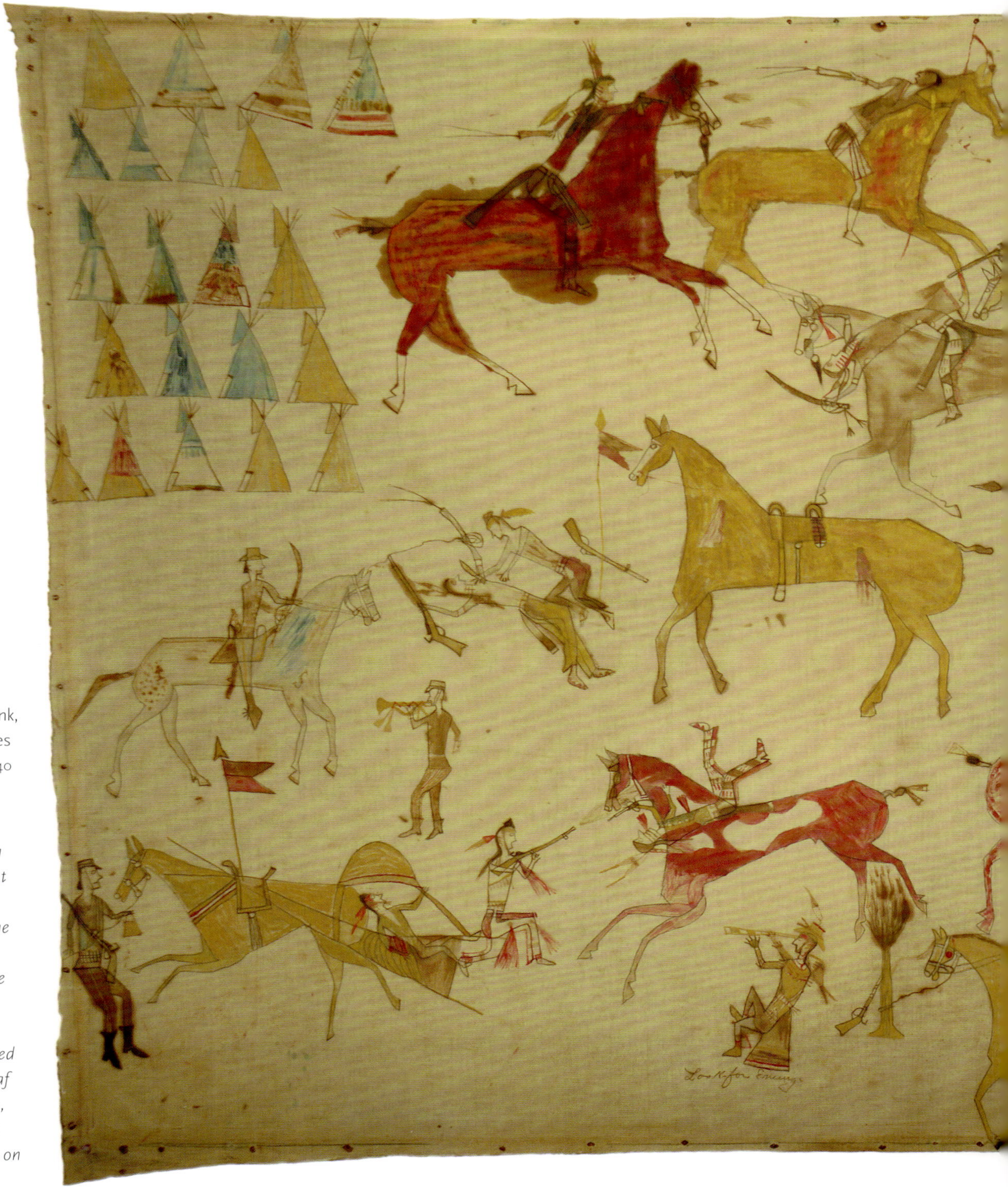

3.3. Mee-nah-tsee-us (White Swan)
Apsáalooke (Crow), Montana, ca. 1887
Painting on muslin, pencil, ink, watercolor; 37¼ × 70½ inches
Plains Indian Museum, NA.702.40

In 1876, Mee-nah-tsee-us, also known as White Swan (ca. 1851–1904), enlisted as a U.S. Army Scout, serving first in the 7th Infantry and later with the 7th Cavalry. On June 25th, 1876, White Swan and other Crow Scouts fought the Lakota and Cheyenne in the Little Big Horn Valley under Major Marcus Reno. Wounded during the battle, he was deaf and mute throughout his life, but recorded his bravery and war deeds through paintings on hide, muslin, and paper.

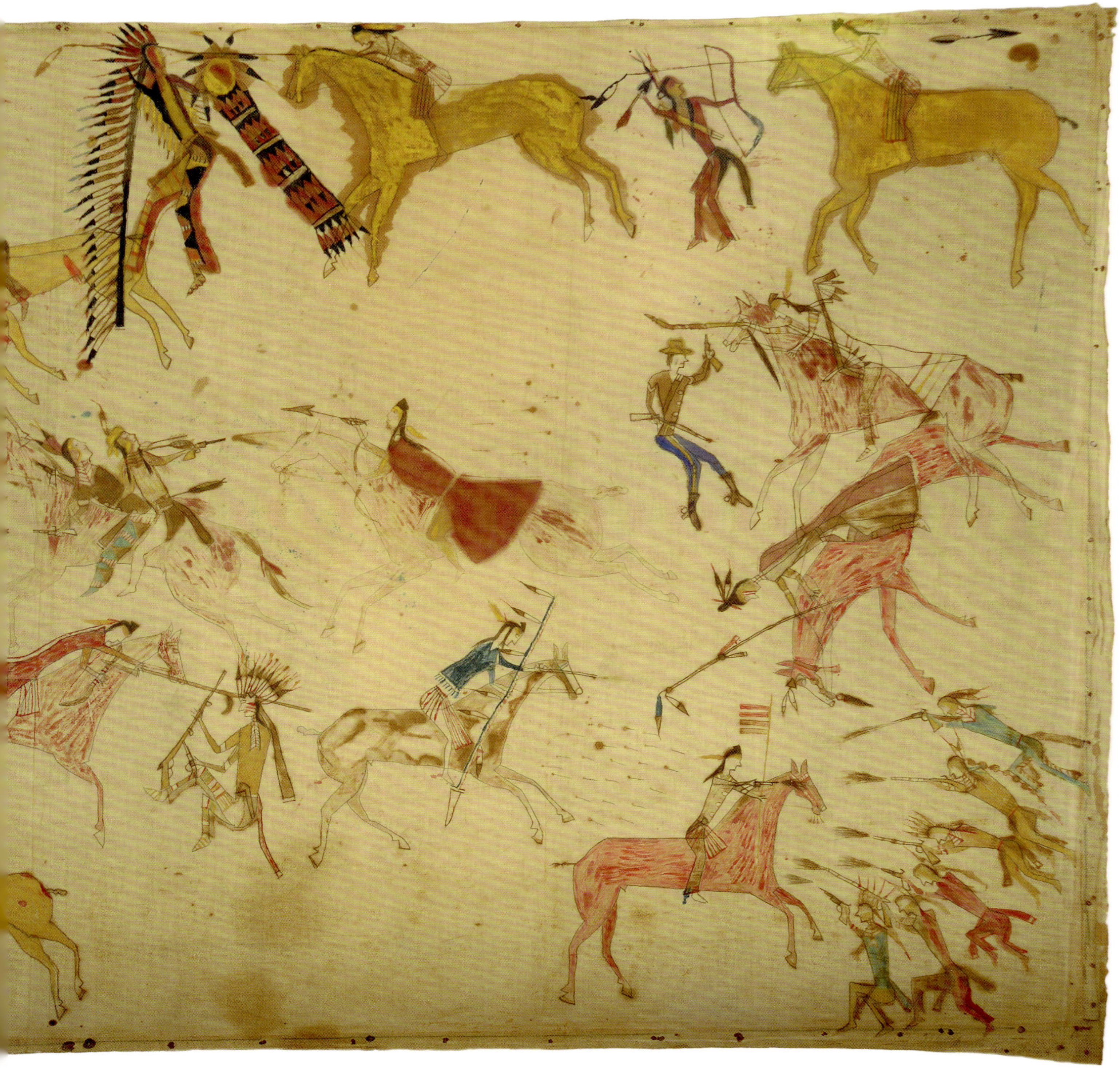

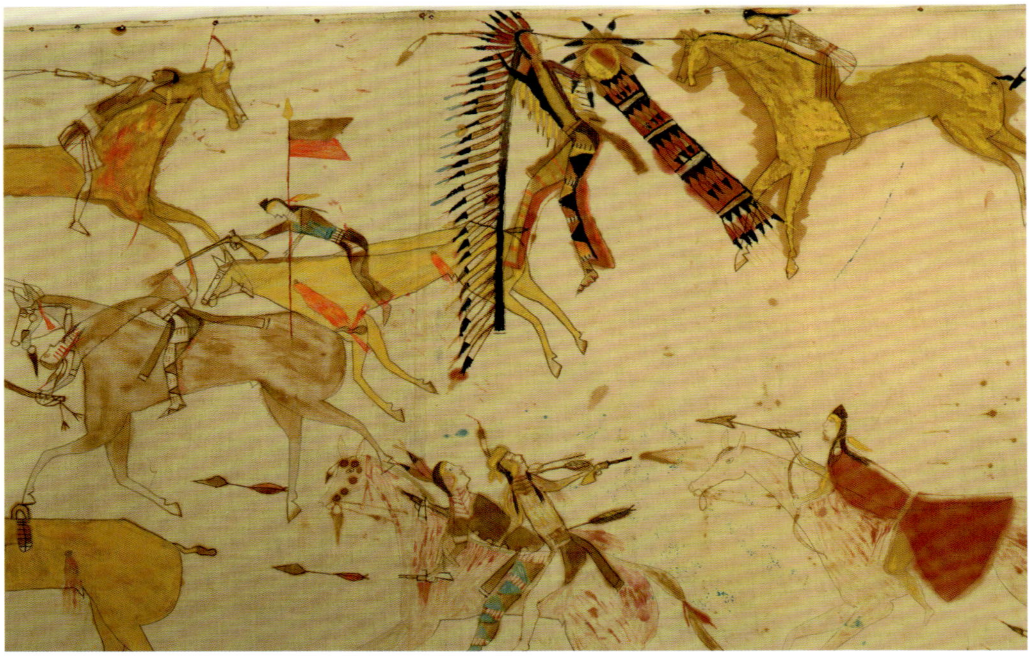

3.4. *(detail)* White Swan painting

White Swan counts coup on a dismounted enemy.

concho headstall, a scalp tied at the chin, a feather on his head, and his tail tied with cloth.

In the next scene, White Swan carries a Seventh Cavalry guidon, indicating that the event occurred during scout duty at Little Bighorn. He has wounded an enemy carrying a saber who has fallen across his horse. The adversary wears a hide shirt, leggings with beaded strips, a long breechcloth, and two eagle feathers in his hair. His horse's tail is tied up with trade cloth, and his ears have been split, an indication of his training and value in buffalo hunting and battle. White Swan's horse is wounded in two places.

Next, White Swan is counting coup on a dismounted enemy (fig. 3.4). He uses a coup stick with an attached eagle feather in an act considered the highest war achievement among the Crow. He rides his yellow horse, whose tail has been tied up in readiness for battle. White Swan's adversary is an accomplished warrior, indicated by his eagle feather bonnet and his painted and feathered shield with a long red wool panel covered in eagle feathers. The enemy wears a fringed and beaded warrior's society shirt with attached ermine tails, cloth breechcloth, and leggings with beadwork strips. Appearing to be disoriented, he turns to face White Swan just as he is hit. Signifying the importance of this action to White Swan, he repeated this narrative in drawings and paintings several times, although with variations in details. In some paintings, another warrior on horseback assists the enemy. In all of the depictions, the enemy is shown as an honored warrior in his eagle feather bonnet and decorated shirt whom White Swan was proud to defeat.

In the upper-right corner of the painting, White Swan on his yellow horse counts coup on an enemy carrying a bow and arrow. His opponent wears a long wool breech cloth and leggings with beadwork strips, carries a bow case and quiver across his body, and holds an arrow in his hand as he prepares to shoot White Swan. He has already missed once, indicated by the arrow flying past White Swan's head.

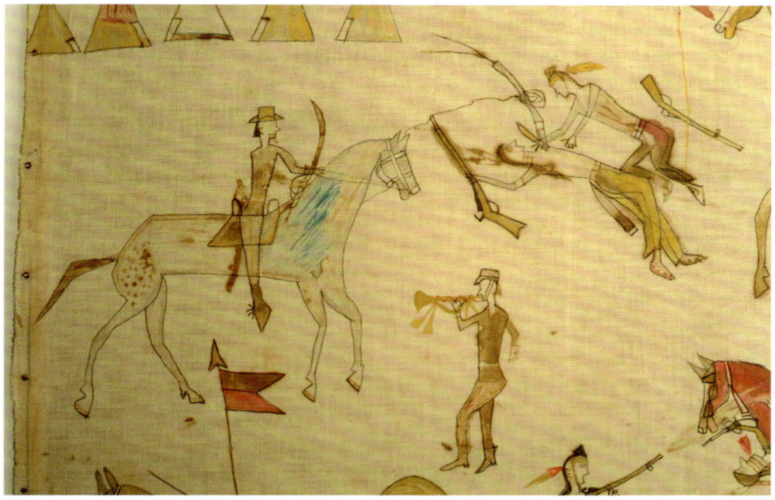

3.5. *(detail)* White Swan painting

A mounted officer, carrying a saber, gives orders as a soldier plays a bugle. White Swan is in hand-to-hand combat with an enemy.

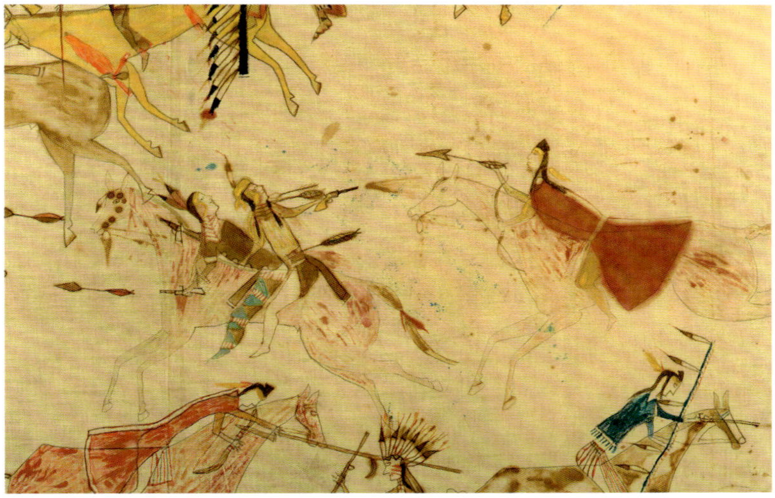

3.6. *(detail)* White Swan painting

Wearing a red cape, White Swan pursues and kills two enemies on a single horse as they return fire.

In the painting's second tier, the first scene on the left shows a mounted officer carrying a saber and giving orders. Another soldier plays a bugle and faces the mounted officer (fig. 3.5). Next, White Swan is shown in hand-to-hand combat with an enemy as his horse, carrying a military McClellan saddle, stands by. White Swan has pinned down the enemy, who holds a quirt in his left hand, and uses his knife while two rifles lie on the ground. This event takes place at Little Bighorn, as indicated by the Seventh Cavalry guidon.

In the second vignette, White Swan, dressed in a long red cape, pursues and kills two enemies on a single horse as his adversaries return fire (fig. 3.6). Next is an interesting scene in which White Swan is shown killing a deserting soldier, in reference to an event that took place at Little Bighorn under orders from Major Reno. White Swan repeated this scene in several of his paintings, perhaps indicating the importance of this event in his life's story.[17]

On the bottom left of the painting, White Swan is shown being carried from the battlefield on the travois built by Half Yellow Face with a soldier leading the horse (fig. 3.7). The horse carries the guidon of the Seventh Cavalry. White Swan's wounds are clearly visible in this

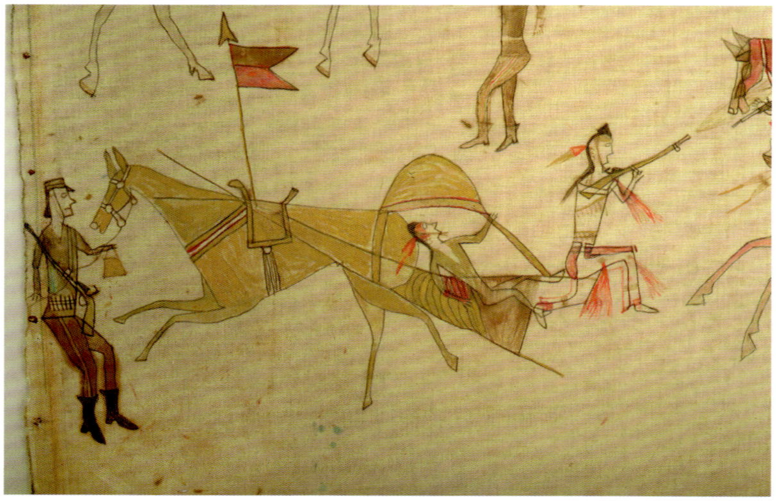

3.7. *(detail)* White Swan painting

White Swan is carried from the battlefield on a travois with a soldier leading the horse.

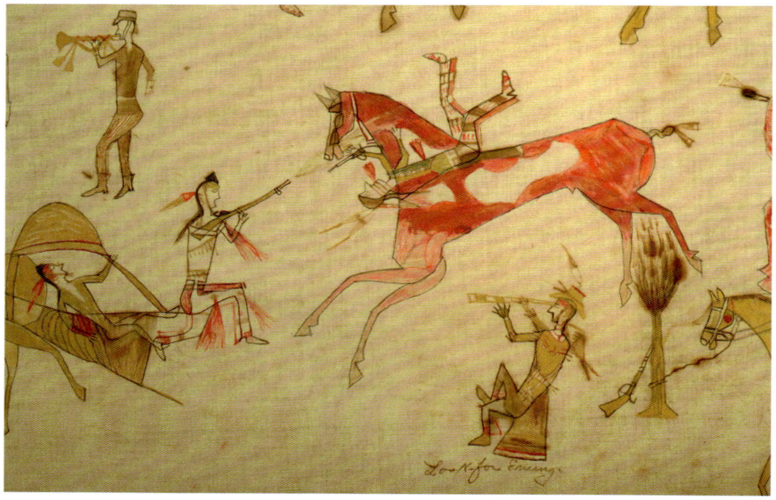

3.8. *(detail)* White Swan painting

White Swan shoots his firearm at a Lakota or Cheyenne enemy tumbling from his horse.

depiction of his rescue. Next, White Swan is shown shooting his firearm at the Lakota or Cheyenne enemy tumbling from his horse. With his wounds in his head, thigh, and knee indicated, White Swan's courage and bravery are clearly on display in this scene.

Below this scene is a vignette labeled "Look for Enemy" (fig. 3.8). This scene, repeated many times in White Swan's paintings, shows the scout using a telescope focusing on the tipi camp above to seek the enemy. His horse, tied to a tree, stands by. Some scholars have suggested that this event took place at Little Bighorn as the scouts gathered at Crow's Nest to see the Lakota and Cheyenne camps. Other scholars disagree because White Swan is shown wearing a woolen capote, winter wear that would be inappropriate for the conflict taking place in June.[18]

In the next vignette, White Swan rides his red horse with his red cape flowing from his shoulders. White Swan records himself striking an enemy with a lance. The adversary, wearing an eagle feather bonnet signifying that he is a prominent Lakota or Cheyenne warrior, carries a rifle. The final scene in the lower-right corner of the muslin is one of the

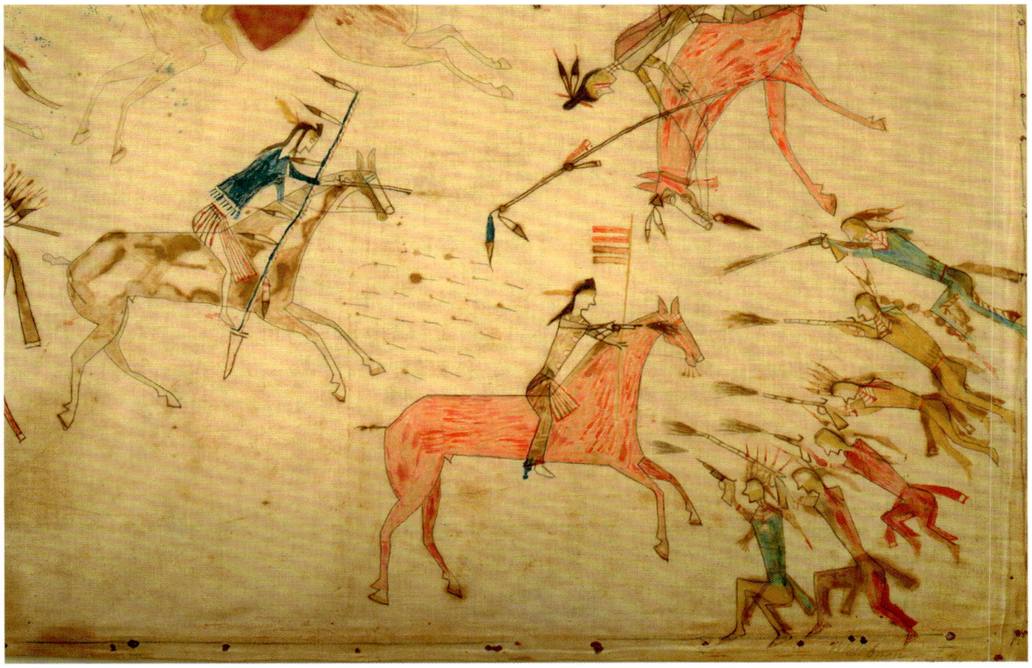

3.9. *(detail)* White Swan painting

White Swan, carrying a flag, fires at a circle of shooting enemies.

most dramatic (fig. 3.9). Here, White Swan, carrying a flag, charges a circle of armed and shooting enemies. The bullets fly by him as he returns fire at the group of warriors. This scene in particular indicates White Swan's pride for his scout duties and power in battle.

Through the muslin painting in the Dyck collection and others, White Swan documented his own war record and his role in significant events in Crow and Northern Plains history. Although Joseph Medicine Crow noted that White Swan was probably the least well known of the Crow scouts among his own people, through his artistry, he has provided for them an autobiography of a heroic and courageous warrior who, despite suffering severe wounds in battle, fought to protect his homeland.[19]

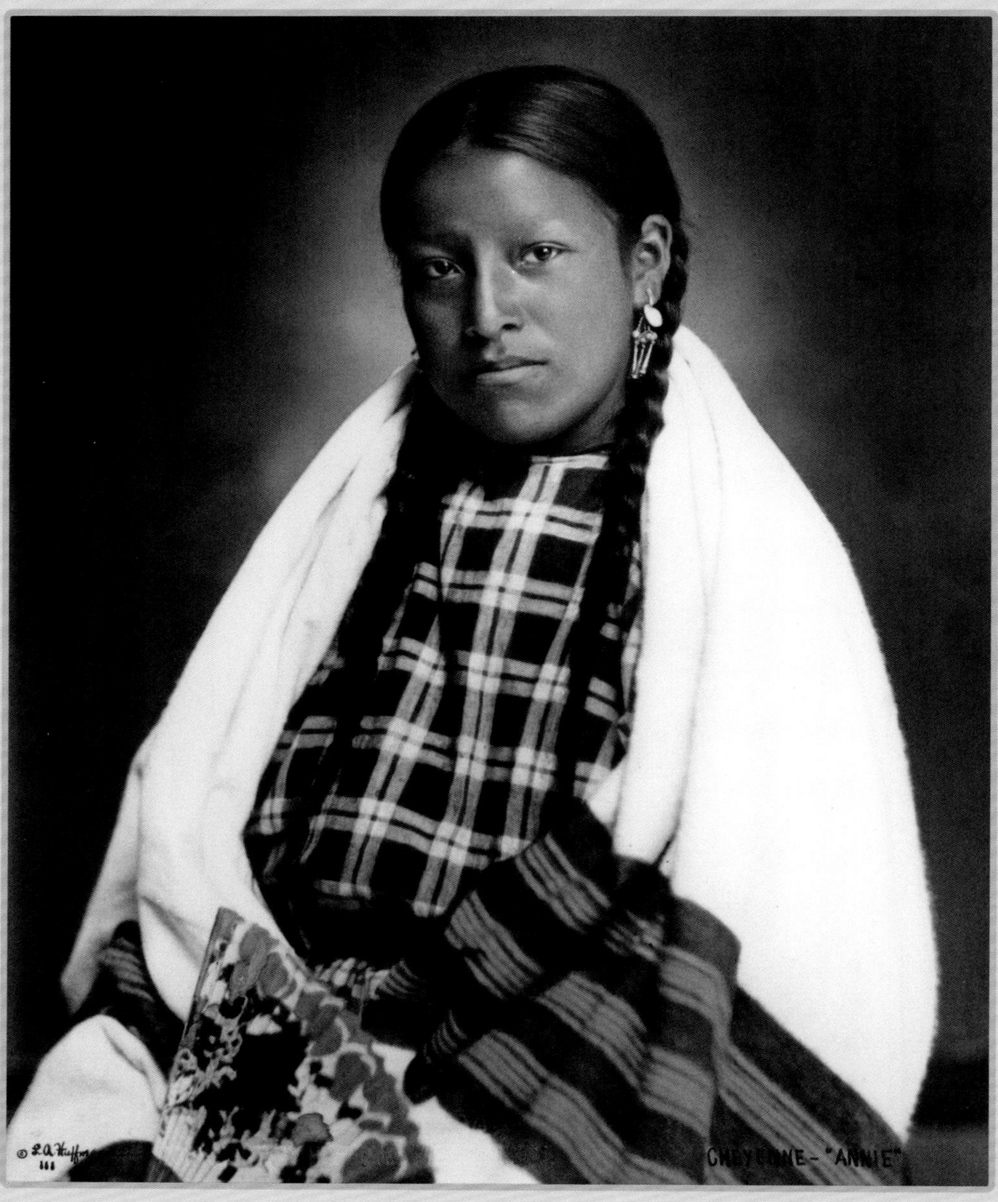
CHEYENNE – "ANNIE"

4 Artistry of Women

Lakota anthropologist Beatrice Medicine devoted her career to research and education about historical and contemporary Plains Indian societies. She emphasized correcting misleading academic and popular stereotypes about the roles and responsibilities of women. Medicine suggested that the identification of Plains Indian peoples as "warrior" societies "has sublimated the contributions of Indian women to the point where such terms as 'drudge, slave, whore, and squaw' have been used by the dominant society. The latter term still resonates in some parts of the country, as evidenced by the current opposition to the naming of places, creeks, and mountains with this word."[1]

> Although women used similar methods to produce goods from raw materials, including fleshing and tanning animal skins for clothing and tipis, preserving the flesh of the hunt, searching for such fruits and vegetables as the ubiquitous "prairie turnip" and medicinal plants and herbs, they did not view this work as drudgery. Their arduous labor was recognized as contributions to family and kin group survival. The woman's skill and efficiency in packing and moving the tipi and possessions also added to her status.[2]

The disparagement of Native American women, together with the popular use of the derogatory terms listed by Medicine, were common in nineteenth-century journals and letters. Christian missionaries and other Euro-American travelers, traders, and government representatives wrote these publications. Most of these primarily male writers were unable to communicate with Plains Native women because of language and cultural barriers. They based their unfavorable opinions on observing women involved in the hard work of butchering and preserving meat; scraping and tanning hides; building and furnishing tipis, earth lodges, and grass houses; moving camp; gathering wild plants, cultivating gardens, and preserving the produce; preparing food and clothing for family members; and taking care of children. Non-Native observers, such as John Dunbar, held predetermined attitudes about the proper role of women and expressed their biases in writings.[3]

4.1. *Cheyenne Annie*, Tsitsistas (Cheyenne) woman
Northern Cheyenne Reservation, Montana, ca. 1890
Photograph by L. A. Huffman
McCracken Research Library, P.100.3578

> The Pawnee women are very laborious. I am inclined to think they perform more hard labor than any other woman on this continent, be they white, black or red. It is rare, they are seen idle. When a Pawnee woman has nothing to do, she seems to be out of her element. They dress the skins for the tent covers, which is done with no small labor,

> sew them together, and fit them for the tents—make all the robes, which are many, both for their own use and the market—cut and bring all the wood on their backs—make all the fires—do all the cooking of course—dry all the meat—dig the ground—plant—hoe and gather all the corn, of which they raise in abundance, as they also do of beans and pumpkins—cut the timber, and build all their dwellings, both fixed and movable—set up and take down the portable tents—bridle and unbridle, saddle and unsaddle, pack and unpack all the horses—make all their moccasins, mats, bags, bowls, mortars, etc., etc. Since the ground has thawed, they have bestowed some hundreds of days of hard labor in digging Indian potatoes. A woman does not succeed in digging more than a peck, laboring diligently from sunrise till sunset. Soon after light, I have seen droves of the women and girls with their hoes and axes on their shoulders, starting off to their day's work. Their women are mere slaves.[4]

As a Presbyterian missionary to the Pawnee from 1834 to 1849, John Dunbar failed to recognize that women exercised power as owners of their earth lodges in which their husbands, unmarried children, and married daughters with husbands and children lived. In addition to their economic contributions from gardening and gathering plants; creating homes; and producing meals, clothing, household goods, and other necessities, Pawnee women cared for and instilled cultural values in children and participated in ceremonial life.

In practical terms, roles and responsibilities of Plains Indian men and women allowed for flexibility and cooperation. Although men were generally in charge of hunting and defense, women were primarily responsible for the home, food preparation, and rearing children. Both men and women were also sometimes involved in each other's work. Men assisted in cutting wood, slicing meat, or preparing corn for drying and spending time with children. They developed the skills necessary for traveling on their own for hunting or raiding, such as food preparation and repairing clothing and moccasins. Women supported men in hunting, warfare, and their associated ceremonies. In the arts, men and women contributed the raw materials, talents, and skills to create decorated tipis, furnishings, clothing, ritual items such as pipes and pipe bags, and other accoutrements. Ella Deloria expressed the attitude of Dakota women about their traditional roles and responsibilities in the following way:

> Outsiders seeing women keep to themselves have frequently expressed a snap judgment that they were regarded as inferior to the noble male. The simple fact is that woman had her place and man his; they were not the same and neither inferior nor superior.
>
> The sharing of work also was according to sex. Both had to work hard, for their life made severe demands. But neither expected the other to come and help outside the customary division of duties; each sex thought the other had enough to do. That did not mean, however, that a man disdained to do woman's work when necessary; or a woman, man's. The attitude on division of work was quite normal, however it looked to outsiders. A woman caring for children and doing all the work around the

> house thought herself no worse off than her husband who was compelled to risk his life continuously, hunting and remaining ever on guard against enemy attacks on his family.[5]

Writers on Plains Native cultures have often emphasized the roles and responsibilities of Plains Indian men as buffalo hunters, warriors, and leaders, which appeared more dramatic, glorious, and respected than those of women. Men were publicly honored through warrior society ceremonies, songs, and oral traditions celebrating their skills as hunters, their courage, and bravery in battle. They also validated their achievements in hunting and warfare through specialized clothing, regalia, and artistic expression, such as pictographic paintings and drawings on hide, muslin, and paper. Women, however, also earned respect through their accomplishments in both practical work and exquisite artistry that enriched and enhanced daily life.

TIPI: SHELTER, SANCTUARY, REFUGE, HOME

As described by Alma Hogan Snell, the youngest granddaughter of the Crow army scout Goes Ahead and his wife, Pretty Shield, the powerful symbolism of the buffalo as provider and protector of the people is conveyed to the shelter created by Plains Indian women from its strong and heavy hides.

> The lodge would be a sanctuary. It actually is a place of refuge. It protects you. It means so much more. I think it means more than a house, actually. It has the animal structure to it, the buffalo animal structure to it that protects us even from other animals that could invade the lodge. You could wrap up in a buffalo robe and stay still. The smell of the buffalo is so overwhelming and yet the hide is so tough. My grandmother says it protected them from many things, the buffalo.[6]

Pretty Shield reared her granddaughter after her mother died when she was a year and a half old. Like other Crow mothers and grandmothers of earlier generations, Pretty Shield taught her granddaughter traditional knowledge about plant uses for foods and medicines and methods of tanning hides and creating tipis and furnishings. Living in a small log house on the Crow Reservation, Pretty Shield and other women of her age had transitioned to a new way of life while keeping many of the old ways alive for their children and grandchildren. As an elder, Alma Hogan Snell reminisced about what her grandmother had taught her about Crow women as lodge keepers in the buffalo-hunting times.

> The lodge keepers were actually the backbone. Like my grandma always said, "If a man stayed in a lodge by himself, it was no good." It just wasn't a home until there was a lodge keeper there. So many things they had to do. Yet, they found time to make beauty of it . . .
>
> Right now, in the spring, I long to be in a tipi. I imagine like I'd like to be in the tipi and I'd like to have some other tipis around. I'd like to hear people talking out there. I like to hear them busy, going back and forth, and a few dogs barking even, you know. I could just imagine myself being in the tipi listening to all this, enjoying it.[7]

For contemporary Plains Native people, tipis, or lodges, as they are sometimes called, are more than nostalgic reminders of eighteenth- and nineteenth-century life. Families often erect and stay in their canvas tipis during annual summer fairs and celebrations such as the American Indian Exposition held in Anadarko, Oklahoma; North American Indian Days, which take place each July at Browning, Montana; Calgary Stampede, located in Calgary, Alberta, in July; and Crow Fair held each year in August at Crow Agency, Montana.

Although Crow Fair, known as the "Teepee Capital of the World," attracts many national and international visitors, it is essentially a reunion for tribal members and a time to commemorate their lives as Plains buffalo hunters and reintroduce this heritage to younger generations. Crow speakers refer to this celebration, consisting of a powwow, parades, rodeo, and exhibition of tribal arts, as *uhba'asaxpiluua*. This term translates as "where they make the noise" and refers to any dance, celebration, or social gathering.[8] For this event, Crow and other Native people from many tribes camp in 1,000 to 1,500 tipis on grounds located along the banks of the Little Bighorn River.[9] Such tipi encampments take place throughout the Great Plains at annual tribal celebrations and in more intimate ceremonial contexts such as Sun Dance and Native American Church meetings.

For Native people, tipis serve as powerful symbols of a unique and creative existence of tribal peoples on the Great Plains before Euro-American colonization, Native depopulation, and confinement to reservations—at a time when buffalo, deer, and elk were abundant and the people had the freedom to move seasonally in search of game to hunt or native plants to gather. As a functional and universal dwelling style on the Plains, the tipi has great cultural significance among Plains tribes and is deeply rooted and inherent in diverse and fundamental tribal values, histories, and traditions. Crow speakers refer to the tipi as *ashé*, meaning "home," or *ashtáahile*, meaning "real home."[10] As the Crow moved into reservation log homes and, later, brick houses, they began to use the term *ashtáale* specifically to refer to the more traditional tipi housing.[11] Crow oral traditions featuring the exploits of Yellow Leggings (Issaatshíilish) illustrate the origin and cultural significance of the tipi itself as well as its tribally specific structure, composed of a framework of twenty-one poles, including a base of four poles. Yellow Leggings brought the tipi to the Crow, who, according to oral tradition, had previously made their homes in the shelter of caves or rock overhangs. Yellow Leggings also introduced to the Crow people the symbolism of the tipi's various elements as well as the respect, values, and protocol associated with it.[12]

The Pawnee, who lived in their earth lodge villages while women cultivated their gardens, created different styles of hide lodging for their winter and summer buffalo hunts. During the winter, they lived in the standard hide tipi (*káracapí* in Pawnee). With the fire burning in the middle of the lodge, the tipi provided protection from the cold. During the summer hunt, Pawnee women used the hide cover of the tipi over a framework of poles and lightweight elm or willow saplings to construct a curved open-faced shelter. With the fireplace near the entrance but outside the shelter, the home was much cooler during long summer days. Traveling with this type of shelter was simplified with the lightweight saplings rather than the heavier tipi poles.[13]

For the Pawnee, constructing the hide cover for a tipi was a major undertaking that needed to be planned at least two years in advance so as to accumulate at least eight buffalo hides, as well as the sinew to sew them together.[14] An experienced lodge maker would supervise the complex work of fitting the hides together, with four or five other women doing the actual sewing over about four days. For this assistance, the lodge owner compensated all of the women with gifts of dried buffalo meat, clothing, and trade goods and provided them with meals for the duration of the work.[15]

Among the Lakota, Cheyenne, Arapaho, and Kiowa, men painted autobiographical hunting scenes and war deeds on tipi covers, which, like hide and muslin paintings, documented their individual honors and tribal histories. Blackfoot men painted on their lodges visionary images of buffalo and other powerful creatures that they regarded as sources of their own supernatural powers. Following the directions received in his vision, a man often called upon other men who were skilled artists to paint the outlines of the figures, which were later painted in by family members. Although the distinctive designs of such paintings are often owned by individuals and families who uniquely understand their full symbolism, there are some tribal conventions. For example, the red band often painted along the bottom of Blackfoot tipis represents the earth. The unpainted circles within the band symbolize fallen stars. The tops of such tipis painted in black represent the night, and unpainted circles within this area indicate constellations such as the Pleiades. The cross at the back of the cover near the top is said to symbolize the morning star.[16] Cheyenne, Arapaho, and Lakota women often decorated their tipi covers with circular hide ornaments covered in beadwork or porcupine quillwork and pendants of small dewclaws wrapped in quillwork.[17] Other tribes such as the Crow preferred that their tipi covers remain undecorated.

For women, who had the primary responsibility for creating and maintaining tipis, the acquisition and preparation of adequate numbers of strong heavy poles required careful planning and, often, assistance from male relatives. Blackfoot women cut new tipi poles of lodge pole pine during the fall months. After locating, cutting, and transporting the poles into camp, a woman often enlisted the help of young men for assistance in peeling the bark from the poles by preparing berry soup and inviting them to a feast.[18]

Southern Arapaho artist Carl Sweezy remembered that the women of his youth took great pride in constructing and maintaining their tipis on the Cheyenne and Arapaho Indian Reservation in southwestern Oklahoma: "The important thing, besides the know-how, was the lodge poles. These must be long and straight and slender, and for a good family lodge, there must be from sixteen to twenty of them. They must be of some wood like cedar that would not rot when they were exposed to rain and snow. Such poles were not easy to find on the Plains, and the women took great care in them."[19] In the 1880s when Sweezy was a child, the Southern Cheyenne and Arapaho were no longer living in buffalo-hide tipis. Hide tipis had disappeared with the decimation of the buffalo herds and were replaced by tipis made of canvas. Born in 1881, Sweezy experienced changes and transitions on the reservation brought about by new government policies. During his early childhood, the family still moved seasonally within the reservation lands. The camps were located in sheltered areas near the North Canadian River for protection from the cold during the winter and on cooler higher ground during the summer. As they did in pre-reservation times, the Arapaho moved their entire camps to hunt game for meat and hides for trade—deer and small game, since buffalo were no longer available—and to camp in areas with good supplies of wood, water, and fresh pasture for the horses. According to Sweezy, although agency buildings and Fort Reno had been established on the reservation, there were few fences and farms to limit their movements. He remembered, "To us who were young, its streams and thickets and prairies seemed to stretch to the end of the world, but when we listened to the talk of the old men and women we knew they considered the Reservation small and the white settlements too close to us."[20]

When the agent Brinton Darlington established the Upper Arkansas Agency in 1870 to administer Southern Cheyenne and Arapaho affairs, he had called all the traditional leaders together to encourage them to abandon their tipis for government-built houses and to begin new lives as farmers. The Arapaho resisted these drastic changes to their way of life: "But, this meant a great change, and one we could not make in a hurry. We liked our tipis, with all of our things around us in a circle. I have heard white people talk, of late, about the modern circular house, with arrangements for heat and plumbing in the center, new as tomorrow, they say. Well, ours were circular, with a central fire, but I never heard an Arapaho boast that the idea was a new one."[21] Some of these leaders, such as Little Raven, eventually accepted government houses built at Cantonment, and plowed and planted some of the land around it. They continued, however, to maintain their tipis along with their government houses and to live close together in family groups.[22]

According to Ella Deloria, the early log reservation houses were "small, one room affairs, low and dark, and dank, because of the dirt floors. Compared with the well-constructed tipis with their manageable wind flaps for ample ventilating, the cabins were hot and stuffy. Germs

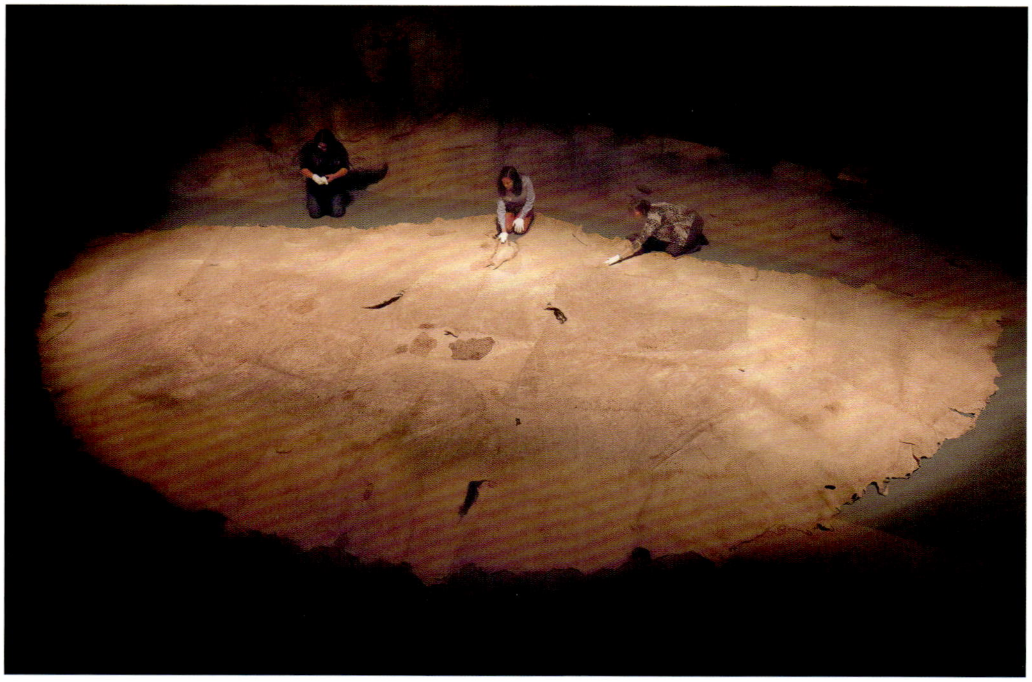

4.2. **Buffalo hide tipi**
Northern Plains, ca. 1860
Tanned buffalo hides and hair, sinew; 413 × 318 inches
Plains Indian Museum, NA.302.269

Plains Indian Museum staff examine and measure a Northern Plains buffalo hide tipi dating from the mid-nineteenth century. Buffalo hide tipis are extremely rare in museum and private collections.

lurked everywhere, causing general sickness, and the death rate increased."[23] After allotment, tribal members were able to build larger and better-constructed houses and began to adapt some elements of tipi living to their new environment. They made large wall coverings of muslin reminiscent of the earlier tipi linings to protect the log houses from drafts and dirt. Men painted pictographic drawings of warfare, hunting, and camp and courtship scenes on the coverings, which were sometimes purchased by collectors for museum collections.[24] Arthur Amiotte has researched Lakota log houses built on the Pine Ridge Reservation during the years of 1880 to 1920. He describes the log house as "more than just a house where people lived. It was an entire experiment wherein Lakota people, who had previously lived in tipis, were now making the transition to living an agrarian lifestyle."[25]

Nineteenth-century buffalo-hide tipis are extremely rare in museum and private collections. As the tipis wore out and hides for replacement became much more difficult to obtain, women turned to using canvas, which was available on the Plains through traders. Canvas was also lighter and easier to work with and transport on a travois. There are actually two full-sized buffalo-hide tipis, three canvas ones, and one made of cow hide in the Paul Dyck Collection. One of the buffalo-hide tipis dates from the mid-nineteenth century (fig. 4.2). The tipi has no painted designs, but has three buffalo tails attached to the exterior.

MAKING A HOME ON THE GREAT PLAINS

Creating and maintaining a fine lodge required collaboration and shared responsibilities that placed high cultural values on women's industriousness and creativity. Living in a tipi involved other shared cultural values for women such as generosity, hospitality, and humility. The Crow woman Pretty Shield recalled a woman named Kills-good who possessed all of these traits as well as a beautifully maintained tipi.

> Its poles were taller, its lodge-skin whiter and cleaner, its lining, beautifully painted, reaching all around it. Its back-rests, three of them, were made with head-and-tail robes; and always Kills-good burned a little sweet-grass, or sweet-sage, so that her lodge smelled nice. . . . Yes, and the shoulder-blades of buffalo that Kills-good used for dishes were bleached snow white, and always she placed a little square of rawhide under each of them when she gave meat to anybody.[26]
>
> How I loved to watch Kills-good pack her things to move camp. The painting on her parfleches was brighter, her bags whiter, than those of any other Crow woman; and, ah, she had so many pretty things. Besides, I thought her favorite horse, a proud pinto, was far and away the best horse in the Crow tribe. And yet Kills-good was not proud. Instead, she was kindly and so soft-spoken that all the people loved her.[27]

Women furnished their tipis with functional, yet often finely decorated, tipi liners made of tanned hide with painted, porcupine quillwork, or beadwork designs; parfleches made of rawhide and incised or painted in geometric designs; soft tanned buffalo robes; backrests made of slender peeled willow sticks laced together with sinew, trimmed with red or blue trade cloth, and embellished with beadwork or porcupine quillwork (fig. 4.3). Other possessions included bowls made from rawhide or carved from wood; carved wood or horn spoons; and bags made from tanned hide and decorated in porcupine quillwork, beadwork, or natural pigments.

Plains Indian tipi furnishings and personal items were transportable, functional, and practical while also often carved, painted, quilled, beaded, and embellished to reflect distinctive cultural traditions. As Euro-American trade items became available in the Plains in the early nineteenth century, iron pots and kettles, metal knives, wool blankets, and other tools and household items were added to this assemblage of necessities. Despite the addition of such items, many people preferred the older, more traditional creations.

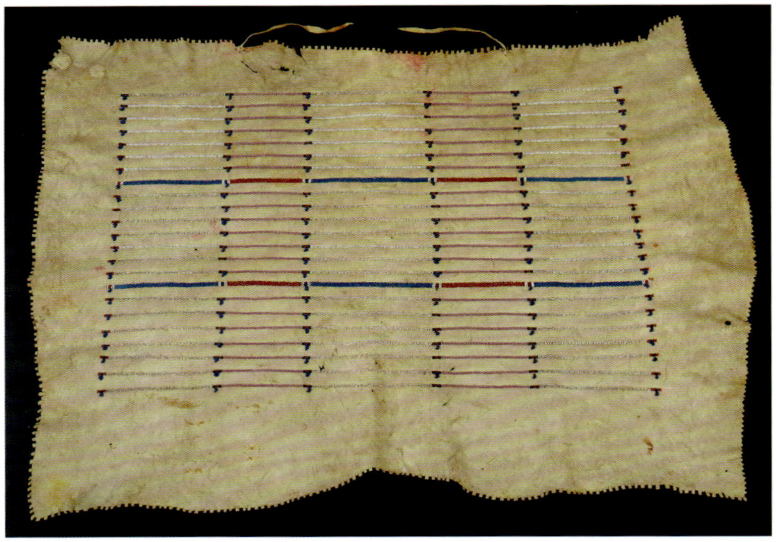

4.3. **Tipi liner**
Northern Plains, ca. 1850
Wool, glass beads, sinew, tanned bison hide; 45 × 68½ inches
Plains Indian Museum, NA.302.286

Parfleches and other rawhide bags were made to accommodate the shapes and sizes of the objects they held, such as the cylinders that protected feather bonnets. Similar painted cylinder parfleches also carried dried herbs and other plants that were used as medicines and in ceremonies (figs. 4.4 and 4.5). The common shape of a parfleche container was an envelope

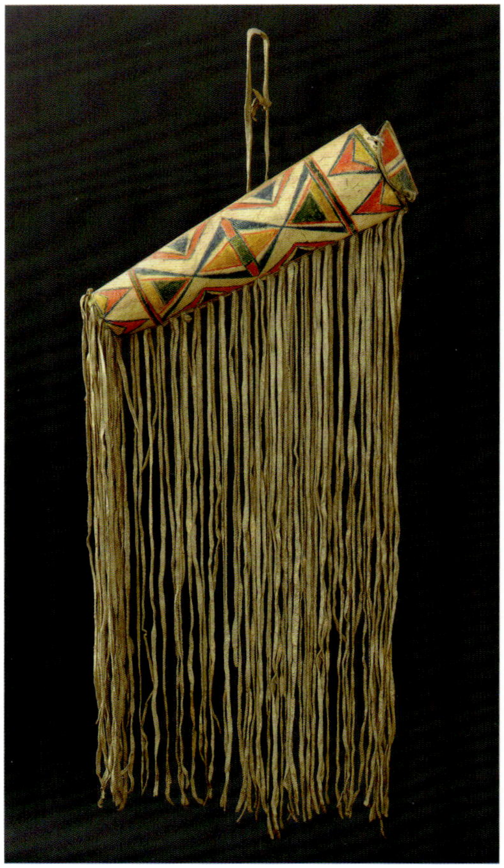

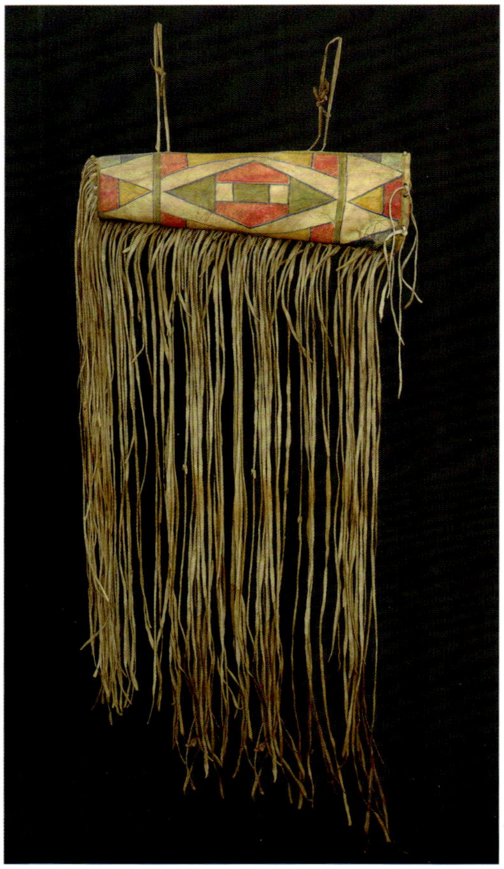

FAR LEFT:
4.4. **Parfleche cylinder case**
Apsáalooke (Crow), Northern Plains, ca. 1880
Rawhide, pigment, tanned hide; 20½ inches, with 6-inch diameter; length of fringe: 40 inches
Plains Indian Museum, NA.106.891

This parfleche cylinder case could have been used to store and carry dried roots, plants, and other medicines.

LEFT:
4.5. **Parfleche cylinder case**
Apsáalooke (Crow), Northern Plains, ca. 1880
Rawhide, pigments, tanned hide; 23 inches, with 6½-inch diameter; length of fringe: 42 inches
Plains Indian Museum, NA.106.890

The cylinder form of this parfleche accommodated a rolled-up eagle feather bonnet for storage and travel.

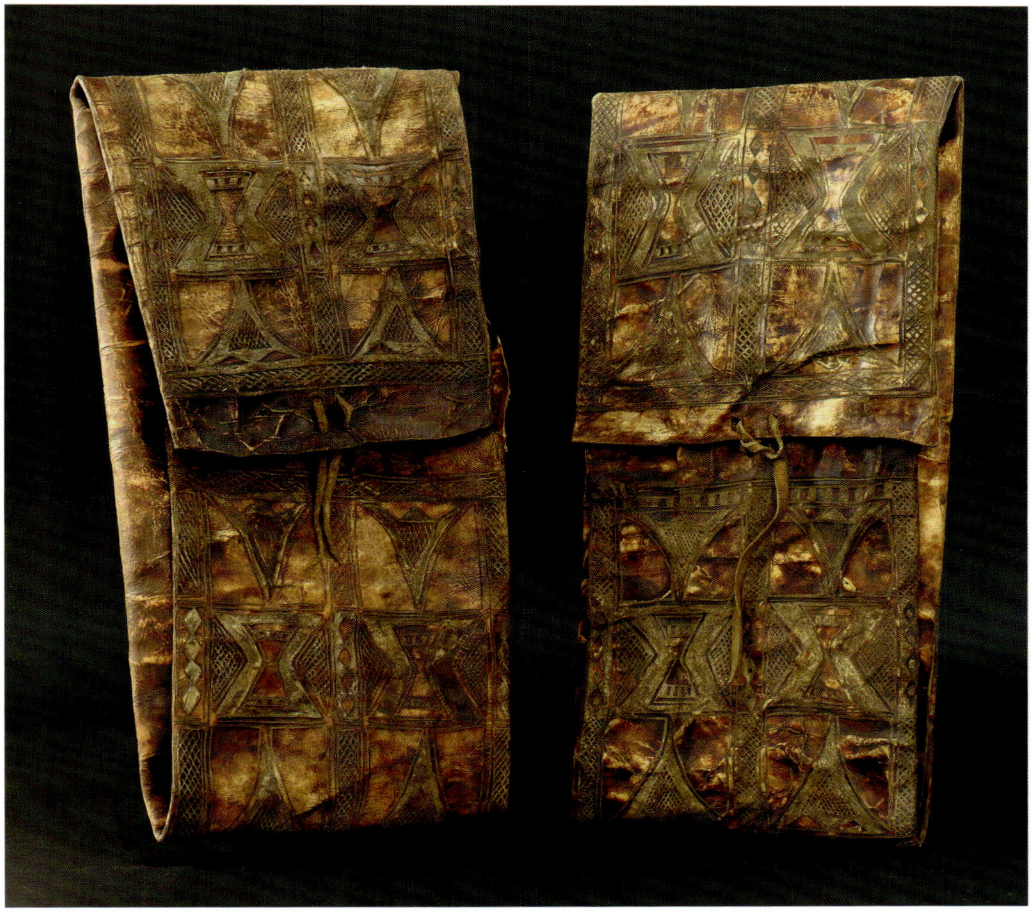

4.6. **Pair of parfleches**
Apsáalooke (Crow), Northern Plains, 1830–1850
Buffalo rawhide, tanned hide;
25 × 14 × 3 inches and
25 × 13 × 2 inches
Plains Indian Museum, NA.106.912.1–2

Women often made parfleches in matching pairs and tied them to horses or travois when traveling. The incised design of these parfleches features diamonds, triangles, and cross-hatching.

made from an oblong section of hide with the long sides folded inward and the short sides folded to meet in the middle. Women painted vibrant geometric designs on the parfleches when the hides were staked out to dry before they were cut.

Some early parfleches were decorated with intricate incised designs made by carving the surface of the hides. Often made in pairs and tied to horses or carried on travois, parfleches were used to store food, utensils, and personal items. In the Dyck collection is a particularly fine pair of Crow parfleches dating from the mid-nineteenth century (fig. 4.6). The incised design of the parfleches features diamonds, triangles, and cross-hatching made by carving into the rawhide while it was still damp. Incised parfleches from the early nineteenth century featuring carved geometric designs likely predate those with painted designs.

After buffalo hide became scarce and the tribes were settled on reservations in the late nineteenth century, women made parfleches and other rawhide bags from the hides of domestic cattle. Manufactured containers were now available for daily life, so parfleches were primarily made for giveaways. Alma Hogan Snell recalls the use of parfleches when she was a girl: "The parfleches are our suitcases, you might say, because I have seen them put clothes in there. I have seen them put even dry meat in there. When they put clothes in there, they usually added a little sweet grass in there and then the next item, whatever it is. And then, tie them up right and then put them against the wall."[28]

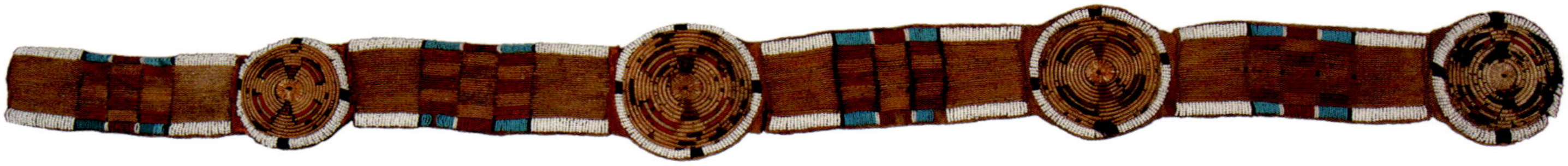

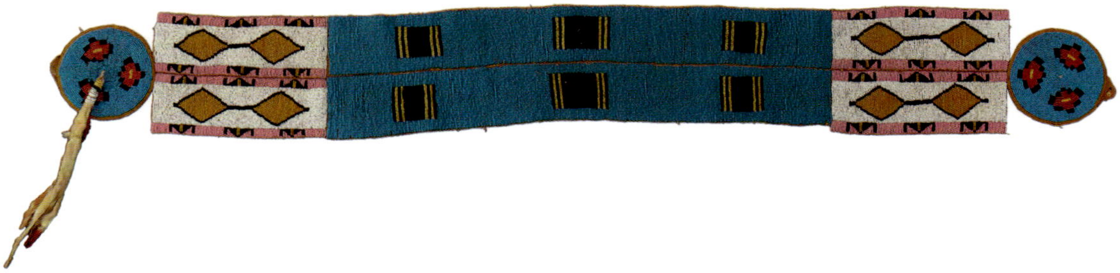

ABOVE:

4.7. **Blanket strip**
Apsáalooke (Crow) or Nimi'ipuu (Nez Perce), Northern Plains or Plateau, ca. 1850
Tanned buffalo hide, porcupine quills, glass beads, horse hair, wool cloth, cotton thread, yarn; 57 × 5¼ inches
Plains Indian Museum, NA.203.1483

The artist who made this blanket strip created its complex pattern by wrapping the porcupine quillwork around small bundles of horse hair.

BELOW:

4.8. **Blanket strip**
Niitsitapi (Blackfoot), Northern Plains, ca. 1880
Tanned hide, glass beads, feather fluffs, yarn, cotton thread, ermine skin; 49½ × 6 inches
Plains Indian Museum, NA.203.1559

OPPOSITE:

4.9. **Dress**
Northern Plains, ca. 1850
Tanned hide, glass beads, wool cloth; dress length: 60 inches; dress width sleeve to sleeve with fringe: 53 inches
Plains Indian Museum, NA.202.1217

Plains Indian women took pride in creating beautiful clothing for themselves and family members. Combining skills in tanning hides of deer, elk, antelope, and mountain sheep with their own artistry in painting, quillwork, and beadwork, they made practical yet beautiful shirts and dresses for daily wear and ceremonies. On this dress, two deer hides form the front and back, with the animal's hind legs folded over to create the shoulders. Parallel bands of beadwork framing the deer's tail follow the contours of the hides.

Women worked long hours cleaning, scraping, tanning, and softening buffalo hides that would serve as warm sleeping and wearing robes. After tanning, the robes could be painted in traditional designs using natural pigments or decorated with porcupine quillwork or beadwork. As commercial wool blankets became available through European and American trading posts during the mid-nineteenth century, they were used like buffalo robes for bedding and outer clothing. Robes and wearing blankets were often decorated with strips of porcupine quillwork or beadwork created in tribally distinctive designs. Traditionally, porcupine quills were dyed with natural plant dyes, but once Euro-American trade materials became available, other more vibrant colors were created from boiling quills with strips of brightly dyed blankets and aniline dyes.

In the Dyck collection, one interesting blanket strip from the Crow or the Plateau region that dates from the mid-nineteenth century is made from a section of tanned buffalo hide (fig. 4.7). The strip's central design is created from porcupine quill–wrapped horse hair, but glass beads form an edging. The design of a later blanket strip from the Blackfoot features a dynamic geometric beadwork pattern of black, yellow, pink, and red beads on a blue background (fig. 4.8).

European glass beads began to appear on the Plains by the early 1800s, brought by Euro-American traders and travelers such as Lewis and Clark. Sometimes called pony beads, they were larger than the later seed beads and came in a limited range of colors, primarily black, white, and blue (figs. 4.9, 4.10, and 4.11). The early beaded designs on leggings, men's shirts, moccasins, women's dresses, pipe bags, and saddle blankets were sometimes combined with painted pigments and quillwork and tended to be relatively simple, consisting predominately of broad bands and blocks of single colors and basic squares, triangles, and rectangles.

In the mid-nineteenth century, smaller Venetian beads became available through long-established trading networks and at centers of trade such as the Mandan, Hidatsa, and Arikara villages of the Upper Missouri River. Manufactured in a wider range of colors, these beads allowed women to create more intricate geometric designs. Porcupine quillwork declined except among the Lakota, Mandan, Arikara, and Hidatsa women, who continued to produce this work into the twentieth century. Mandan, Hidatsa, and Arikara women preferred the vibrant red, yellow, orange, and violet dyes they obtained from the Fort Berthold traders for blanket strips and decorations on men's clothing, pipe bags, and other materials (figs. 4.12 and 4.13).

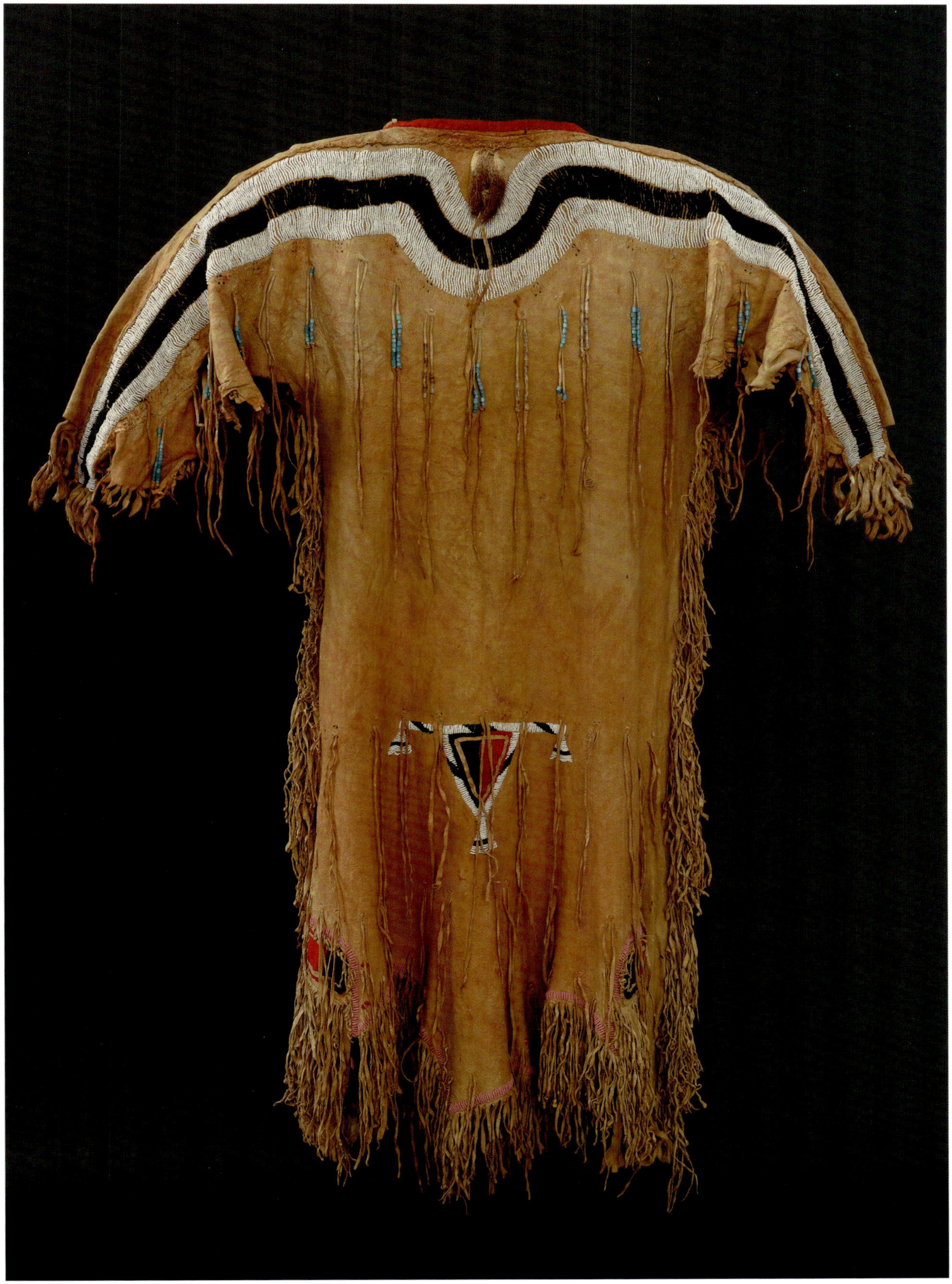

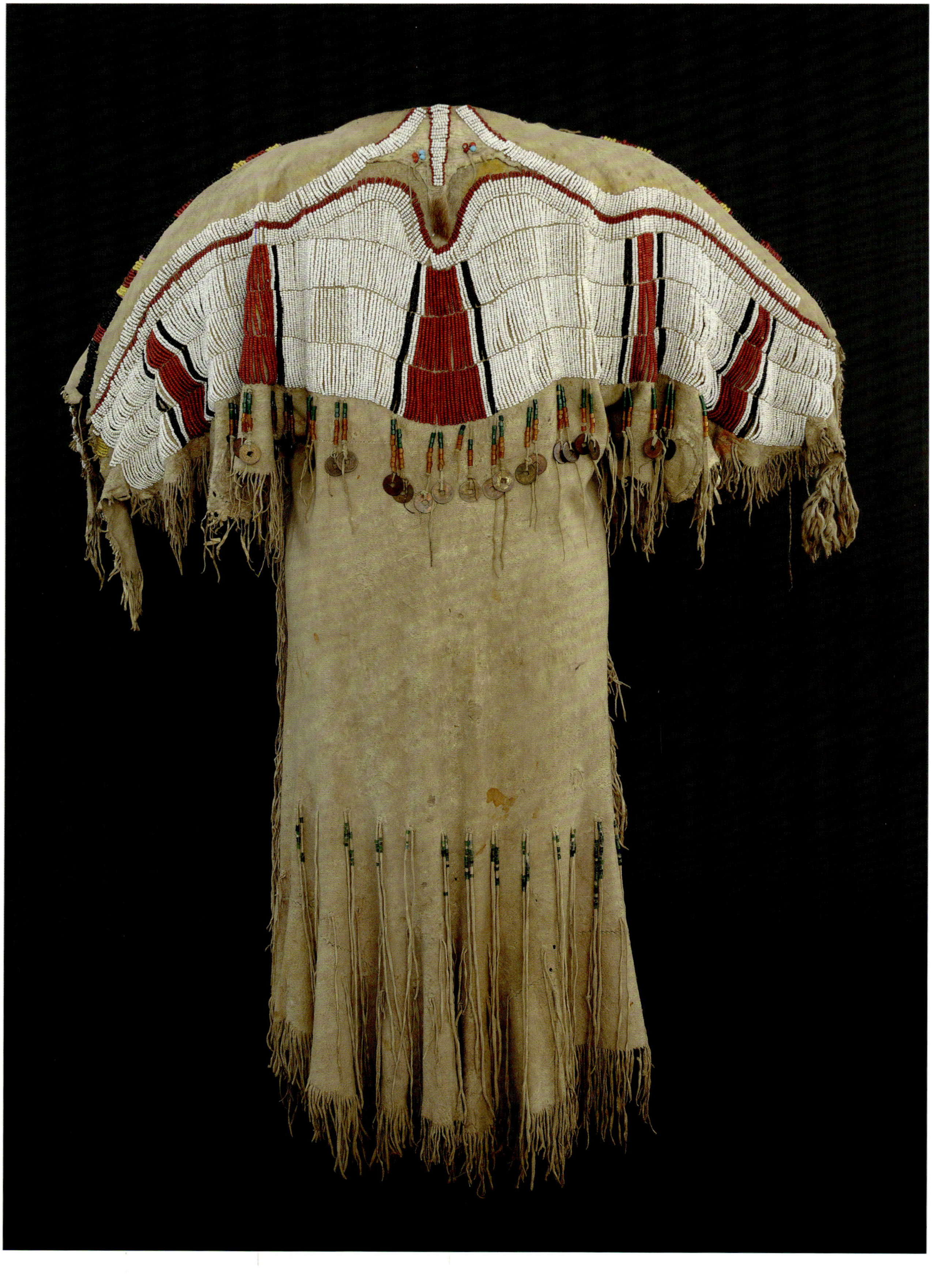

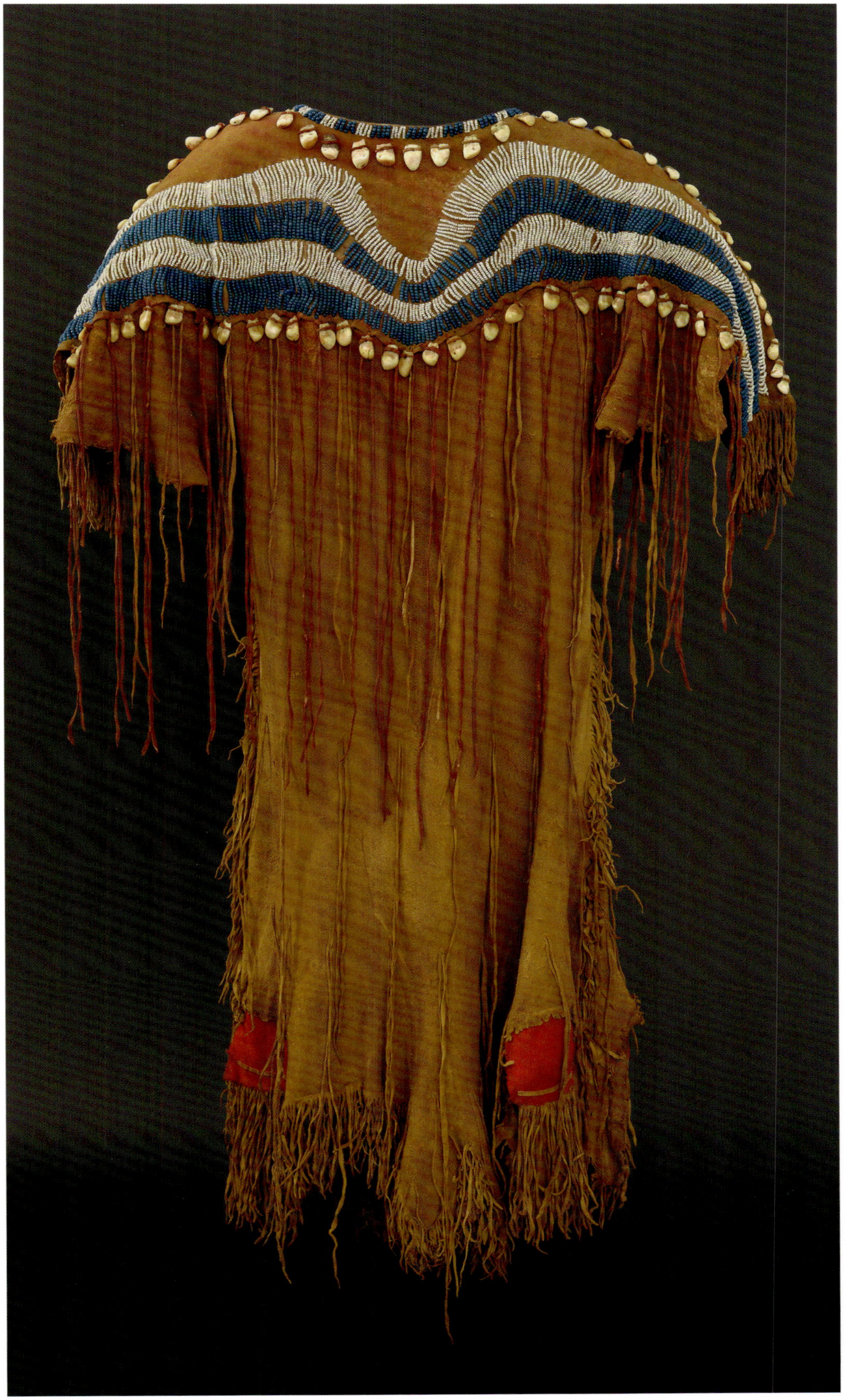

OPPOSITE:

4.10. **Dress**
Plateau, ca. 1830–1850
Tanned deer hide, glass beads, brass coins, sinew; dress length: 49 inches; dress width sleeve to sleeve with fringe: 63 inches
Plains Indian Museum, NA.202.1198

The deer tail remains on this two-hide dress and is bordered by bands of pony beads creating a geometric design. Chinese coins hang from fringe below the bodice of the dress.

4.11. **Dress**
Northern Plains, ca. 1880
Tanned hide, elk teeth, glass beads, pigment, tin cones, wool cloth; dress length: 57 inches; hem width: 30 inches; sleeve to sleeve: 44½ inches
Plains Indian Museum, NA.202.1249

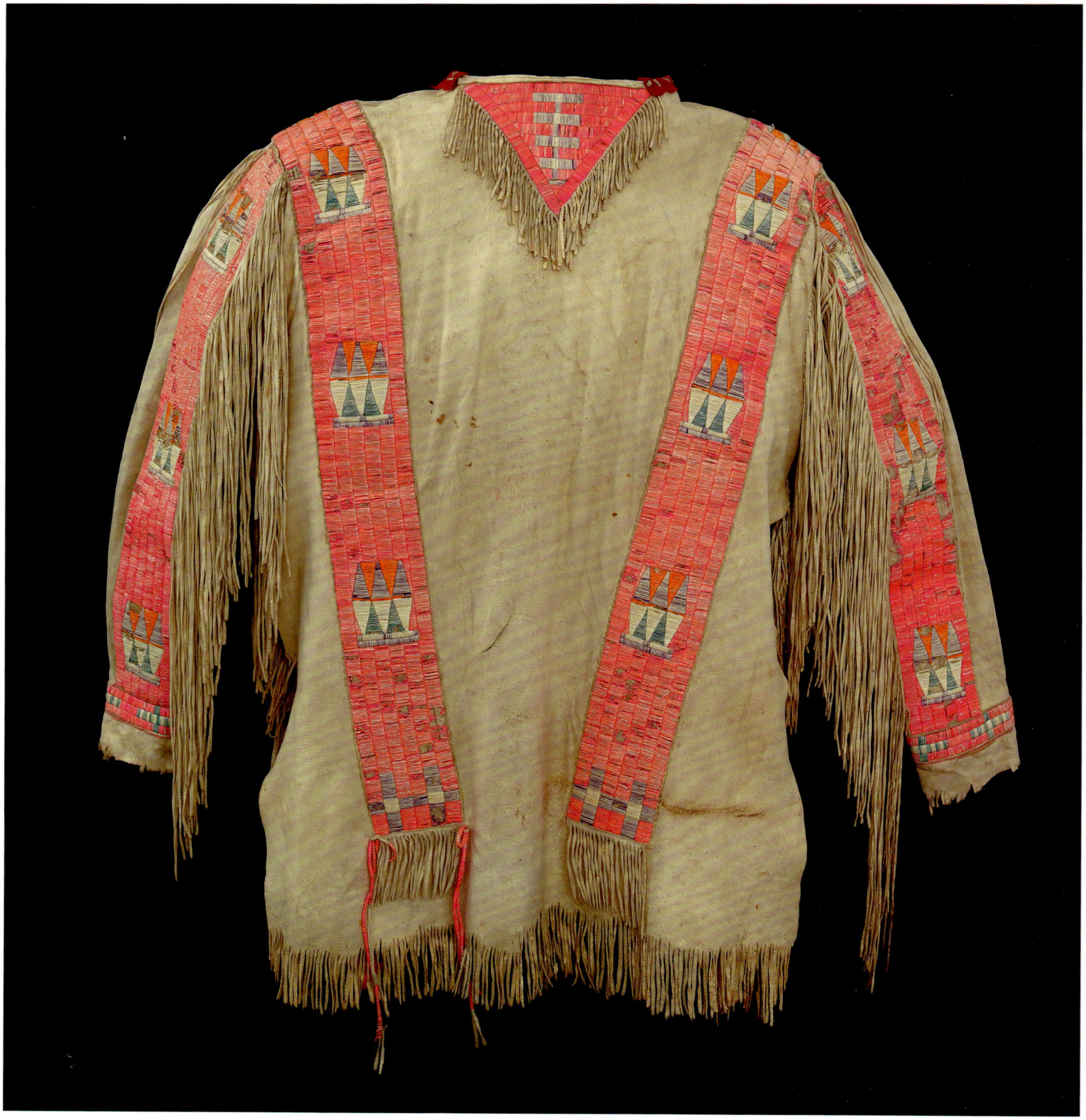

4.12. **Shirt**
Arikara, Hidatsa, Upper Missouri Region, ca. 1900
Porcupine quills, tanned hide, wool cloth, cotton thread, metal cones, dyed feather fluffs; 28½ × 19½ inches
Plains Indian Museum, NA.202.1310

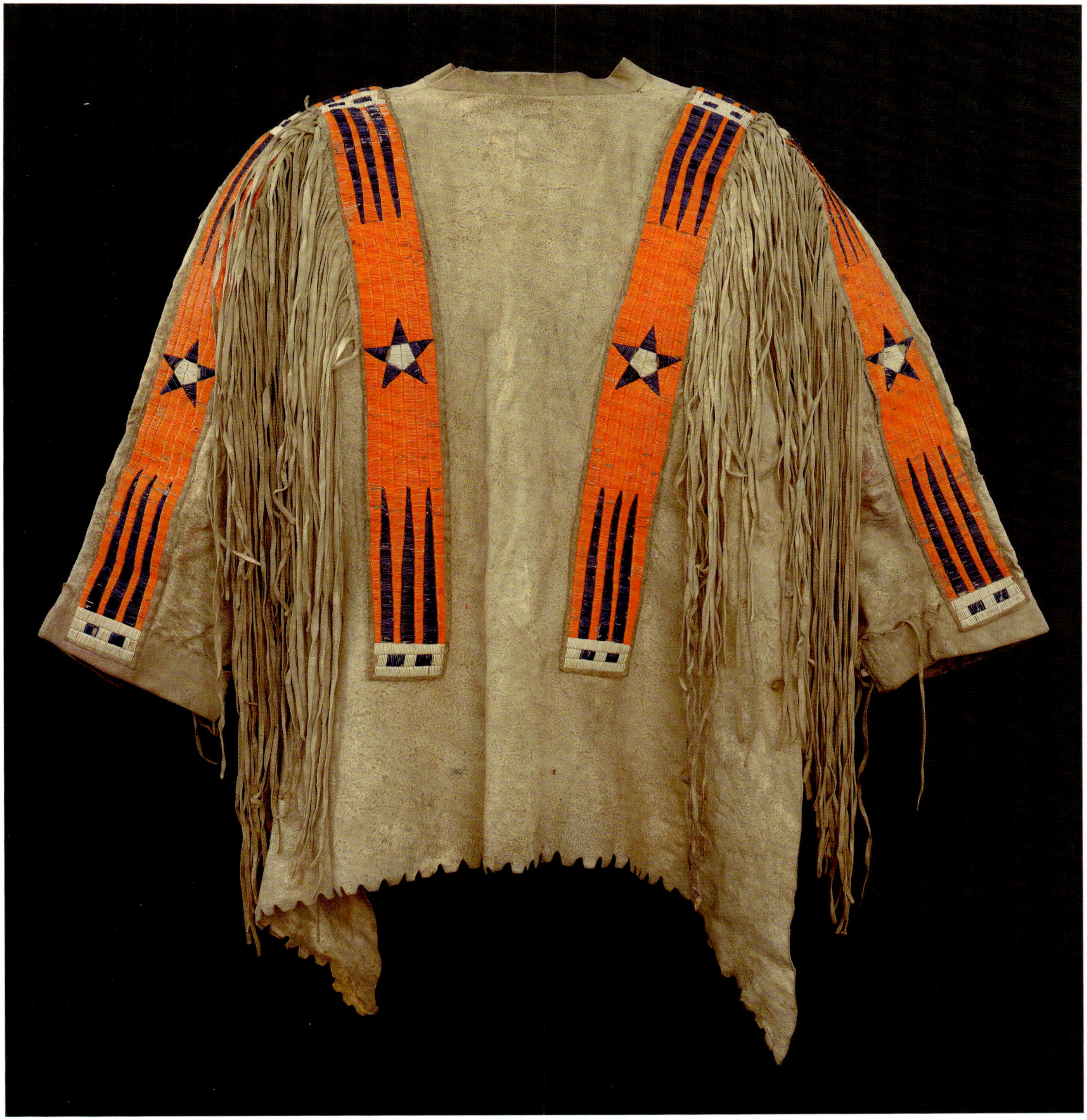

4.13. **Shirt**
Mandan, Hidatsa, or Arikara, Upper Missouri Region, ca. 1890
Porcupine quills, tanned hide, cotton thread; 29 × 19 inches
Plains Indian Museum, NA.202.1308

ARTISTRY OF CREATING CLOTHING

Women spent considerable time making clothing, moccasins, bags, and accessories for themselves and their families. Using skills in tanning deer, antelope, and mountain sheep hides and artistry in painting, quillwork, and beadwork, women produced functional but beautiful and culturally meaningful clothing for everyday use and special ceremonial occasions (figs. 4.14 and 4.15).

By the mid- to late 1800s, women also readily used new materials available through Euro-American trade, including cotton and wool cloth, metal ornaments, and silk ribbons in making clothing for themselves and family members. Two dresses in the Dyck collection created from red and blue wool trade cloth have traditional elk teeth decorations. The numerous elk teeth on the Crow example (fig. 4.16) symbolize wealth and prosperity and the hunting skills of the

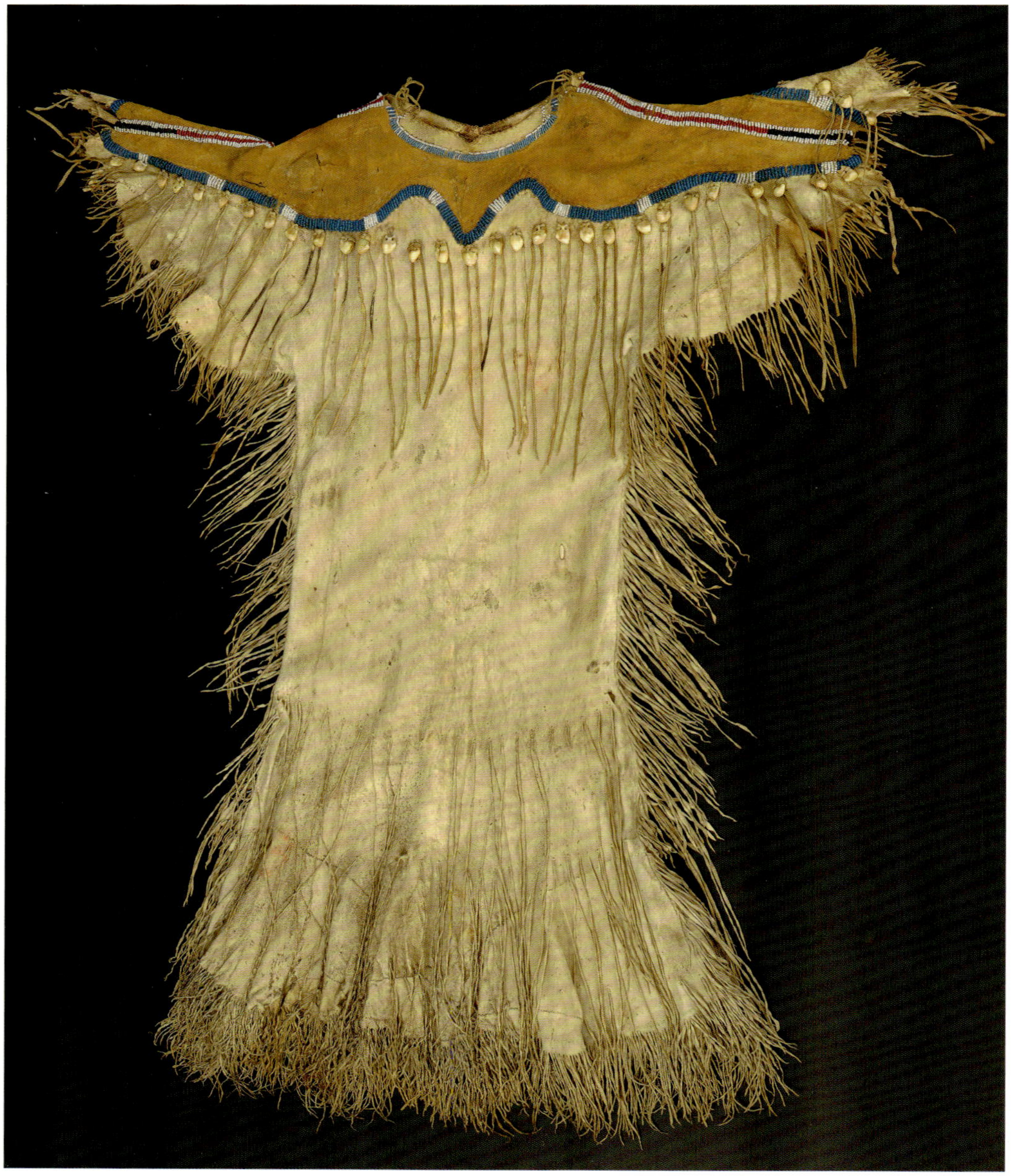

4.14. **Dress**
Tsitsistas (Cheyenne), Southern Plains, ca. 1860
Tanned hide, pigment, glass beads, sinew, elk teeth; dress length: 49 inches; width sleeve to sleeve: 43 inches
Plains Indian Museum, NA.202.1048

husband or other male relative who provided them. According to Crow dressmaker Mardell Hogan Plainfeather, "If a wife and all her female children were attired in these dresses, it was a sign of a family of means, one with a good provider. The dress, which was sometimes given to a newly married bride, meant high honor and acceptance by the bridegroom's family. It also showed their prestige in the tribe."[29]

Women only used the two upper canines or "ivories" of an elk to decorate their clothing. Since a single dress fully covered in elk teeth would require the killing of numerous elk, reservation-era artists also carved additional bone "teeth," that were combined with the ivories to more fully cover dresses.

As seed beads became widely available, the diversity of tribal styles and designs greatly increased. These artistic styles became markers of cultural identity that seemed to intensify

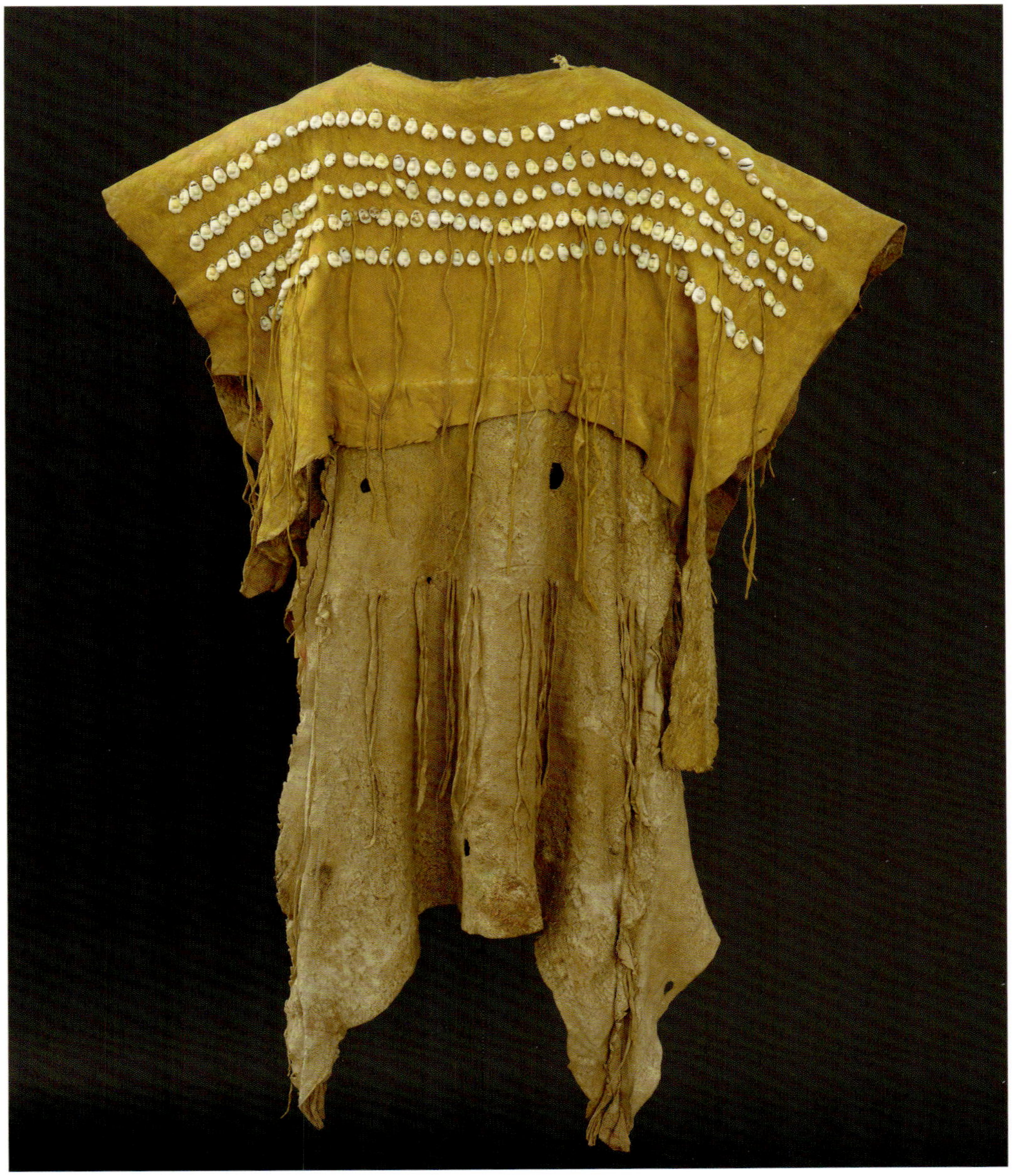

4.15. **Dress**
Kaigwa (Kiowa), Washita River area, Oklahoma, ca. 1890
Tanned hide, pigment, cowrie shells; dress length: 29½; width at shoulders: 27 inches
Plains Indian Museum, NA.202.1285

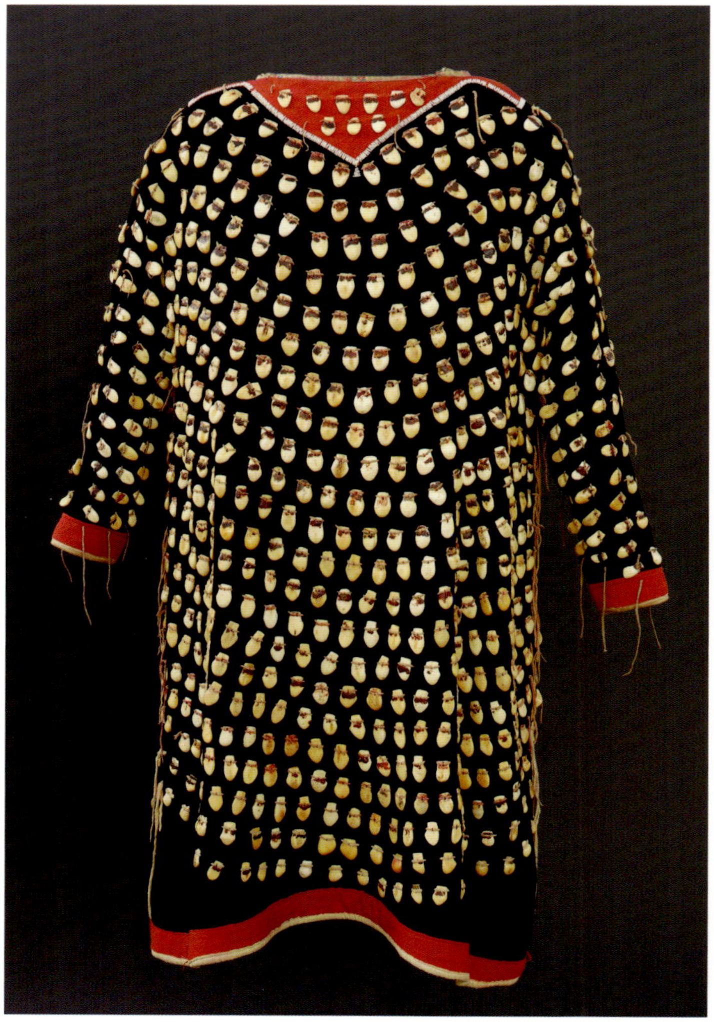

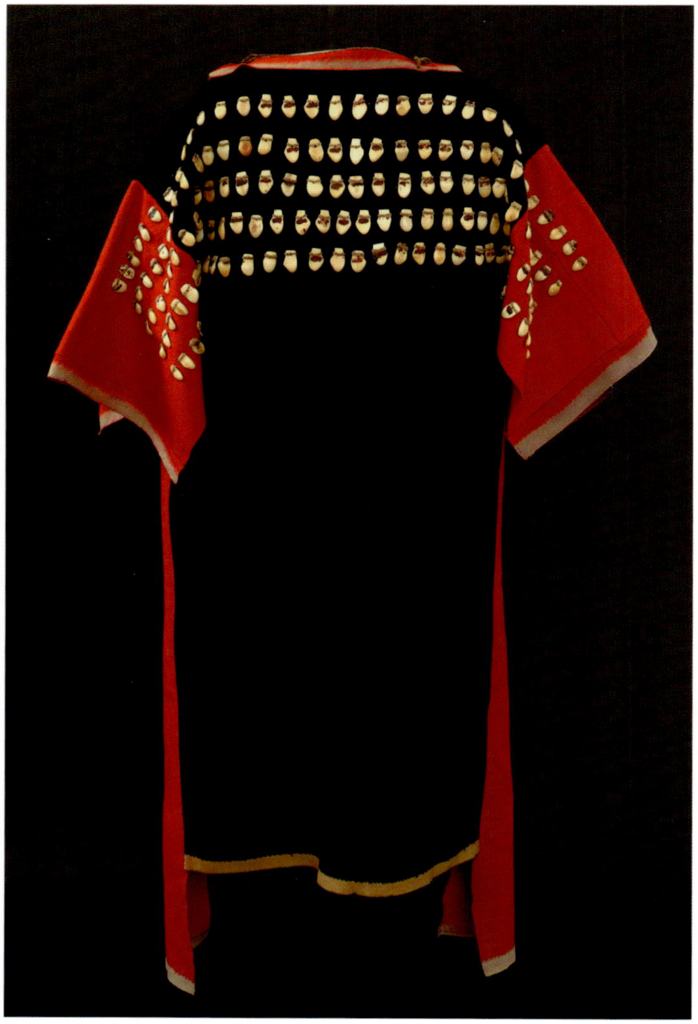

LEFT:

4.16. **Dress**
Apsáalooke (Crow), Northern Plains, ca. 1880
Wool cloth, elk teeth, thread; dress length: 43½; hem width: 37 inches; width sleeve to sleeve: 62 inches
Plains Indian Museum, NA.202.1181

The many elk teeth on this dress demonstrate the hunting ability of the husband of the woman who wore it.

RIGHT:

4.17. **Dress**
Tsitsistas (Cheyenne), Northern Plains, ca. 1860
Wool, elk teeth; dress length: 56½ inches; hem width: 38 inches; sleeve to sleeve: 50 inches
Plains Indian Museum, NA.202.1239

during the early reservation period. Kiowa, Comanche, Arapaho, and Cheyenne people of the Southern Plains created dresses, shirts, leggings, and moccasins from beautifully tanned hides with modest beadwork centered on single motifs or narrow bands along hems and sleeves of dresses and edges of leggings and moccasins (figs. 4.18 and 4.19). Long fringes and painting added to the design of Southern Plains garments.

Northern Plains people such as the Lakota preferred more heavily beaded clothing, such as dresses with fully beaded yokes and moccasins with fully beaded tops and, sometimes, soles. A Lakota dress in the Dyck collection is an exquisite example of early reservation clothing (fig. 4.20). The yoke of the dress is covered in beadwork, with commonly used blue beads forming the background and geometric designs in red, greasy yellow, and black beads. Early Lakota dresses left the deer tail of the hide in the central lower section of the yoke. In this later version, the dressmaker replaced the tail with a U-shaped beaded motif. Lakota women said that this form represented the turtle, which was said to have power over women's health, including conception, birth, and the infancy of their children. The turtle was associated with fertility and

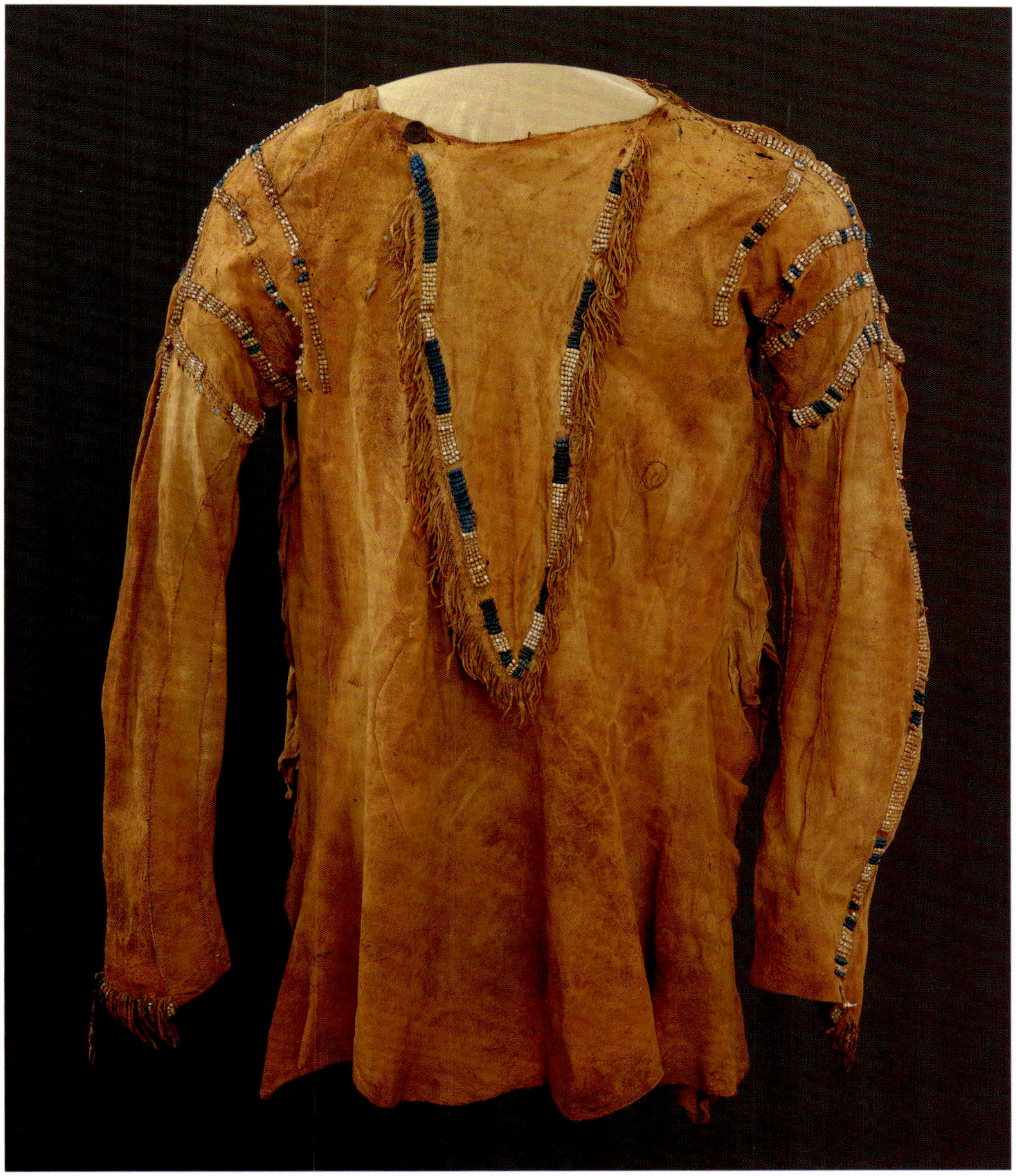

4.18. **Boy's shirt**
Southern Plains, ca. 1850
Glass beads, sinew, tanned hide, cotton thread, metal buttons; length: 29 inches; width at shoulders: 22 inches
Plains Indian Museum, NA.202.1282

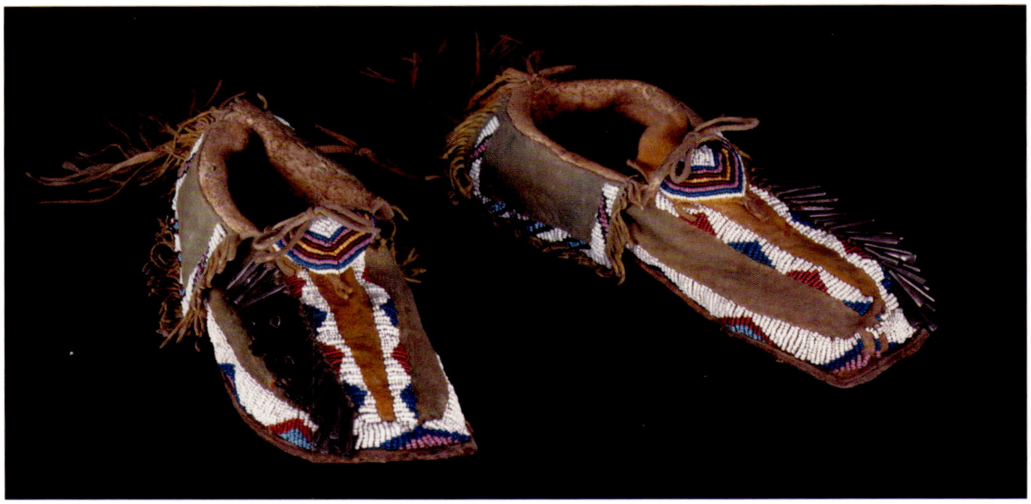

4.19. **Moccasins**
Numunu (Comanche), Oklahoma, ca. 1880
Glass beads, pigment, tin cones, tanned hide, rawhide;
9 x 3¾ x 3 inches
Plains Indian Museum, NA.202.1182

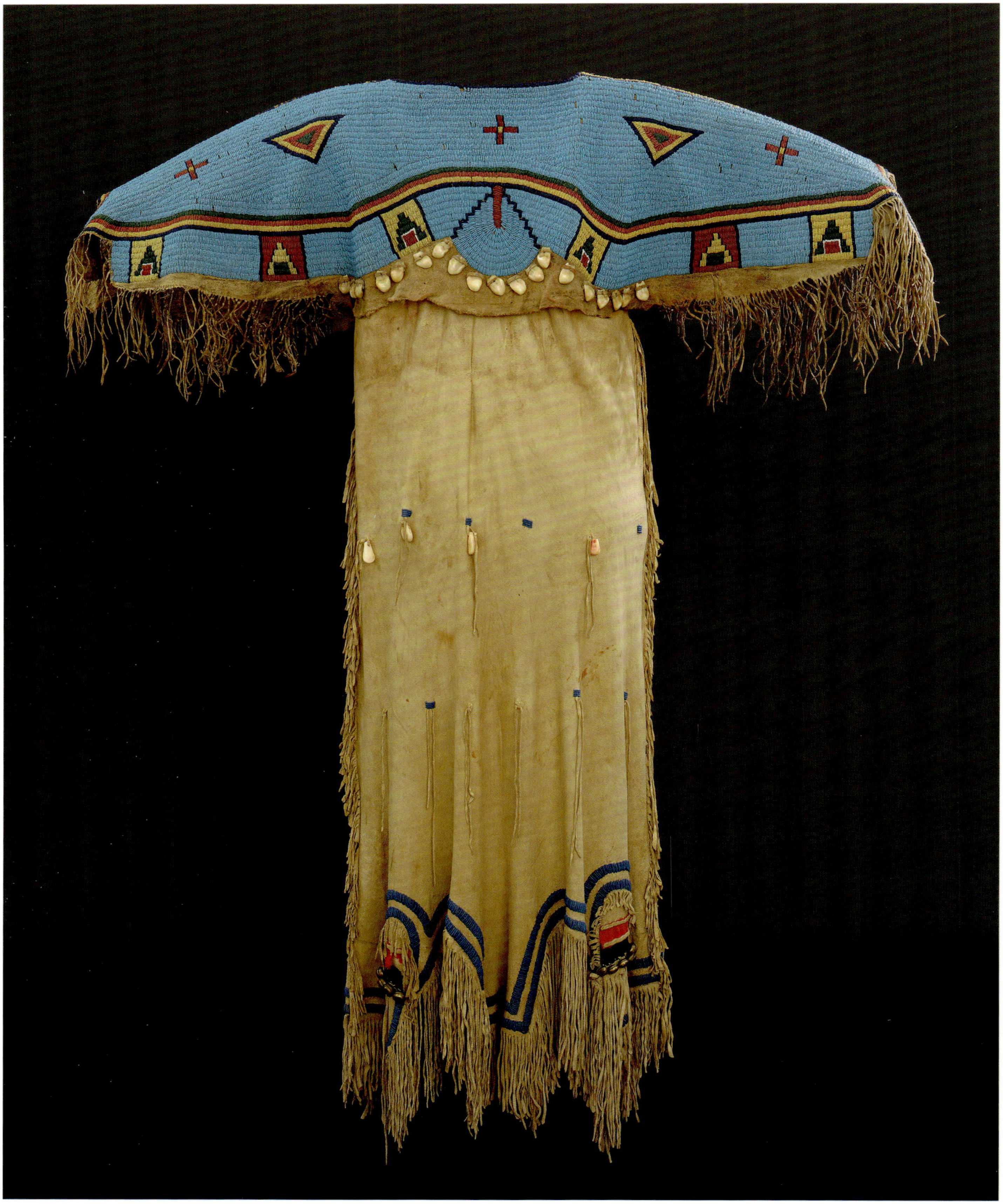

long life in Lakota traditions.[30] The beadwork that covers the yoke represents a lake with the narrow bands of beadwork that form the border symbolizing the shores where the turtle seems to emerge from the water. The yoke is also edged with elk teeth.

OPPOSITE:
4.20. **Dress**
Lakota (Sioux), Northern Plains, ca. 1880
Tanned hide, wool cloth, glass beads, elk teeth, brass bells, cotton thread; length: 56 inches; width sleeve to sleeve with fringe: 53 inches; hem width: 35 inches
Plains Indian Museum, NA.202.1254

Around 1850, Euro-American traders brought small glass beads called "seed beads" to the Plains. During the early reservation period, beadwork on clothing became more elaborate. Lakota and Cheyenne women created dresses such as these featuring fully beaded bodices with geometric designs. Women wore such dresses—beautiful, yet too heavy for daily wear—for ceremonies, parades, and other special occasions.

The use and significance of moccasins with fully beaded soles have often been misinterpreted (figs. 4.21 and 4.22). Because moccasins with beadwork on the bottom would not have been practical in daily life, it is assumed that they were made for burial. Arthur Amiotte has pointed out that Lakota tradition calls for burial at the end of a four-day period. Such elaborately beaded moccasins could not conceivably have been completed in that period.[31]

According to Amiotte, the moccasins were made for ceremonial use such as ear-piercing ceremonies for babies that took place during the time of the Sun Dance and the Hunka ceremony. The Hunka ceremony was held for children of both genders to bestow blessings upon and dedicate participants to the highest ideals of Lakota society. A young woman might also have worn fully beaded moccasins at marriage when she and her family brought gifts as she joined her husband's family. On all of these occasions, the honorees were carried by other participants, and the beaded soles were visible to all. If the owners of fully beaded moccasins should pass away, they likely would be buried in their best clothing, including the moccasins. In that way only could they be considered burial moccasins.[32]

The heavily beaded dresses and moccasins produced by Lakota artists are part of a trend that occurred on the Plains beginning in about 1880 and lasting into the twentieth century. During this time, an unexpected and remarkable flowering of tribal arts transpired, with the creation of beautiful works in hide, beadwork, and porcupine quillwork combined with newly introduced materials, including fabrics, silk ribbons, tin cones, brass bells, and other items available through trading posts and stores. Lakota and Cheyenne women began to illustrate men's war exploits in representational images in quillwork and beading, an innovation from earlier and predominately geometric designs. They beaded and quilled images of men on horseback and wearing eagle feather bonnets with long trailers, along with figures of horses, buffalo, deer, and elk.

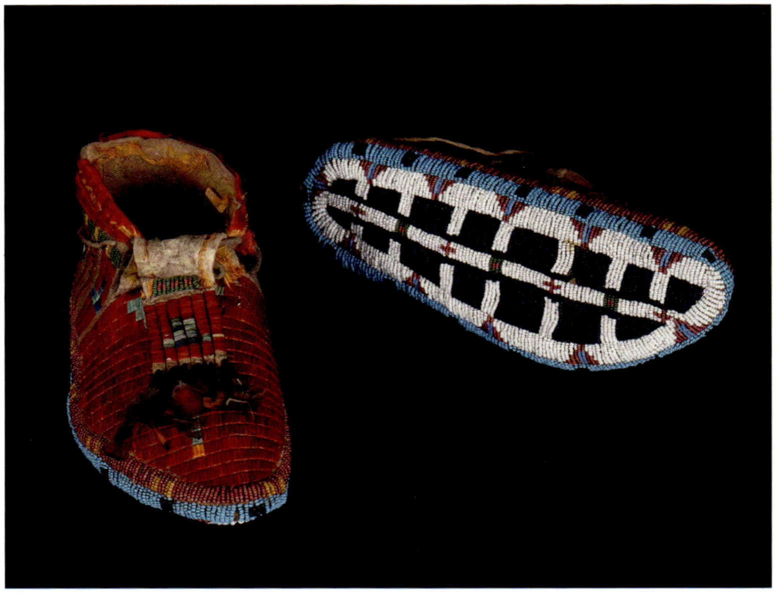

4.21. **Moccasins**
Lakota (Sioux), Northern Plains, ca. 1880
Tanned hide, dyed porcupine quills, glass beads, pigment, silk ribbon, tin cones, feathers; 11 × 4½ x 3¼ inches
Plains Indian Museum, NA.202.1183

Everyday moccasins had little or no decoration. This ornate pair of moccasins with the upper portion covered in porcupine quillwork also has beadwork covering the soles. A man wore these moccasins for special occasions or rites of passage.

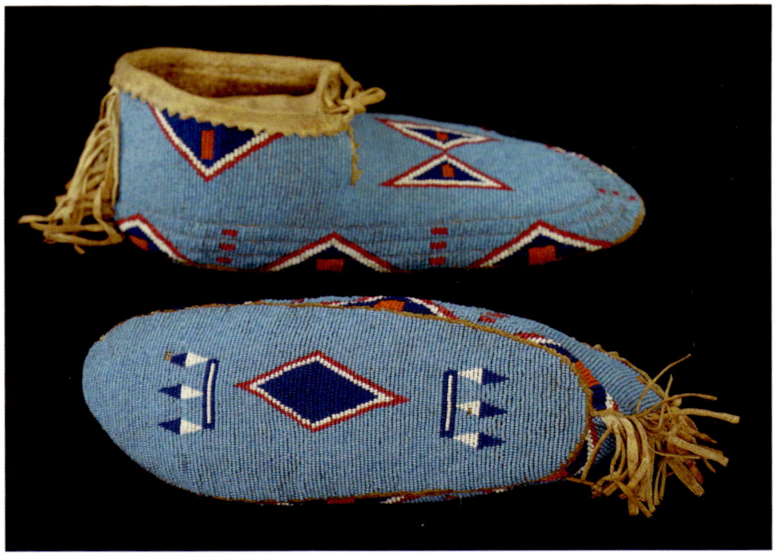

4.22. **Moccasins**
Lakota (Sioux), Northern Plains, ca. 1900
Tanned hide, glass beads, tanned hide, cotton thread; 10½ × 4 × 3¾ inches
Plains Indian Museum, NA.202.1381

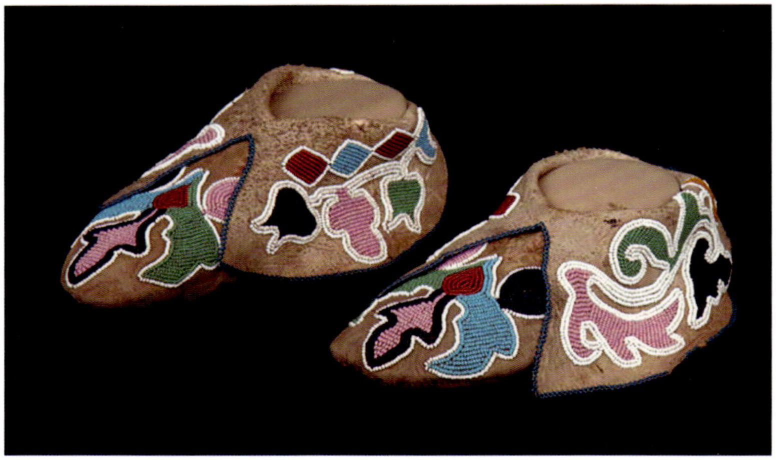

4.23. **Moccasins**
Meskwaki, Prairie, ca. 1875
Glass beads, tanned hide, cotton thread; 9 × 4 × 2½ inches
Plains Indian Museum, NA.202.1372

On the Southern Plains, as tribes from the Northeast and Great Lakes regions were relocated to reservations in Indian Territory (Oklahoma), they brought with them floral designs that influenced Kiowa, Otoe, and other Plains bead workers (fig. 4.23). The Crow, Dakota, and Blackfoot had earlier adopted floral designs from Eastern peoples who had accompanied nineteenth-century fur traders to their regions (figs. 4.24 and 4.25). Fabrics with floral patterns may also have been inspirations for innovative beadwork designs.

Scholars have suggested that Plains Indian women produced beautifully embellished examples of material culture once they were settled on reservations simply because they had more time without the traditional time-consuming duties associated with the buffalo-hunting way of life and easier access to commercial materials. It is also likely that the motivations for early reservation artistry in the Plains, which has come to symbolize excellence in Native American arts, developed in reaction to the hardships and culturally destructive influences of the reservation experience. Reservation arts, manifested in beautifully embellished creations in tribal designs, became a means of establishing and maintaining cultural identities and survival through these difficult times.

OPPOSITE:
4.24 and 4.25. **Coat**
Dakota (Eastern Sioux), ca. 1850
Tanned hide, glass beads, metal chain, silk ribbon, silk cloth, cotton cloth, wool cloth, tanned otter hide, brass buttons; 43 × 24 inches
Plains Indian Museum, NA.202.1476

The woman who made this coat fashioned it after a European-style man's coat. The elegant design of the coat features beautiful floral beadwork on both front and back with silk cloth and ribbon and otter hide trimming.

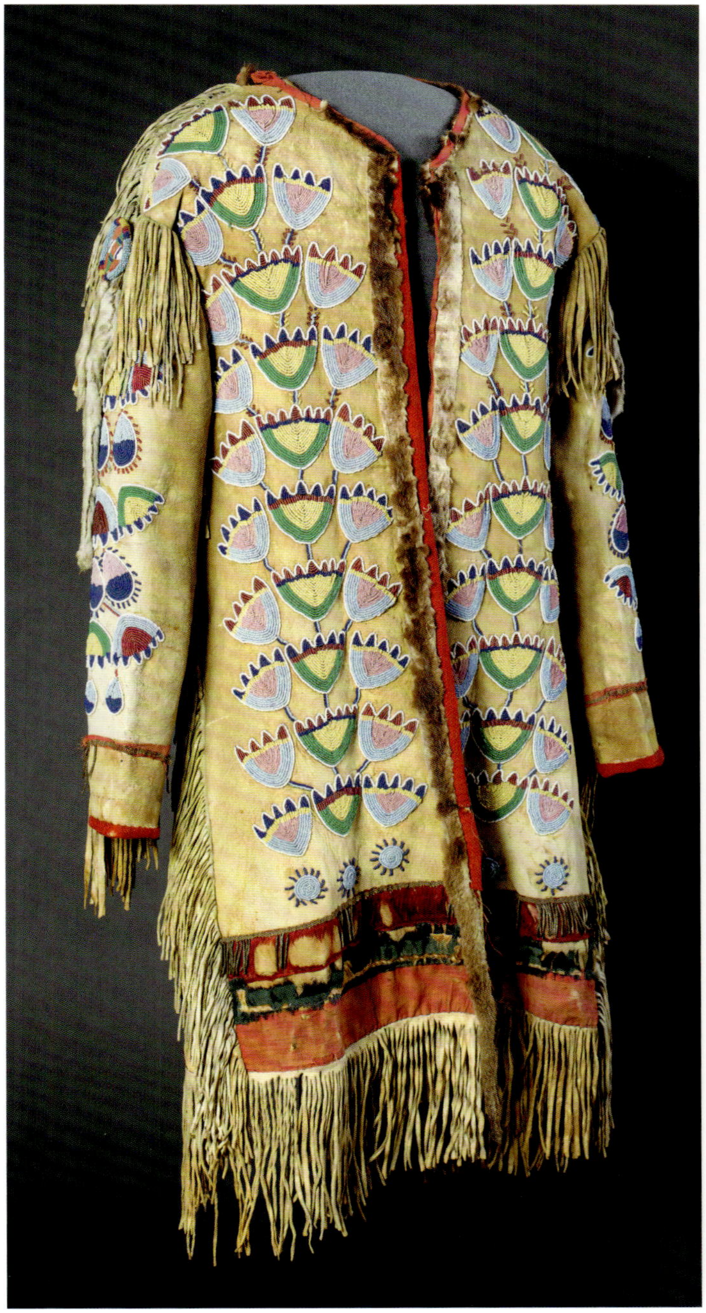

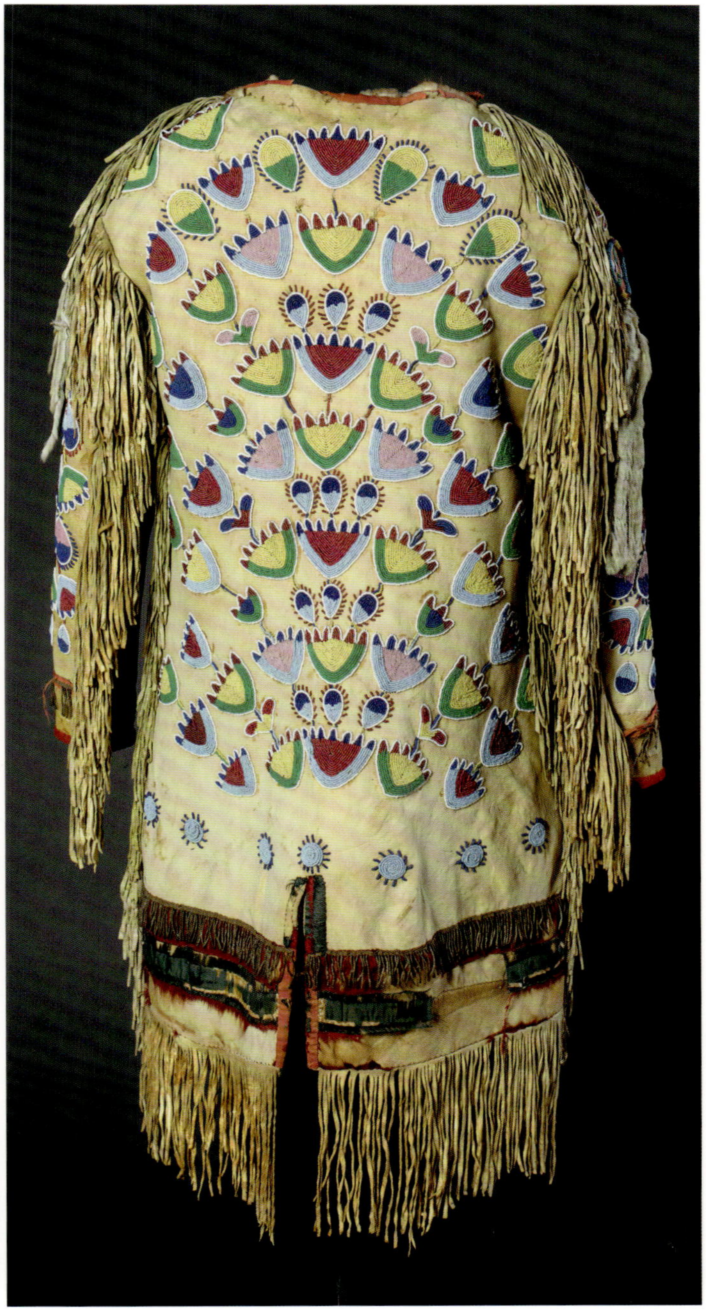

CHILDREN: HOPE FOR THE FUTURE

In the following passage about Kiowa and Comanche families, N. Scott Momaday expresses the universal appreciation and value placed on children as the hopes for the future, especially through difficult times:

> The Kiowas and Comanches had always loved their children above all else. From the dim beginnings, it was understood that their way of life, predicated upon migration, hunting, and a warrior ideal, was always in the keeping of their children, one generation at a time. As long as their children came into the world, survival was a prospect no matter how fragile it might be. The women began to make cradles, not so much for the sake of utility, but in thanksgiving and love for the children, that they might live full lives and carry on the blood of their ancestry beyond the moment in which extinction seemed most imminent. They made the cradles with profound love and faith, and they placed in them the whole strength and beauty of their spirit.[33]

Children naturally embodied this hopefulness and signified the continuation of cultural traditions, the family, and the tribe even when prospects appeared bleak. In the intimate setting of a Plains Indian village, responsibilities of child-rearing and teaching were supported by the shared values of the community and an extended kinship system that tied individuals together through descent, marriage, and spiritual and social affiliations. Children of Plains Indian tribes learned their future roles in life with the guidance and counsel of older family members. Through play, they learned the adult responsibilities of men and women and skills needed to sustain life. They also received spiritual instruction from grandparents and other elders.

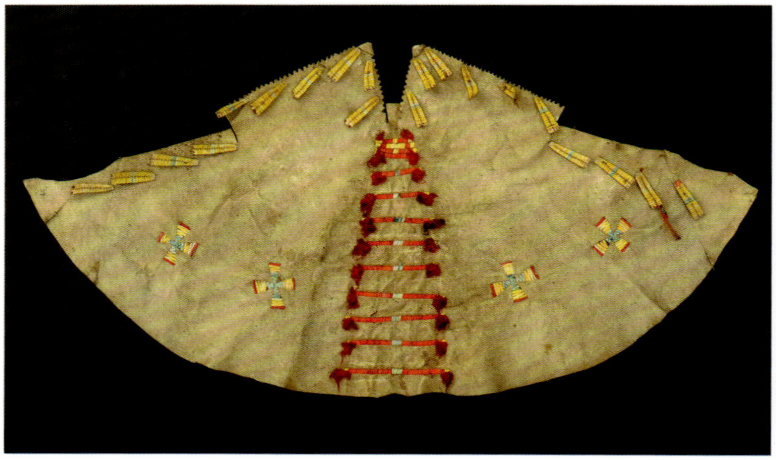

4.26. **Toy tipi**
Northern Plains, ca. 1890
Tanned hide, porcupine quills, yarn, cotton thread; 13 × 26½ inches
Plains Indian Museum, NA.507.65

Young boys were taught by fathers and other male relatives to make bows and arrows and encouraged to practice hunting, beginning with small animals around their village. When a boy brought home his first game, this important milestone was celebrated as his mother cooked and shared the meat with as many people as possible. From an early age, girls were taught by their mothers and grandmothers to make moccasins, clothing, and lodge covers and to help prepare food, carry water, and do other daily work. They played with miniature tipis, dolls, and toy cradles, which prepared them for their roles as adult women and mothers (figs. 4.26 and 4.27). Iron Teeth from the Northern Cheyenne remembered her childhood play in this way.

> Our dolls were made by tying a stuffed buckskin head on the end of a forked stick. Such a doll had hair glued to the head, beads for eyes, and a face painted on the buckskin. The stuffing for the head was buffalo hair. The clothing was of beaded and fringed buckskin. We girls built playhouse tepees for ourselves and our dolls. We would hang little pieces of meat out upon bushes and play like we were drying meat, the same as our mothers did

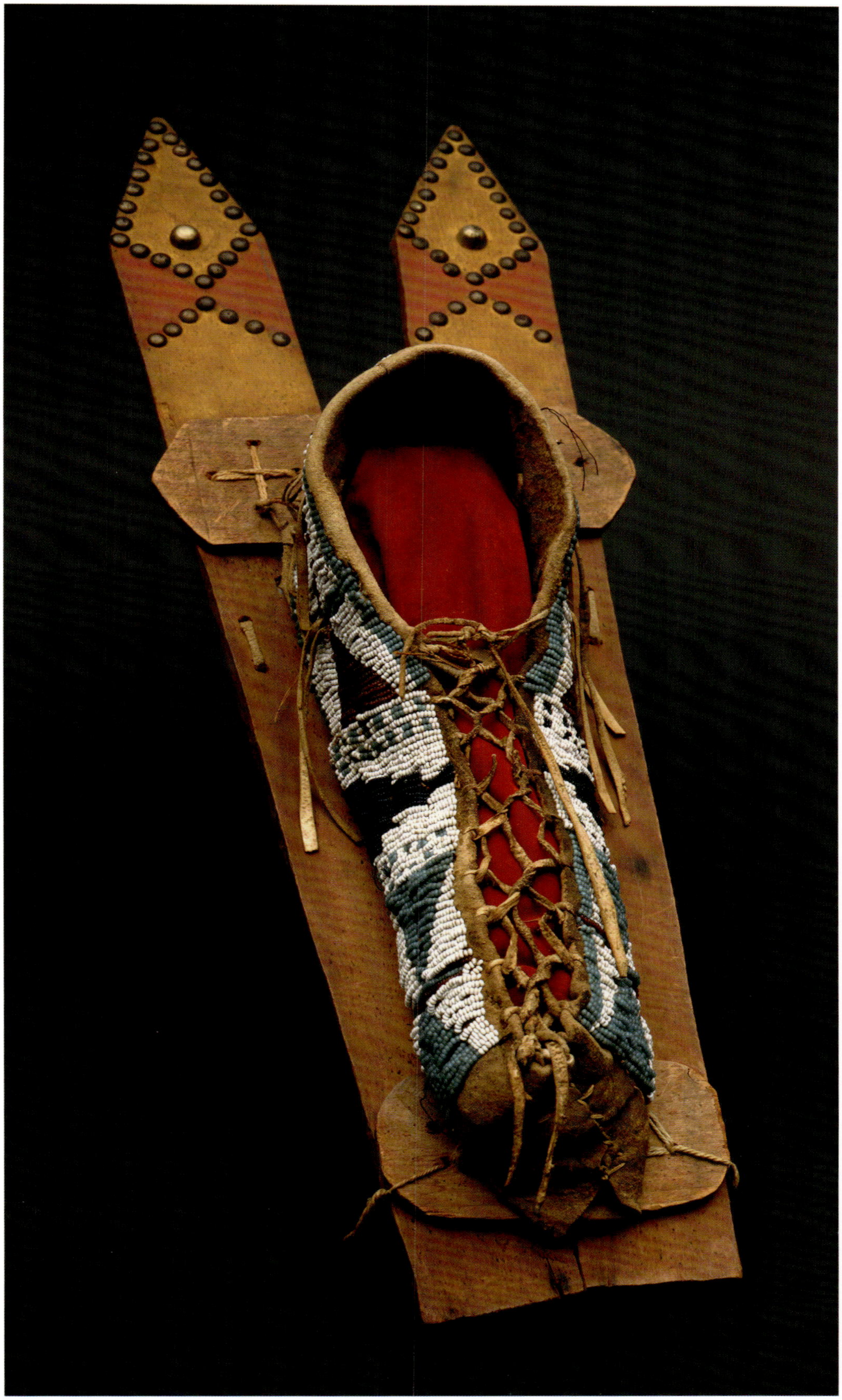

4.27. **Toy cradle**
Kaigwa (Kiowa) or Numunu (Comanche), Oklahoma, ca. 1900
Tanned hide, glass beads, wood, brass tacks, pigment, cotton thread; 22 × 7½ inches
Plains Indian Museum, NA.507.126

at the home lodges. Sometimes we would play at moving camp. The boys would come with willow baskets. Everything would be put into the baskets and then the boys would drag them to wherever we might want to go. We would ride stick horses. The doll might ride on a stick horse beside the play-mother, or it might be carried on her back.[34]

As girls matured, they were given the tools they would need to produce clothing and household furnishings needed for their families. At puberty she might be given a small work bag with sinew, an awl, and a needle in it, and she was taught to make her first pair of moccasins. She was also expected to practice skills like tanning, quillwork, and beadwork. Her first achievement—making moccasins, a piece of clothing, or a bag—would be celebrated through a feast and a giveaway with a presentation of gifts to family and friends who had supported her.

Grandparents were fundamentally involved in rearing children by providing spiritual and practical guidance. Grandmothers cared for children and made them toys and beautiful clothing following the designs of adult clothing (figs. 4.28, 4.29, and 4.30). As elder matriarchs, they were significant sources of cultural knowledge and wisdom, which they passed on through instruction, stories, and games.

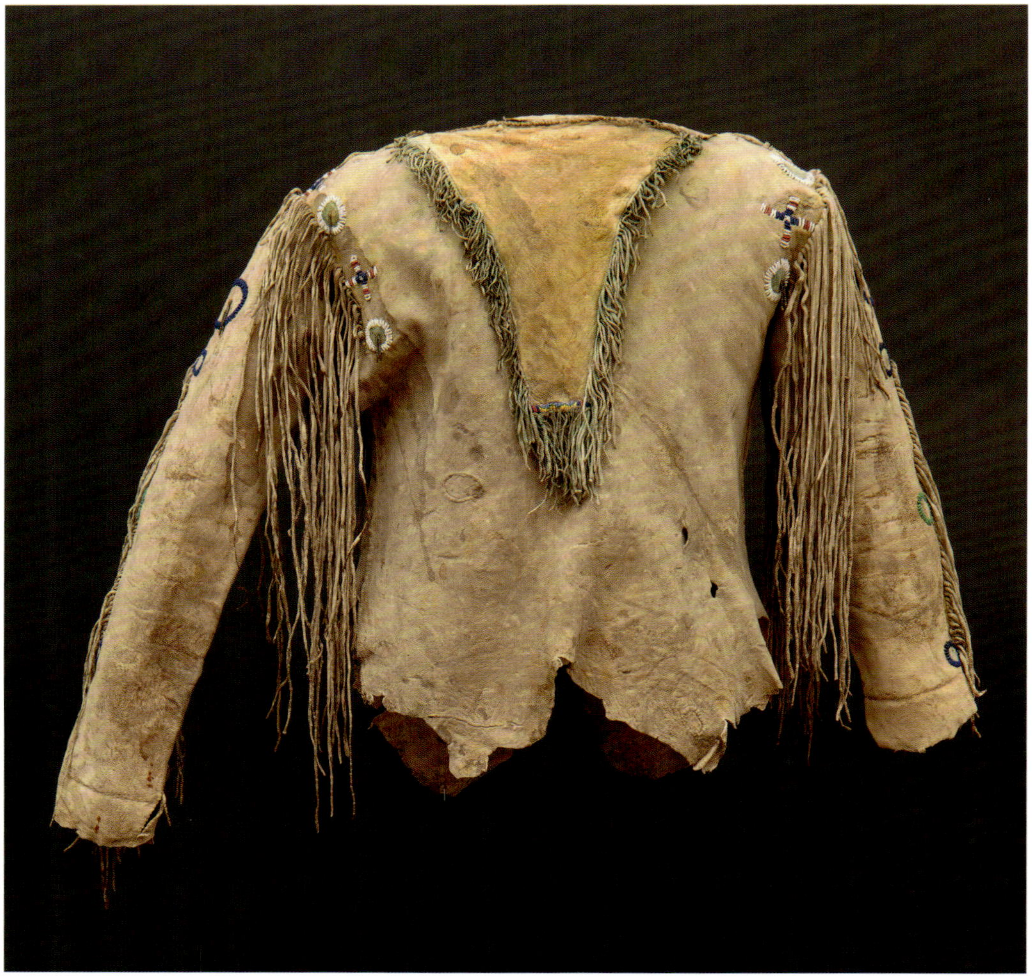

4.28. **Boy's shirt**
Tsitsistas (Cheyenne), Southern Plains, ca. 1880
Tanned hide, glass beads, pigment, sinew; 23 × 42 inches
Plains Indian Museum, NA.202.1272

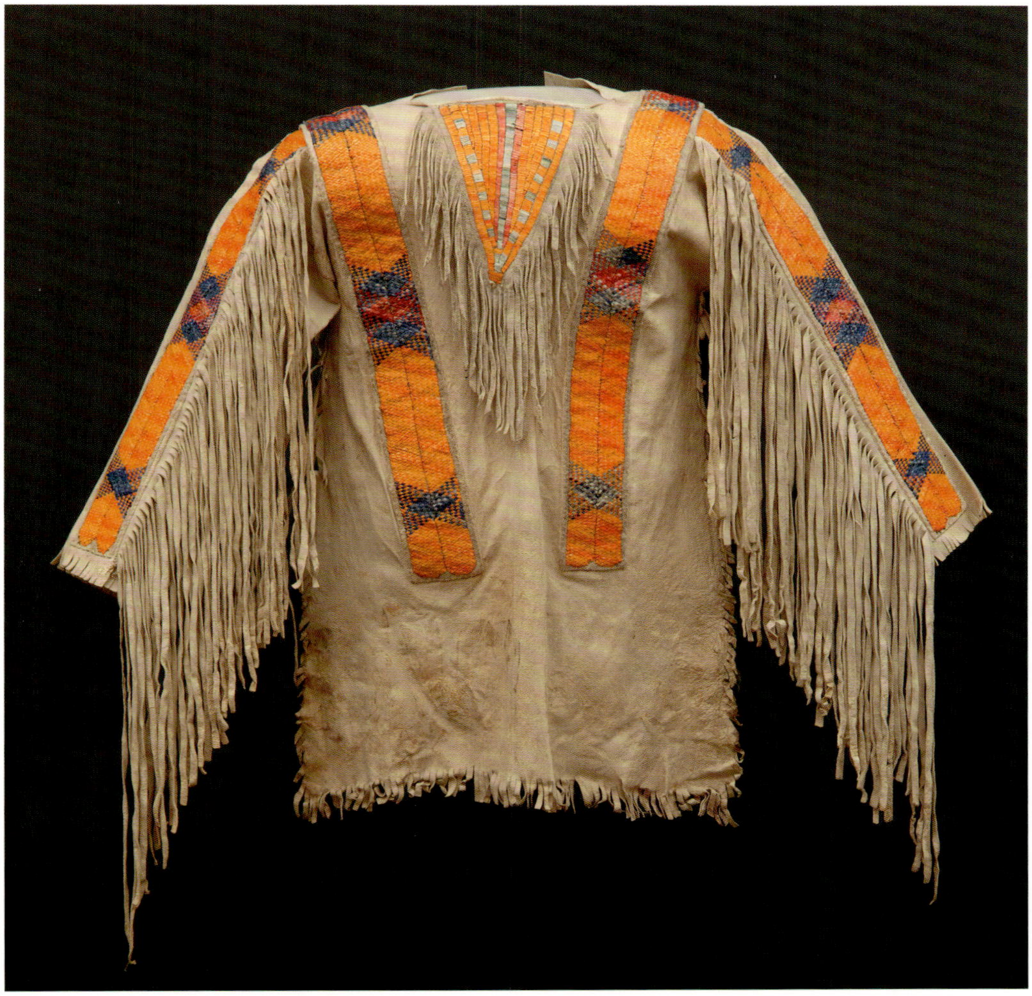

4.29. **Boy's shirt**
Hidatsa, Upper Missouri Region, ca. 1890
Tanned hide, dyed porcupine quills, cotton thread; 22 × 38½ inches
Plains Indian Museum, NA.202.1273

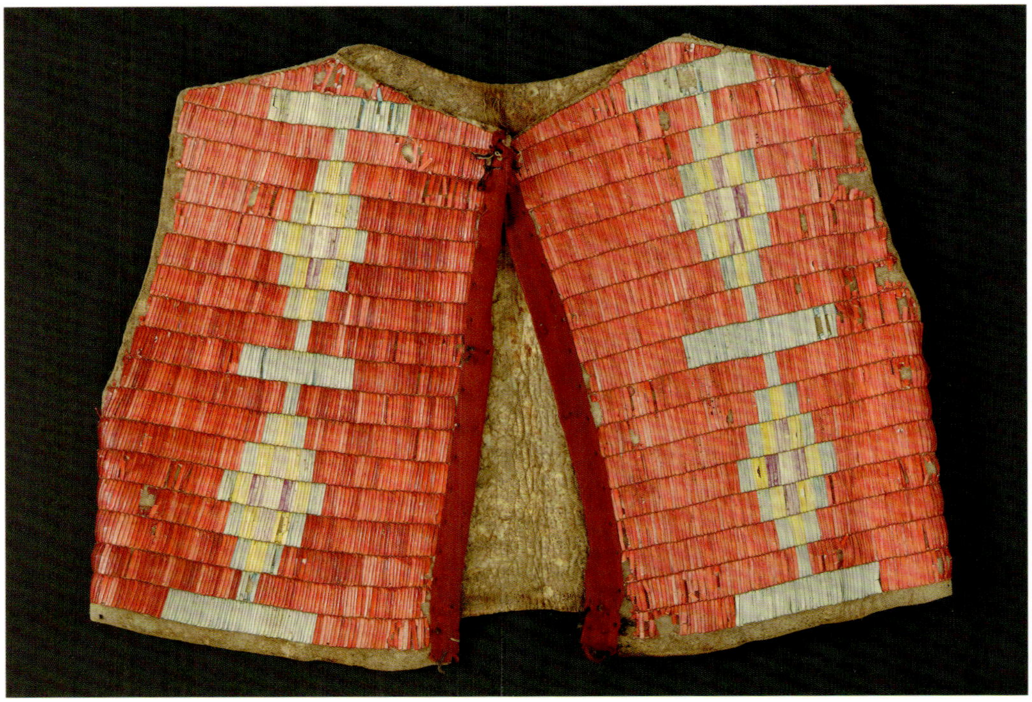

4.30. **Child's vest**
Lakota (Sioux), Northern Plains, ca. 1870
Tanned hide, dyed porcupine quills, satin ribbon, sinew, cotton thread; 9½ × 12¼ inches
Plains Indian Museum, NA.202.1023

The highest form of artistry of Plains Native women is epitomized in a cradle, described by some as "a house for the beginning of life."[35] The creation of a beautifully decorated cradle in anticipation of a baby's birth was a powerful expression of family love and symbolic of the practical and spiritual importance of children. With the babies tightly wrapped and laced into cradles when they were a few months old, they were safe and secure when families traveled or when mothers and other female relatives were cooking or working around the camp. Propped upright or carried on the mothers' backs, babies could also see the activities around them, providing engagement with family life.

The creation of a cradle was a spiritual endeavor accompanied by prayers, blessings, and thanks for the raw materials from which it would be made as well as for the newborn. Cradles were typically made by grandmothers, aunts, and other female relatives. Three of the cradles in the Dyck collection—all made by Northern Cheyenne and Lakota artists in the early reservation period—exhibit the distinctive artistry of Plains Indian women (figs. 4.31, 4.32, and 4.33). All three cradles are of lattice style, a type with documented use beginning in the 1860s among the Kiowa, Comanche, Arapaho, Lakota, and Cheyenne.[36]

A lattice cradle is made from a hide cover wrapped around rawhide supports at the head and foot and a rawhide backing, all laced to a board frame. This sturdy construction protected the baby, with a rawhide hood around its face and strong boards and rawhide at its back. The V shape formed by the lattice framework provided an opening for the mother's head while she carried the cradle on her back. When she leaned it against a tree or post, the boards on either side prevented the cradle from slipping.[37] Each of the collection's cradles features fully beaded covers with white backgrounds and geometric patterns in green, red, yellow, black, and blue beads. The cradles express a melding of functionality and artistic elegance.

Plains artistic traditions are characterized by the transmission of cultural ideals, knowledge, and skills from one generation to another. Kiowa beadwork artist and cradle maker Vanessa Paukeigope Jennings expressed her admiration for her ancestors and appreciation for her grandmother, who taught her the essential lessons of life.

> I started beading when I was eleven years old. One lesson that has stayed with me all these years is in words of my grandmother Jeanette: "No one lives forever. Pay attention because you are the one who will take my place!" . . . Now I understand that she was teaching me a culture that would form the foundation of my life. I understand now that culture is a conscious, consistent, deliberate passing on of knowledge taught every day by an older generation to the next generation. Her instructions were always prefaced with the words, "You tell your grandchildren that it's done this way because that's how my grandmother showed me!"[38]

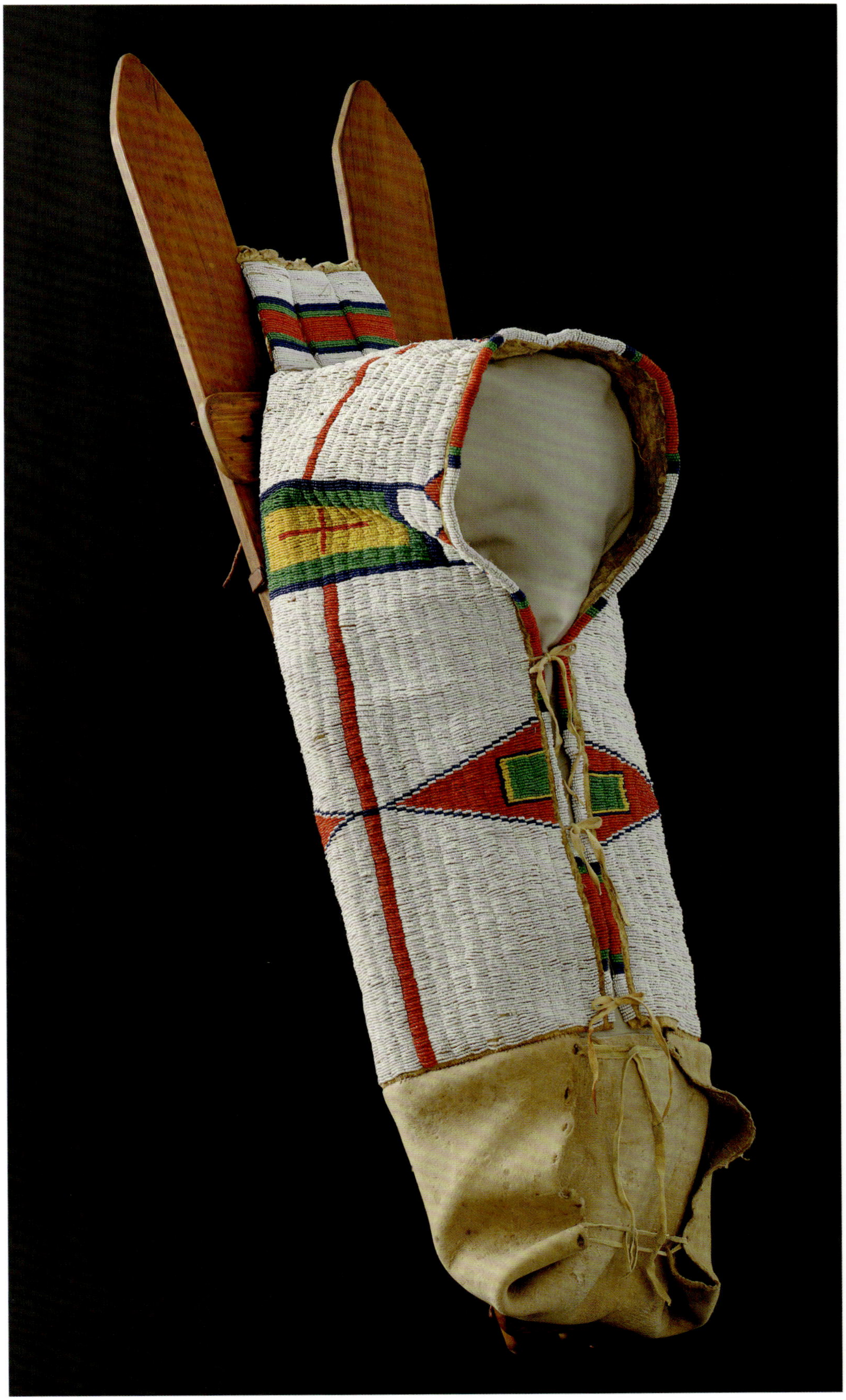

4.31. **Cradle**
Tsitsistas (Cheyenne), Northern Plains, 1880–1890
Wood, rawhide, glass beads, tanned hide, cotton thread; $42\frac{1}{2} \times 10\frac{7}{8}$ inches
Plains Indian Museum, NA.111.32

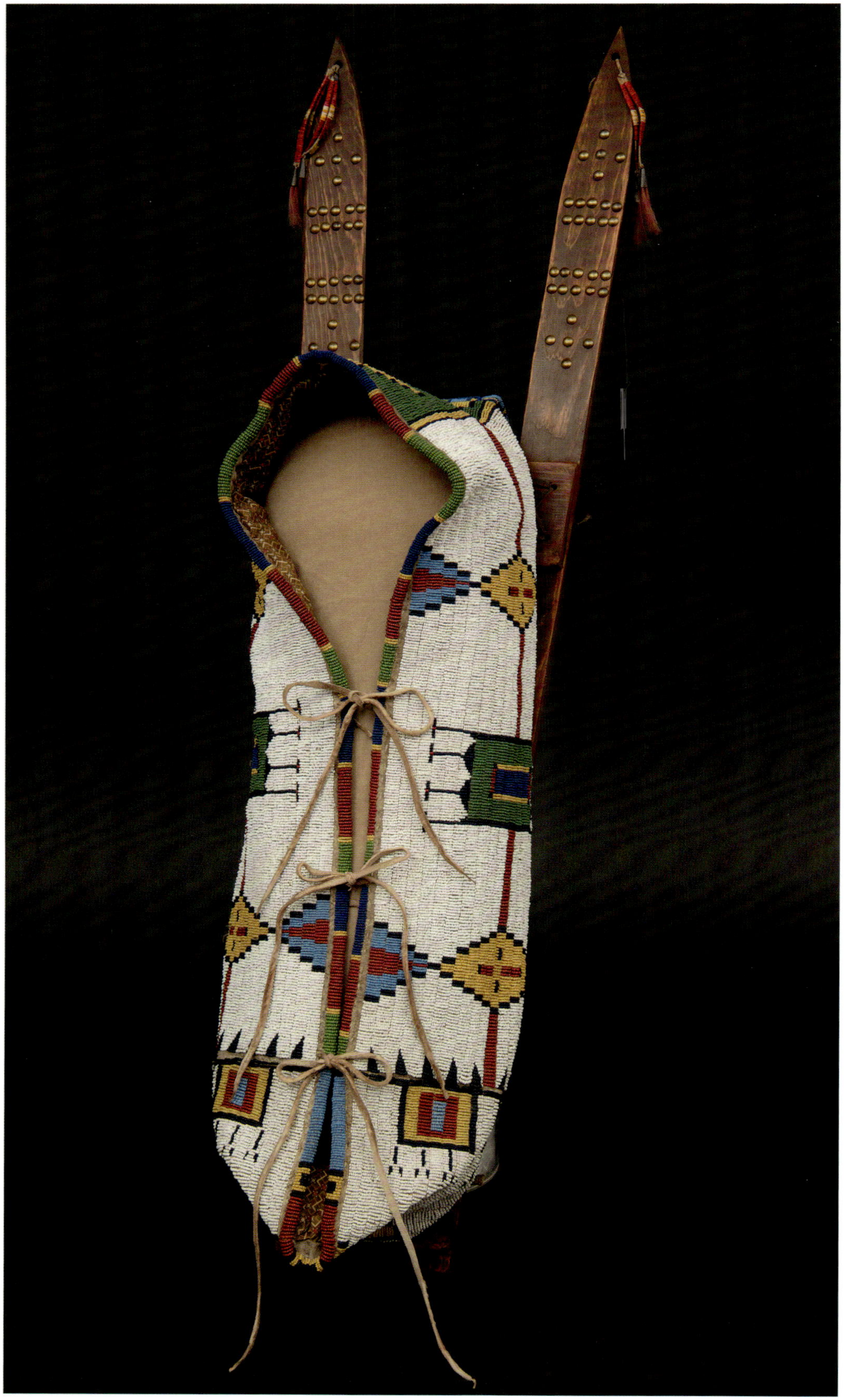

4.32. **Cradle**
Tsitsistas (Cheyenne), Northern Plains, ca. 1880
Wood, tanned hide, cotton cloth, glass beads, brass tacks, tin cones, died porcupine quills, dyed horse hair; 43 × 11½ inches
Plains Indian Museum, NA.111.61

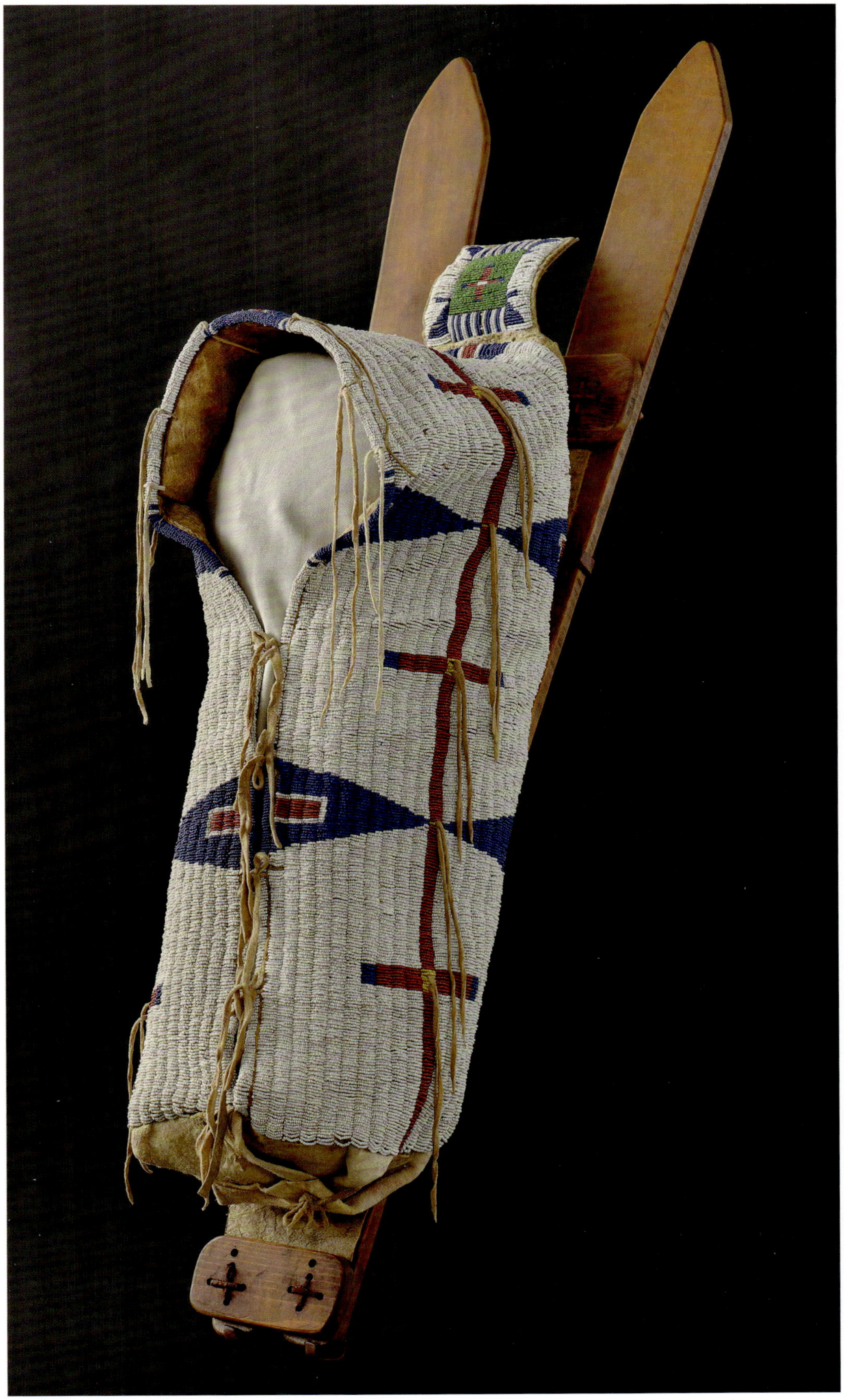

4.33. **Cradle**
Lakota (Sioux), Northern Plains, ca. 1890
Wood, rawhide, glass beads, sinew, tanned hide, cotton thread; 41¾ × 11 inches
Plains Indian Museum, NA.111.63

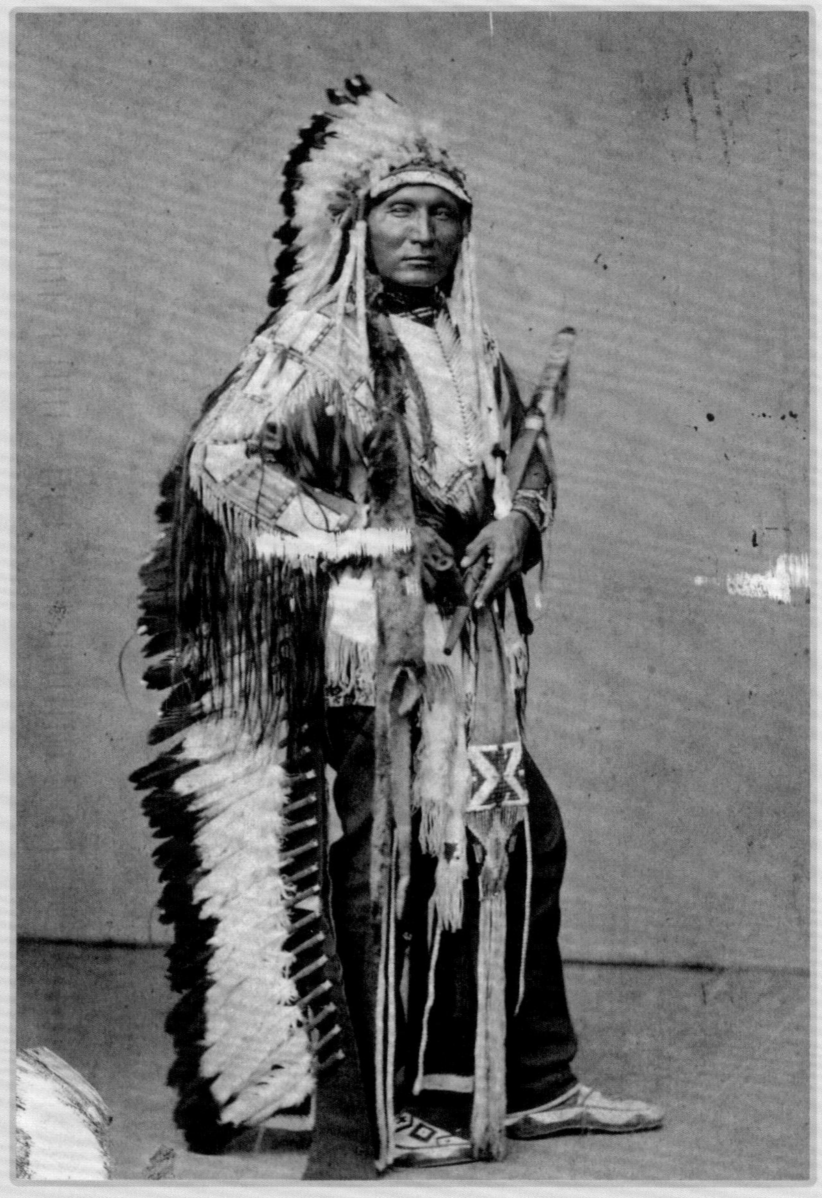

5 Leadership, Respect, and Ceremony

In an essay on significant leaders among the Crow Nation, Joseph Medicine Crow emphasized key moments in Crow history when capable men stepped forward, made decisions, led warriors into battle, and represented the tribe in negotiations with U.S. government officials to protect the people and their homelands. He begins his story with the founding of the Crow as a distinctive people with a culture that formed as they separated from their Hidatsa relatives living near Devils Lake (in present North Dakota) and journeyed over many years until settling in new homelands in present southern Montana and northern Wyoming.

> A leader emerges because of the conjuncture of an event or a situation, a person possessing innate capabilities, and this person's definition of the situation. Since 1600 A.D., when a man called No Insides, or No Vitals, seceded from the Earthen Lodges, now called Hidatsa, and migrated westward, there have been many great leaders, or chiefs, ruling a fledgling new tribe eventually called "Crow Indians" by white men. These people called themselves Apsáalooke, meaning "children of a large beaked bird."[1]

According to Medicine Crow, No Vitals received a vision while fasting at Devils Lake. Through the vision he was given a bundle of sacred tobacco seeds and told to take the seeds to the high mountains in the west for planting. He was told that as long as the Crow people followed the sacred ways of planting and harvesting the seeds, they would have a good place to live and become a rich and powerful nation. Medicine Crow went on to say that "No Vitals was the first of a succession of great leaders of the Apsáalooke, the progenitor of a new tribe which may be regarded as the forerunner of creating the so-called Northern Plains Indian Culture Area."[2]

SYMBOLS OF LEADERSHIP

In his memoir, Plenty Coups recalled his ambitions as a young warrior: to become a prominent leader and a man of authority, "to count coup, to wear an eagle's feather in my hair, to sit in the council with my chiefs holding an eagle wing in my hand."[3] As a warrior, war leader, and prominent man of authority as the recognized chief of the Crow people during the difficult early reservation era, he achieved his ambitions and earned the rights to wear an eagle-feathered bonnet and carry an eagle wing fan at tribal ceremonies as insignias of honor and distinction. Although Plains Indian men like Plenty Coups achieved leadership positions by following

5.1. Touch the Clouds
Minneconjou Lakota (Sioux), 1877
McCracken Research Library, Paul Dyck Photograph Collection, P.320.429

different paths, they shared culturally desired characteristics. Leaders possessed the ability to provide food for the family through hunting, exhibited courage and bravery in warfare through counting coup, and expressed generosity and concern for others. The concept of chief among Plains Indian people has often been misinterpreted by Euro-American representatives and government officials, who preferred to deal with one or a few leaders who had absolute authority to negotiate and sign treaties on behalf of entire tribes. In practice, however, such leaders had no such authority and made major decisions by consulting with other senior advisors to arrive at a consensus and, consequently, to ensure the support of their followers.

The path to political leadership for Plains Indian men required participation in warrior societies that trained and encouraged warriors, organized war expeditions, and celebrated victorious outcomes. Societies were responsible for policing and carrying out the decisions of the chiefs, although they also advised leaders on matters related to peace and war, movement of camps, and details of the buffalo hunts. They maintained order on buffalo hunts and when bands traveled, built the medicine lodge for the annual Sun Dance, and sponsored their own dances held to prepare for war and celebrate their victories.

Plains Indian men achieved prestige through their exploits in war and through the hunt. As men accumulated more honors and accomplishments, they might be given the authority of leading hunting and war expeditions, which made them responsible not only for the success of the undertaking but also for the safety of all the participants. Such leadership tended to be fluid and was neither permanent nor absolute. Leaders were continually required to demonstrate their influence and abilities as warriors and hunters. With age and experience, men could rise to the level of band headmen, or chiefs, which brought additional responsibility for looking out for the well-being of their followers.

Among the Lakota, the Akicita was a specialized soldier society with responsibilities for enforcing laws. The Akicita maintained order, particularly during the summer buffalo hunt, the Sun Dance, and other large tribal gatherings. There were six Akicita societies in all, each with its own distinctive organization and ceremonies. Any young man who had experienced at least one hunting or war expedition could join one of the societies.[4] Black Elk described the role of the Akicita as the band traveled in search of buffalo.

> Then we are started for where the bison were. The soldier band went first, riding twenty abreast, and anybody who dared go ahead of them would get knocked off his horse. They kept order, and everybody had to obey. After them came the hunters riding five abreast. The people came up in the rear. Then the headmen of the advisors went around picking out the best hunters with the fastest horses, and to these he said, "Good young warriors, my relatives. Your work I know is good. What you do is good always; so today you should feed the helpless. Perhaps there are some old and feeble people without sons, or some who have little children and no man. You shall help these, and whatever you kill shall be theirs." This was a great honor for young men.[5]

As Black Elk explained, in addition to prowess in hunting and war, leaders demonstrated generosity by providing buffalo meat, lending horses to people in need, and assisting the elderly. Men aged forty and older who demonstrated these qualities belonged to a governing council termed the Chiefs' Society. Seven selected chiefs known as *wica^sitancan,* "leaders of men," headed this council. They delegated authority to four younger men as *wica^sayatanpi,* or "praiseworthy men." These men were also called "Shirt Wearers," because of their distinctive symbol of office, a shirt fringed with human and sometimes horse hair.[6] Older leaders presented the shirts, which were decorated with representations of the warriors' individual war exploits, to the Shirt Wearers in a formal ceremony. They were expected to lead in battle and to act for the benefit of all the people.[7] The Chiefs Society and the Shirt Wearers together appointed four men, *wakicunze,* who, working through the Akicita, were responsible for organizing and controlling the camps. All such leaders governed by consensus and influenced policy and decisions made through councils.

Among the Cheyenne, leadership was entrusted to the Council of Forty-Four, a tribal council of peace chiefs representing all of the bands. Peace chiefs were proven warriors who had resigned from membership in military societies as a requirement of their positions. These men were known to have courage, wisdom, generosity, and a concern for the security of all the people. These men were also expected to be even-tempered and deliberative in decision making.[8]

Hidatsa, Mandan, and Arapaho men and women followed separate paths through hierarchical stages, or societies, from childhood to old age. Through this progression, individuals accumulated knowledge and skills, as well as prestige and authority in both sacred and secular matters. Much of this knowledge came with accompanying responsibilities and expectations of appropriate behavior for each stage of life. Age-graded systems for males of these tribes consisted of a series of warrior societies, each with its own name, symbols of membership, ceremonies, songs, dances, rights, and responsibilities. The societies reflected the fact that warfare was interwoven with ceremonial and spiritual life.

The path to leadership also required supernatural protections and blessings that men received through visions or dreams. As a young man, Plenty Coups undertook a vision quest in an isolated high place in the Crazy Mountains. His vision, earned through fasting and personal sacrifice, came to him through a spiritual intermediary in the form of a buffalo bull. He saw the end of the buffalo era and their replacement by cattle that eventually dominated the Crow homelands.[9] This vision significantly influenced Plenty Coups' life, and because of his prominence, affected the lives of many other Crow people. He led the Crow through the transitions of the late nineteenth and early twentieth centuries until his death in 1932.

Not all Plains tribes practiced the vision quest, although dreams and revelations came to men, and women, under other special circumstances. Sometimes visions brought curative powers from spiritual emissaries such as eagles, hawks, bears, elk, deer, and buffalo, who taught the individual how to heal people. Such healers were greatly respected among Plains Indian people.

Specialized regalia, insignia, and other symbols of office signified the honors, abilities, and status of the men who wore them. During the nineteenth century, honored men in the Plains and Plateau regions wore shirts made of deer, elk, antelope, or mountain sheep hide decorated with strips of dyed porcupine quillwork or beadwork sewn on the shoulders and sleeves. Two shirts in the Dyck collection worn by honored men of the Upper Missouri River region of the Northern Plains (figs. 5.2 and 5.3) are characterized by complex patterns of plaited porcupine quillwork. The painted designs on the shirts likely represent hail stones of the powerful thunderstorms that can sometimes move across the Plains. Shirts such as these, created to honor male relatives, also reinforced respected roles of talented women who earned prestige and honors for their exceptional artistry in processing soft and beautiful hides and designing and completing intricate patterns in the porcupine quillwork that adorned them.

Women also embellished men's shirts of honor with bundles of human and horse hair, often providing their own hair for the decorations. The overall design and instructions for making such shirts may have originated from dreams or visions of the owners. As with the Lakota Shirt Wearers, the shirts symbolized the wearers' accomplishments and respected

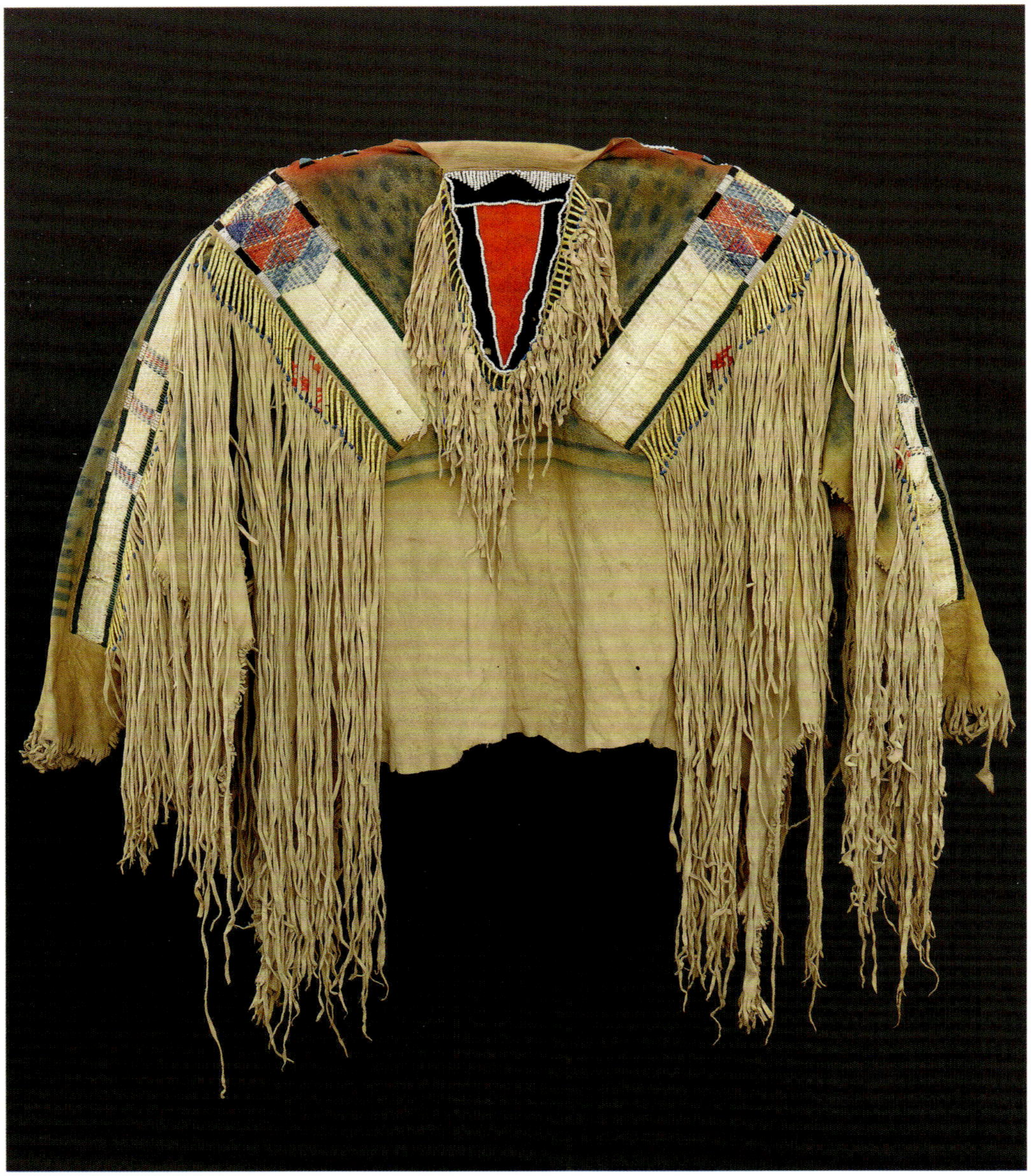

5.2. **Shirt**
Upper Missouri River Region, Northern Plains, ca. 1850
Tanned hide, porcupine quills, pigments, yarn, trade cloth; 37 × 34 inches
Plains Indian Museum, NA.202.1247

positions within Plains societies. The hair embellishments signified the people represented by the leaders as well as men's coups and the enemies they had defeated in battles. Some of the shirts exhibited biographical paintings illustrating the war deeds of their owners, including coups counted, horses captured, or enemies defeated. Painted images of powerful elements of the earth and sky provided spiritual support and protection and exemplified the fortitude, valor, and leadership of the men who wore them.

During the early reservation period, when men were no longer actively involved in warfare and had few opportunities to hunt, the former warriors continued to wear decorated hide shirts as symbols of their achievements. Women continued to make the shirts with beadwork strips, human hair, and horse hair for their male relatives to wear at ceremonies, parades, and other social events. Chiefs and other leaders of tribal delegations sometimes wore these shirts when they conferred with government representatives in Washington, D.C., and other locations as

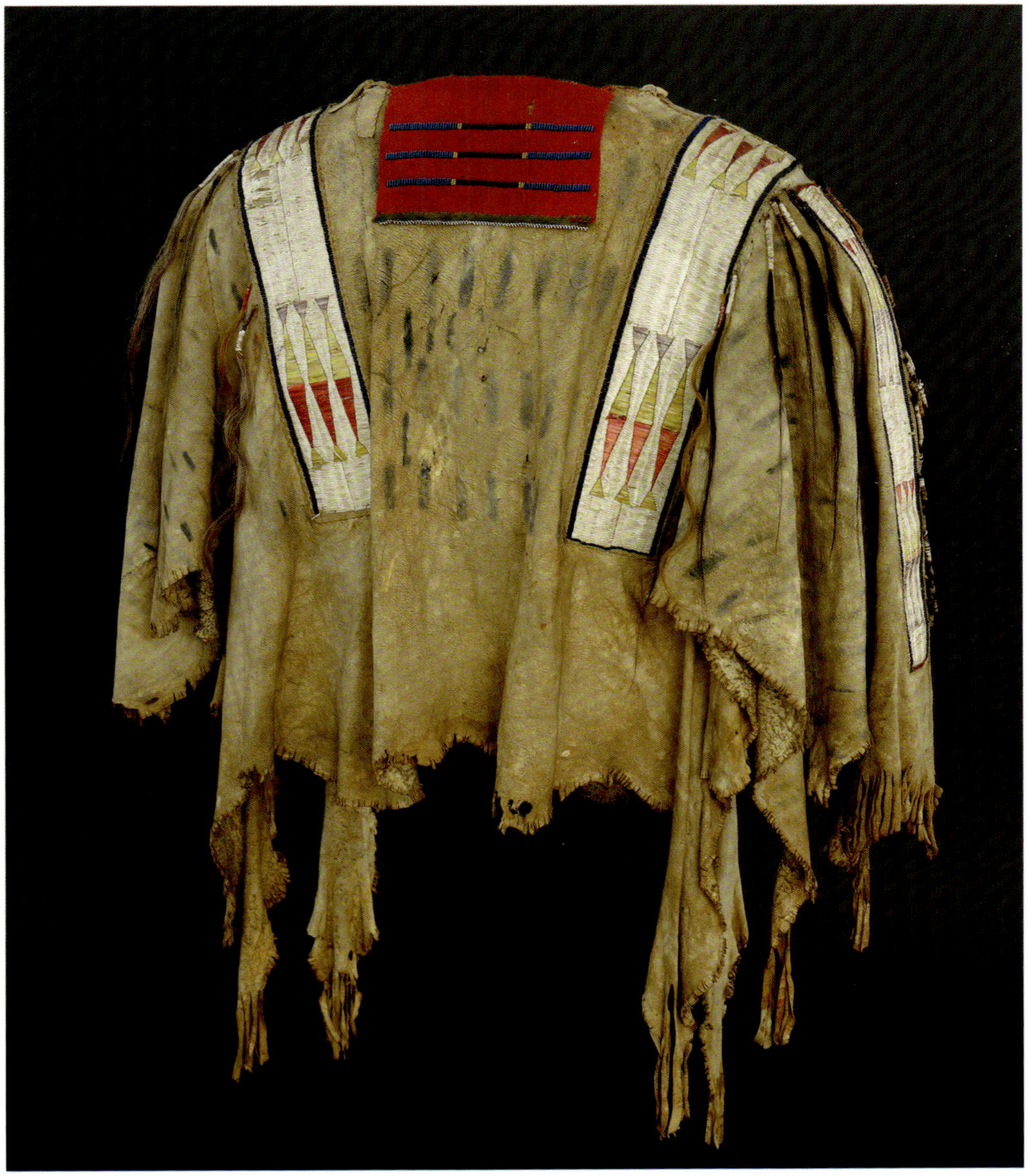

5.3. **Shirt**
Upper Missouri River Region, Northern Plains, ca. 1870
Tanned hide, porcupine quills, pigments, wool cloth, human and horse hair, sinew, cotton thread; 22 × 19½ inches
Plains Indian Museum, NA.202.1309

symbols of cultural identities, as well as indications of their individual status as leaders in their communities.

An Oglala Lakota shirt in the Dyck collection (fig. 5.4) exhibits the characteristics of a warrior society shirt that would have been worn by an honored and respected man. Painted in yellow, blue, and red pigment, it features strips of blue, white, and red beadwork on the arms and shoulders fringed with bundles of human hair wrapped in porcupine quills. Golden eagle and northern flicker feathers are tied on one shoulder, perhaps imparting personal spiritual power. The blue and yellow paint are said to symbolize Sky and Rock, two of the major supernatural powers in the Lakota cosmos. The dark blue upper half of the shirt could also

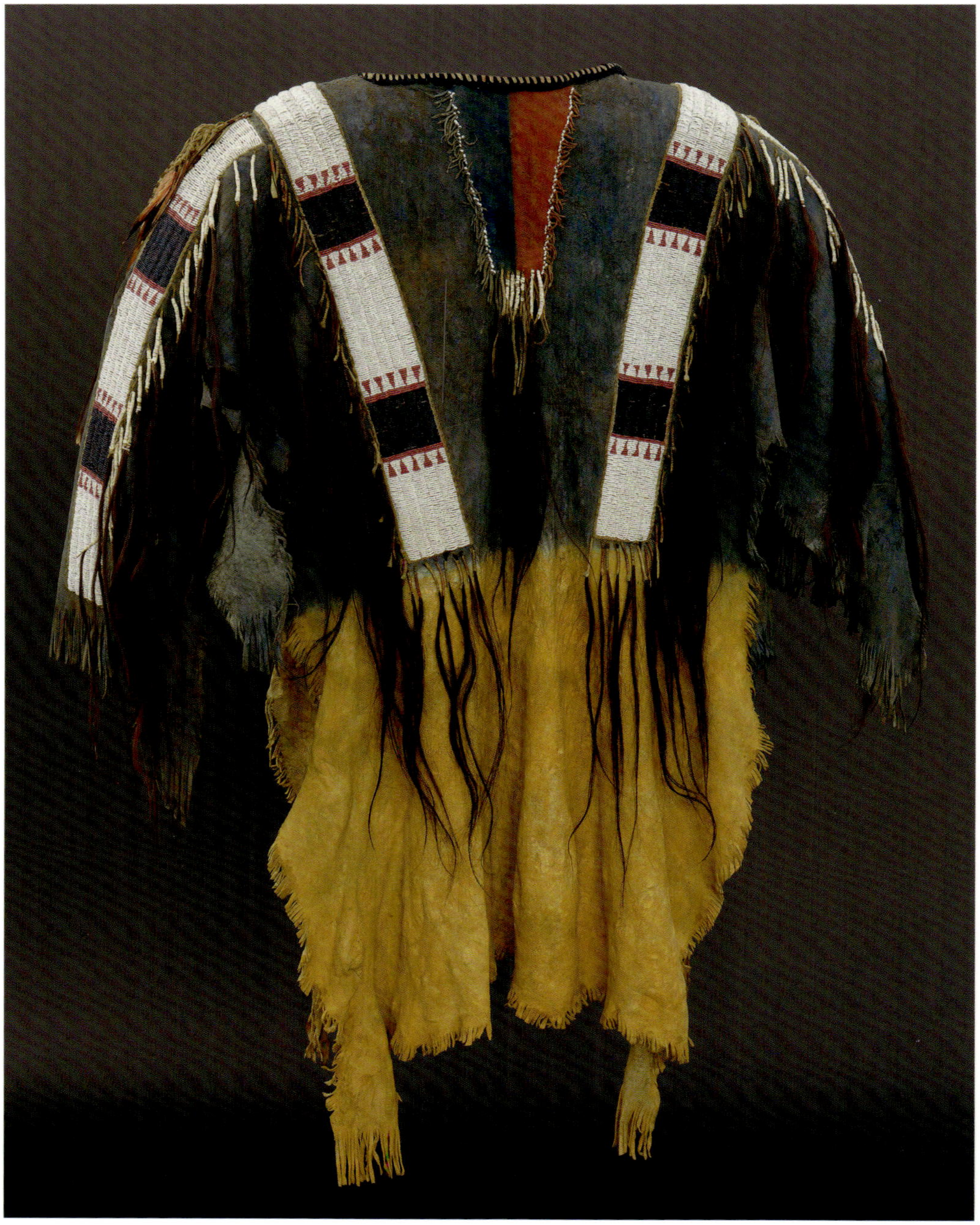

5.4. **Shirt**
Oglala Lakota (Sioux), Northern Plains, ca. 1868
Tanned hide, wool cloth, pigments, glass beads, dyed porcupine quills, golden eagle feathers, northern flicker feathers, human hair, sinew; 38½ × 19 inches
Plains Indian Museum, NA.202.1052

represent the black body paint of warriors returning from a successful raid.[10]

Another example of a shirt worn by a man of honor is from the Crow and dates from around 1870 (fig. 5.5). The shirt is painted in red ochre and has beadwork strips composed with a background of blue beads. The shirt features geometric designs in pink, yellow, and other colors traditionally favored by the Crow. Ermine skins hang from the beadwork strips. Ermine, human, and horse hair drape from the neck flap.

In like manner, a Nez Perce warrior in the middle of the nineteenth century would have worn another notable shirt in the collection (fig. 5.6). The shirt is made of tanned deer hide and decorated with strips of beadwork that use blue and white pony beads on the shoulders

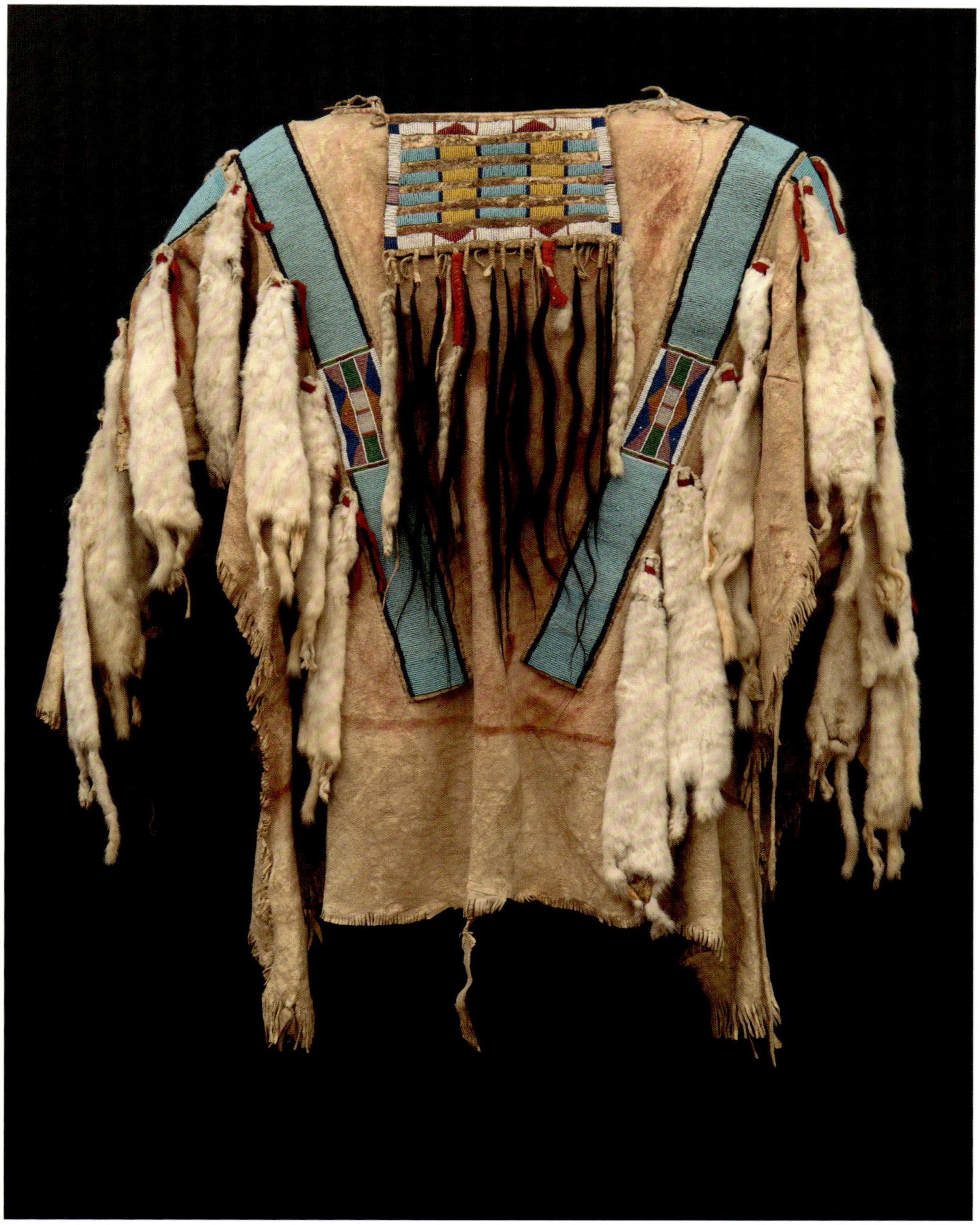

5.5. **Shirt**
Apsáalooke (Crow), Northern Plains, ca. 1870
Tanned deer hide, glass beads, ermine, wool cloth, horse and human hair, pigment, porcupine quills; 32 × 30 inches
Plains Indian Museum, NA.202.1185

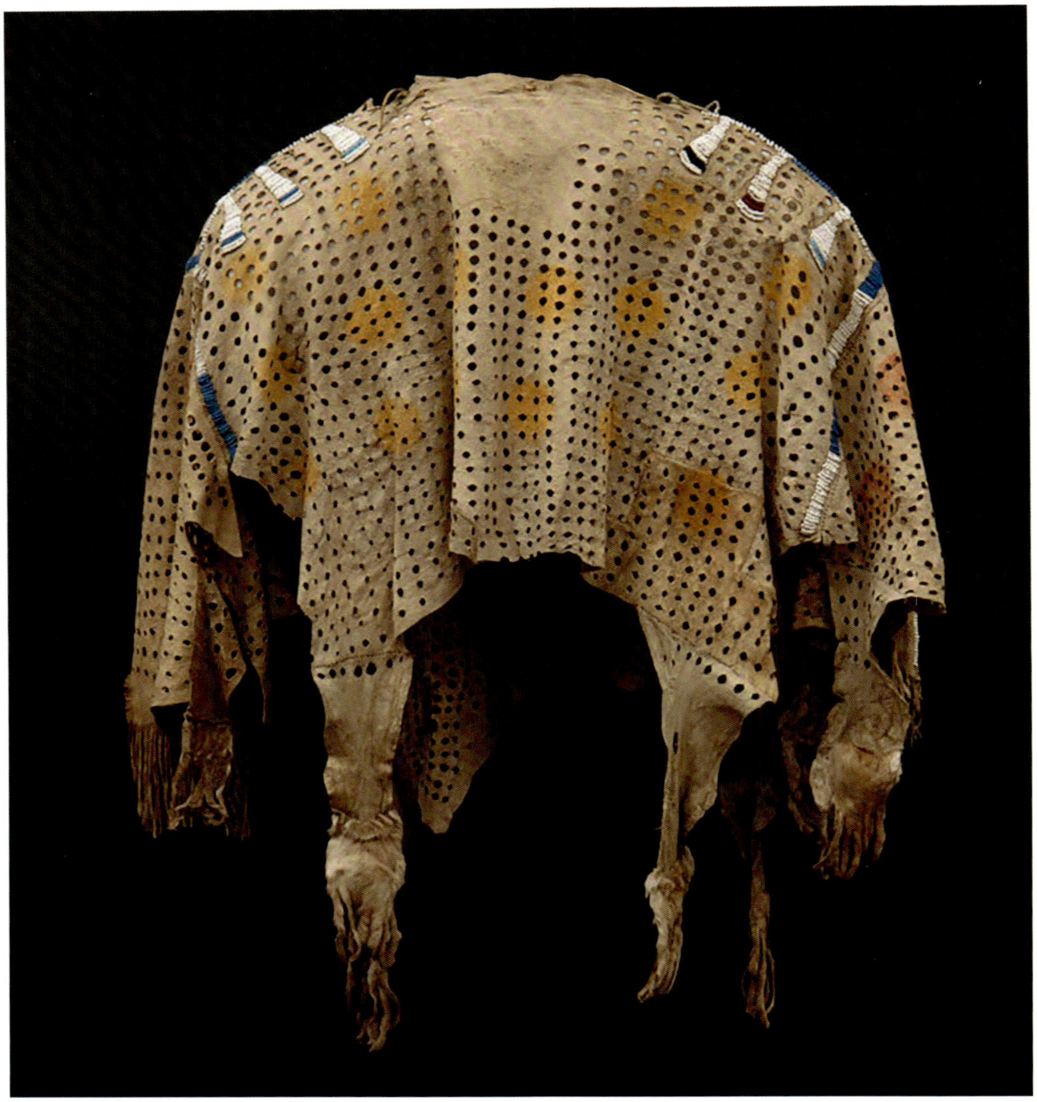

5.6. **Shirt**
Nimi'ipuu (Nez Perce), Plateau, ca. 1850
Tanned hide and fur, pigment, glass beads, human hair, sinew; 30 × 28½ inches
Plains Indian Museum, NA.202.1209

Nineteenth-century warriors of the Plateau and Northwestern Plains sometimes wore shirts covered with small cuts or punctures in the hide for ceremonial and formal occasions. Such shirts signified membership in a military society or honored the wearer's victories in battle.

and sleeves. It also features yellow and red pigments and fringes at the end of the sleeves. Nez Perce shirts, as well as those of other Plateau tribes and the Blackfeet and Gros Ventre of the Plains, sometimes feature many perforations, as seen on this example. Shirts of this type, with quillwork instead of beadwork, are documented in early journals and ethnographies concerning the Nez Perce.[11] Although the shirt lacks embellishments made from bundles of horse or human hair, a perforated or "punctured" shirt would signify the owner's membership in a Nez Perce warrior society and represent his bravery and leadership position.

In addition to shirts, warriors sometimes wore leggings with painted images, markings, beadwork, quillwork, and hair attachments representative of their accomplishments in war or with spiritual significance. One pair in the Dyck collection from the Lakota has markings in brown and ochre around each of the leggings, perhaps indicating the number of coups completed by the wearer (fig. 5.7). A second pair is painted overall in dark green/blue pigment and fringed with bundles of human hair (fig. 5.8). Images of turtles are painted in yellow on the

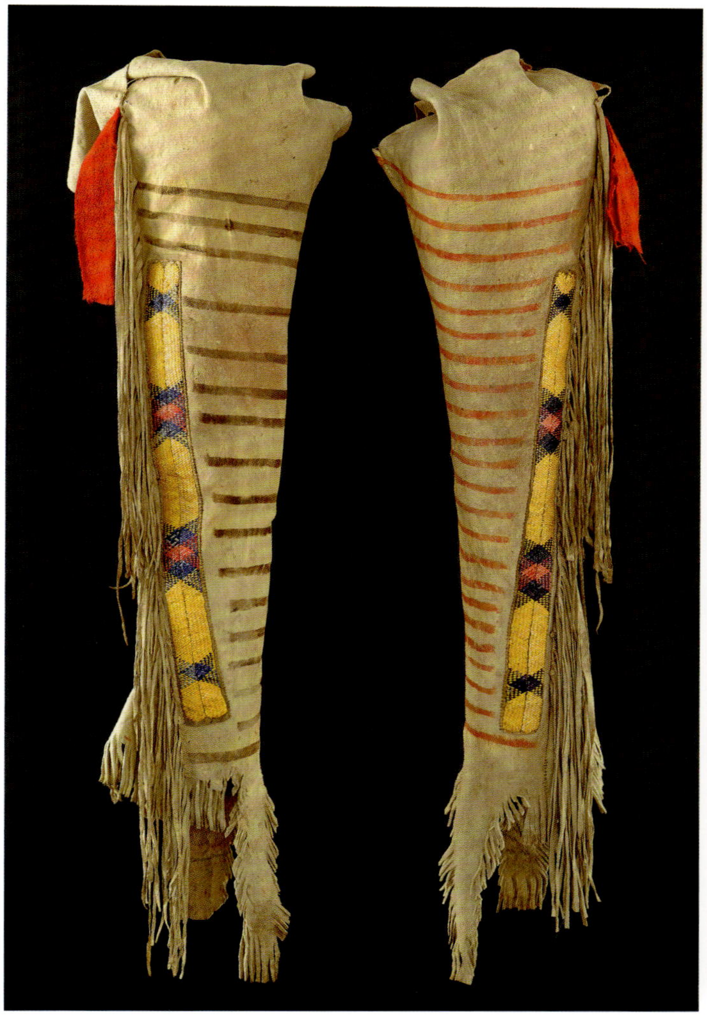

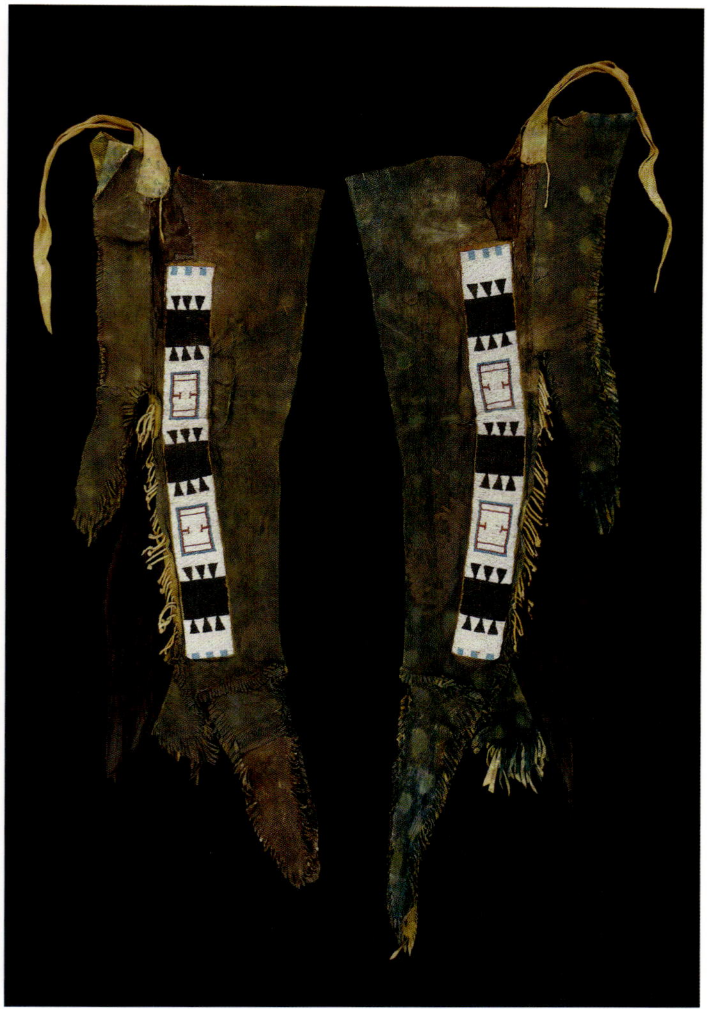

LEFT:
5.7. Man's leggings
Lakota/Dakota (Sioux), Northern Plains, ca. 1860
Pigment, dyed porcupine quills, sinew, tanned hide, wool cloth; 44 × 12 inches
Plains Indian Museum, NA.202.1303

RIGHT:
5.8. Man's leggings
Tsitsistas (Cheyenne), Northern Plains, ca. 1870
Tanned elk hide, glass beads, human hair, pigments, sinew; 39 × 12 inches
Plains Indian Museum, NA.202.1304

backs of the leggings, perhaps indicating their spiritual significance as representatives of the earth and symbols of long life.

An eagle feather was a mark of distinction, the highest honor that a Plains Indian man could attain. The feather's specific symbolism, whether painted, cut, or worn in a particular manner, varied among tribes. Eagles were considered the most powerful birds that flew highest in the sky, and warriors were encouraged to emulate them by demonstrating their strength, abilities, and valor in battle. The eagle itself was symbolic of the thunderbird, the creature of the sky that controlled the storms. The Northern Cheyenne elder John Stands In Timber recalled, "They say an eagle can take in nearly the whole world with his eyes, and see it as clearly as a man looks at the ground by his feet."[12] Because of eagles' inherent physical and spiritual powers, only certain men attempted to capture them in an effort that required fasting, prayers, and spiritual assistance.

A bonnet created from the eagle's tail feathers and often elaborated by a magnificent flowing trailer of many feathers is among the most recognizable of Plains Indian icons. In the popular imagination, the image of an eagle feather bonnet or a warrior on horseback wearing such a bonnet is generalized to represent all Native Americans. Distinguished warriors and leaders wore such feathered bonnets as symbols of their own personal acts of bravery or of the combined war honors of many men under their leadership. Men wore eagle feather bonnets in battle to inspire bravery and remind other men of past war honors. The feather bonnet could also summon supernatural power to defeat the enemy. The feathers within the bonnet were considered by the Lakota to hold the protective power of the eagle, which prevented men from being hit by bullets or arrows.

Wooden Leg recalled that eagle feather bonnets were not worn by all warriors, but only by a few distinguished men in each Cheyenne warrior society. Such men were experienced and capable fighters, some of whom had been told by distinguished senior warriors and leaders that they had earned the right to wear eagle feather bonnets. According to Wooden Leg, "After a man had been accepted as a war bonnet man he remained so throughout his lifetime."[13]

After tribes were settled on reservations, distinguished men continued to wear eagle feather bonnets as symbols of their achievements and to remind people of their tribal histories. In the late nineteenth and early twentieth centuries, as Lakota and Cheyenne men wearing eagle feather bonnets performed in Buffalo Bill's and other Wild West shows in the United States and Europe, their dramatic appearances became the public personifications of all Native people. This image has been reproduced in countless books and films. Over time, Native leaders from outside the Plains adopted eagle feather bonnets to represent their own accomplishments and identification as Native Americans. In modern practice, Plains Indian people continue to honor their leaders in this way, by bestowing an eagle feather bonnet or gifting an eagle feather upon returning soldiers, college graduates, and other tribal members who have achieved significant goals.

The predominant style of eagle feather bonnets on the Plains was the swept-back form based on caps of tanned hide or cut from commercial felt hats. This is the style of bonnet most often worn in the Wild West shows as well as in later depictions of Plains Indian men in films. With a crown of eagle feathers and an attached beaded brow band, some of the bonnets had trailers of tanned hide and, later, trade cloth decorated with additional eagle feathers. One eagle feather bonnet attributed by Dyck to Chief Joseph of the Nez Perce is built on a tanned hide crown and made up of golden eagle feathers, eagle fluffs, and flicker feathers (fig. 5.9). Ermines, strips of ermine hides, and hawk feathers hang from each side of the bonnet, and ermine covers the brow band.

A later swept-back bonnet is also from the Nez Perce and built on a rawhide band covered with red wool cloth (fig. 5.10). The bonnet consists of a crown of golden eagle feathers with ermine pieces attached on each side of the brow band. This bonnet also has a long red wool trailer, with a green wool strip and a row of brass bells sewn to the center. Thirty-one feathers, tipped with ribbon and yellow-dyed horse hair, are attached to the trailer.

Blackfoot leaders wore a distinctive style of eagle feather bonnet, consisting of a crown of upright eagle feathers in a rawhide headband, covered in red cloth and decorated with pieces of ermine skin. Stand-up bonnets, imbued with supernatural protection, were worn in battle, during ceremonies, or in dress parades. The design for the bonnet was said to have originated

5.9. **Eagle feather bonnet**
Nimi'ipuu (Nez Perce), Plateau, ca. 1870
Rawhide, tanned hide, golden eagle feathers, hawk feathers, flicker feathers, ermines, and ermine hide, pigment, horse hair; 27 inches (height)
Plains Indian Museum, NA.203.1547

According to a paper tag attached to this bonnet, Chief Joseph of the Nez Perce wore this bonnet during the Nez Perce War of 1877. The tag also states that in 1897 Chief Joseph gave the bonnet to Ralph Armstrong, who attended Carlisle Indian School in 1890–98.

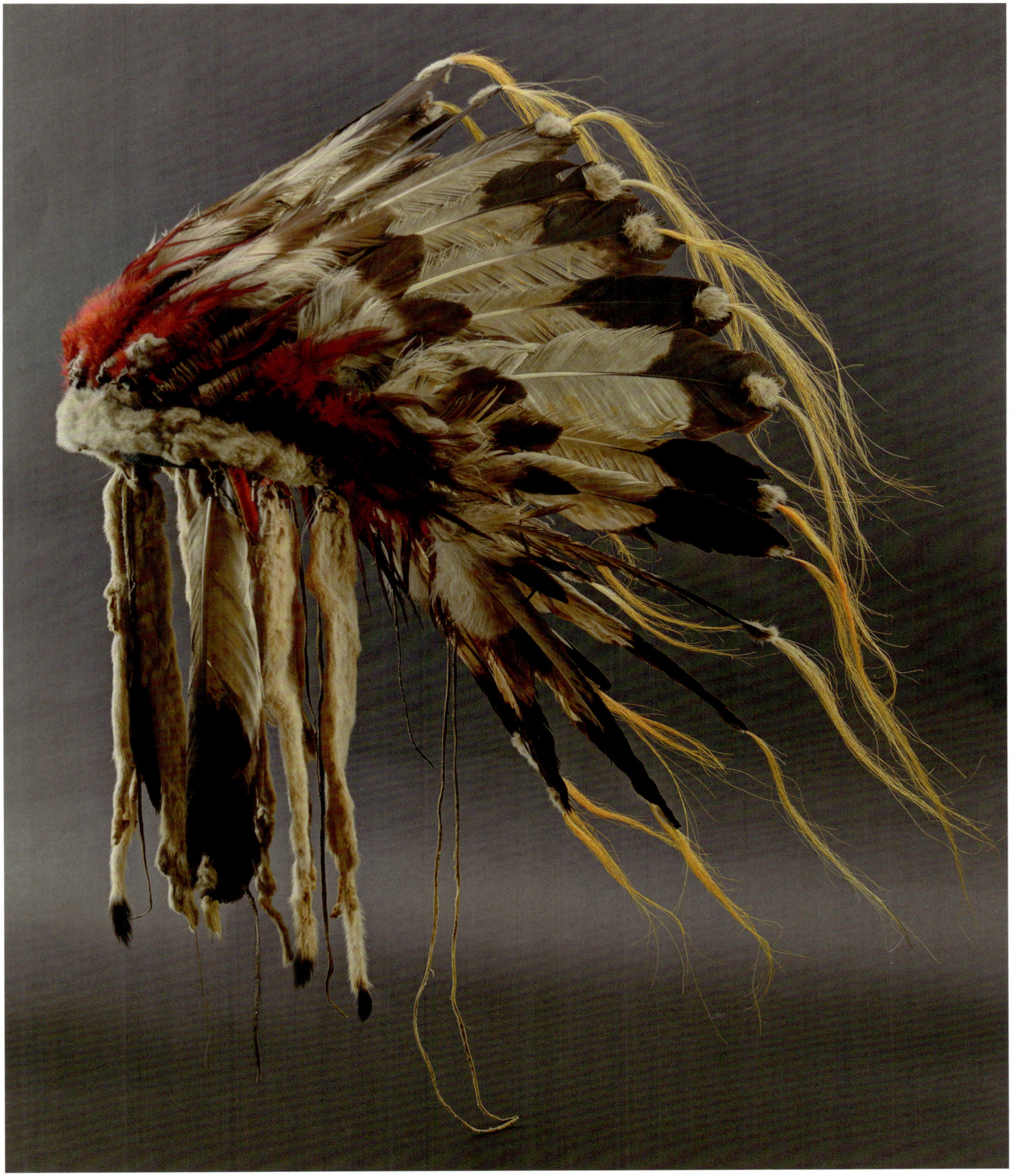

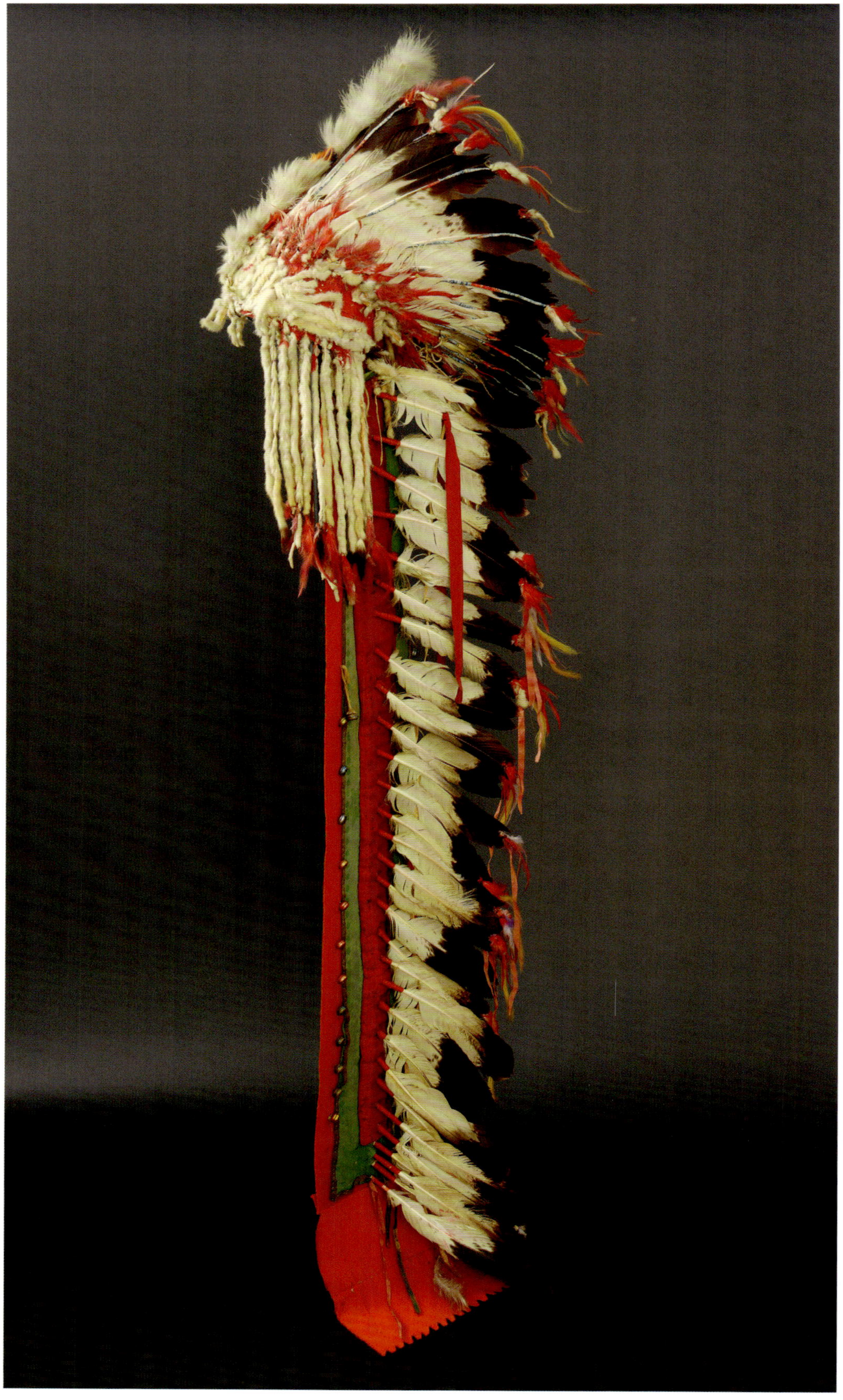

5.10. **Eagle feather bonnet and trailer**
Nimi'ipuu (Nez Perce), Plateau,
ca. 1900
Rawhide, tanned hide, golden eagle feathers, feather fluffs, horse hair, ermine, satin ribbon, porcupine quills, brass bells, wool cloth, silk ribbon, metallic ribbon;
bonnet: 28½ inches (diameter);
trailer: 63¼ × 10¾ inches
Plains Indian Museum, NA.203.1557

Eagle feather bonnets symbolized the status, honor, and accomplishments of the men who wore them. After tribes were settled on reservations, distinguished leaders continued to wear eagle feather bonnets as emblems of their achievements and to remind people of their tribal histories.

RIGHT:

5.11. **Stand-up bonnet**
Niitsitapii (Blackfoot), ca. 1860
Rawhide, tanned hide, bald eagle feathers, eagle fluffs, ermine, wool cloth, cotton cloth, ochre; 18½ inches (height) and 28 inches (diameter)
Plains Indian Museum, NA.205.127

FAR RIGHT:

5.12. **Eagle feather bonnet and trailer**
Niitsitapi (Blackfoot), Northern Plains, ca. 1850
Rawhide, wool cloth, eagle feathers and fluffs, ermine, cotton cloth, glass beads, cotton thread, porcupine quills, brass beads; bonnet: 22½ × 7¾ inches (diameter); trailer: 57½ × 17¼ inches
Plains Indian Museum, NA.203.1500

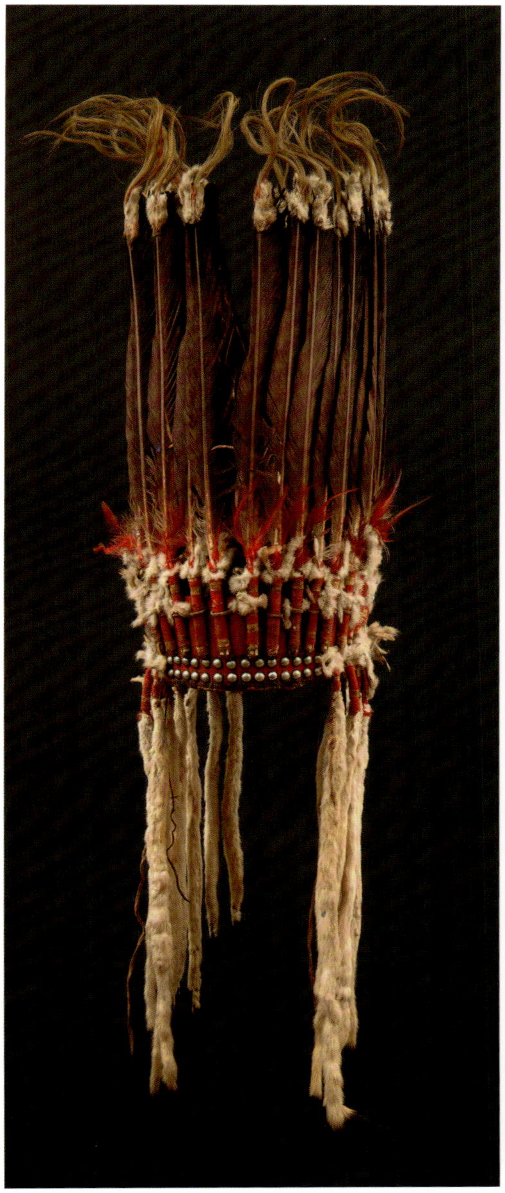

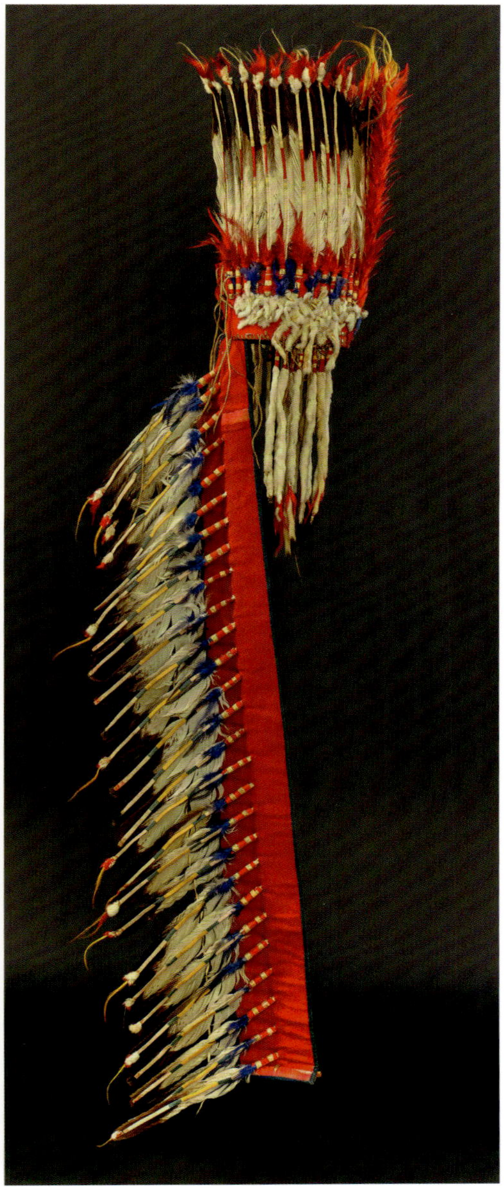

in a vision experienced by Many Tail Feathers at the time of the last Blackfoot buffalo jump in the mid-nineteenth century. There are two stand-up bonnets in the Dyck collection. One is made of bald eagle feathers, some of which have been trimmed to create narrow profiles attached to a headband, covered in red trade cloth, and decorated with metal tacks (fig. 5.11). The feathers have also been painted in red ochre. The bonnet has ermine strips attached to the headband at each side. The second Blackfoot bonnet of this style is made of golden eagle feathers and has a long feathered trailer (fig. 5.12).

Similar to the status symbolism of eagle feather bonnets, bear claw necklaces were worn by Pawnee, Otoe, Ponca, and Omaha men as emblems of their accomplishments, honors, and roles as leaders (figs. 5.13, 5.14, and 5.15). Pawnee men, in particular, specialized in creating bear claw necklaces made from the long broad claws of prairie grizzly bears, which once roamed

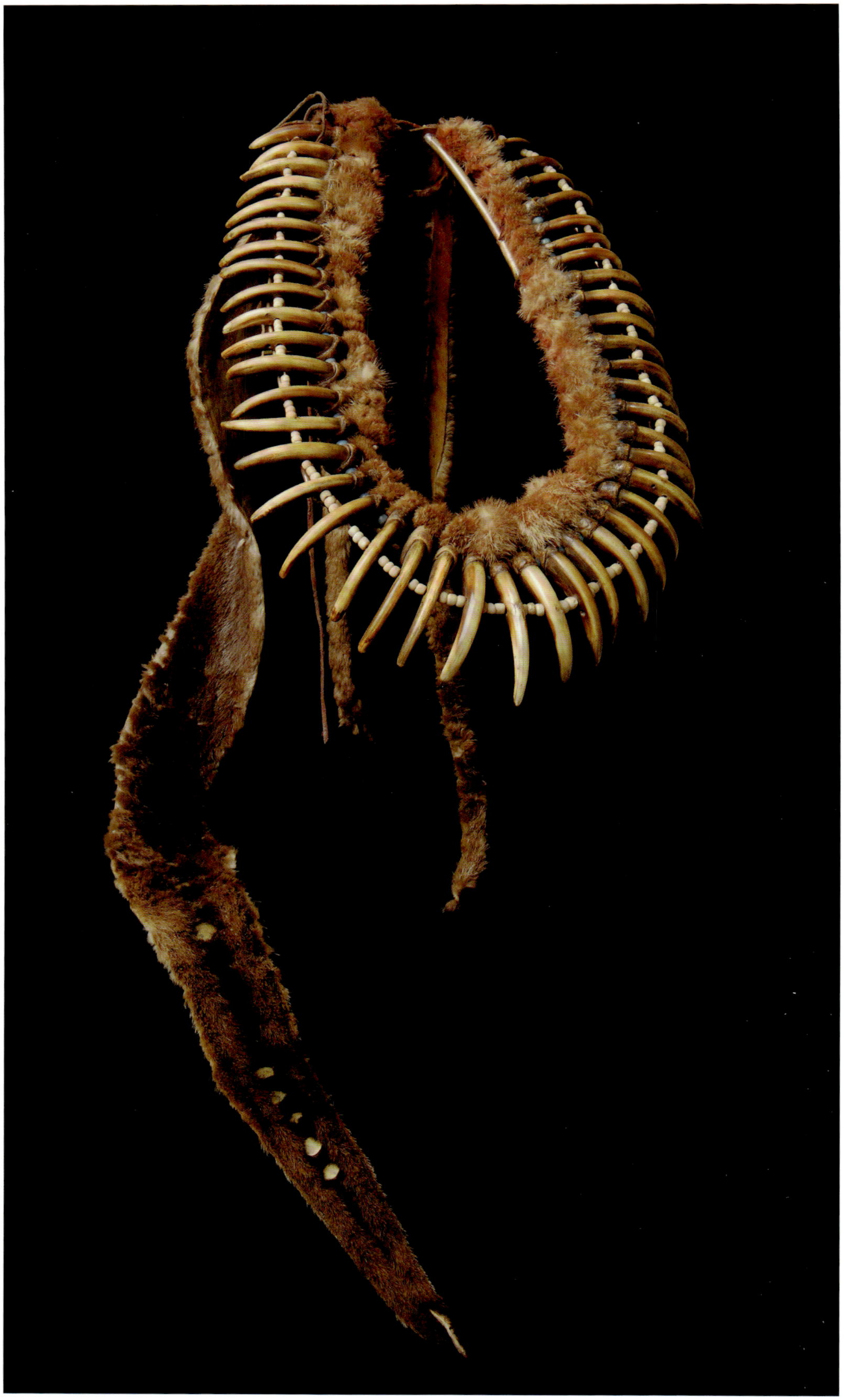

5.13. **Bear claw necklace**
Central Plains, ca. 1850
Tanned otter hide, tanned deer hide, grizzly bear claws, ochre, glass beads, sinew, brass buttons; necklace: 18 × 14 inches; trailer: 56 × 5 inches
Plains Indian Museum, NA.203.1476

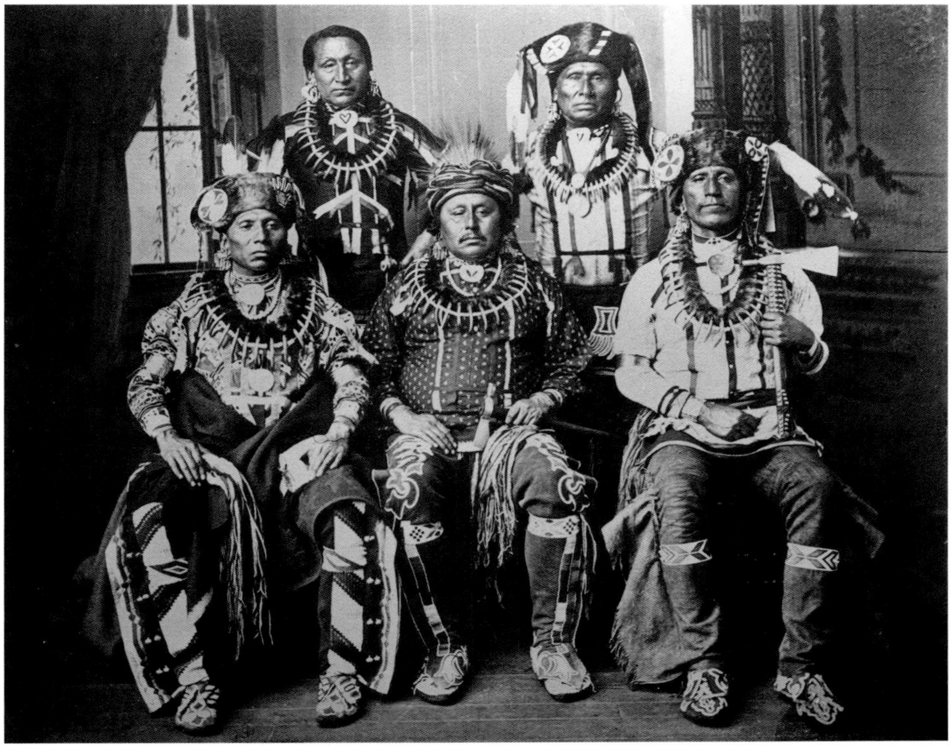

5.14. **Otoe delegation**
Washington, D.C., January 1881
Photograph by John K. Hillers
Plains Indian Museum, Adolf Spohr Collection, P.42.203

All of the men in this photograph of a delegation of Otoe leaders to Washington, D.C., wear bear claw necklaces as symbols of their leadership status.

the Central and Eastern Plains.[14] The Pawnee held grizzly bears in high esteem because of their strength, power, and fighting abilities, qualities universally admired by Native warriors. Before going into battle, Pawnee warriors sought the sacred protection of four animal spirits—wolves, eagles, mountain lions, and bears. Each animal had its own unique powers. According to Pawnee cosmology, the four great powers are represented by the stars and constellations of the sky. Pawnee men believed that success in war required the defining characteristics of these four animals: the stealth and craftiness of the wolf, the spiritual power of the eagle, the magnetic or drawing power and cunning of the mountain lion, and the strength of the bear.[15]

In addition to the bear's great strength, Pawnee warriors admired the animal for its ferocity and invulnerability. Through visions, spiritual teachings, and ceremonies, men could learn about and, eventually, possess the special powers of the bear. This included the ability to cure wounds and sickness. Men believed that by wearing the bear claw necklaces they could protect themselves from being hit by arrows or bullets in battle.[16] The Pawnee scholar James R. Murie recounted a story told by Big Star, about how a man could come to possess the power of the bear. According to the story, a man wounded in battle was found by bears. The bears took care of him and cured him of his wounds. Upon restoring his strength, they taught him about their special abilities. As one of the bears escorts the man back to his village, he speaks of the special powers of the bears:

> You have my claw. It is my spirit. As long as you keep the claw, no diseases will trouble you. In battles no harm will come to you, and if it does, my power will be with you so that you will again get well. If I should be killed or die of old age, then you must also go.

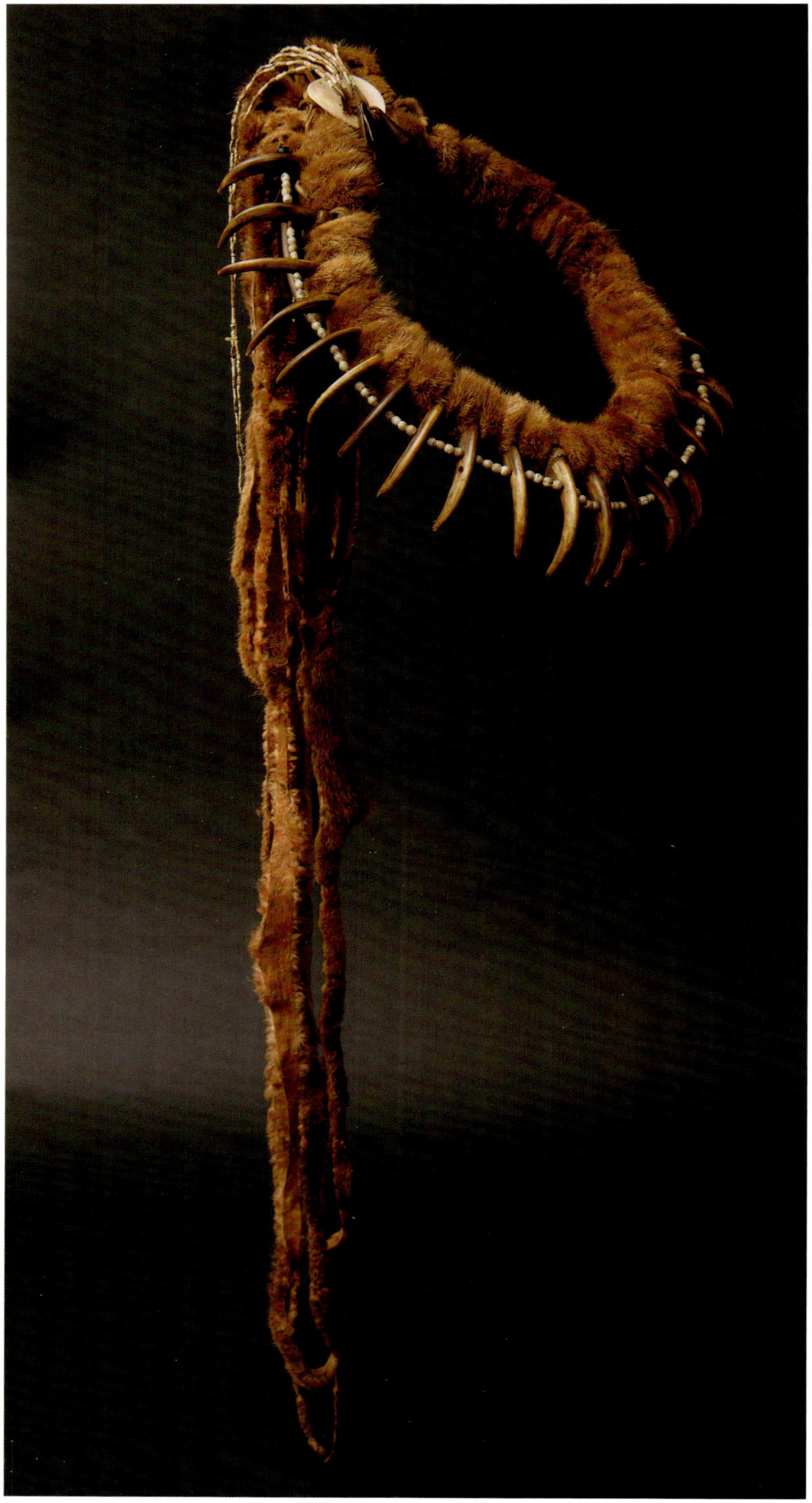

5.15. **Bear claw necklace**
Central Plains, ca. 1860
Tanned otter hide, grizzly bear claws, red ochre, abalone shell, porcupine quills, glass pony beads; 63 × 12 × 2 inches
Plains Indian Museum, NA.203.1585

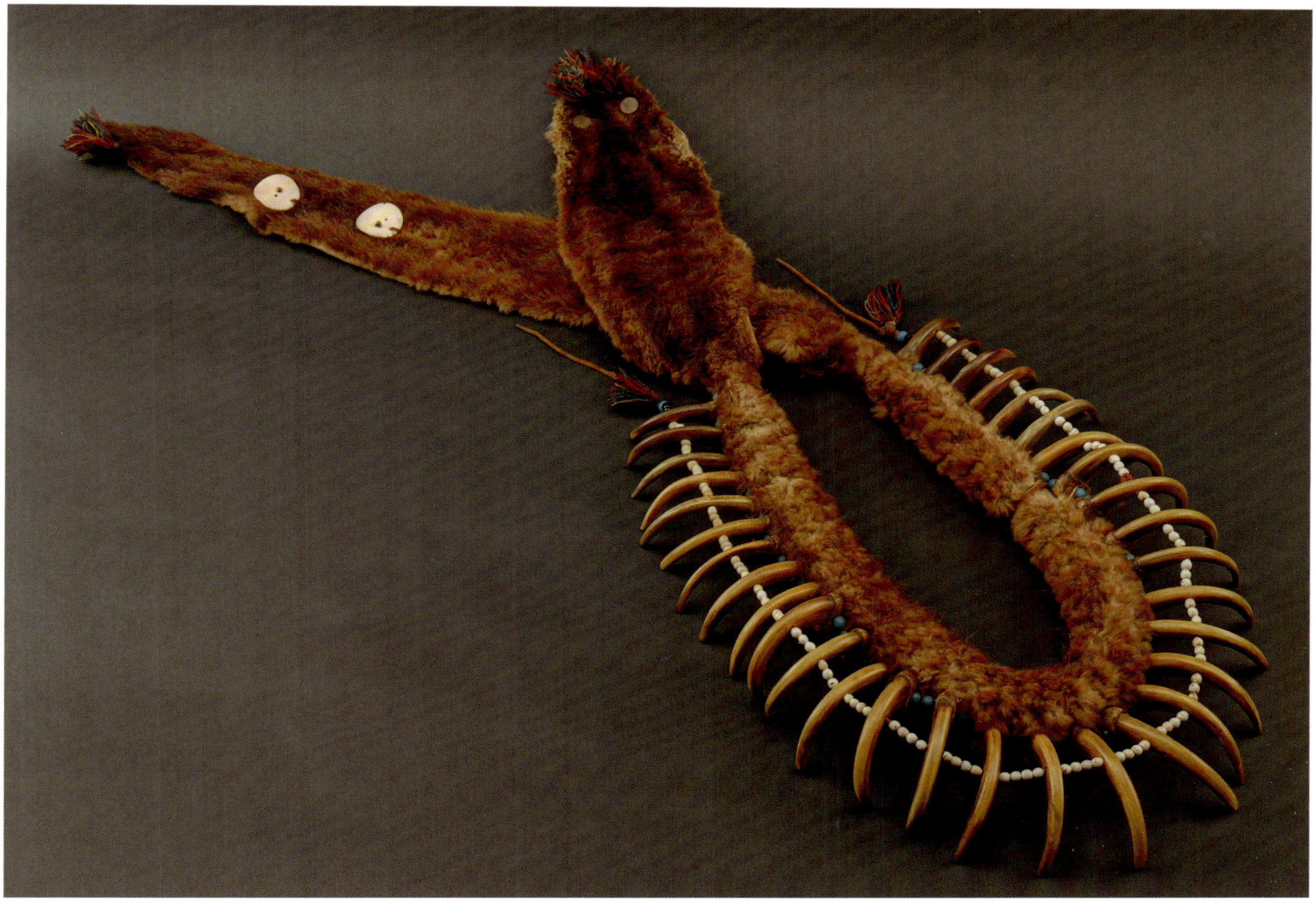

5.16. **Bear claw necklace**
Chaticks si Chaticks (Pawnee), ca. 1830
Otter fur and hide, grizzly bear claws, glass beads, abalone shells, tanned hide, brass tacks, wool cloth;
left: 32 inches; right: 45 inches;
width: 18 inches
Plains Indian Museum, NA.203.1413

Distinguished Pawnee men wore bear claw necklaces made from otters and the long, broad claws of grizzly bears that once roamed the Central and Eastern Plains. The necklaces were emblems of their honors and roles as leaders. Plains Indian people held grizzly bears in high esteem because of their power and fighting abilities. The claws on the necklace represent the bear's strength and courage, and the otter hide signifies power over both land and water. Both animals' qualities guided the wearer during warfare, treaty negotiations, and ceremonies.

> We are now near your people. I can smell them; that is why I snorted. Tomorrow we will approach your village; then I must leave you. I will remain among the hills so that when you get strong you can come to me. Then I will teach you more of our mysteries.[17]

Murie described a renewal ceremony for a bear claw necklace that had once belonged to Sky Chief, a prominent leader of the Pawnee. The ceremony took place in the 1920s, after the necklace had been returned after being held out of Pawnee ownership for decades. Through the ceremony, the necklace was remade using a new otter hide and replacing the strip of bear hide, tobacco, and dried cedar leaves that had been rolled in the old hide. After attaching the bear claws to the otter hide and restringing the glass beads, the necklace was formed into a circle, with the head and tail of the otter made to hang down the wearer's back.[18]

Paul Dyck had four spectacular bear claw necklaces in his collection. One necklace is made in the style of the Pawnee, and dates from around 1830 (fig. 5.16). On this necklace, the bear claws—interspersed with white glass beads—are attached to a circle of otter hide that forms the base for the necklace. Abalone shells also decorate the tail of the otter, which would flow from the back of the neck between the wearer's shoulders. While the bear claws represent the bear's strength and courage, the otter hide signifies power over both land and water. Both animals' qualities guided the wearer during warfare, treaty negotiations, and other important events.

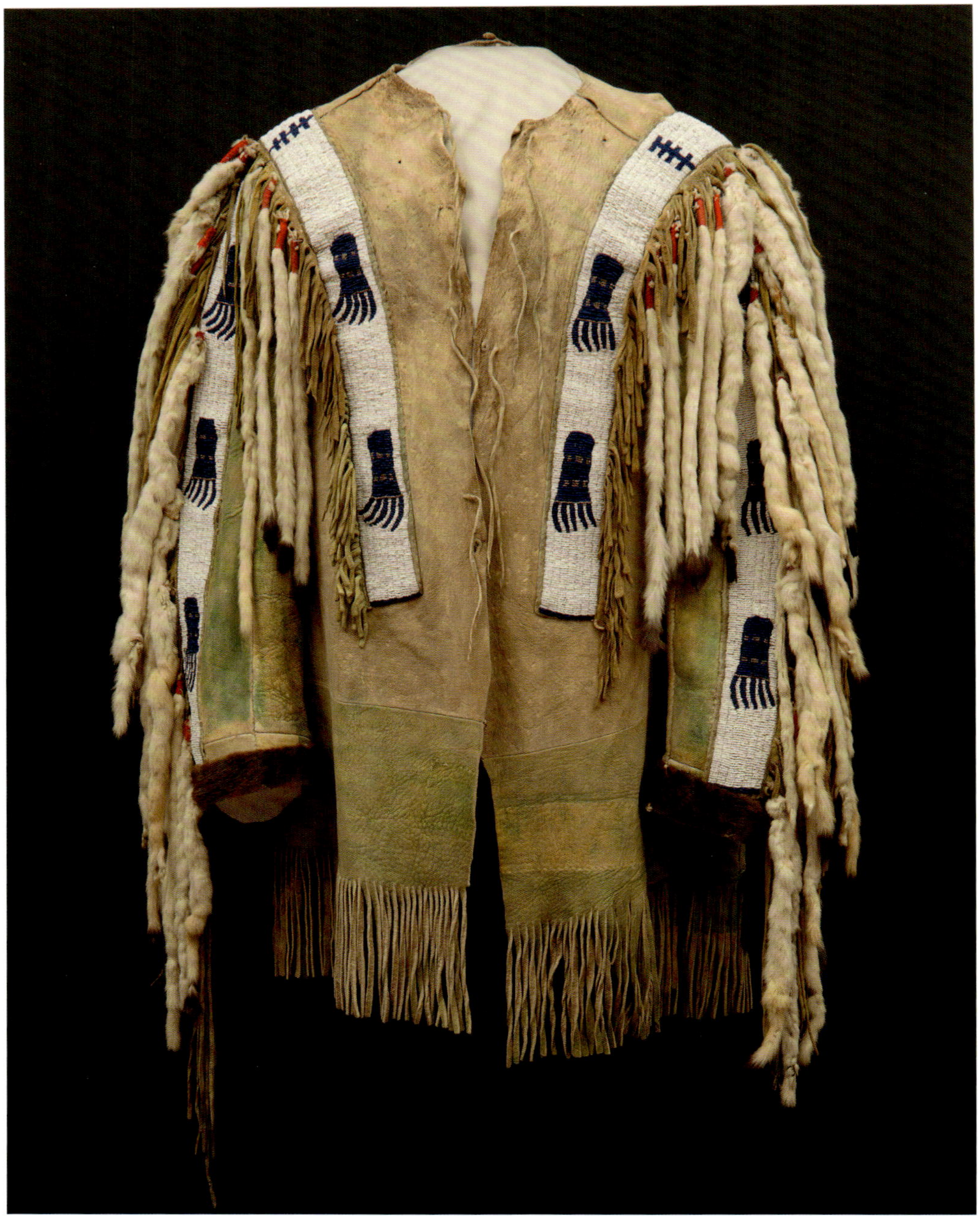

5.17. **Shirt**
Chaticks si Chaticks (Pawnee), ca. 1890
Tanned hide, otter hide, glass beads, ermine, horse hair; shirt length: 38 inches; width sleeve to sleeve: 71 inches
Plains Indian Museum, NA.202.1186

This shirt also reflects the respect the Pawnee held for the power of the bear. The design of the beadwork strips on the shoulders and arms of the shirt features elegant beaded bear paws and claws. The shirt is also trimmed at the shoulders with ermine.

The strength and power of bears are also symbolized in beadwork and porcupine quillwork on men's leggings, moccasins, and shirts (fig. 5.17). In a similar manner, the significance of eagles to Plains cultures is also represented in a necklace composed of forty-one eagle talons attached to a circle of tanned hide trimmed with red wool cloth (fig. 5.18).

Other symbols of leadership came to Plains Indian men from sources outside their cultures. When Plains nations came together to confer or trade, reciprocal gift exchanges served to establish relationships and to sanction agreements that occurred during the meetings. Early visitations between European representatives and traders followed this pattern, with gifts being presented to Plains Indian leaders in recognition of their positions. Such exchanges also

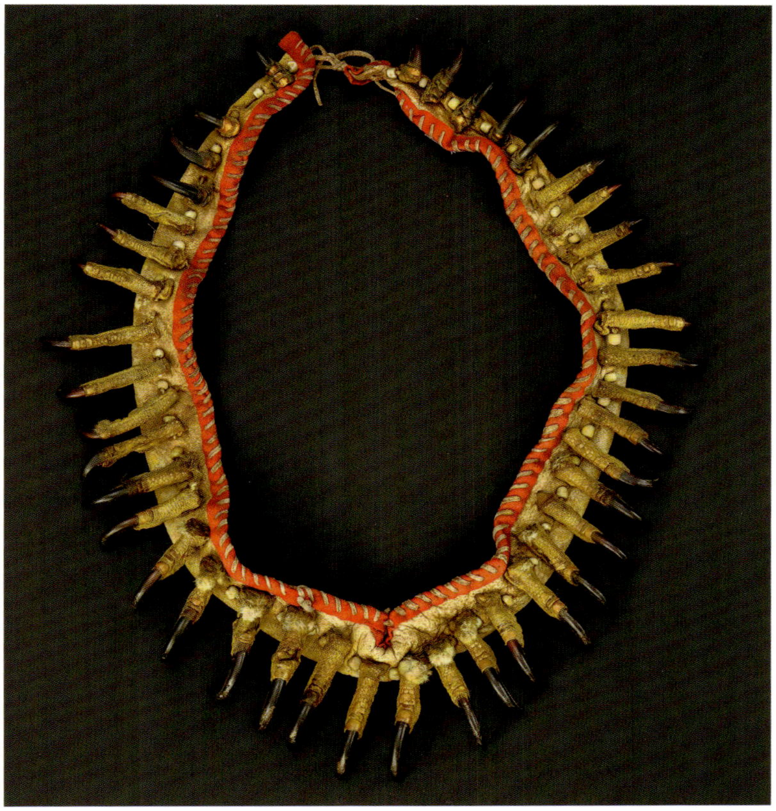

5.18. **Necklace**
Plains, ca. 1879
Bald eagle talons, tanned hide, wool cloth, glass beads; 21 × 13 inches
Plains Indian Museum, NA.203.1474

With forty-one eagle talons on this necklace, the man who wore it carried with him the power of the eagle.

established and strengthened future relations. Representatives of the U.S. government also provided presentation objects of diplomacy. Notably, these were presidential peace medals and pipe tomahawks, items highly desired by Plains Indian men.

As a ceremonial weapon, the pipe tomahawk combined the significance of the pipe in Native spiritual practices with the symbolic importance of warfare (fig. 5.19). Pipe tomahawks were first manufactured by the English for Native American trade in the seventeenth century, followed by the French and the Americans. Pipe tomahawks were introduced to Native peoples of the Plains by the earliest Euro-American expeditions to the region. Manufactured of steel, brass, or pewter, pipe tomahawks had handles of ash, walnut, hickory, or maple. Pipe tomahawks sometimes were decorated by their Native owners with brass-headed tacks on the handles and attachments of cloth, beadwork, and other materials.

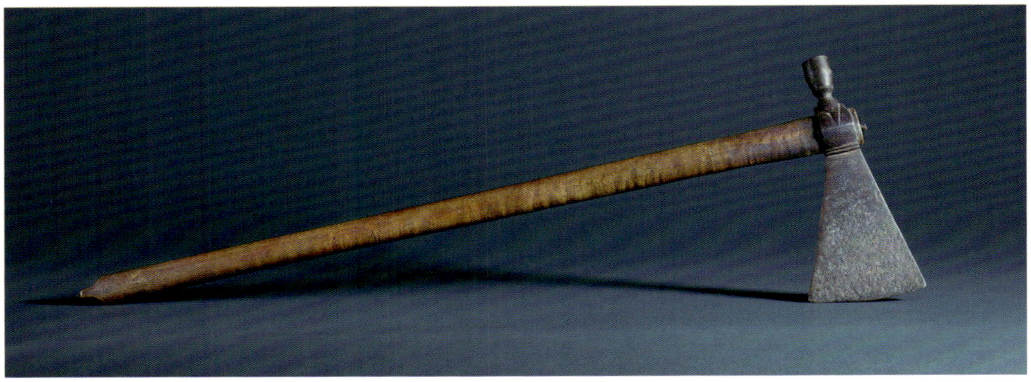

5.19. **Pipe tomahawk**
Hunkpapa Lakota (Sioux), Northern Plains, ca. 1870
Wood, metal: 28½ × 9½ inches
Plains Indian Museum, NA.504.375

Paul Dyck collected this pipe tomahawk at Grand River, South Dakota, during his first visit to the Standing Rock Reservation. His notes attributed the ownership of the pipe tomahawk to Kills Enemy of the Hunkpapa Lakota.

WOMEN'S HONORS

Just as men were respected for their achievements in hunting and warfare and as leaders, Plains Indian women were also honored for instilling values in the children they cared for, for their work in the arts, and for their roles in ceremonial life. In her writings, Beatrice Medicine emphasized the fundamental importance of women as culture bearers that guide children in understanding and respecting Lakota ideals from one generation to the next: "The fact that women are the primary socializers of children underlies their duties as teachers of values, language, culture, world view, rituals, and practices, and underlies the beliefs and behaviors of the Lakotas. As Lakota women and men, we must constantly keep in mind the meaning of our word for children, the 'sacred ones.' By valuing the Lakota way and teaching it to our children, we will ensure that this lifestyle that we cherish will continue."[19] All of these elements mentioned by Medicine are embodied in the Lakota ethos—values, language, culture, worldview, rituals, and practices—and underlie the unique and distinct artistry of the Lakota and other Plains Indian people. Plains Indian women taught their daughters, nieces, and granddaughters to produce tipis, buffalo robes, furnishings, clothing, and moccasins that were essential to "living in a good way" in the Great Plains while at the same time instructing them on the protocols and sacred rituals that guided the creation of these materials.[20]

Women created a good portion, if not most, of the Plains Indian art of the nineteenth and early twentieth centuries now residing in museums and private collections in the United States and Europe. Members of their own communities admired and respected their exquisite artistry, skills, and knowledge of cultural values that made possible the careful creation of objects for daily use or for ceremony that were embellished with beautiful designs in painting, porcupine quillwork, and beadwork. Unfortunately, these women artists today remain largely anonymous outside of their own communities, as most of the collectors and museum representatives who purchased or traded for these materials failed to record their names.[21]

Although there were exceptions, ethnographers of the late nineteenth and early twentieth centuries, when major museum collections were assembled, rarely recorded information about the daily lives of women and their influences and positions in ceremonial and political realms. Perhaps the researchers were unable to communicate directly with women because of cultural and linguistic constraints, or, possibly, researchers were just uninterested in recording this information.

Within communities, however, women did have paths to honor by means of formal recognition for their excellence in hide tanning, sewing, porcupine quillwork, and beadwork. Women's societies or guilds devoted to the decorative arts fostered and encouraged excellence in tanning and working with hides, creating tipis and their furnishings, and in porcupine quillwork. Such societies operated in much the same way as men's warrior societies, with their own ceremonies, initiations, feasts, and sponsored events. Also like the men's societies, these associations provided venues for recognizing and celebrating those women who had attained the highest level of achievement in their artistic production. For example, Cheyenne women who had tanned thirty buffalo robes and decorated them with porcupine quillwork or made a

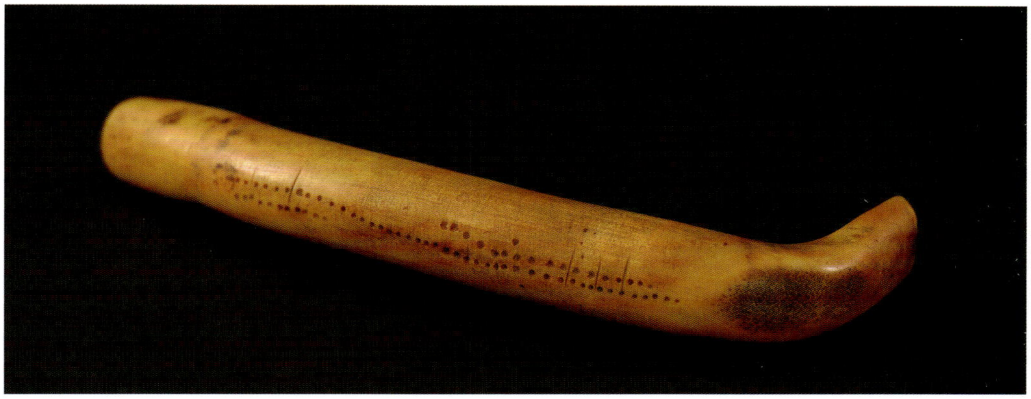

5.20. **Hide scraper**
Plains, 1850–1890
Animal bone; 11 × 4 inches
Plains Indian Museum, NA.106.960

Women treasured their hide scrapers and work bags of tools needed for tanning, sewing, and doing quillwork and beadwork. The notches on this scraper represent the owner's artistic accomplishments.

complete tipi by tanning and softening buffalo hides, fitting them together and sewing them, and preparing the lodge poles were considered to be at the highest level of arts producers. Therefore, they were worthy of special recognition.[22] Skilled women artists cherished their hide-working tools used to clean, scrape, work, and soften buffalo, deer, elk, and other hides that would be used for clothing, robes, bags, tipis, and other items (see fig. 5.20).

Membership in the societies was limited to experienced, knowledgeable, and skilled women who had reached significant artistic milestones. One of the most important societies, the women's quilling society, was dedicated to the production of the sacred arts by ceremonial decoration in quillwork of buffalo robes and other objects made of hides. Members of this association were expected to be highly moral and virtuous in their personal lives. Among the Northern Cheyenne, women were ranked within the society according to the degree of difficulty associated with the items they had produced. Ranging from lowest degree to highest were moccasins, baby cradles, tipi decorations, buffalo robes and tipi linings, backrests, and storage bags.[23] According to George Bird Grinnell, Cheyenne women considered quillwork "of high importance and, when properly performed, quite as creditable as were bravery and success in war among the men. The guild of quill workers included the best women in the camp. Its ceremony and ritual have been handed down from mythic times."[24]

One means of gaining membership in this society was for a young woman to pledge to complete an object, such as a buffalo robe decorated with quillwork, to achieve good fortune for a family member, such as a husband or brother going to war or an ill child or other relative. The young woman would approach a member of the women's quilling society, most often a family member, and ask for instruction in completing the work properly. The process of beginning work on the robe and fulfilling the woman's vow involved rituals, a ceremonial feast, and giveaways as women of the society came together to support the young woman in her first endeavor. The actual quilling of the robe was a sacred undertaking that required that the artist follow specific procedures and restrictions.[25]

With the completion of the robe, the young woman was admitted to the society and could attend its feasts and other ceremonies. She also earned the right to teach other potential candidates. Grinnell noted that during the ceremonies, the women of the society described the quillwork they had completed in much the same way as men publicly recounted their coups.

Later, women of the society would provide detailed instruction and patterns for the design of the quillwork.[26]

Members of such societies had special designs with accompanying rituals that they precisely reproduced on robes, cradles, tipi decorations, moccasins, and other items. Like men, women also had dreams or visions in which they received new designs considered to be the individual's personal property, which were not to be copied.

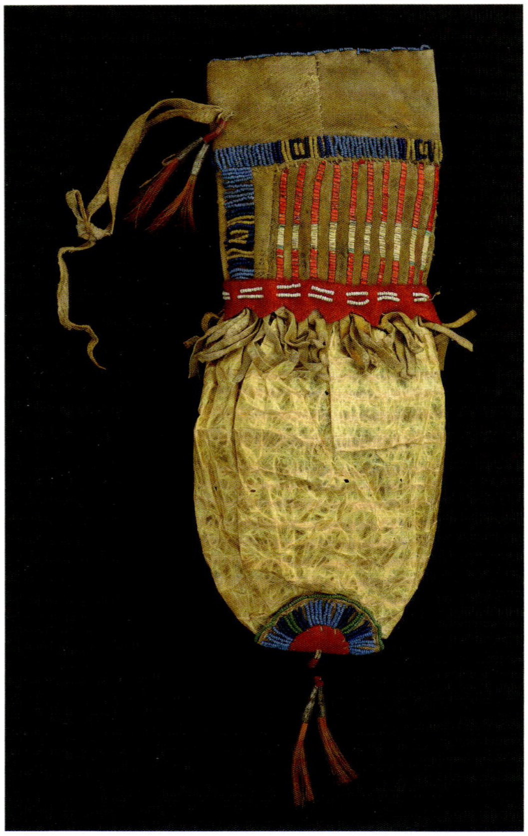

5.21. **Bag**
Lakota (Sioux), ca. 1870
Buffalo bladder, glass beads, tanned hide, tin cones, dyed horse hair, dyed porcupine quills, wool cloth, cotton thread; 13 × 5 inches
Plains Indian Museum, NA.202.1408

Women used decorated bladder bags to store the sharp quills of a porcupine.

Northern Arapaho women learned the skills and associated rituals of quillwork through apprenticeship with an older woman who was a holder of one of seven sacred medicine bags. The bags, which contained the tools needed for quillwork and for tipi painting, signified the high ritual authority of the women who held them.[27] Like the Cheyenne women, a Northern Arapaho woman could vow to create a cradle or a buffalo robe decorated with a quillwork design to earn supernatural assistance for a family member in need. After the completion of this undertaking, and additional work that demonstrated her skill and artistry, she could eventually inherit the bag, along with the right to instruct other women in the art of quillwork, including the required rituals. A Northern Cheyenne woman named Firewood inherited a sacred medicine bag from her mother in about 1885, and her parents encouraged her to begin quilling in order "to keep her home surroundings and honor her kindred."[28] In time, Firewood earned honors through the completion of sixty baby cradles, fourteen buffalo robes, five decorated tipis and several plain ones, ten calf robes, and one buffalo backrest cover. She made these works as gifts for relatives, to honor war deeds, to fulfill vows for a loved one's recovery from illness, or as prayers for long life.[29]

Lakota and Blackfoot quillers also recognized the sacred connotations of their art. Lakota women who excelled in quillwork and in hide work were said to have received their abilities through a vision of Double Woman. Associations of such women were sometimes called together under the leadership of older women for feasts and to exhibit their works to one another. Proficient hide tanners and tipi makers also came together for the cooperative making of tipis.[30] Blackfoot women began working in quillwork only after initiation and ceremonies that protected them from going blind or experiencing swelling in their finger joints.[31]

After tribes were moved to reservations, women's artisan societies diminished in importance. Traditional family-based methods of teaching were disrupted by children being sent away to government or missionary boarding schools, often for years at a time.[32] Women concentrated on creating finely beaded clothing for ceremonial use and household items for giveaways. In a less formal structure than the quilling societies, older women continued to instruct their younger relations in the art of beadwork and to come together to display their creations. According to Barbara Hail, "Their art continues to combine the cultural ideals of beauty, sacredness, and harmony."[33]

CEREMONY

Plains Indian ceremonial life followed and supported the yearly seasonal cycle of hunting buffalo; gathering plants; preserving and storing foods; traveling to new camps and trade gatherings; and for farming peoples, planting, tending, harvesting, and preserving their crops. Each tribe followed its own ceremonies, accompanied by specific songs and dances, which were deeply rooted in cultural traditions that provided spiritual meaning and reinforcement for their values, traditions, and ways of life. One of the yearly ceremonies, the Sun Dance, was a significant component of the ceremonial cycle for many Plains tribes. Held during the summer, when abundant grass supported large herds of buffalo, the Sun Dance provided an opportunity for many bands and small family groups to come together to renew kinship ties and celebrate as a people. It was a time when leaders met in tribal councils and men's societies came together to discuss common

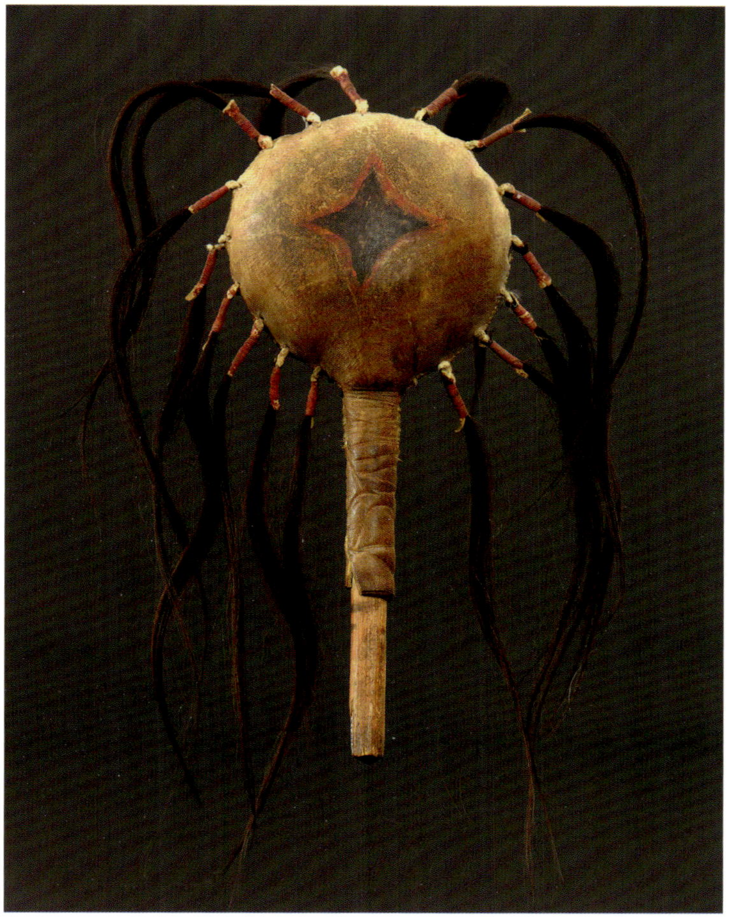

5.22. **Rattle**
Lakota (Sioux), Northern Plains, ca. 1860
Rawhide, minerals, wood, pigment, human hair, sinew; 10 × 4 inches
Plains Indian Museum, NA.505.90

According to Dyck, a member of the Buffalo Bulls, a Lakota warrior society, used this rattle with the central design of the morning star.

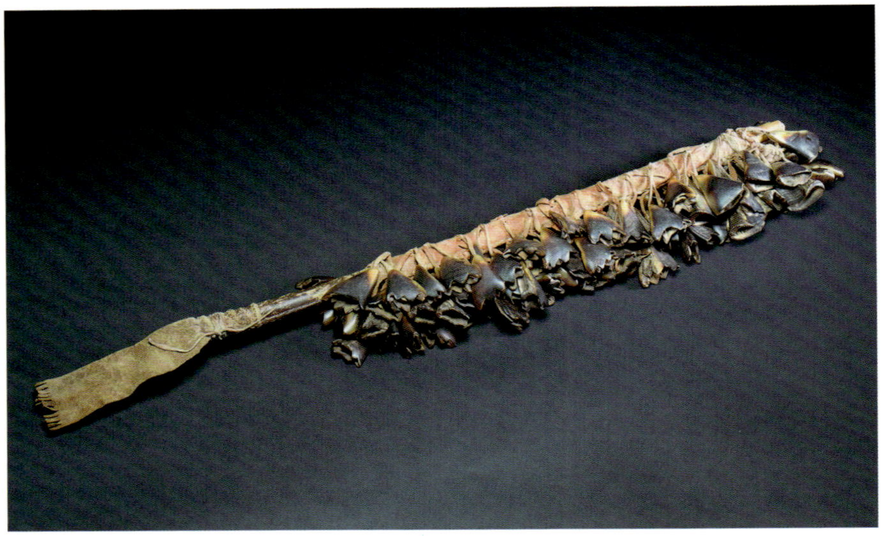

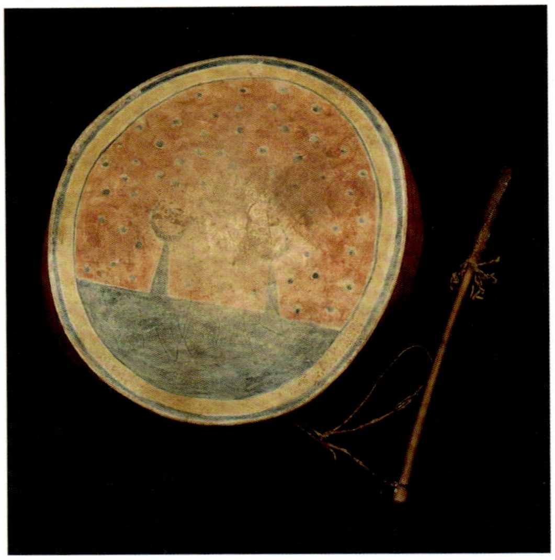

LEFT:
5.23. **Rattle**
Nueta (Mandan), Upper Missouri River Region, ca. 1880
Wood, pigment, tanned hide, deer dewclaws, deer hooves; 24 × 4 inches
Plains Indian Museum, NA.502.288

RIGHT:
5.24. **Drum and stick**
Amskapi Pikuni (Blackfeet), Montana, ca. 1880
Metal, wood, rawhide, pigment, tanned hide, cotton thread; drum: 19 inches (diameter) × 3¼ inches (height); stick: 17½ inches
Plains Indian Museum, NA.505.87

Plains Indian men who performed songs at ceremonies and military society dances accompanied themselves on hand drums painted with spiritually significant images derived from visionary experiences.

interests. Trading took place, and young men and women courted while families made marriage arrangements.

However, not all Plains Indian tribes followed the rituals of the Sun Dance. The Pawnee observed a rich and complex ceremonial cycle that was intertwined with preparation for and celebration of hunting, planting, growing, and harvesting corn and other crops. Ceremonies recognized the place of the people within the great universe and all elements of the earth and sky. The significance of corn, or Mother Corn, was the overriding element of many of the ceremonies, reflecting its importance in the survival of Pawnee people.

Widespread throughout the continent, the smoking of ceremonial pipes as a means of prayer is considered one of the earliest forms of spiritual expression among Native Americans. Native people believed tobacco was a gift from the supernatural powers to men, and the act of smoking was a message or prayer to the heavens. Ceremonial smoking took place when giving thanks, establishing new relationships, and sealing agreements. Its practice also marked significant passages in ritual life and the beginning of new undertakings such as war expeditions.

Men carved pipe bowls from bone, steatite, shale, limestone, and catlinite (also called pipestone) and stems made of a variety of woods (figs. 5.25, 5.26, and 5.28). Women dressed the stems with porcupine quillwork, beadwork, and sometimes feathers (figs. 5.27). Women also made pipe bags in which to store the pipes and tobacco out of soft, tanned hide with painted, beaded, and quillwork designs (5.29, 5.31, and 5.32). According to Curly Bear Wagner, pipes continue to have a significant role in contemporary Plains spiritual life.

> The pipe is one of our most sacred instruments of our people. We were guided by the pipe. We use it in all our ceremonies, the pipe. To us the bowl of the pipe is made of stone and to us that represents the earth. The stem of the pipe is made of wood and so, to us, that represents all the different things on the earth. When we smoke the pipe, the smoke that goes out of the pipe, that's our prayers going up to the Creator because the smoke is like a spirit. You see it for a minute and then it disappears.[34]

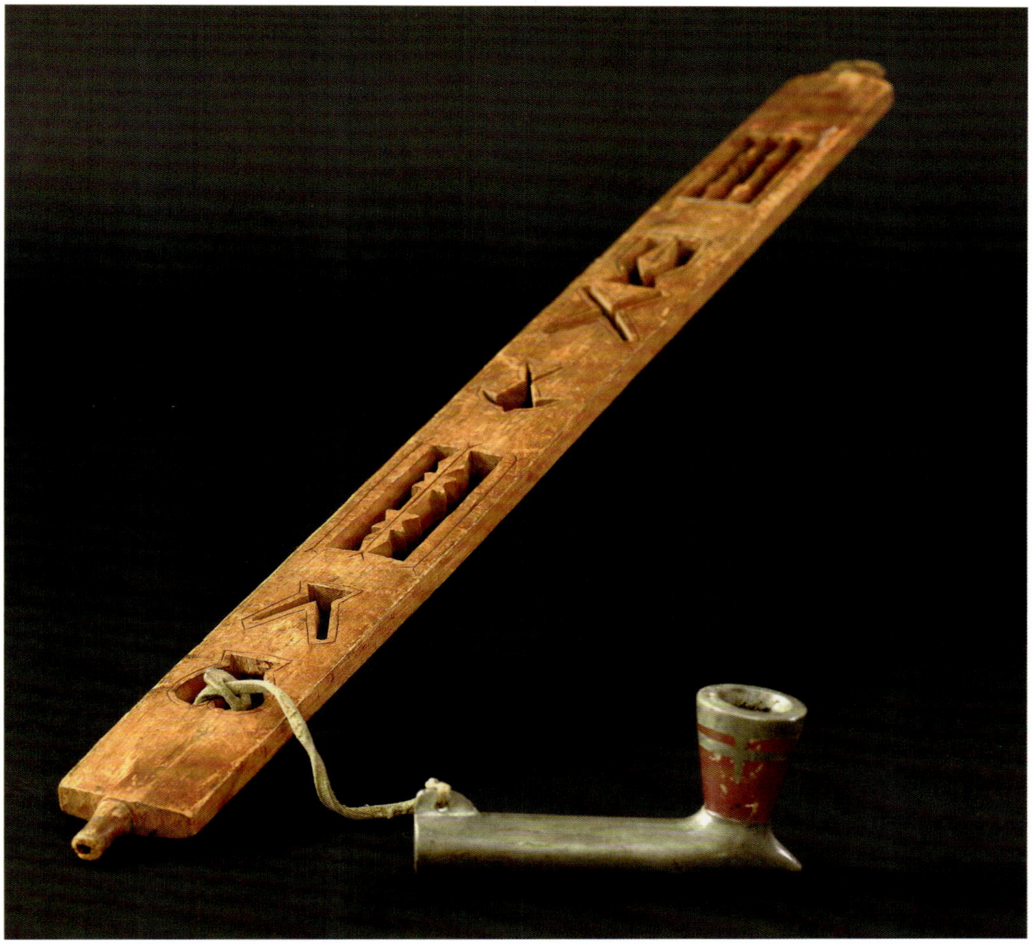

5.25. **Pipe bowl and stem**
Dakota (Eastern Sioux), Plains, ca. 1840
Wood, lead, pipestone (catlinite), tanned hide; bowl: 5¾ × 2¾ inches; stem: 30¾ × 2¼ inches
Plains Indian Museum, NA.504.471

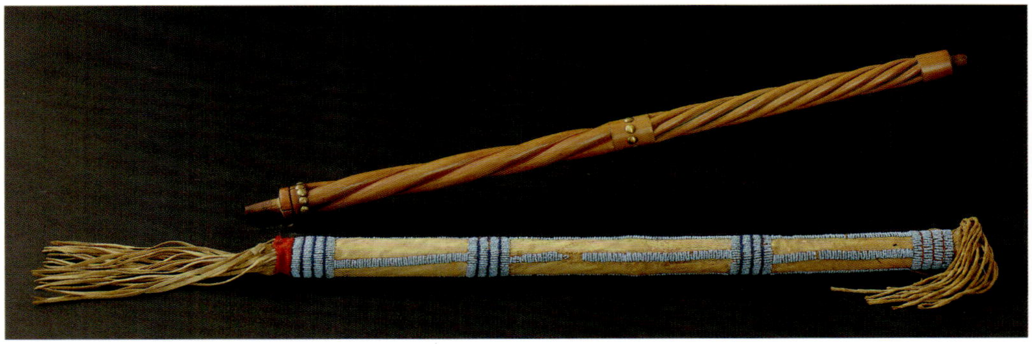

5.26. **Pipe bag and pipe stem**
Eastern Plains, 1890–1920
Brass tacks, metal, wood, pigment, glass beads, tanned hide, wool cloth; bag: 36 × 3⅞ inches; stem: 25 inches
Plains Indian Museum, NA.504.406

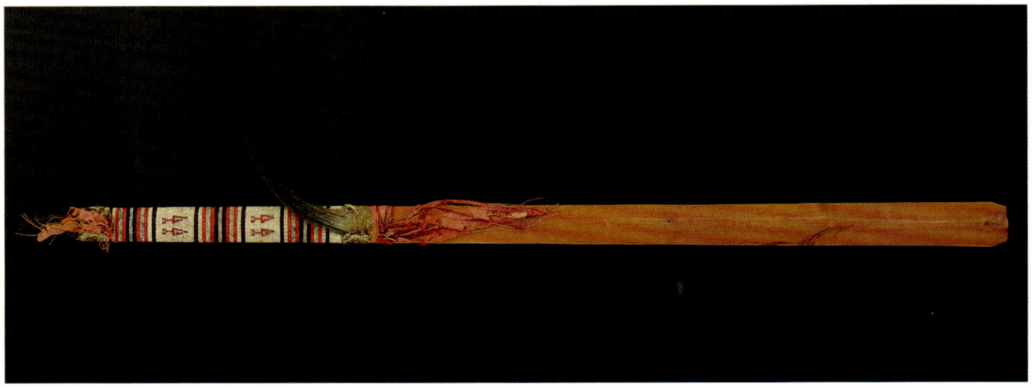

5.27. **Pipe stem**
Lakota (Sioux), Northern Plains, ca. 1870
Metal, wood, silk, pigment, glue, porcupine quills, horse hair, sinew; 39 × 2 inches
Plains Indian Museum, NA.504.357

For Plains Indian men, the smoking of pipes was an integral part of all ceremonies. They carved wooden pipe stems, and women dressed the stems with quillwork, beadwork, feathers, horse hair, and hide or cloth wrappings.

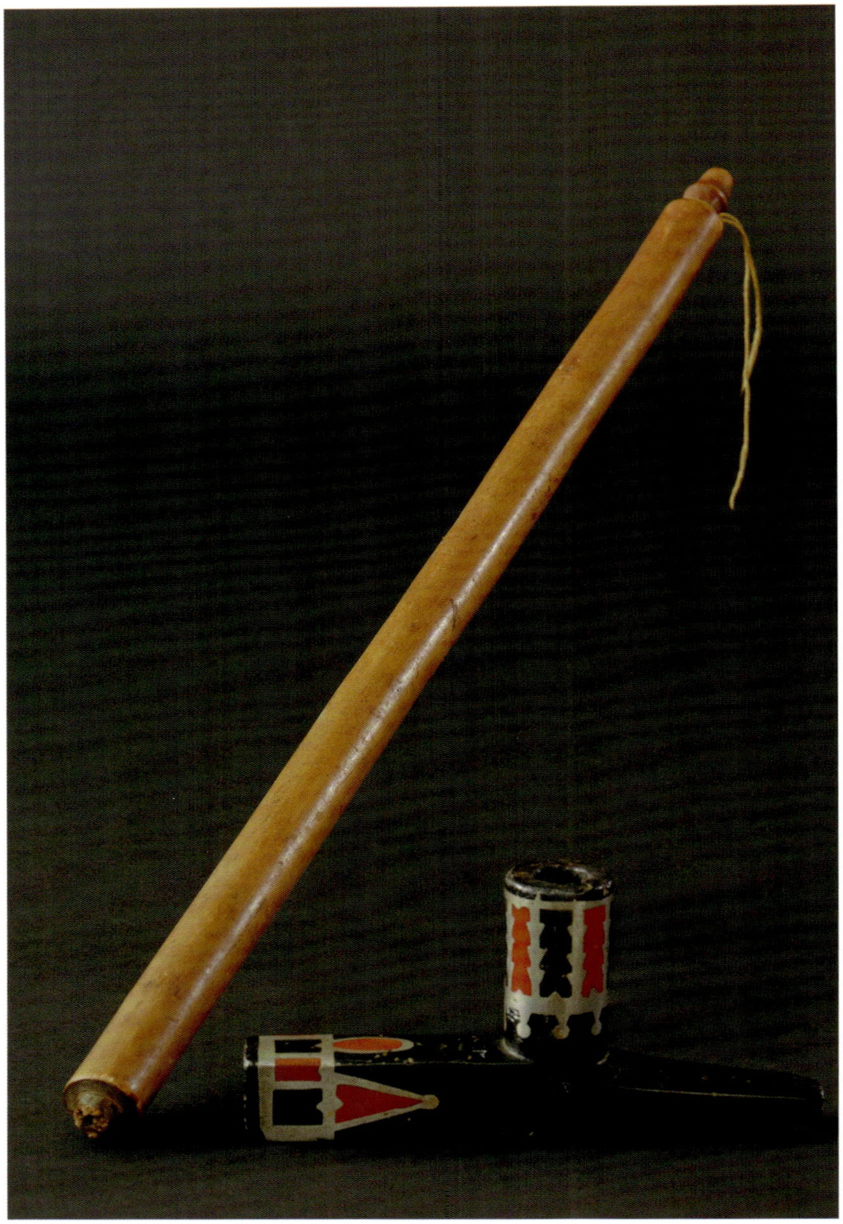

5.28. **Pipe bowl and stem**
Mandan, Upper Missouri Region, ca. 1850
Wood, steatite, catlinite, lead; bowl: 7 × 3¼ inches; stem: 20¾ inches
Plains Indian Museum, NA.504.468

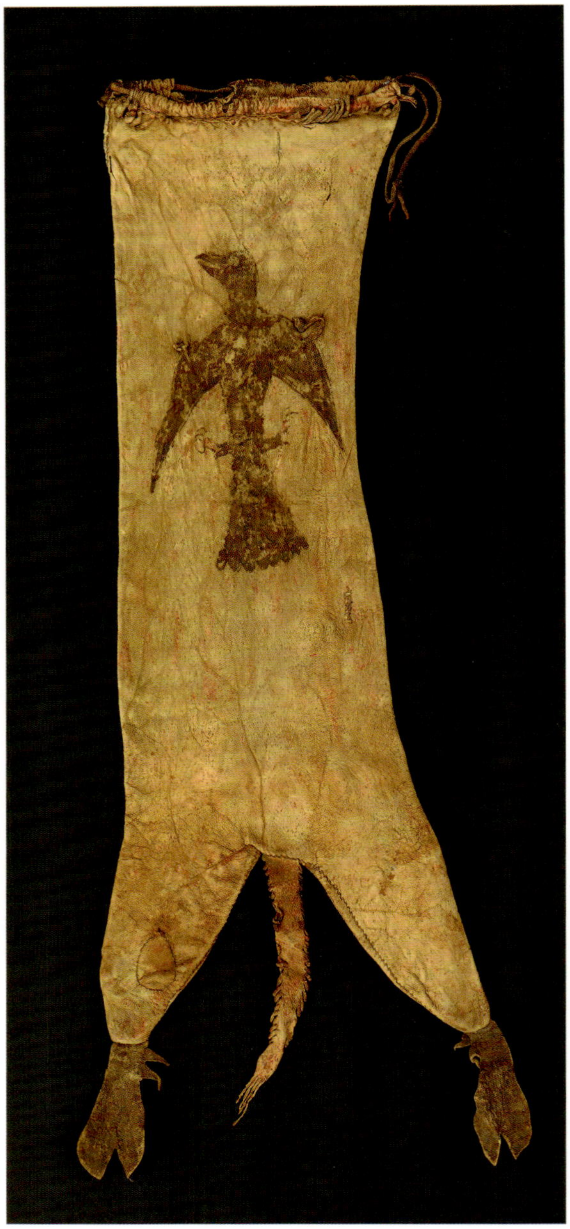

5.29. **Pipe bag**
Lakota (Sioux), Northern Plains, ca. 1860
Tanned hide, pigment, sinew; 25¾ × 8¾ inches
Plains Indian Museum, NA.504.398

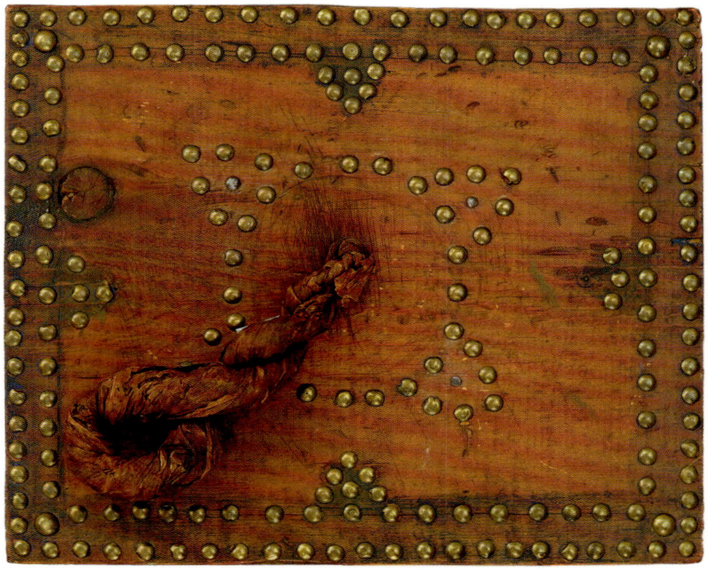

5.30. **Tobacco cutting board**
Niitsitapi (Blackfoot), Northern Plains, ca. 1880
Brass tacks, wood, pigment, metal nails; 11½ × 9½ inches
Plains Indian Museum, NA.504.409

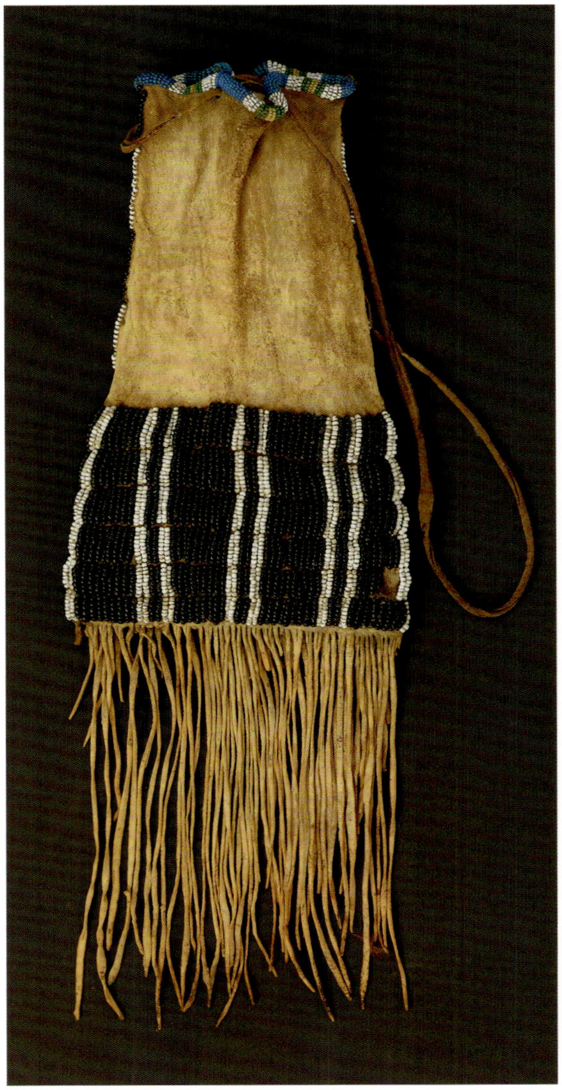

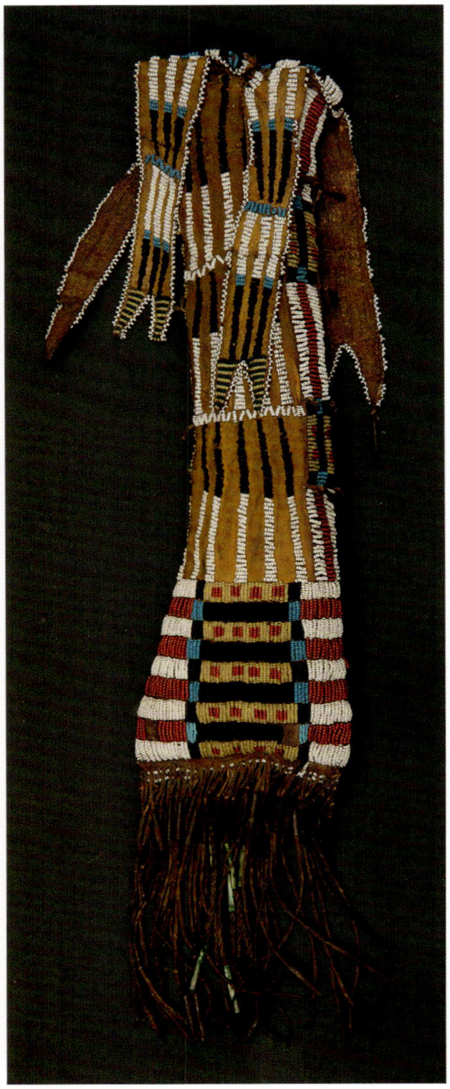

LEFT:
5.31. **Tobacco bag**
Niitsitapi (Blackfoot), Northern Plains, ca. 1850
Glass beads, sinew, tanned hide; 10¾ × 6¾ inches
Plains Indian Museum, NA.504.402

RIGHT:
5.32. **Pipe bag**
Hinono'ei (Arapaho), Southern Plains, ca. 1870
Tanned hide, glass beads, pigments, cotton thread; 31½ × 5 inches
Plains Indian Museum, NA.504.405

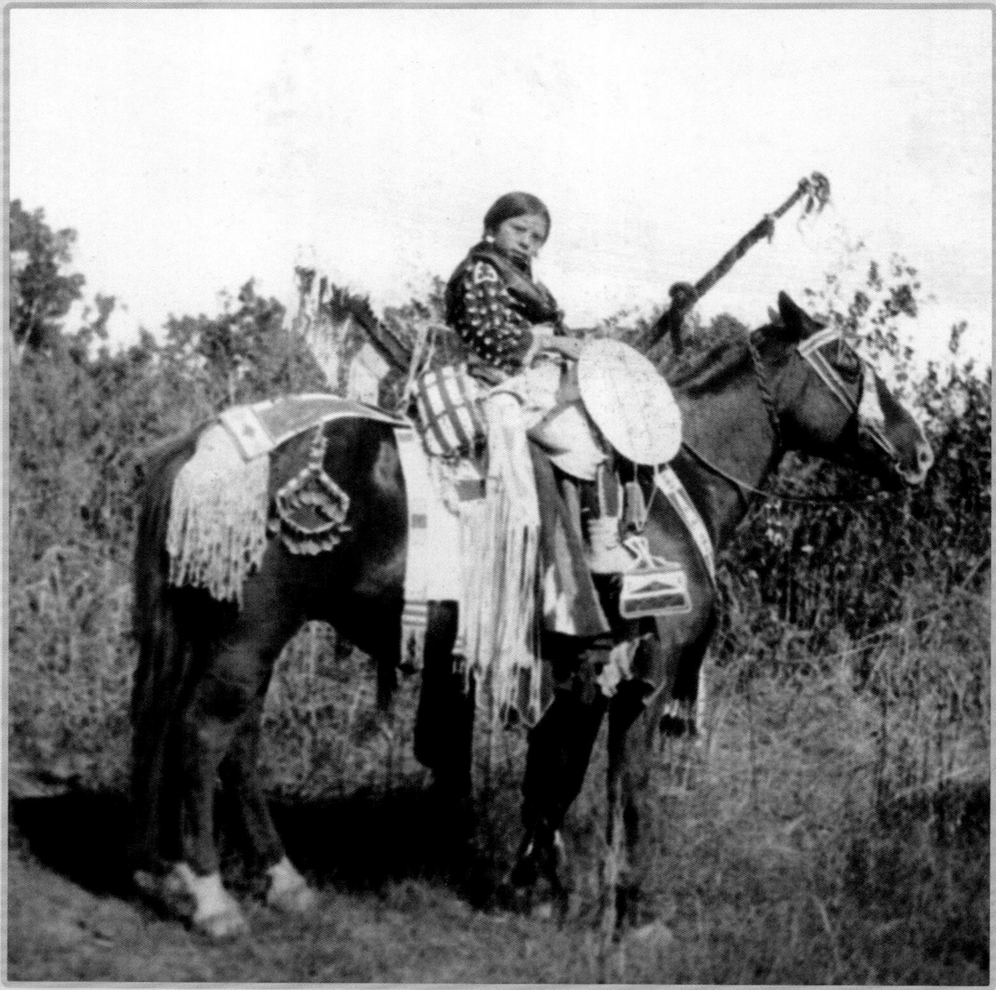

6 Plains Indian People and Their Horses

Two Shields sang the following song for the ethnomusicologist Frances Densmore during her research on Lakota and Dakota music during 1911–1914 on the Standing Rock and Sisseton Wahpeton Oyate (Lake Traverse) Reservations of present-day North and South Dakota.

see them
prancing
they come
neighing
they come
a Horse nation
see them
prancing
they come
neighing
they come[1]

This song of the Horse Society, possibly derived from a vision, evokes a lively image and conveys the pride and admiration of a warrior for the kindred spirit of a horse. The horse aided Two Shields in buffalo hunting, migration, and warfare; and as a Lakota, not only enhanced his way of life but made it possible.

CENTAURS IN THEIR SPIRIT

For centuries, Native people traveled the Plains to hunt, gather plants, and trade visits, with their dogs dragging lodge poles, and carrying their tipis and other belongings in packs or on travois. Natives adapted this means of travel with the acquisition of horses, which they acquired from Southwestern settlements after the Pueblo Revolt of 1680 when the Spanish were driven out of the region.[2] By the end of the eighteenth century, horses had spread throughout the Plains from southwestern pueblos along established trading networks and through intertribal horse raiding.

For Native groups already living on the Plains, including Mandan, Hidatsa, Arikara, Pawnee, Crow, Plains Apache, and Blackfoot, horses provided a more efficient means of travel.

6.1. Crow girl and her horse, ready for a parade
Crow Agency, Montana, ca. 1900
Photograph by William A. Petzoldt
McCracken Research Library, Petzoldt Collection, LS.95.303

They allowed the bands to move more frequently and farther to hunt or trade, and to carry greater food supplies and more belongings. Hunters on horseback could travel farther and much faster in search of the buffalo herds, and kill them more expeditiously. For most of the tribes with previous homelands outside of the Great Plains, such as the Lakota, Dakota, Cheyenne, Arapaho, Kiowa, Comanche, and Shoshone, horses dramatically transformed their cultures as they moved into the region and adopted the buffalo-hunting way of life.[3]

Likening Kiowa men on horseback to the centaurs of Greek mythology, N. Scott Momaday describes the flowering of the tribe's culture in the early nineteenth century as "particularly vital, native, and distinct, however vulnerable and ill-fated."[4] According to Momaday's narrative, "Now it must have seemed to them that in the Southern Plains of 1800, they had reached the time and place of their fulfillment; and so it was indeed. In the course of their long journey they had acquired horses, the sun dance religion, and a certain love and possession of the prairies. They had become centaurs in their spirit."[5]

Many tribal stories recount the first time Native people encountered horses, and as they provided numerous advantages for travel and in warfare, how they became an essential part of their lives. A Piegan (Blackfoot) story tells of their first close view of a horse that had been killed in battle with the Shoshone: "Numbers of us went to see him and we all admired him; he put us in mind of a stag that had lost his horns; and we did not know what name to give him. But as he was a slave to Man, like the dog, which carried our things, he was named the Big Dog."[6] Piegans and other Blackfoot people also referred to the horse as "elk dog." Among the Lakota, the horse was called "sacred dog." The Crow named the horse *iichiile,* which means "to search with," perhaps referring to its use in searching for enemies and game.[7] Other names for the horse among Native people that emphasize its spiritual qualities include "mystery dog," "medicine dog," and "sky dog," reflecting the belief of some people that horses descended from the sky.[8]

Dogs continued to be useful and valued among Plains Indian people. Women used their dog travois in daily tasks for carrying light loads and gathering firewood. Dogs were particularly efficient in deeper snows where horses often struggled. They also continued to play important roles as companions and guardians of the villages, even as horses assumed much of their significance in terms of practicality, spirituality, and symbolism. For some tribes, dogs were eaten as a sacred food during healing and other ceremonies.[9] For others, dogs were sources of food when game was scarce. Artists carved and painted images of dogs, wolves, or coyotes in pipestone and on rock bluffs, caves, and rock shelters.

Horses had several beneficial qualities that were valuable for the buffalo-hunting peoples of the Plains. In addition to their practical uses and advantages of increased mobility, large herds of horses afforded increased social status, wealth, and power. Hunters on horseback could pursue buffalo much faster and at greater distances than on foot. Killing the buffalo from horseback was also more efficient than previous methods. Families were able to carry larger amounts of food and heavier belongings, as well as larger tipis made of many more buffalo hides. They were able to travel to trading centers such as those established at the Hidatsa, Mandan, and Arikara villages on the Upper Missouri River and Euro-American trading posts. They were also able to more easily transport small children, elders, and relatives who were ill or injured. Wooden Leg of the Cheyenne told of riding in a travois as a small boy when his family traveled:

> As a little boy I used to ride in a travois basket when the tribe moved camp. Two long lodge poles were crossed over the shoulders or tied to the sides of a horse. Thus they were dragged over the country. Buffalo skins were used to stretch across between the widely gaping poles behind the horse. Upon or into these bagging skins were placed all of the family property, in rawhide satchels or as separate loose articles. The smaller children also rode there. I have fond recollections of this kind of traveling. Many an hour I have slept in that kind of gentle bed.[10]

Men worked to build their personal horse herds, not only for their practical advantages but also for the associated prestige they bestowed. Throughout the Plains, Native people universally recognized the value of horses. Plains Indians considered the ownership of many horses, primarily acquired through capture from other tribes, as a symbol of wealth. Losses of horses to enemies, especially horses of high prestige such as those used in running buffalo, were serious matters to be avenged through reciprocal raiding. In acts of generosity required for leadership positions, men also increased their status through providing horses to less fortunate individuals and families in need.

Two Leggings of the Crow recounted the story of one successful horse raid against a Lakota camp and his excitement about his homecoming that would be commemorated in a celebration and recognition of the honors, prestige, and praise he would receive for his achievements.

> We had captured over a hundred head, the night was still early, and we had a good chance to get away. It would bring me greater honors to lead them back safely without having killed a man, and I did not want to spoil this. I felt that my medicine had kept the Sioux's attention off their horses. . . . Now there was no danger of being overtaken and we all felt good. As I rode I thought of the celebration waiting for us and of the praise I would receive for being leader. I pictured the older men leading me through camp, singing songs about me, and calling out my name. I was so happy I sang my medicine song: "Anywhere I go, I thank you." The bunch of horses running before us looked so fine I could not help myself and sang my song again.[11]

Representing the Lakota point of view, in about 1913 on the Standing Rock Reservation, Frances Densmore recorded a song by Jaw, also known by the name His Battle (Okícize-táwa). The song extols his success in capturing horses from the Crow as a young man:

> Friend
> be alert
> any way
> I wish
> to roam about
> horses
> I will seek[12]

In one night raid on the Crow, Jaw captured seventy horses, and later told Densmore that "I did not waken nor kill any of the Crows; I just took their horses. No Sioux ever took more horses than that in one night."[13]

Men trained horses that were used in buffalo hunting to maneuver in and out of buffalo herds, bringing the hunter closer to the animals, and quickly veering away. Men also practiced riding on horses trained for warfare. War horses were seen as extensions of their owners, with whom they had developed special relationships. "To be alone with our war-horses . . . teaches them to understand us and us to understand them," said the Crow leader Plenty Coups. He also recounted, "My horse fights with me and fasts with me, because if he is to carry me in battle he must know my heart and I must know his or we will never become brothers."[14]

Women also owned horses, which they received from relatives or through trade and used for riding and pulling travois. Among the Blackfoot and other tribes, women were free to give their horses away, trade, or loan them as they wished.[15] The Northern Cheyenne elder Iron Teeth recalled her skills in riding and breaking horses:

> The first time I rode alone on horseback occurred when I was about ten years old. My father gave me a yearling colt. When we were traveling, my mother would put packs upon the colt with me. Usually I had two badger skins filled with dried chokecherries behind me, swinging down the colt's sides. Boys teased me by riding up close and lashing my colt to make it jump. At first I was frightened and they laughed at me. But I soon got used to it and after a little while I became a good rider.
>
> After I grew older I liked to break horses. When I became a woman I never asked any man to tame my horses for me . . . Lots of wild horses used to be running loose on the plains to the southward. I had a good running horse when I was a young woman, and I always carried with me a lariat rope made of spun and plaited buffalo hair . . . One time, after my marriage, I was riding with my baby strapped to my back when I saw some wild horses. I put the baby in its cradle board down on the prairie and got after the herd. That day I caught two horses.[16]

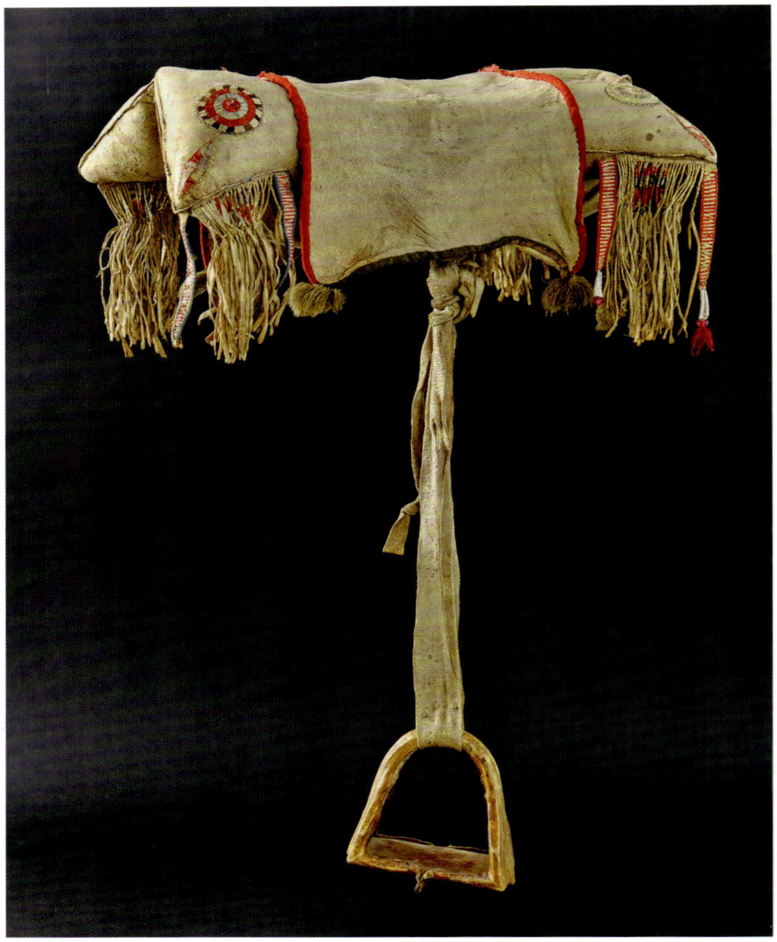

6.2. **Pad saddle**
N'hilaw' (Plains Cree), Northern Plains, ca. 1865
Tanned hide, rawhide, wood, dyed porcupine quills, velvet cloth, dentalium shells, glass beads, cotton cloth, silk, cotton thread, sinew; 21½ × 20½ × 3¾ inches
Plains Indian Museum, NA.403.222

Both men and women developed specialized equipment for riding and handling horses. Although men often rode bareback, women made pad saddles of tanned buffalo, deer, or elk hide for their male relatives (fig. 6.2). Women also made saddle blankets of tanned hide, some of which were undecorated with the hair remaining, while others were embellished in porcupine

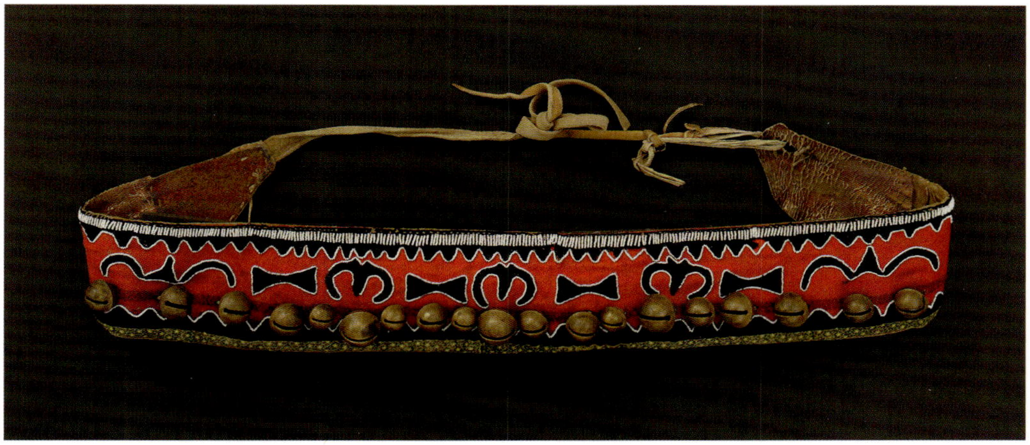

6.3. **Martingale**
Niitsitapi (Blackfoot) or Cayuse, Northern Plains or Plateau, ca. 1880
Tanned hide, cotton cloth, glass beads, brass bells, wool cloth, cotton thread; 48 × 4 inches
Plains Indian Museum, NA.403.265

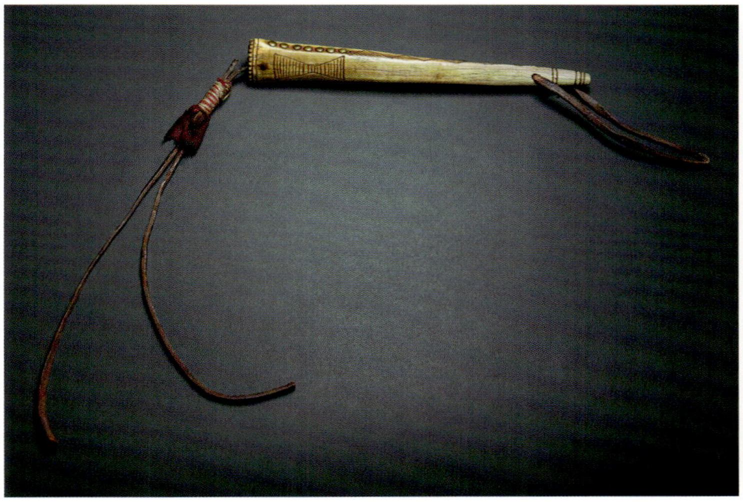

6.4. **Quirt**
Niitsitapi (Blackfoot), Northern Plains, ca. 1860
Elk antler, brass tacks, metal, wood, pigment, nails, sinew, tanned hide, wool cloth; 31¾ inches, with 4½-inch diameter
Plains Indian Museum, NA.403.242

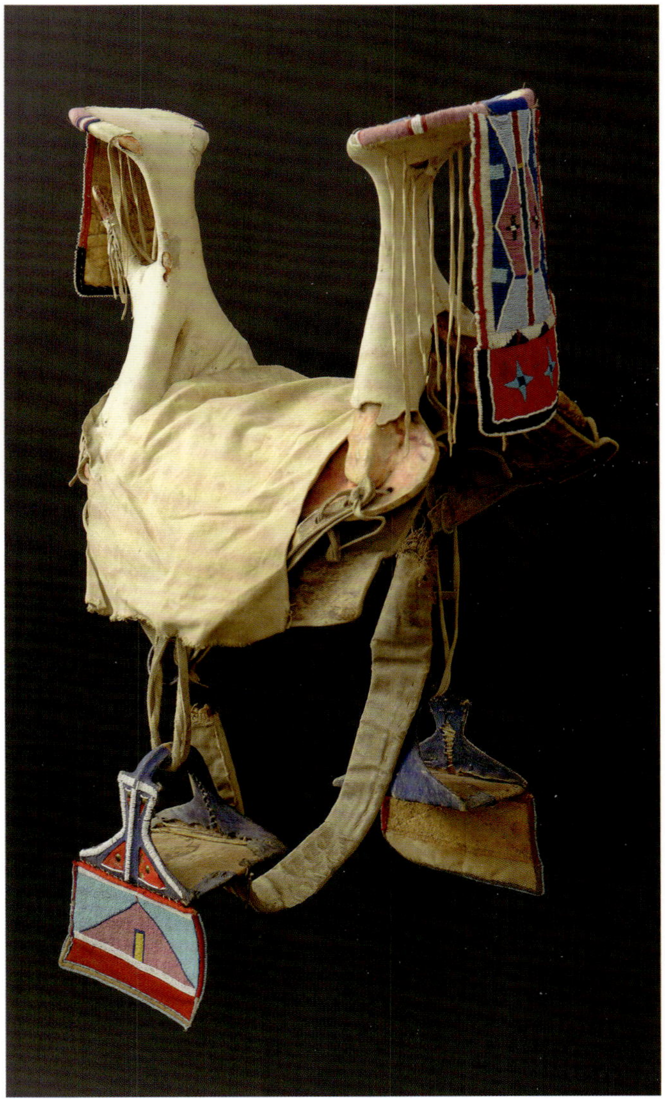

6.5. **Saddle and stirrups**
Apsáalooke (Crow), Northern Plains, ca. 1900
Wood, rawhide, cloth, beads, burlap, pigment, thread, tacks, tanned hide; 17½ × 26½ × 19 inches
Plains Indian Museum, NA.403.281

Among Northern Plains people, horse pageantry became more elaborate as the use of horses in warfare and hunting decreased. For Crow parades, full horse regalia included a saddle, beaded crupper, bridle, forehead ornament, saddle blanket, stirrups, and a martingale.

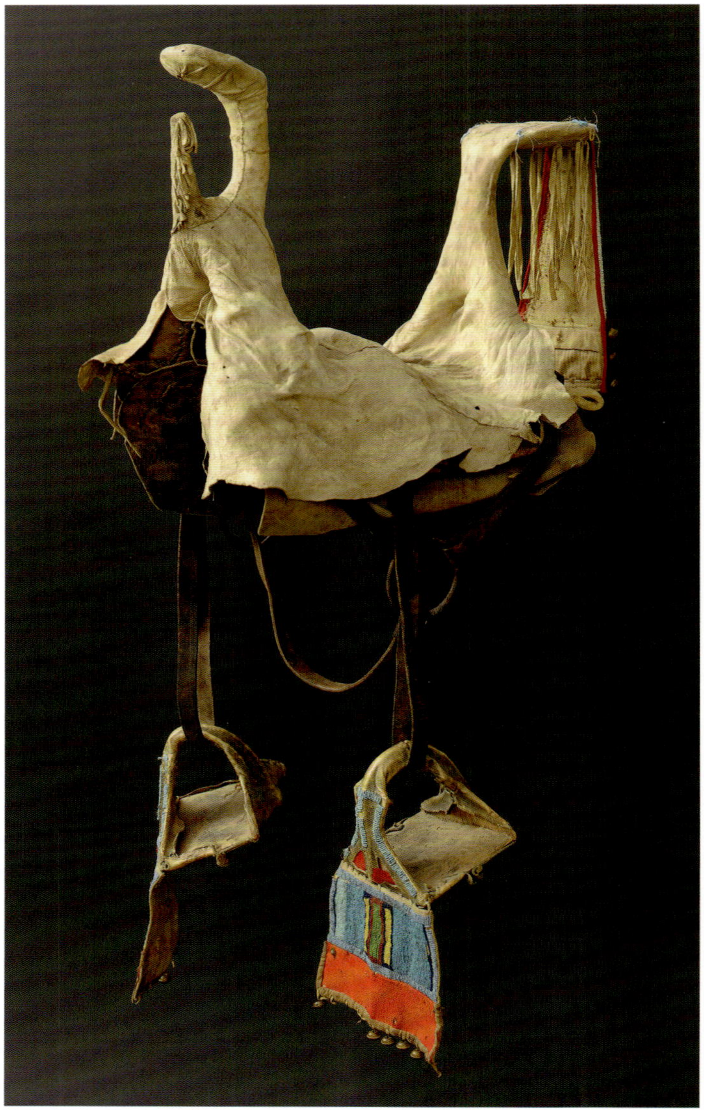

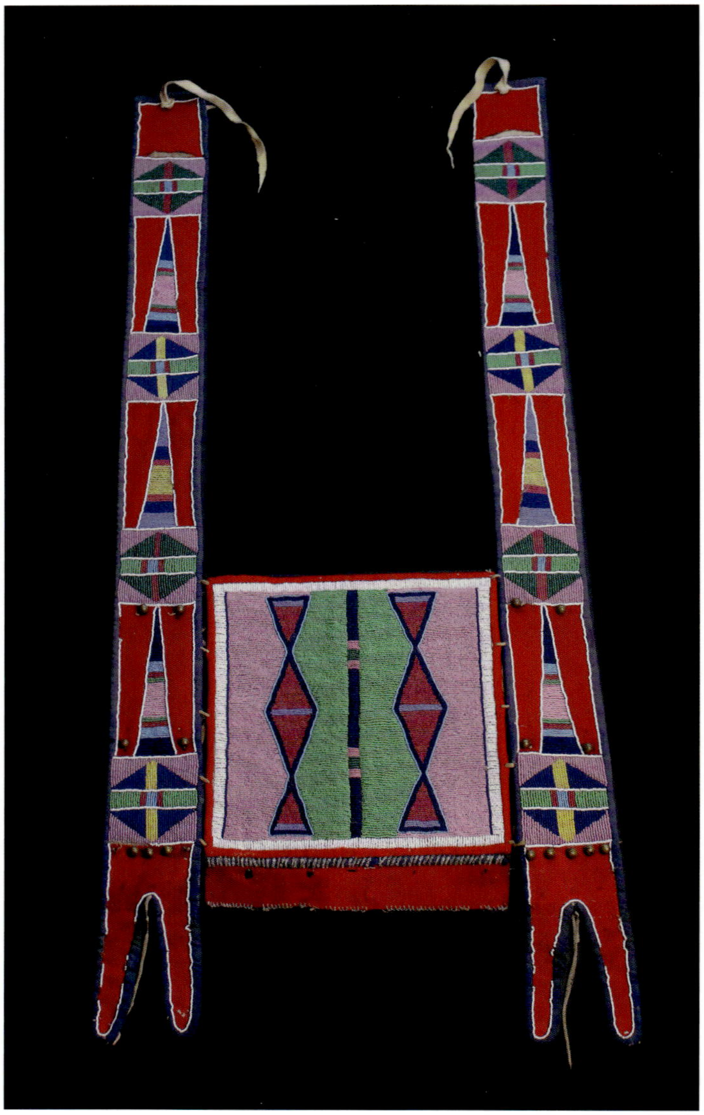

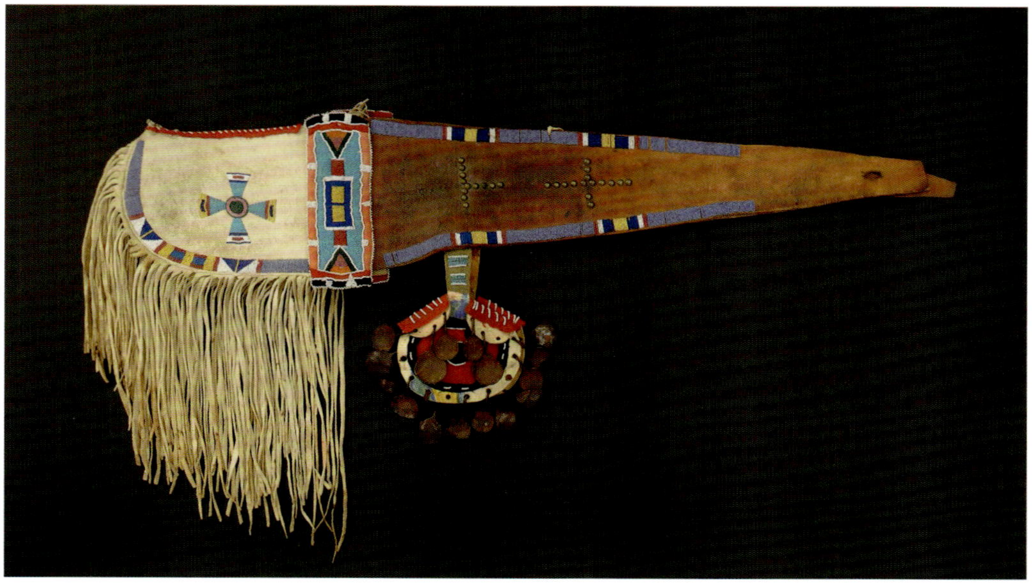

6.8. **Crupper**
Apsáalooke (Crow), Northern Plains, ca. 1890
Brass tacks, metal, rawhide, leather, pigment, glass beads, sinew, tanned hide, wool cloth, cotton thread; 42 × 9½ inches
Plains Indian Museum, NA.403.217

quillwork and beadwork. Saddles made of elk antler or wood covered in rawhide had high pommels and cantles and stirrups made of bent wood covered in rawhide. Other specialized horse gear included wood or bone quirts, decorated head ornaments and masks, bridles and headstalls, martingales, cruppers, and saddlebags (figs. 6.3 and 6.4).

In the Dyck collection are superb examples of Crow horsemanship and distinctive artistry, including two women's saddles, a martingale, a crupper, and a bridle dating from 1880 to 1900 (figs. 6.5, 6.6, 6.7, 6.8, and 6.9). During this period on the reservation, the Crow began their tradition of having parades at special events and on holidays.[17] During the parades, Crow men and women dressed in their finest regalia and rode horses decorated with beautifully made saddles, bridles, cruppers, and other accoutrements. The parades had origins in earlier periods when the bands moved in organized processions to new locations or on seasonal buffalo hunts. There were antecedents also in the rides of victorious warriors returning to their camps after successful raids and battles with their horses painted and decorated with feathers. The parade tradition continues today at the annual Crow Fair, when a procession of men, women, and children and their horses, all adorned in beautiful beaded regalia, ride daily through camp.

Plains Indian people conveyed the significance of horses through images painted and beaded on clothing, carved in stone for pipe bowls, and carved in wood for dance sticks and

OPPOSITE, LEFT:
6.6. **Saddle and stirrups**
Apsáalooke (Crow), Northern Plains, ca. 1880
Commercially tanned leather, metal, wood, rawhide, horsehair, cotton cloth, glass beads, tanned hide, brass bells, wool cloth, cotton thread, velvet cloth;
saddle: 17 × 21¾ × 13 inches;
stirrups: 25 × 8 ½ inches
Plains Indian Museum, NA.403.216

OPPOSITE, RIGHT:
6.7. **Martingale**
Apsáalooke (Crow), Montana, ca. 1890
Cotton cloth, glass beads, brass buttons, tanned hide, wool cloth, cotton thread, commercial canvas;
38 × 16½ inches
Plains Indian Museum, NA.403.288

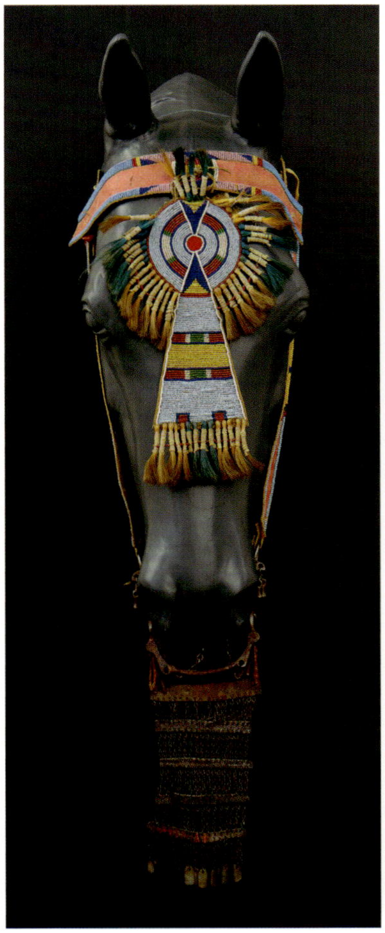

6.9. **Bridle**
Apsáalooke (Crow), Montana, ca. 1880
Iron, dye, cotton cloth, glass beads, parfleche, horse hair, tanned hide, wool cloth, cotton thread, pigments;
28 × 14¼ inches
Plains Indian Museum, NA.403.243

Parades in which Apsáalooke men and women rode horses decorated in beautifully made gear were an important part of early reservation life. The parades were reminiscent of pre-reservation life when the bands moved seasonally.

6.10. **Pipe bowl and stem**
Otoe, Central Plains, ca. 1880
Wood, pipestone (catlinite), pigment;
bowl: 5 × 2¾ inches; stem: 10½ × ⅞ inches (diameter)
Plains Indian Museum, NA.504.466

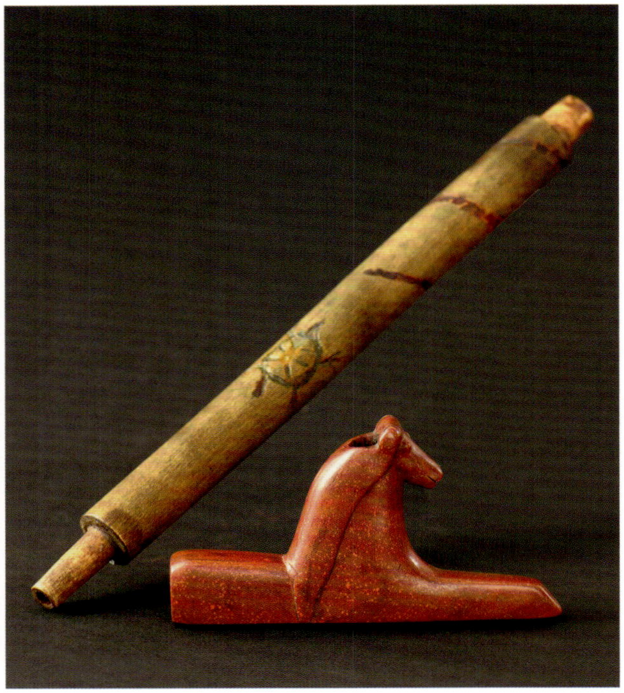

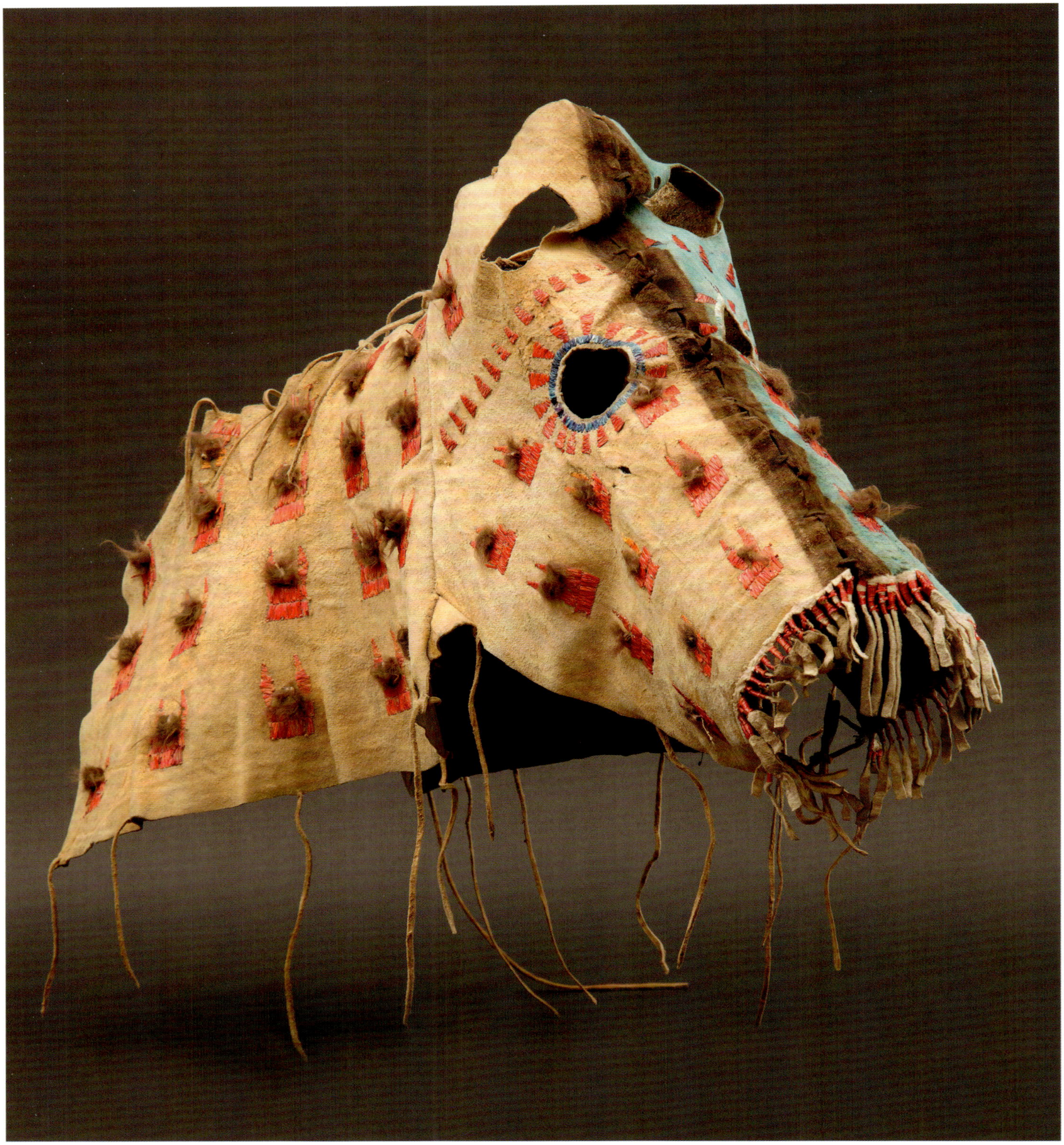

war clubs. Men recorded successful horse raids on lodge covers, war shirts, hide paintings, and, later, ledger drawings (fig. 6.10).

Drawing from visionary experiences, men painted and adorned their fastest and finest horses with feathers, medicine bags, amulets, and strips of wool cloth to enhance their swiftness, agility, and endurance in battle. According to Densmore, before going into battle, Jaw painted a red crescent over his mouth with the ends extending upward, and painted both his feet and hands red as well. He also painted a large red crescent on the horse's chest, a smaller one on the horse's left hip, and the entire end of the horse's nose in yellow. If the horse performed well in battle, he put a feather in its mane or tail or a strip of red trade cloth around its neck. He also carried two medicine bags with herbs for himself and his horse, with the horse's bag tied on the bit of his bridle.[18]

Men demonstrated respect for their best horses, those who were specially trained to perform well in warfare or in chasing buffalo, by adorning them in beautiful regalia. For special horses, with the help of female relatives, they created beaded, painted, and porcupine-quilled horse

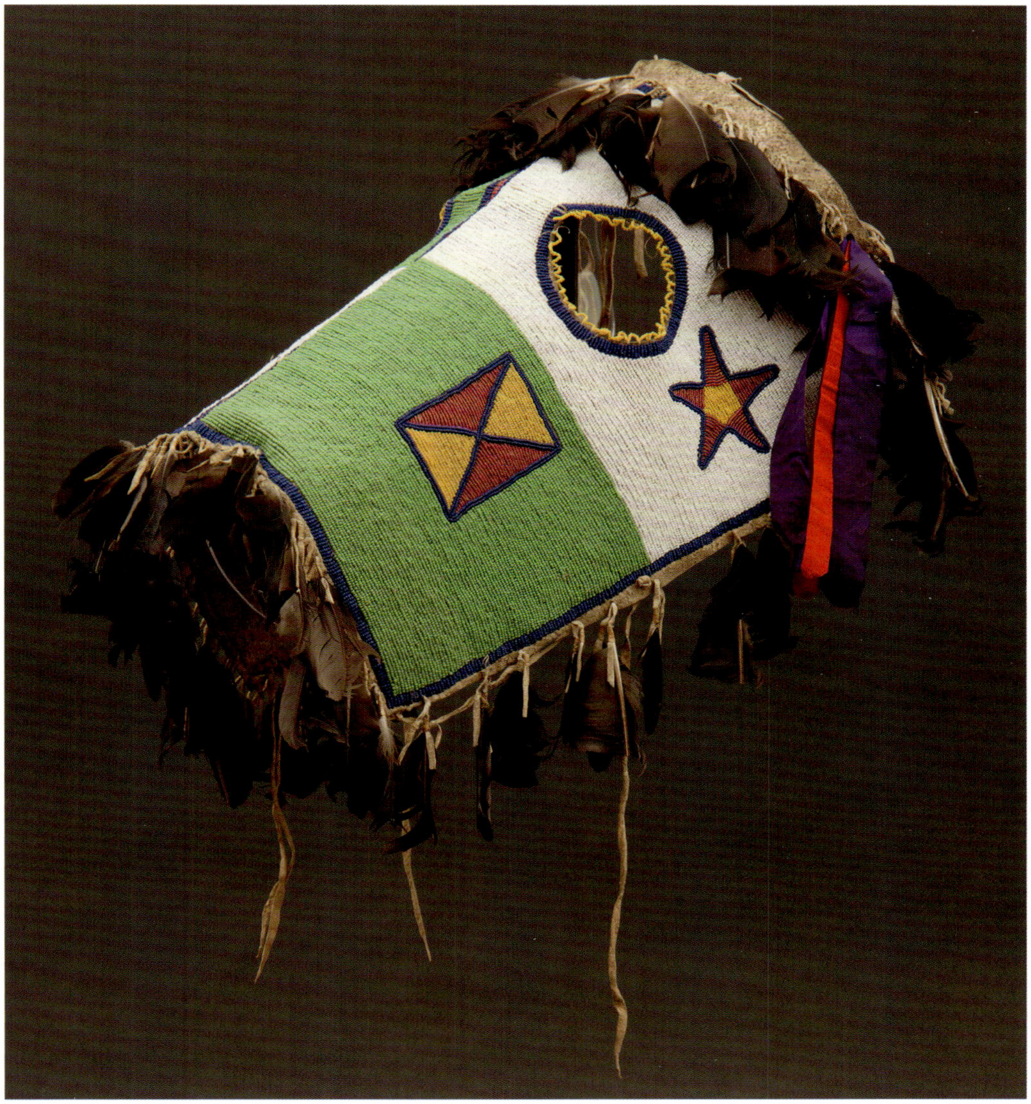

OPPOSITE:
6.11. **Horse mask**
Niitsitapi (Blackfoot), Northern Plains, ca. 1850
Tanned buffalo hide, buffalo hair, pigments, dyed porcupine quills, sinew; 35 × 20½ inches
Plains Indian Museum, NA.403.226

6.12. **Horse mask**
Kainai (Blood), Northern Plains, ca. 1870
Tanned hide, glass beads, silk ribbon, raven feathers; 20 × 13 inches
Plains Indian Museum, NA.403.221

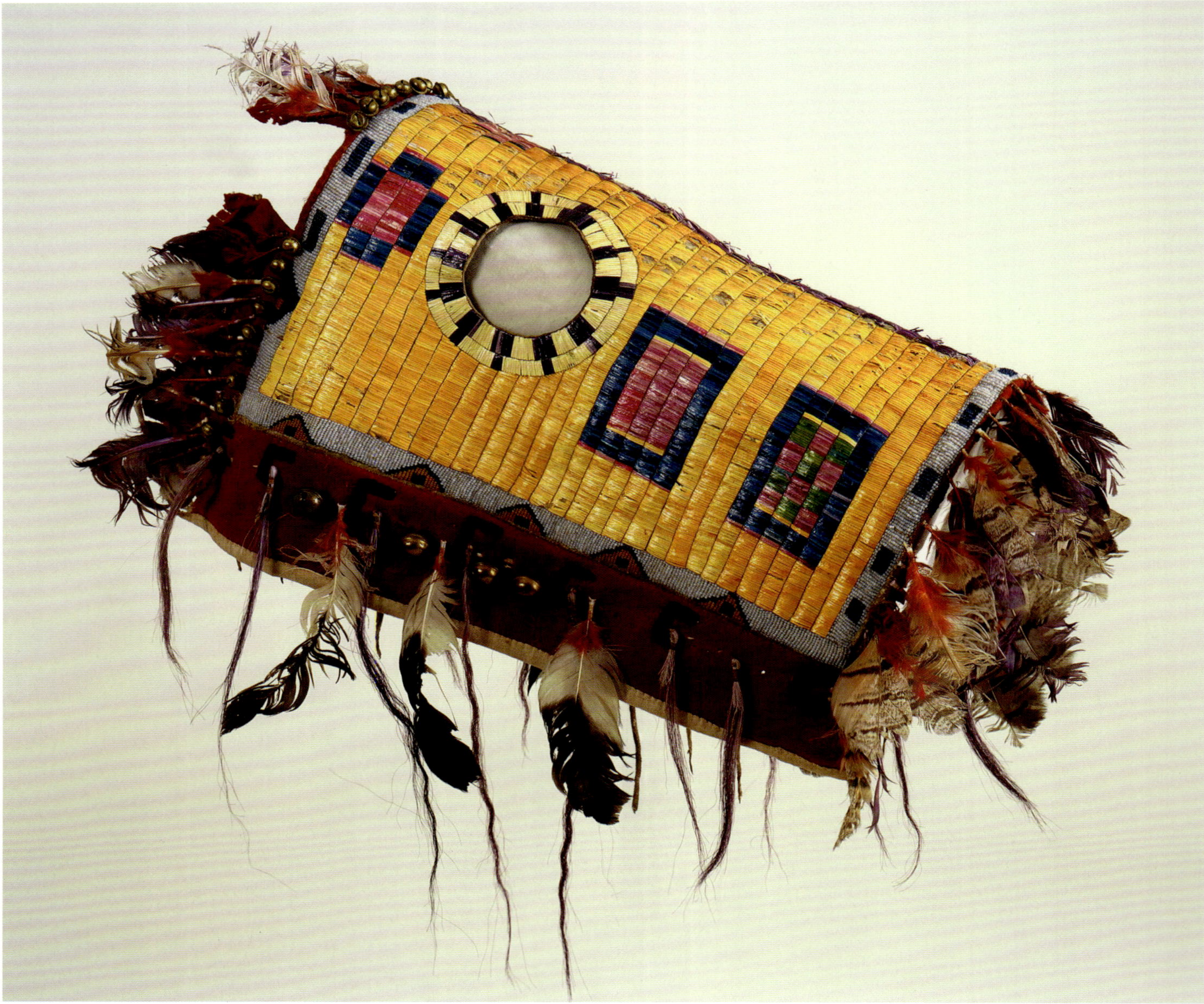

6.13 and 6.14.
Medicine Owl (1966–1919)
Horse mask
Amskapi Pikuni (Blackfeet), Blackfeet Reservation, Montana, ca. 1896
Dyed porcupine quills, leather, cloth, pigment, feathers; 23½ × 24 inches
Plains Indian Museum, NA.403.214

According to Dyck, Medicine Owl made and used this mask.

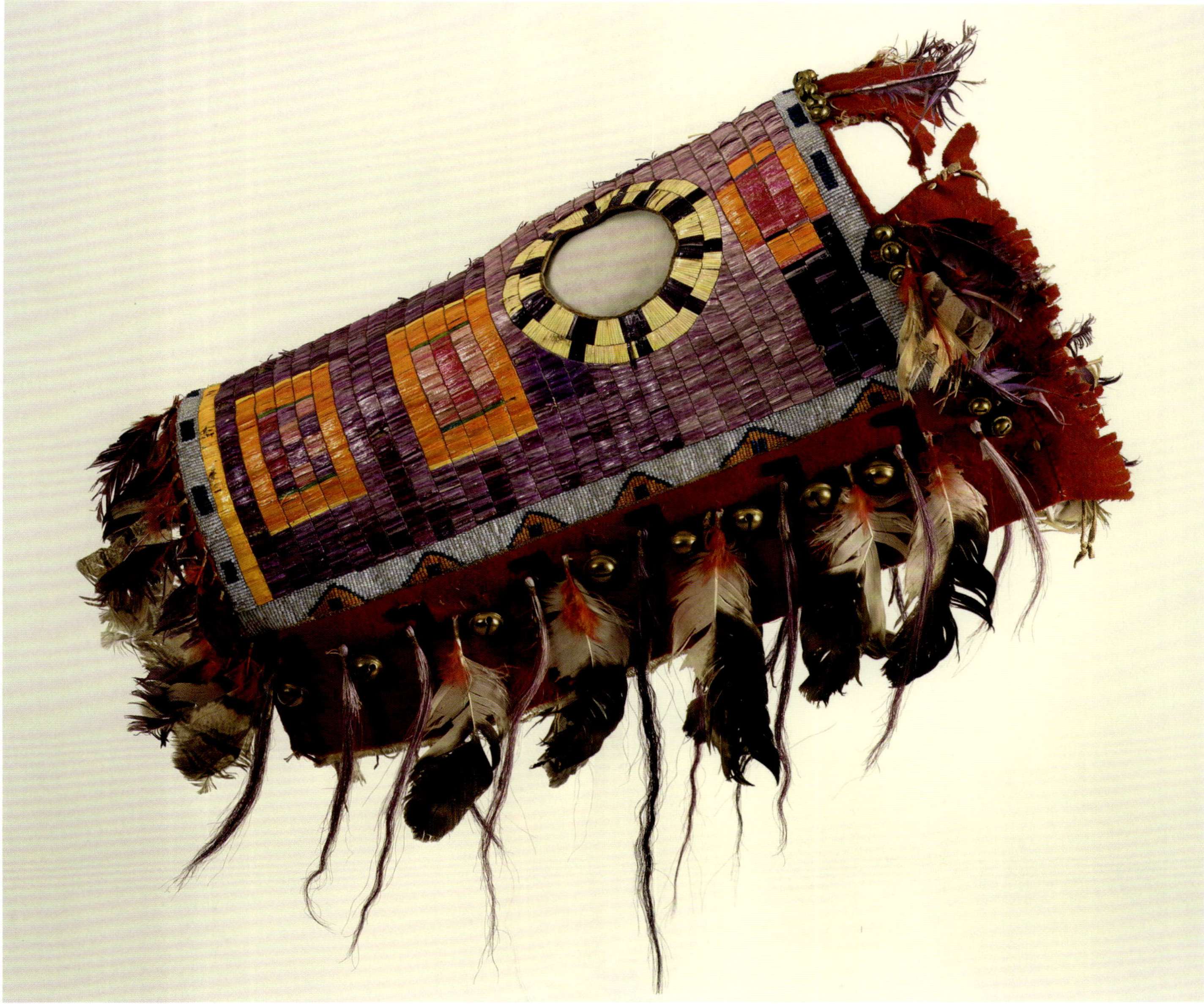

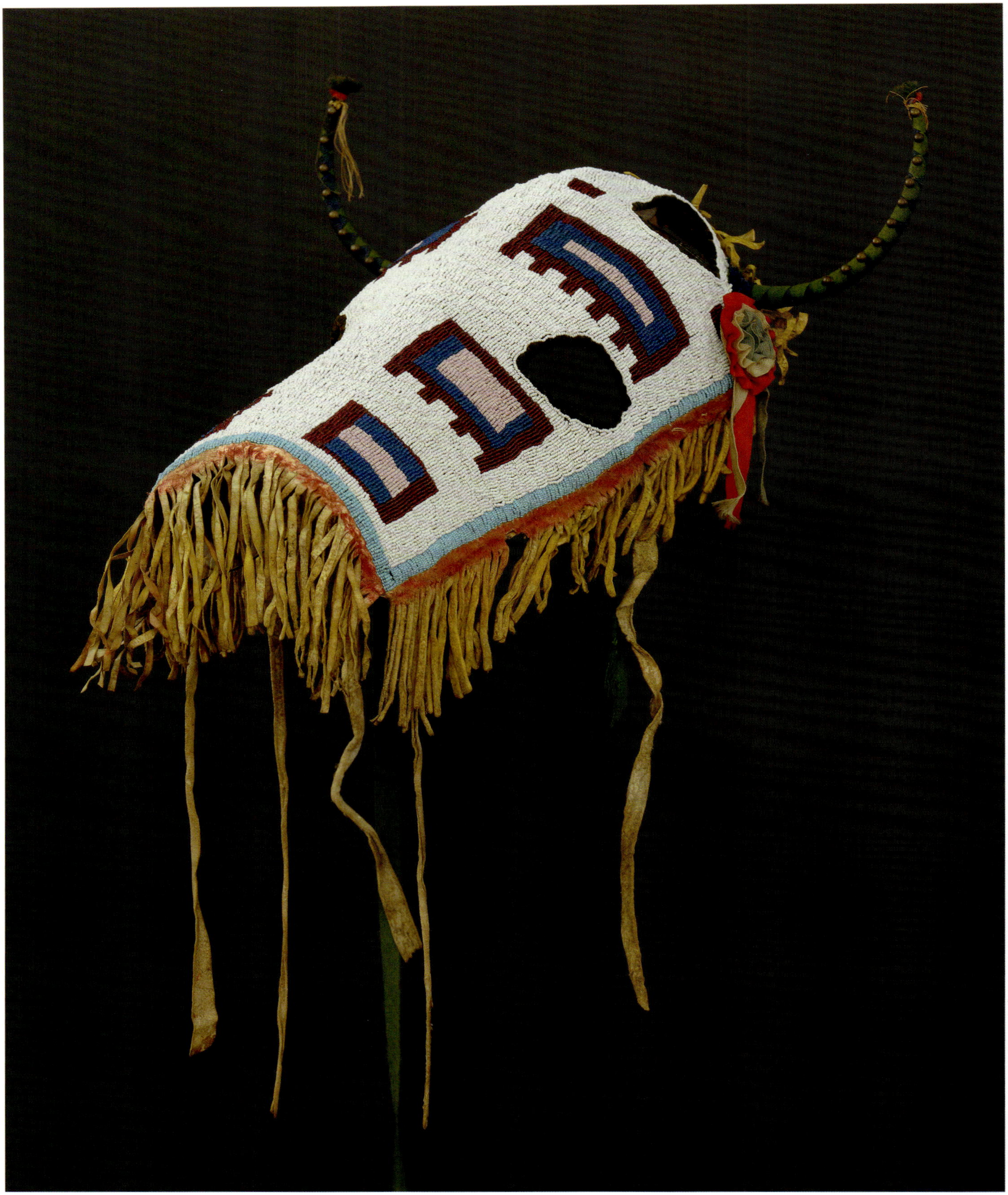

hoods and masks, bridles, and other equipment for parades. Horse adornment took place as men prepared to leave for battle, returned from successful raids, and during public celebrations.

There are four spectacular horse masks in the Paul Dyck Collection, all attributed to the Blackfoot. An early mask dating from the mid-nineteenth century was made of tanned buffalo hide divided into two halves: one painted blue; and the other unpainted (fig. 6.11). The design possibly represents night and day. The halves are connected by lacing made of strips that were painted brown, as is the center line that separates the two sides. Over most of the mask are sixty-four forked motifs in red porcupine quillwork symbolizing buffalo hooves. Tufts of buffalo hair are attached to the top of each quilled hoof. Blue quillwork circles bordered by red arrow-shaped designs surround the eye openings of the mask. This design may symbolize the flashing eyes of the thunderbird that were capable of producing lightning. Fringe wrapped in red porcupine quills hangs from the nose of the hood. The design of this mask is unusual because, unlike others from the Blackfoot, it would have covered the entire head and a large part of the neck of the horse who wore it.

A second mask, from the Kainai people and dating to around 1870, is covered fully in vibrant red, green, yellow, and dark blue beadwork in star and rectangular designs (fig. 6.12). Cut raven feathers fringe the borders, and silk ribbons hang from the top of the mask. Another mask also features fringing of cut raptor feathers around the borders, a characteristic of nineteenth-century Blackfoot examples. In this case, the feathers are from golden eagles and owls. Again, the mask is divided into two halves: one predominately covered in yellow porcupine quillwork, and the other in purple, with parallel rectangular designs on each side and circular highlighting of the eye openings (figs. 6.13 and 6.14). The quillwork body of the mask is edged in beadwork and red wool cloth decorated with brass bells. According to Dyck's notes, Medicine Owl (approximately 1866–1919), who lived on the Blackfeet Reservation in present-day northern Montana, made the mask. Medicine Owl was a member of the Crazy Dog Society, and, like other warrior society members, belonged to the Blackfeet tribal police, serving as captain in 1899.

The fourth horse mask in the Dyck collection, dating from about 1875, features horns carved of wood and wrapped with black cotton cloth (fig. 6.15). Brass upholstery tacks, silk ribbons, and feather fluffs decorate the horns. The horns are reminiscent of earlier nineteenth-century Blackfoot horse masks made with buffalo horns, hide, and, sometimes, the head. The entire mask is covered in elegant beadwork with a white background and blue, dark red, and pink rectangular designs. The artist who made this mask painted the edges in red ochre, which is a sacred paint among the Blackfoot and many other Plains peoples. Silk ribbon rosettes hang from each side of the mask below the ear openings, and hide fringes edge the borders of the mask.

6.15. **Horse mask**
Niitsitapi (Blackfoot), Northern Plains, ca. 1875
Tanned buffalo hide, glass beads, brass tacks, wood, cotton cloth, silk ribbon; 25 × 18 inches
Plains Indian Museum, NA.403.215

Like other significant and powerful beings, horses appeared to men through dreams and visions. Horse visions brought men power that ensured their success in capturing and training horses, hunting, and warfare. Such visions also brought healing powers to individuals, such as the ability to cure illness, or to those who had been wounded. According to Joseph Medicine Crow, in speaking of the significance of horses among the Crow, horse medicine was a blessing characterized by the power, stamina, speed, and agility of a horse. Men with horse medicine also had an unusual ability for finding and owning good horses for hunting, warfare, and racing.[19]

> A man with horse medicine had special songs about horses that he would sing in certain ceremonies and dances. Whenever he was asked to name a child, he would invariably use the word *horse* in the name. By so doing, he expressed a wish and prayer that the child would grow to live up to the meaning of the name. Among the Crows today there are many family names such as Takes a Horse, Rides a Horse, Good Horse, and so on.[20]

To Plains Indian people, horses were gifts that made their lives as buffalo hunters on the Great Plains possible. The introduction of the horse also brought them spiritual blessings. Through prayers, ceremonies, and songs, they asked that the gift of many horses and their associated powers be bestowed upon them, as in this Lakota song.

In a sacred manner
I live
To the heavens
I gazed
In a sacred manner
I live
My horses
are many[21]

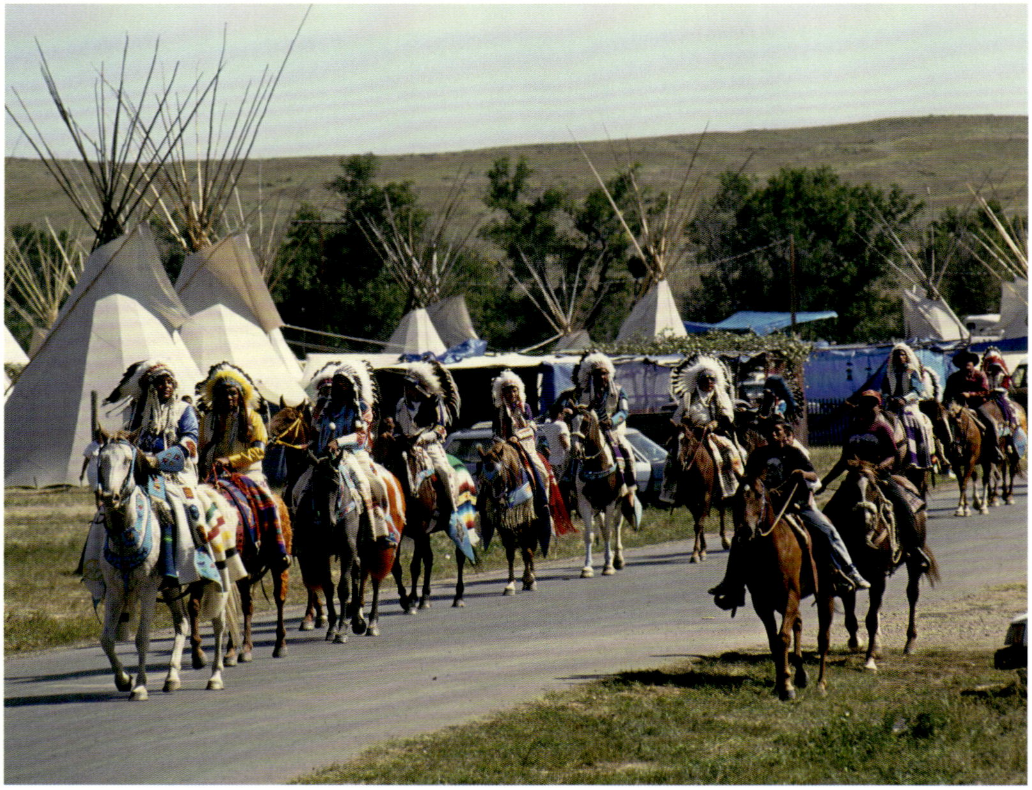

6.16. **Parade riders**
Crow Fair, Crow Agency, Montana, August 1992
Photograph by Ken Blackbird
McCracken Research Library, P.426.26784

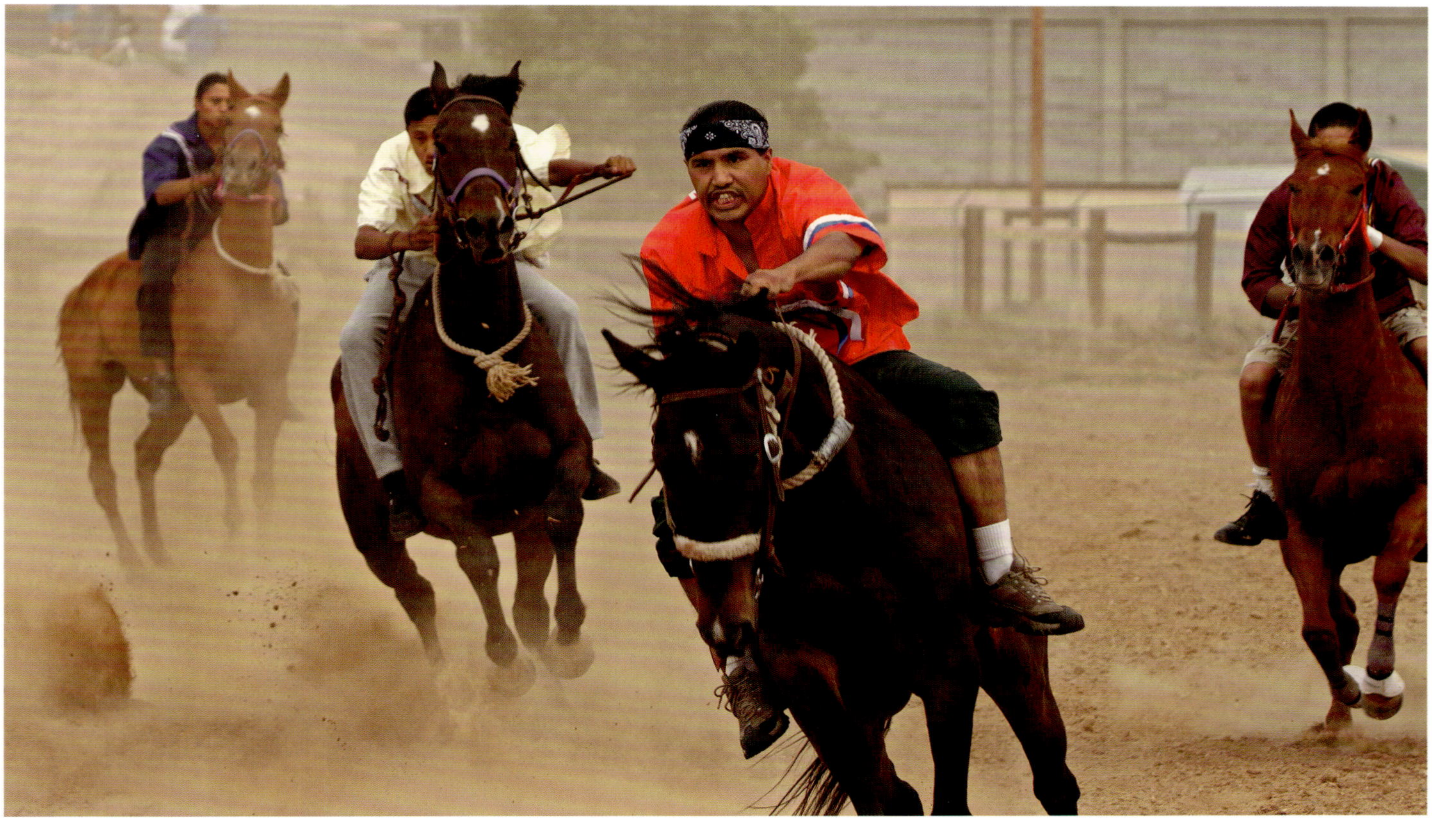

6.17. **Indian relay race**
Wind River Reservation, Ethete, Wyoming, June 2005
Photograph by Ken Blackbird
McCracken Research Library, P.426.05381

Contemporary Native people continue to acknowledge and celebrate the significance of the horse at parades at the annual Crow Fair, the Pendleton Round-Up, Calgary Stampede, North American Indian Days at Browning, Montana, and tribal celebrations throughout the Plains and Plateau regions (fig. 6.16). Native ranchers breed and raise horses used for rodeos and racing. Indian cowboys and cowgirls compete in Native American rodeos held during annual tribal celebrations and other such events. Indian relay races, now held in towns and cities near reservations, have proliferated in recent years and attract large general audiences (fig. 6.17). The races provide opportunities for Native men and women to demonstrate their horsemanship and skills, such as those first developed by their ancestors beginning in the eighteenth century. In ceremonial life, horses and their regalia are prized gifts bestowed during giveaways and ritual adoptions. Artists continue to produce images of horses in their work, with some returning to the old pictographic hide painting and ledger art techniques. Through such artistry and creative endeavors endowed with pride, tradition, pageantry, and respect, Native people of the Great Plains acknowledge the many gifts received by their people through the coming of the horse.

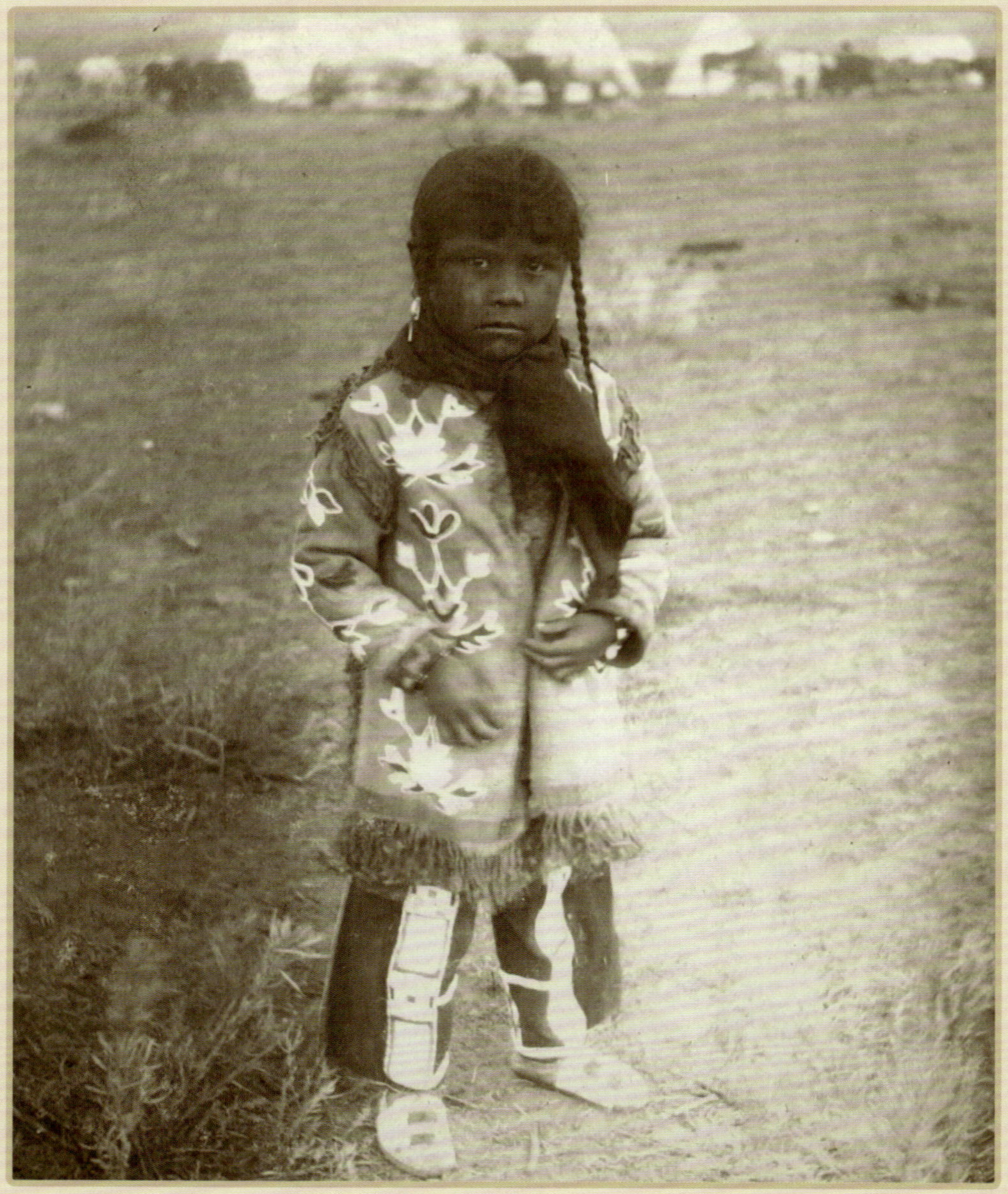

7 Enduring Legacies of the Paul Dyck Collection

Through generations prior to the arrival of Euro-Americans, Native people living in the Great Plains experienced and survived many changes and challenges as the Euro-American frontier moved west, people from the Great Lakes and other regions arrived, and new conflicts as well as trading and diplomatic alliances formed. Beginning with the successive devastating epidemics of European-introduced diseases in the late 1700s that weakened and killed massive numbers of people, the challenges multiplied and threatened indigenous cultural and physical survival. With the near extinction of the buffalo and destruction of the traditional economic pursuits of hunting, gathering, and cultivation of plants adapted for the Plains environment, Native people could not provide for themselves and their families. Government agents and missionaries prohibited Native cultural and spiritual rituals and ceremonies and attempted to compel Plains Indian people to abandon their traditional economies, languages, values, and beliefs and assume the lives of Christian farmers, ranchers, and homemakers. To hasten this process of assimilation, federal officials and religious denominations separated children from their parents, families, and communities by sending them far from home to residential boarding schools. Arthur Amiotte described the repercussions on Plains Indian societies resulting from the changes, conflicts, and environmental destruction of the late nineteenth century as follows:

> The treaty-making period that began around 1851 marked rapid and sometimes violent change from the autonomy the Plains Indian tribes had known to confinement and profound adversity. By the later 1860s and early 1870s, reservations were slowly being occupied by some tribal people willing to live the new life, though some notable leaders like Crazy Horse of the Oglala Lakota, Sitting Bull of the Hunkpapa Lakota, and Chief Joseph of the Nez Perce continued to resist relocation. But the destruction of animal and plant species on which the tribes relied prior to and after resettlement dealt them a critical blow, depriving them not only of food, but also of materials for clothing, shelter, and their traditional arts. The physical accoutrements and patterns of life would change, and in the process, give rise to new traditions and art forms.[1]

7.1. **Crow boy in beaded coat**
Crow Reservation, Montana, ca. 1898
Photograph by Fred E. Miller
McCracken Research Library, Edward Becker Collection of Crow Indian Photographs, P.32.10

Just as the introduction of the horse to the Native people of the Great Plains generated the Buffalo Culture Era for the Native people of the Great Plains, the almost complete annihilation of the once-powerful buffalo that had provided both physical and spiritual nourishment for generations brought this period to a devastating conclusion. By the middle of the nineteenth century, the herds of buffalo that once covered the tallgrass prairies were visibly declining in numbers. The diminishment was increasingly apparent to Plains Indian hunters who had to travel far beyond their traditional territories to locate the scarce and scattered herds.

Explanations for this destruction range from periodic droughts that limited grazing forage; competition from introduced cattle, horses, and sheep; wolf depredation; overhunting by Native and Euro-American commercial hide hunters; and premeditated mass killings sanctioned and encouraged by the U.S. government. The destructive effects of commercial hide hunting, however, can be assessed through the recorded numbers of hides shipped from the Great Plains to eastern U.S. and European cities for processing. For example, by the late 1840s in the Missouri River region, the American Fur Company was shipping approximately 110,000 robes a year to St. Louis.[2] In the 1850s, buffalo became scarcer and the Upper Missouri River hide trade began to decline. The establishment of railroad lines throughout the Plains greatly increased the number of buffalo killed. Hides were shipped to market in the 1870s and early 1880s until there were essentially no remaining herds.[3] By 1875, market hunting had obliterated the herds of the Southern Plains, and by 1883, wild buffalo herds were nearly eradicated everywhere. The last commercial shipment of hides took place in 1889, and by 1894 the only free-roaming buffalo remaining in the United States could be found in Yellowstone National Park. By 1902, poachers had reduced the Yellowstone herd to only twenty-eight buffalo.[4]

Reports from travelers as well as photographs—showing piles of hides and bones at railroad depots awaiting shipment and images of numerous skinned buffalo on the Plains—documented the mass destruction of the herds. Plains Indian people also documented the killings through oral histories. Pretty Shield described the desolation of the Crow after seeing the mass slaughter of buffalo. She recalled, "Ahh, my heart fell down when I began to see dead buffalo scattered all over our beautiful country, killed and skinned, and left to rot by white men, many, many hundreds of buffalo. The first I saw of this was in the Judith basin. The whole country there smelled of rotting meat. Even the flowers could not drown the bad smell. Our hearts were like stone."[5]

Other oral and written histories recount the last buffalo hunts of several Plains tribes, during which they traveled hundreds of miles into formerly abundant hunting territories to find just a few scattered remnants of the herds. For the Pawnee, their last documented hunt occurred in 1879 after they had moved from a reservation located along the Loup River in present-day Nebraska to a new one in northern Indian Territory in 1874–75. The conditions on the reservation were so poor that Pawnee leaders petitioned and received permission from the Indian agent for a buffalo hunt. In May 1879, a small group of hunters and their families traveled hundreds of miles to Fort Elliott in the Texas Panhandle in search of buffalo. Driven from that destination by hostile Texans, the Pawnee traveled on to Fort Supply, where they camped for a few days. There, the hunters found and killed some remaining buffalo from a small herd.[6]

Accounts from other "last buffalo hunts" appearing in historical publications and tribal winter counts also document these significant events that occurred in the late 1870s and

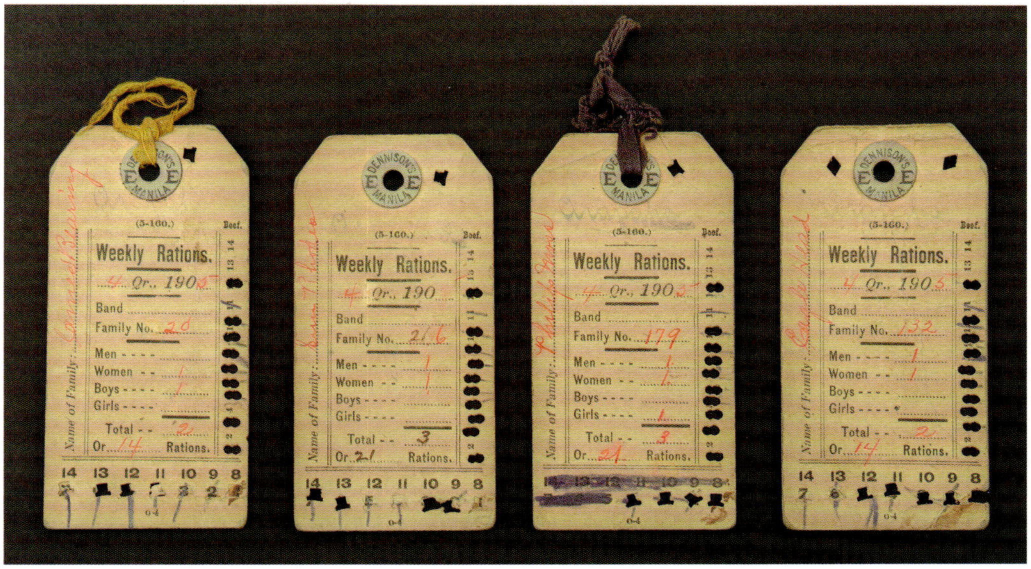

7.2. **Ration cards**
Used by Hinono'ei (Northern Arapaho) Families, Wind River Reservation, Wyoming, 1905
Paper, ink, string; 3⅞ × 1⅞ inches
Plains Indian Museum, NA.704.23.

early 1880s.[7] Tribal leaders and historians from that period associated the decimation of the buffalo with the near destruction of their traditions and communities. Plenty Coups eloquently described the unspeakable sadness this destruction brought to the people: "When the buffalo went away the hearts of my people fell to the ground, and they could not lift them up again. After this nothing happened. There was little singing anywhere."[8]

Because of the centrality of the buffalo to Plains Indian life, their destruction influenced not only physical and economic but also social, cultural, artistic, and spiritual domains. During the same period, in many regions of the Plains other game diminished along with the buffalo, and reservation restrictions on hunting limited the availability of these resources. Likewise, for the village farming people such as the Pawnee, efforts to continue growing their traditional varieties of corn, beans, and squash were thwarted by agency rules and restrictions, droughts, and destructive swarms of grasshoppers.

In other cases, government agents attempted to introduce cattle ranching and farming to tribes settled on reservations. Many of the essential prerequisites for such occupations were not provided, however, and individuals were slow to adopt this new way of life. Tribes found themselves dependent on rations provided by government agents, often in trade for other concessions on the parts of leaders, individuals, and families (fig. 7.2). On some reservations, issuance of cattle as part of the rations provided much-needed nourishment and a rare opportunity for excitement among the men, as they sometimes resurrected their traditional hunting methods to provide meat for their families. Notwithstanding the uneven quality of government-issued rations, this system was a poor substitute for buffalo hunting. The system also failed to fulfill the peoples' spiritual necessities earlier attained through ceremonies, dances, and songs related to the buffalo. These ceremonies became less frequently performed, which created a spiritual void in the lives of the people.

The overall health of Plains Indian people by the beginning of the twentieth century is revealed through alarming statistics documenting tribal depopulation. In 1800, Pawnee population estimates range from 10,000 to 12,500 people, but by 1900 they had declined to 650 individuals.[9] Old World diseases such as smallpox, cholera, mumps, influenza, and measles, which were especially pernicious for farming people living in densely populated earth lodge villages, were primarily responsible for this depopulation. These diseases had already taken their toll on Plains populations during the eighteenth century, and beginning with the 1801–2 smallpox pandemic, became even more widespread and destructive. Researchers have documented thirteen smallpox epidemics affecting North American Indians during the nineteenth century, as well as five of measles, three of cholera, and two of influenza.[10]

A major smallpox epidemic recorded in several Plains winter counts swept through the Plains, the Northwest, Canada, and Alaska between 1836 and 1840. The epidemic resulted in thousands of Native American deaths. The epidemic was brought to the Northern Plains in the summer of 1837 by travelers on the American Fur Company steamboat *St. Peter's* to Fort Union. In only a few short weeks, smallpox caused the deaths of approximately 10,000 people.[11] In July, the disease reached the Mandan, who lived in two earth lodge villages on either side of the Missouri. Smallpox reduced their population from an estimated 1,600–2,000 individuals to only 138 by October of that year.[12] Smallpox came to the Crow in 1840 and resulted in the deaths of approximately one-third of their total population of 3,000.[13] An estimated 6,000 to 8,000 Blackfeet, Piegan, and Blood individuals died from this epidemic.[14] Mike Bruised Head of the Kainai (Blood) described the effects of the smallpox. He characterized the "vast and enormous" smallpox epidemic as a "price the Blackfoot paid for the fur trade."

> Smallpox affected every core of our being. As a result of the smallpox, we lost a large body of knowledge from our people, the old people. You can consequently say that the disease had a profound impact on the Blackfoot physically, culturally and spiritually. Their whole being was affected. The smallpox outbreak reduced the number of society members for years. It affected society transfers of bundles and sacred items. Sacred items could not be transferred because they became infected. Pipes and bundles were buried with the people, if the people were buried at all. There was a fear that touching these sacred articles would transmit the disease and affect more people.[15]

Smallpox continued to devastate Plains populations throughout the nineteenth century. Vaccinations existed by the early 1800s, and were sometimes provided for in treaties, but were only intermittently available until the late nineteenth century.[16] Diseases such as cholera, malaria, measles, tuberculosis, scarlet fever, whooping cough, mumps, and influenza spread throughout tribal communities, abetted by malnutrition, poor medical treatment, and generally unhealthy reservation environments. These conditions incapacitated Plains peoples during the nineteenth and early twentieth centuries. As the Buffalo Culture Era came to a close, the conditions on reservations for Plains Indian people were dire as they adapted to new realities, here described by Arthur Amiotte:

> The people, for one and sometimes two decades, lived near agency headquarters camped in tattered skin tipis, and tipis and tents hand-sewn from canvas issued as annuities (treaty payments). Various kinds of cloth—canvas, wool broadcloth, cotton muslin, and

factory-made blankets distributed as annuities—provided clothing. Cattle purchased by the agency, slaughtered and distributed as rations, provided a new source of hide and sinew for making moccasins, along with remnants of pre-reservation leather goods, were recycled to provide a modicum of continuity of traditional material culture.[17]

The history of Plains Indian people has been one of endurance and survival, despite seemingly overwhelming adversities. On reservations, tribal members struggled for physical survival as they also attempted to maintain their cultural identities. Government agents, missionaries, and schools pressured them to set aside their languages, beliefs, ceremonies, and communal lives. Men and women developed new means of supporting their families through ranching and farming, working as paid laborers, selling beadwork and other arts, and traveling the world with Buffalo Bill and other Wild West shows (figs. 7.3, 7.4, and 7.5).[18]

Reservation arts, manifested in beautifully embellished creations in tribal designs, became a means of establishing and maintaining cultural identities. Through perseverance, Plains Indian people continued to endure the hardships of the late nineteenth and early twentieth

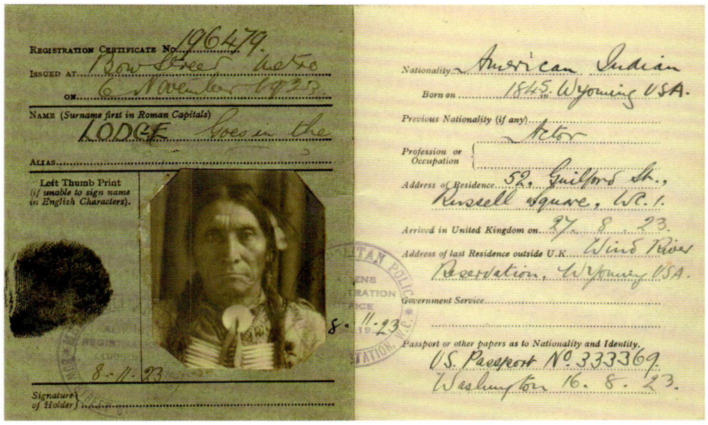

Registration Certificate No. 196479
Issued at Bow Street Metro
on 6 November 1923
Name (Surname first in Roman Capitals) LODGE Goes in the
Alias
Left Thumb Print (if unable to sign name in English Characters).
Signature of Holder
Nationality American Indian
Born on 1845 Wyoming USA
Previous Nationality (if any)
Profession or Occupation Actor
Address of Residence 52, Guilford St., Russell Square, W.C.1.
Arrived in United Kingdom on 27. 8. 23.
Address of last Residence outside U.K. Wind River Reservation, Wyoming USA.
Government Service
Passport or other papers as to Nationality and Identity. U.S. Passport No 333369 Washington 16. 8. 23.

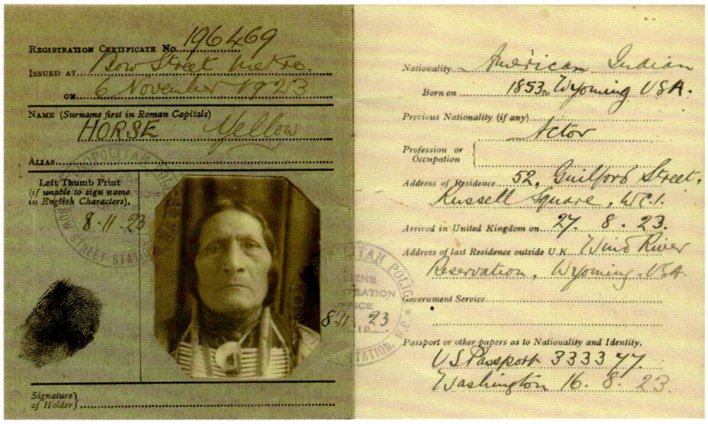

Registration Certificate No. 196469
Issued at Bow Street Metro
on 6 November 1923
Name (Surname first in Roman Capitals) HORSE Yellow
Alias
Left Thumb Print (if unable to sign name in English Characters).
Signature of Holder
Nationality American Indian
Born on 1853 Wyoming USA.
Previous Nationality (if any)
Profession or Occupation Actor
Address of Residence 52, Guilford Street, Russell Square, W.C.1.
Arrived in United Kingdom on 27. 8. 23.
Address of last Residence outside U.K. Wind River Reservation, Wyoming USA.
Government Service
Passport or other papers as to Nationality and Identity. U.S. Passport 333377 Washington 16. 8. 23.

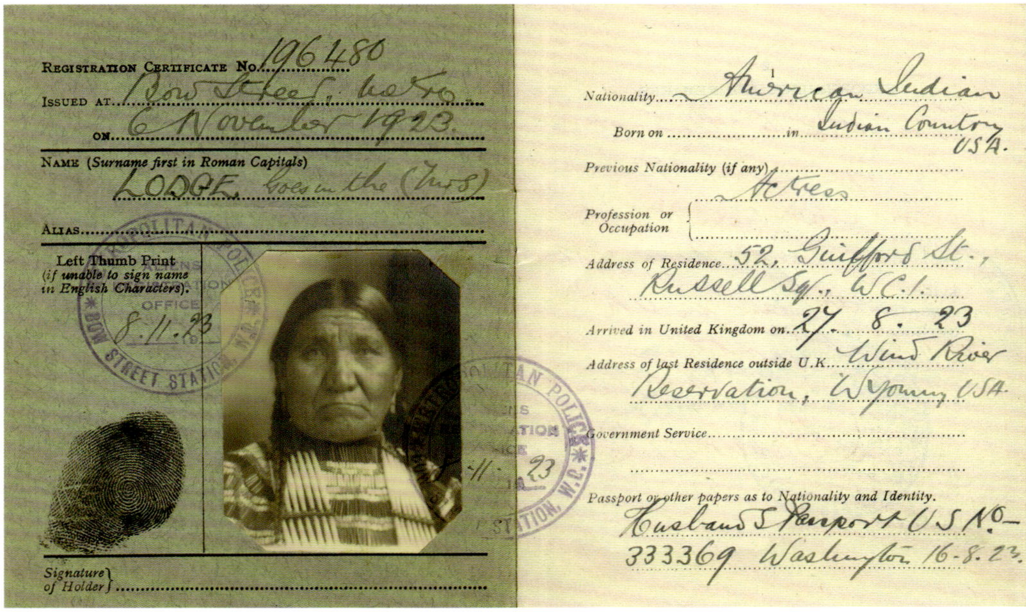

Registration Certificate No. 196480
Issued at Bow Street Metro
on 6 November 1923
Name (Surname first in Roman Capitals) LODGE Goes in the (Mrs)
Alias
Left Thumb Print (if unable to sign name in English Characters).
Signature of Holder
Nationality American Indian
Born on ... in Indian Country USA.
Previous Nationality (if any)
Profession or Occupation Actress
Address of Residence 52, Guilford St., Russell Sq., W.C.1.
Arrived in United Kingdom on 27. 8. 23
Address of last Residence outside U.K. Wind River Reservation, Wyoming USA.
Government Service
Passport or other papers as to Nationality and Identity. Husband's Passport U.S. No. 333369 Washington 16-8-23.

7.3, 7.4, and 7.5. **Passports**
Goes in the Lodge, 1923; Yellow Horse, 1923; Mrs. Goes in the Lodge, 1923
McCracken Research Library, MS320.AO1920.196479; MS320.AO1920.196469; MS320.AO1920.196480

These passports belonged to residents of the Wind River Reservation who traveled as performers in the Miller Brothers 101 Ranch Show.

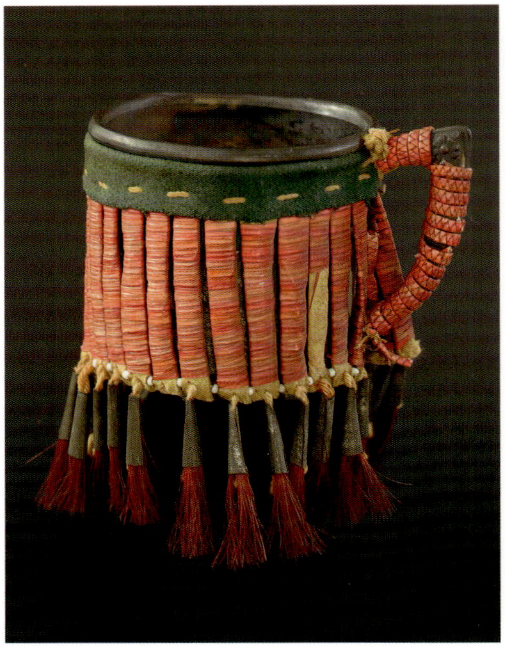

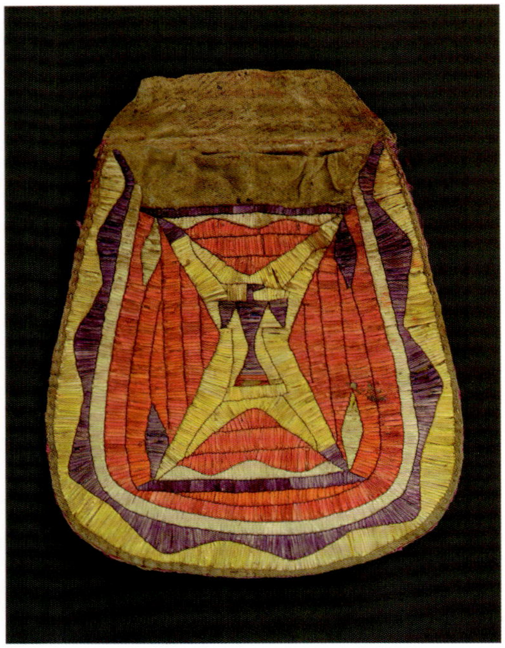

7.6. **Cup**
Lakota (Sioux), Northern Plains, ca. 1900
Metal, rawhide, tin cones, glass beads, dyed porcupine quills, tanned hide, wool cloth, cotton thread, dyed horse hair; 3½ inches (height) x 2¼ inches (diameter)
Plains Indian Museum, NA.506.146

Lakota women living on the reservation continued to do quillwork, often using quills dyed in vibrant red. There are still artists among the Lakota who carry on this artistic tradition.

7.7. **Bag**
Lakota (Sioux), Northern Plains, 1890–1920
Tanned hide, cotton thread, dyed porcupine quills, satin ribbon; 8¾ x 7 inches
Plains Indian Museum, NA.202.1401

centuries. Through artistry and creative innovations as traditional raw materials were lost and new trade materials became available, Plains Indians renewed and expressed their cultural identities and heritages. Paul Dyck was primarily interested in Plains Native arts from the earlier "Buffalo Culture" period that he considered to be less affected by Euro-American influences. He collected relatively few objects dating from the early twentieth century, but some representative works of the period reflect traditions and transitions as Plains Indian artists continued to create clothing and other items for giveaways, dances, parades, ceremonies, and other special occasions (figs. 7.6, 7.7, 7.8, 7.9, 7.10, and 7.11).

Later, as new opportunities became available, Plains Indian people developed professions in education, law, business, and the arts. They also reintroduced buffalo to their reservation lands, promoted tourism, and even built casinos to bring new employment to their communities. Through each generation, they continue to reaffirm and preserve their cultural identities, values, arts,

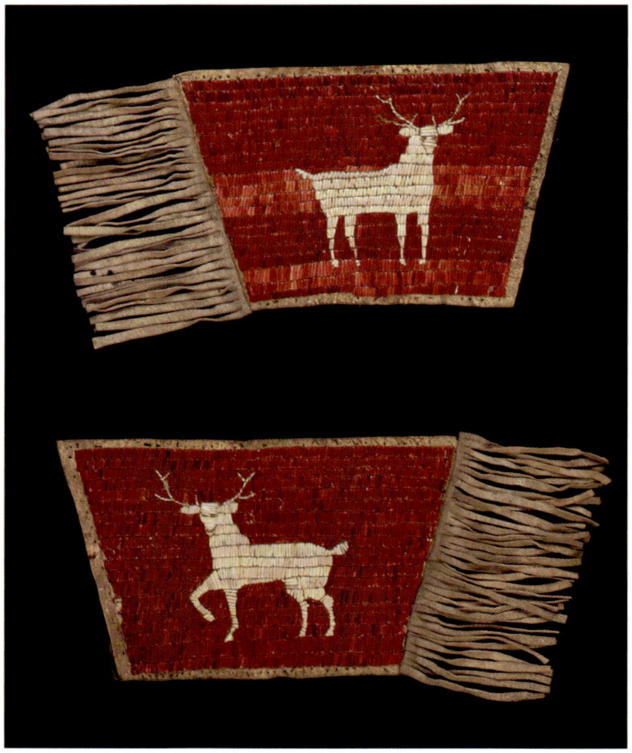

7.8. **Cuffs**
Lakota (Sioux), Northern Plains, ca. 1890
Dyed porcupine quills, tanned hide; 6½ x 13 inches
Plains Indian Museum, NA.203.1414

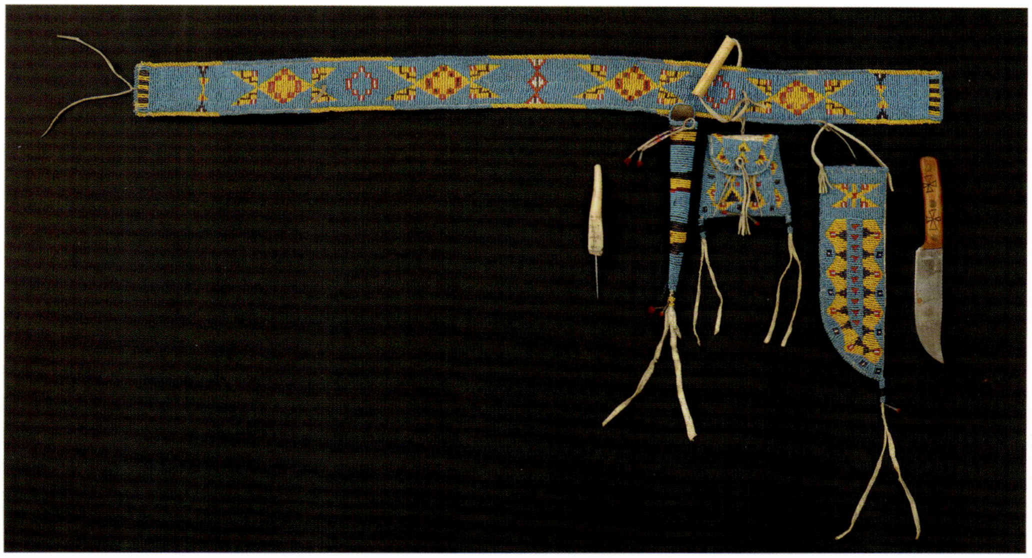

7.9. **Belt**
Northern Plains, 1930s
Metal, feather fluffs, wood, bone, cardboard, glass beads, tanned hide, cotton thread, metal cones, dyed porcupine quills; 33½ × 2⅜ inches
Plains Indian Museum, NA.102.227

The owner of this belt probably made it for wearing with traditional clothing at powwows or other celebrations. The bags on the belt, including a pouch, awl case with awl, and knife sheath with knife, represent a woman's traditional arts.

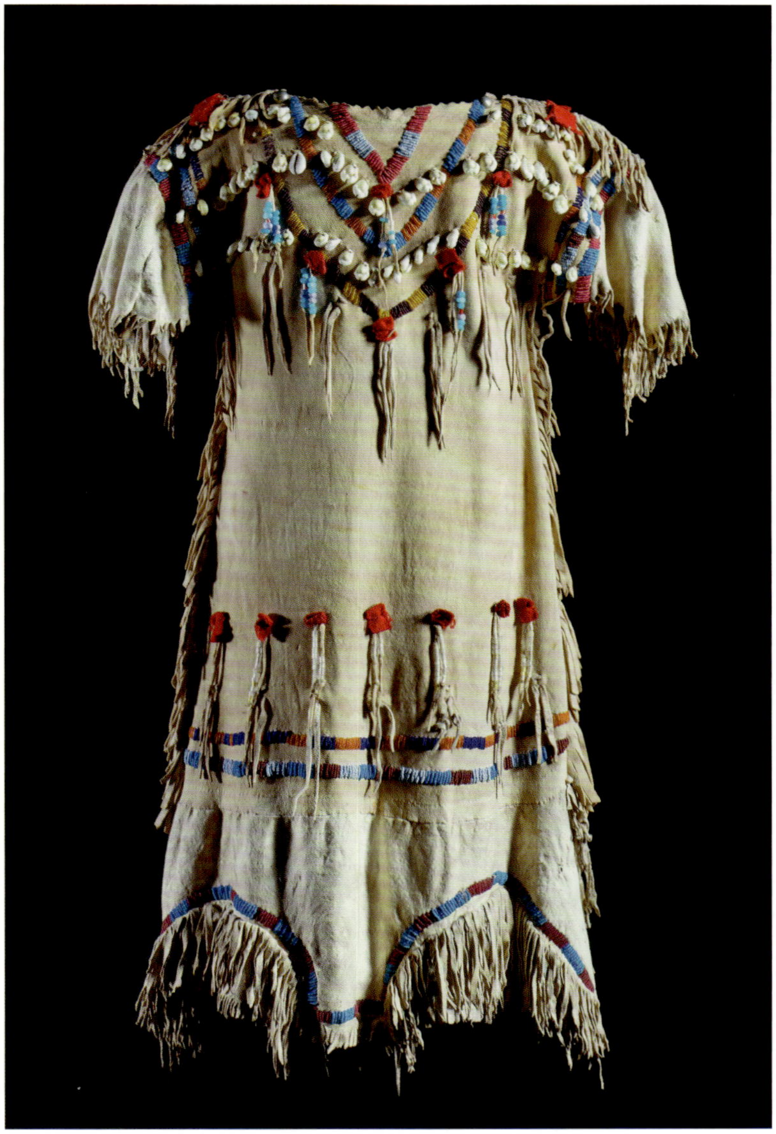

7.10. **Dress**
Amskapi Pikuni (Blackfeet), Montana, ca. 1903
Tanned hide, glass beads, cowrie shells, wool cloth, stone, brass bells, metal buttons, glass tube beads, cotton thread, leather; dress length: 34 inches; width sleeve to sleeve with fringe: 29 inches; hem width: 24 inches
Plains Indian Museum, NA.202.1223

Mothers and grandmothers continued to create beautifully decorated clothing for children to wear to ceremonies, dances, and other formal occasions. This tradition continues among Plains Indian people today. A tag attached to the dress states that it belonged to Crow Eyes, which is the surname of a family living on the Blackfeet Reservation in Northern Montana at the turn of the century.

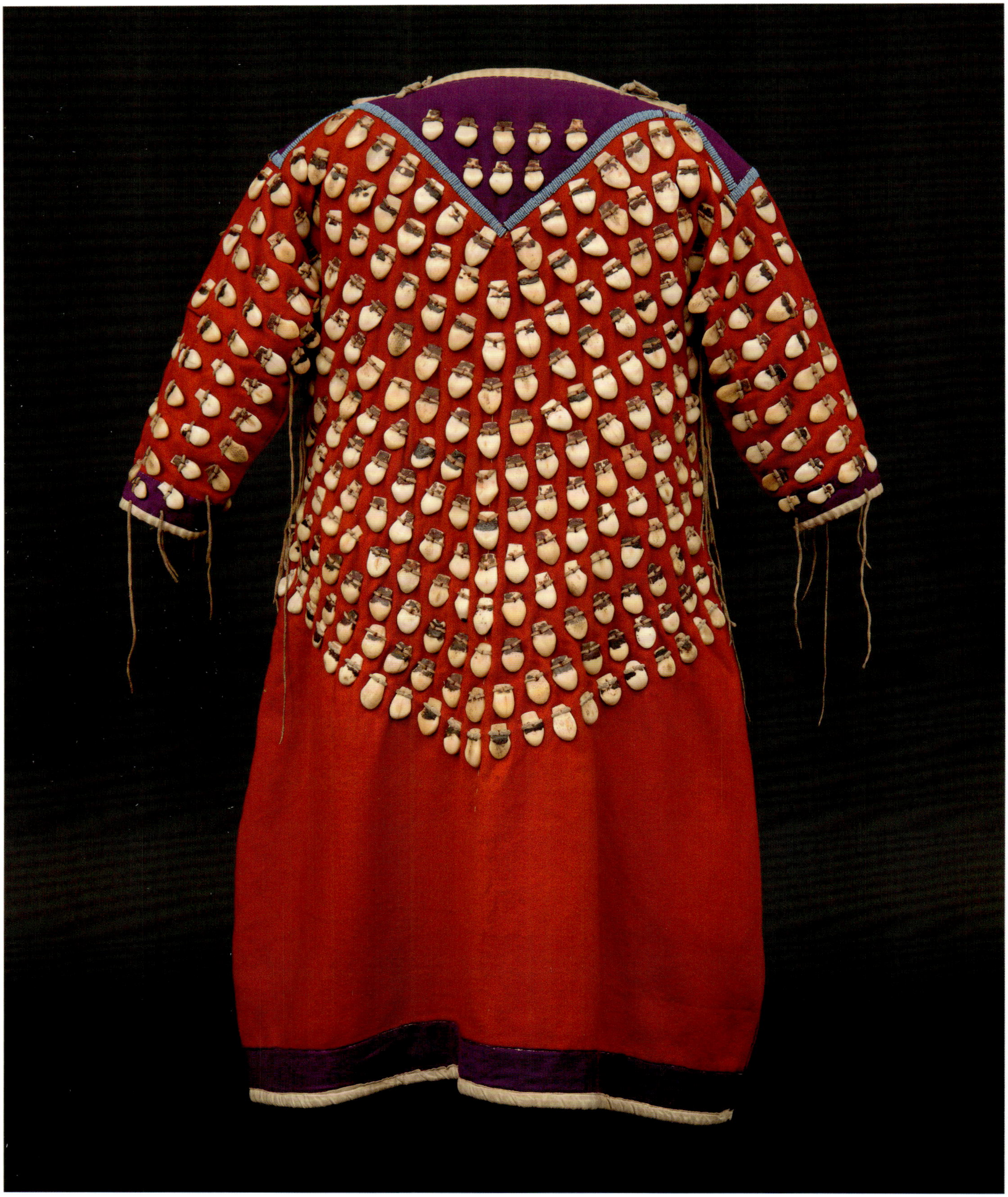

traditions, and heritages. Tribes created inventive means to convey their knowledge and beliefs to their descendants. Colin Calloway describes the history of the people of the Great Plains in the following way:

> Life on the Great Plains has always required resilience in the face of adversity. It has required building anew as opportunities beckoned or disasters demanded, and it has been possible to weather the changes by drawing strength from core values. Native people have always had to find new ways of preserving traditions in times of change and upheaval. . . . The values and beliefs that continue to give meaning to Plains Indian life have proven more difficult to destroy than the buffalo herds. And today the buffalo are returning.[19]

ENDURING LEGACIES

Those of us who have sought out family or tribal collections that represent one's own history, culture, and artistic traditions are sometimes astonished to learn that those materials are stored in distant cities such as Chicago; New York; Washington, D.C.; London; Paris; Edinburgh; and Berlin—far from the Great Plains and home communities that produced them. There, items are preserved for future generations, but in practical terms within reach of only a few Native people who are able to travel to the museums to view, research, pray over, or merely spend time with them. In recent years, Native American scholars, museum professionals, and community members have initiated efforts to make such collections available and accessible to Indian people. Museums have begun to respond to those efforts. Northern Arapaho tribal member Jordan Dresser expresses the ambivalent attitudes of many Native American people toward museums, collections, and collectors:

> It was a little baffling to me that there weren't a lot of artifacts on the reservation. Most old style items that belonged to the people of the Wind River were stored in sites away from the reservation. You look at museum websites and you see these great collections. How did they get them? These museums are keepers now of items that belonged to tribal people. . . . There was this idea that these items belonged to the world so, therefore, you move them and you place them in these museums, but these objects are away from the people who can interpret them best.[20]

The foundations of North American anthropology and the development of natural history museums in the United States in the decades before and after 1900 were intertwined with field research among Native American peoples. During this period, tribes experienced catastrophic changes and disruptions in their traditional lives. Researchers of the time viewed ethnographic studies and field collecting on American Indian reservations as significant and essential documentation of what they considered—based on grave existing circumstances and projected future prospects of Native American peoples—vanishing arts and cultures. They traveled to reservations in Montana, Wyoming, North and South Dakota, Nebraska, and Oklahoma

7.11. **Girl's dress**
Apsáalooke (Crow), Northern Plains, ca. 1890
Wool cloth, carved bone elk teeth, leather, glass beads, cotton cloth, cotton thread; 32½ x 16 inches
Plains Indian Museum, NA.202.1286

within the Great Plains and other regions to record ceremonies, songs, and traditions and to acquire representative ethnographic objects. Clothing, implements, personal belongings, and sacred materials became part of collections intended for study as a historical record of Plains Indian cultures. Many of the anthropologists cited in this and other publications, such as Clark Wissler, George Dorsey, Alfred L. Kroeber, and Robert H. Lowie, were leading scholars who acquired major Plains Indian collections for museums during their reservation visits. James R. Murie and other Native scholars sometimes collaborated in this research. Natural history museums considered it their mission to preserve the collections and the accompanying research for future generations to learn about Native North Americans of the past. Museums categorized and exhibited such materials as specimens of seemingly static and unchanging nineteenth-century buffalo cultures. Beatrice Medicine described this methodology as "laundry list anthropology" through which "parfleche designs, moccasin types, and medicine bundles assumed more dynamic qualities than the people themselves." She also said, "Many Indians were seen as living museum pieces."[21] Art historians and broader audiences began to recognize the intrinsic artistry of American Indian artifacts, highlighted by the benchmark exhibition *Indian Art of the United States,* which opened in 1941 at the Museum of Modern Art. As art museums and galleries acquired American Indian art, they tended to exhibit these creations as singular works of beauty apart from cultural contexts.

An undeniable tension can exist between museums; private collectors of Native American art whose interests may focus on the artistry, craftsmanship, marketability, age, or tribal representation of specific pieces; and contemporary Native people who, additionally, may view the same objects as manifestations of the spirit and endurance of tribal cultures. For museums and collectors, Native arts may be material remnants of past cultures that should be documented and preserved. In Paul Dyck's case, he was also interested in exhibiting the collection in a contextual, sympathetic, and innovative portrayal of eighteenth- and nineteenth-century Plains tribal arts, cultures, and histories based on his research and longtime experiences with Native American elders.

Contemporary Native people who are interested in their traditional arts and cultures may perceive such arts as enduring legacies of tribal heritages. Together with memories and oral histories, collections of Native art have the potential to provide a sense of place, social cohesion, and cultural and spiritual foundations for Indian communities as they strive to gain control over their lands, the education of their children, traditional spiritual practices, and the interpretation of their own lives. Jordan Dresser describes this perspective in the following way:

> Our sacred objects are what carried us through and helped us survive. Growing up on the Wind River Reservation, I learned that story telling was important to our tribe. Objects are a big part of how we tell our stories. They are a living part of our culture. They carry on the memories of the maker. As a kid I always heard singing. I always heard the drum. It's humbling to hear that because you are a part of the bigger picture. You're a part of this long rich history and you always had that respect for these items. You treated them like you would treat another human being.[22]

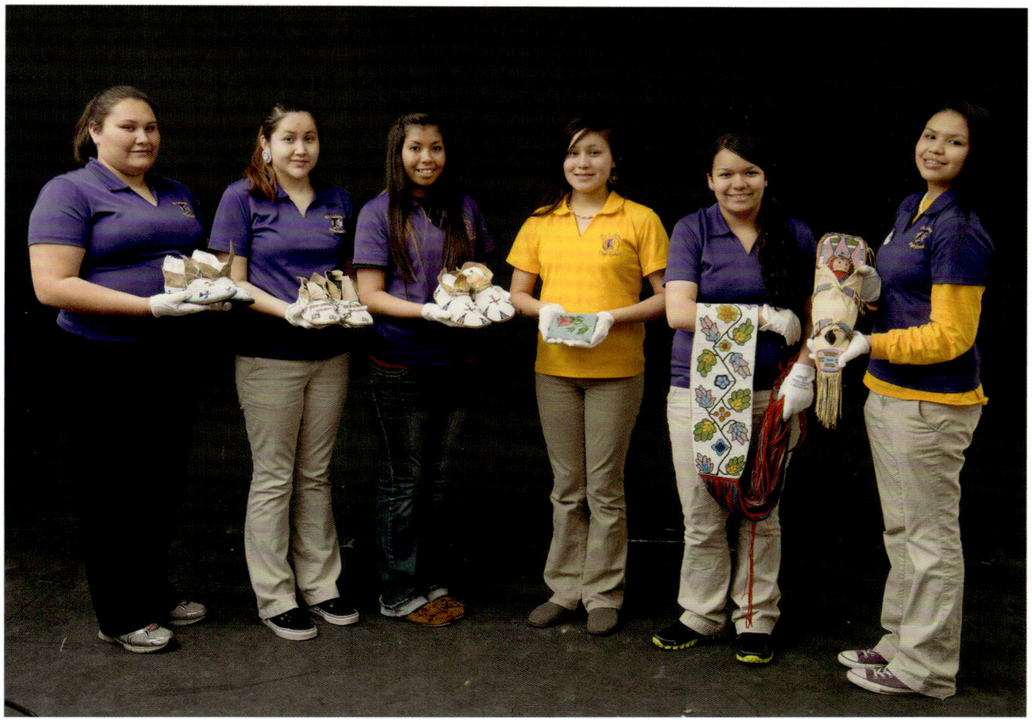

7.12. **St. Labre students**
Plains Indian Museum, May 2013
(*Left to right*): Chalisa Littlebird, Allarie J. Old Coyote, Halle Standing Elk, Tianna Two Moons, Mckenzie Wind, and Cordelia G. Falls Down
Plains Indian Museum

Many Plains tribal members today remember, research, and renew elements of that older way of life—the continuous threads that have been passed down through generations—for the education, cultural and spiritual grounding, and welfare of their own children and grandchildren. They revere and honor the accomplishments of their elders and those who came before them, while living as vital members of their own communities. Tribal arts in museum and private collections, as expressions of cultures, histories, and traditions, can be valuable components for research and understanding, maintaining, and providing cohesion to Plains Indian identities.

The Plains Indian Museum is located in northwestern Wyoming within the heart of the Great Plains and near Crow, Northern Cheyenne, Eastern Shoshone, Northern Arapaho, and other tribal communities and reservations. As Native American scholars, artists, teachers, and community leaders learned that the Paul Dyck Collection is now preserved in the museum, many have visited to study selected collection objects. In recognition of the spiritual significance of such materials, tribal elders have visited, smudged, and offered prayers for the collection. Consultation with spiritual leaders concerning repatriation of sacred objects has also occurred as mandated under the Native American Graves Protection and Repatriation Act. Efforts to increase the accessibility and availability to Plains Indian communities and other interested researchers of the Dyck and other collections are ongoing through exhibitions, educational programming, publications, and online databases.

Over the past decade, classes from St. Labre Indian School in Ashland, Montana, which educates Crow and Northern Cheyenne high school students, have visited the museum twice a year (fig. 7.12). During these two- to three-day visits, museum staff work with the students in providing hands-on experiences in many aspects of museum studies. In recent years, the Paul

Dyck Collection has been a focus of instruction as students learn to document, record, photograph, and interpret collection objects representing their own cultures. Community spiritual leaders accompany the students and teachers on these visits to provide guidance.

Museum interns from Plains Indian communities have also been essential in recording, storing, exhibiting, and consulting on the collection. Hunter Old Elk, a museum intern in the summer of 2016 and currently a Plains Indian Museum curatorial assistant, described her thoughts about the Paul Dyck Collection (fig. 7.13).

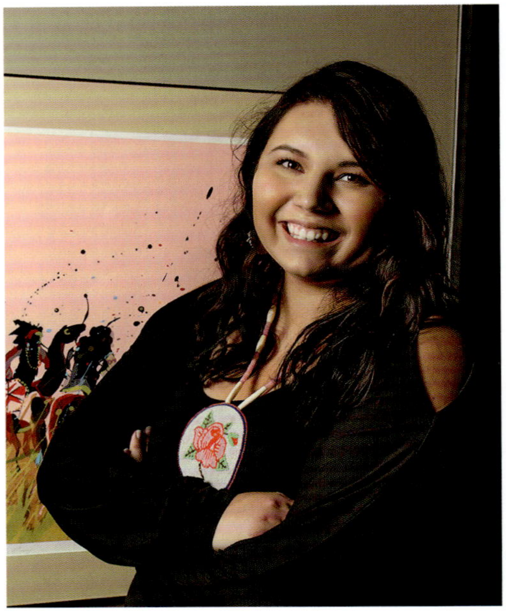

7.13. **Hunter C. Old Elk**
Plains Indian Museum
September 2016
Plains Indian Museum

> Growing up Apsáalooke and Yakama, I have heard many times in my life about returning to one's roots. May that be going off and getting an education, or exploring cultures not of our own. However, when I say returning, I really mean, "coming home." This too is said about the Dyck Collection's new home, at the Plains Indian Museum. Museum objects such as the Dyck pieces, goes through these same experiences. The belongings of my people have seen many places and many people, such as on the Plains or in the hands of collectors. When the Dyck collection was acquired by the Museum, it opened up opportunities to study the ethnographic history of my people for young and eager scholars, such as myself. However more importantly, it afforded the objects a permanent resting place. For both reasons, I am fortunate to have the Dyck collection at the Museum.[23]

Plains Indian elders from earlier centuries through the present day realized it was important to preserve and pass on tribal histories, traditions, and values as elements of the entire fabric of cultural life through a continual oral retelling as well as visual recording and interpretation through art. Joseph Medicine Crow, whose words are used throughout this narrative, was one of those elders who, like others, continued to contribute to their own tribal communities through education and guidance to younger generations (fig. 7.14). He remained interested in Crow

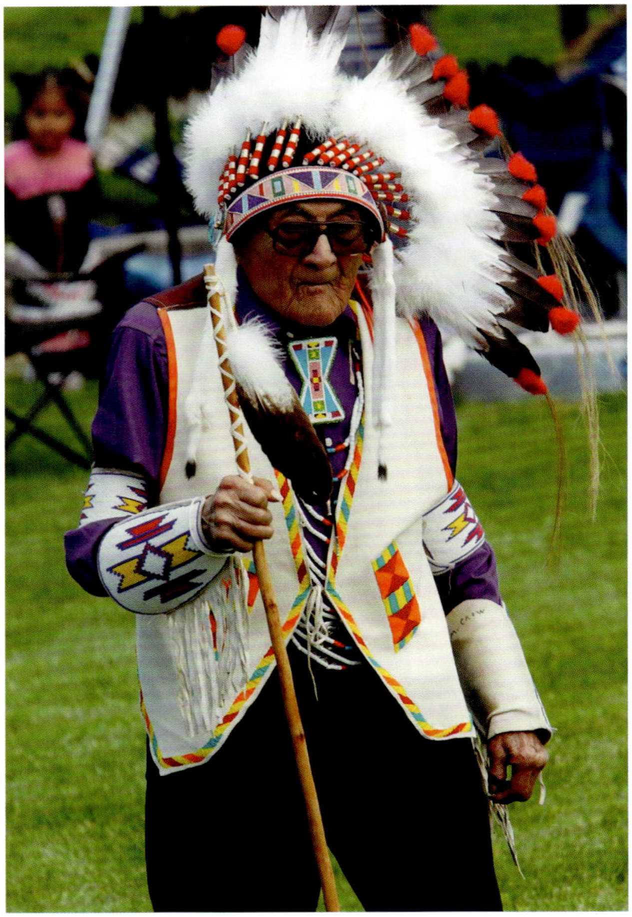

7.14. **Joseph Medicine Crow**
Crow elder and scholar from
Lodge Grass, Montana
Plains Indian Museum Powwow,
Cody, Wyoming, June 21, 2015
Photograph by Ken Blackbird

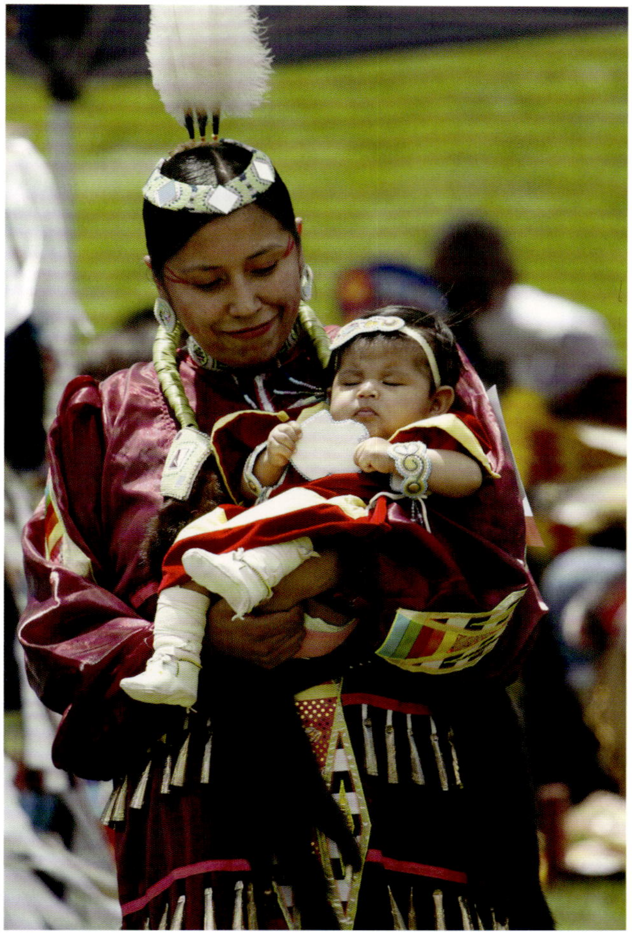

7.15. Jocelyn Bearcomesout and Natahnii Bearcomesout, Northern Cheyenne and Nez Perce mother and daughter from Lame Deer, Montana
Plains Indian Museum Powwow, Cody, Wyoming, June 21, 2014
Photograph by Ken Blackbird

history and traditions, beginning with his early life interests in nineteenth-century warriors and leaders, until his passing in 2016.

Artists have always had integral roles and responsibilities within historic Plains cultures as providers of both secular and sacred materials, recorders and interpreters of cultures and events, and visionaries of the future. They have long adapted materials and technologies to produce multifaceted works that were functional and relevant to cultural and spiritual lives. Plains Indian arts and cultures endure and are expressed in traditional ceremonies and contemporary powwows, fairs, and other celebrations of Native life (fig. 7.15).

Considered in its entirety, the art of the Paul Dyck Collection can be viewed as symbolizing the traditions, transitions, adaptations, and innovations in Plains Indian lives from the freedom of the buffalo-hunting days to the struggles of the late nineteenth century. Research and study of the Plains Indian art of the Paul Dyck Collection generate a renewed appreciation for the superb artistry of singular works and the aesthetic milieus that produced them. In addition to their intrinsic artistry and creativity, such works are powerful and multilayered expressions by Native artists of cultural knowledge and understandings, biographical and historical experiences, and a spirituality that guides all aspects of life.

NOTES

INTRODUCTION

1. John Dyck, e-mail to the author, April 19, 2017.
2. For additional biographical information on Paul Dyck, see Lorna Thackeray, "Arizona Collector Dyck Preserved Plains Indian History," *Billings Gazette*, June 9, 2013; and "Paul Dyck," *Arizona Republic*, February 19, 2006.
3. Historically, the Blackfoot Confederacy (Niitsitapi) consisted of four bands: the Siksika, Kainai (Blood), Northern Pikuni (Piikani) or Northern Peigan (Apa'tosee), and the Blackfeet Nation or Southern Pikuni (Piikani) or Southern Piegan (Amskapi Pikuni). In this writing, the term "Blackfoot" refers to any of the four bands of the Confederacy. "Blackfeet" refers specifically to members of the Blackfeet Nation.
4. Paul Dyck, "A Passion for the Indian," Attachment C to *Plains Indian Buffalo Culture Collection Feasibility Study* (Rimrock, Ariz.: The Paul Dyck Foundation, 1994), C9, Paul Dyck Papers, McCracken Research Library, Buffalo Bill Center of the West. Reprinted from Abe Chanin and Mildred Chanin, *This Land, These Voices: A Different View of Arizona History in the Words of Those Who Lived It* (Flagstaff, Ariz.: Northland Press, 1977), 246–53.
5. Ibid.
6. Ibid., C7.
7. In a June 2013 conversation with the author, Heywood Big Day, a Crow elder and Sun Dance leader from Pryor, Montana, described some of Dyck's visits to his childhood home to attend the family-sponsored Sun Dance. He remembered that Dyck usually arrived by motorcycle for the annual ceremony. In July 1941, Big Day's father, William Big Day, led the return of the Sun Dance to the Crow after an absence of the ceremony for about seventy years. Two years before, William Big Day had vowed to bring the Sun Dance back to his people if the ailing Heywood lived through an illness. See Heywood Big Day's foreword to Michael Crummett's *Sun Dance: The 50th Anniversary Crow Indian Sun Dance* (Helena, Mont.: Falcon Press, 1993), vii. Heywood Big Day renewed his friendship with Paul Dyck in 1992 when he visited the ranch with a group of Crow tribal members. He continued to visit with Dyck periodically during his travels to Arizona.
8. "Paul Dyck," *Arizona Republic*, February 19, 2006.
9. Paul Dyck, *Brulé: The Sioux People of the Rosebud* (Flagstaff, Ariz.: Northland Press, 1971).
10. Dyck, "A Passion for the Indian," C9.
11. Beginning in 1962 and continuing until 1972, Southwest Museum archaeologists excavated the Dyck Rockshelter, located on the ranch. In 2014, the Paul Dyck Foundation and John and Cindy Dyck, Dyck's son and daughter-in-law, contributed the artifact collection to the Verde Valley Archaeology Center in Sedona, Arizona. Publications about the site include *The Dyck Rockshelter*, exhibition guide (Sedona, Ariz.: Verde Valley Archaeology Center, 2015); Todd W. Bostwick, Charles E. Rozaire, and George Kritzman, "The 1962–1972 Excavations of the Dyck Rockshelter along Wet Beaver Creek, Central Arizona: An Archival Reconstruction," *Verde Valley Archaeology Center Occasional Papers* No. 2 (Camp Verde, Ariz., 2015); and Paul R. Fish and Suzanne K. Fish, *Verde Valley Archaeology: Review and Perspective*, Research Paper No. 8 (Flagstaff, Ariz.: Museum of Northern Arizona, 1977).
12. See *Plains Indian Buffalo Culture Collection Feasibility Study*, 1994, 10; and Christian F. Feest, "American Indians and Ethnographic Collecting in Europe," *Museum Anthropology* 16, no. 1 (1992): 7.
13. Paul Dyck, transcript of interview with the *Tucson Arizona Daily Star*, September 1975, McCracken Research Papers, Buffalo Bill Center of the West, Cody, Wyoming.
14. Statement from the Paul Dyck Foundation Research Institution of American Indian Culture, Rimrock, Arizona, June 25, 1987; Paul Dyck Papers, McCracken Research Library, Buffalo Bill Center of the West.
15. Ibid.
16. Arthur Amiotte, statement made during a meeting in June 2009.
17. Marilyn Hudson, statement in letter to "Save America's Treasures," January 2009.

CHAPTER 1 BUFFALO CULTURE ERA

1. Joseph Medicine Crow and Herman J. Viola, *Counting Coup: Becoming a Crow Chief on the Reservation and Beyond* (Washington, D.C.: National Geographic, 2006), 18–19.
2. Joseph Medicine Crow passed away in April 2016 at one hundred and two years of age. Throughout his long, distinguished life, as scholar and tribal historian for the Crow Nation, he recorded, researched, and wrote about Crow history. His publications include Medicine Crow and Viola, *Counting Coup;* and Joseph Medicine Crow, *From the Heart of the Crow Country: The Crow Indians' Own Stories* (New York: Orion Books, 1992).
3. Medicine Crow and Viola, *Counting Coup*, 60–61.
4. Arthur Amiotte, "Artists of Earth and Sky," in *The Plains Indians: Artists of Earth and Sky*, edited by Gaylord Torrence (Paris: Skira Rizzoli, 2014), 35–36.
5. Major Stephen H. Long of the U.S. Army Engineers, who traveled the Missouri River in 1819 and the Platte River region in 1820, characterized the area as "almost wholly unfit for cultivation, and uninhabitable by a people depending upon agriculture for their subsistence," despite his meeting with Pawnee, Otoe, and Omaha people who had farmed this region for centuries. In 1805, William Clark had earlier characterized the Upper Missouri region in the same way, followed by Zebulon Pike in 1806, who compared the Central Plains to the deserts of Africa. See Edwin James, "Account of an Expedition from Pittsburgh to the Rocky Mountains, Performed in the Years 1829, 1820, under the Command of Major S. H. Long," in *Early Western Travels, 1748–1846*, edited by Reuben Gold Thwaites (Cleveland, Ohio: Arthur H. Clark, 1905), 17:147; Zebulon Montgomery Pike, *The Expeditions of Zebulon Montgomery Pike to Headwaters of the Mississippi River through Louisiana Territory, and in New Spain, during the Years 1805–1807* (Minneapolis, Minn.: Ross and Haines, 1965), 8; Carolyn Gilman, *Lewis and Clark: Across the Divide* (Washington, D.C.: Smithsonian Books, 2003), 31.
6. Gilman, *Lewis and Clark*, 57–58.
7. Curly Bear Wagner, author interview, January 20, 2000, Plains Indian Museum, Cody, Wyoming.
8. Keith H. Basso, "Wisdom Sits in Places: Notes on a Western Apache Landscape," in *Senses of Place*, edited by Steven Feld and Keith H. Basso (Santa Fe, N.M.: School of American Research Press, 1996), 54.
9. Although protested by tribal leaders and members, construction of Garrison Dam, begun in 1947 under the Flood Contract Act (Public Law 78–534) of 1944, resulted in the flooding of the homelands of the Three Affiliated Tribes. In 1936, the Mandan, Hidatsa, and Arikara developed a joint governing constitution and adopted the formal name of the "Three Affiliated Tribes of the Fort Berthold Indian Reservation" under the Indian Reorganization Act of 1934. See Mary Jane Schneider, "Three Affiliated Tribes," in *Handbook of North American Indians*, Vol. 13, Pt 1, *Plains*, edited by Raymond J. DeMallie (Washington, D.C.: Smithsonian Institution, 2001), 391–98.
10. Marilyn Hudson, "'We Are Not Here to Sell Our Land': The Mandan, Hidatsa, and Arikara People and the Flood Control Act of 1944," presentation at Plains Indian Museum Seminar, Buffalo Bill Center of the West, October 1, 2005.
11. Ibid.
12. George Parker Winship, "The Coronado Expedition, 1540–1542," *14th Annual Report of the Bureau of Ethnology to the Secretary of the Smithsonian Institution, 1892–1893*, Pt. 1 (Washington, D.C: Smithsonian Institution, 1896): 329–613.
13. Raymond J. DeMallie and John C. Ewers, "History of Ethnological and Ethnohistorical Research," in *Handbook of North American Indians*, Vol. 13, Pt. 1, *Plains*, edited by Raymond J. DeMallie (Washington, D.C.: Smithsonian Institution, 2001), 23.
14. For a description of Hidatsa and Mandan horticultural traditions, see Gilbert Wilson, "Agriculture of the Hidatsa Indians: An Indian Interpretation," University of Minnesota Studies in the Social Sciences No. 9 (November 1917); reprinted as *Buffalo Bird Woman's Garden: Agriculture of the Hidatsa Indians* (St. Paul: Minnesota Historical Society Press, 1987); and George F. Will and George E. Hyde, *Corn among the Indians of the Upper Missouri* (Lincoln: University of Nebraska Press, 1964). Pawnee women cultivated several varieties of corn, beans, and squash. See Gene Weltfish, *The Lost Universe: Pawnee Life and Culture* (Lincoln: University of Nebraska Press, 1965), 119–23.
15. Alice C. Fletcher, assisted by James R. Murie, "The Hako: Song, Pipe, and Unity in a Pawnee Calumet Ceremony," in *Twenty-second Annual Report of the Bureau of American Ethnology* (Washington, D.C.: U.S. Government Printing Office, 1904; reprint, Lincoln: University of Nebraska Press, 1996), 305. Here and throughout, page numbers pertain to the reprint editions of works cited.
16. Ibid., 81.
17. Joseph Medicine Crow, interview, January 20, 2000.
18. Gerard Baker, "The Buffalo as Part of the Mandan-Hidatsa Way of Life," in *Memory and Vision: Arts, Cultures, and Lives of Plains Indian People*, by Emma I. Hansen (Seattle: University of Washington Press, 2007), 146.
19. Lone Man, quoted in Frances Densmore, *Teton Sioux Music, Bureau of American Ethnology Bulletin* 61 (Washington, D.C.: U.S. Government Printing Office, 1918): 63–66.
20. John (Fire) Lame Deer and Richard Erdoes, *Lame Deer, Seeker of Visions: The Life of a Sioux Medicine Man* (New York: Simon and Schuster, 1972), 119.
21. Morgan Baillargeon and Leslie Tepper, *Legends of Our Times: Native Cowboy Life* (Vancouver: UBC Press and University of

Washington Press, 1998), 41. See also Hugh A. Dempsey, "Blackfoot," in *Handbook of North American Indians*, Vol. 13, Pt. 1, *Plains*, edited by Raymond J. DeMallie (Washington, D.C.: Smithsonian Institution, U.S. Government Printing Office, 2001), 606.

22. Baker, "The Buffalo," 146. For a description of the Buffalo Bull Society among the Mandan and Hidatsa, see Robert H. Lowie, "Societies of the Crow, Hidatsa and Mandan Indians," *Anthropological Papers of the American Museum of Natural History*, Vol. 11, Pt. 1, edited by Clark Wissler (New York: American Museum of Natural History, 1913), 291–93, 315–17.
23. Alfred W. Bowers, *Mandan Social and Ceremonial Organization* (Chicago: University of Chicago Press, 1950; reprint, Moscow: University of Idaho Press, 1991), 315–28; Alfred W. Bowers, "Hidatsa Social and Ceremonial Organization," *Bureau of American Ethnology Bulletin* 194 (Washington, D.C.: Smithsonian Institution, 1965; reprint, Lincoln: University of Nebraska Press, 1992): 433–66. George Catlin, *Letters and Notes on the Manners, Customs, and Conditions of the North American Indians: Written During Eight Years' Travel (1832–1839) amongst the Wildest Tribes of Indians in North America* (New York: Wiley and Putnam, 1844; reprint, New York: Dover Publications, 1973), 127.
24. See George Catlin, *O-kee-pa: A Religious Ceremony, and Other Customs of the Mandans* (London: Trubner, 1867; reprint, New Haven, Conn.: Yale University Press, 1967, edited by John C. Ewers), 54–55; Catlin, *Letters and Notes*, 155–77; Bowers, *Mandan Social and Ceremonial Organization*, 111–63.
25. Clark Wissler, "Societies of the Plains Indians," *Anthropological Papers of the American Museum of Natural History* (1916), 430–35; John C. Ewers, *The Blackfeet: Raiders on the Northwestern Plains* (Norman: University of Oklahoma Press, 1958), 106. Extensive Notes on the Motoki Society can be found in John Canfield Ewers Papers, Series II, Box 6, Glenbow Museum Archives, Calgary, Alberta.
26. Alfred L. Kroeber, "The Arapaho," *Bulletin of the American Museum of Natural History* 18 (1907; reprint, Lincoln: University of Nebraska Press, 1983): 210–26.
27. See Paul Dyck, "The Plains Indian Shield," *American Indian Art Magazine* 1, no. 1 (1975): 34–41.
28. Alma Hogan Snell, author interview, January 22, 2000, Plains Indian Museum, Cody, Wyoming.
29. Baker, "The Buffalo," 147.

CHAPTER 2 PROTECTING THE LAND AND THE PEOPLE

1. Amiotte, "Artists of Earth and Sky," 37.
2. For descriptions of early pedestrian buffalo-hunting methods, see Emma I. Hansen, *Memory and Vision: Arts, Cultures, and Lives of Plains Indian People* (Seattle: University of Washington Press, 2007): 107–11.
3. Frances Densmore, *Teton Sioux Music, Bureau of American Ethnology Bulletin* 61 (Washington, D.C.: Smithsonian Institution, 1918): 442.
4. Although Plains Indian people viewed hunting and warfare as men's responsibilities, women also had well-defined roles in both occupations. There are stories of warrior women who served courageously in battle, often saving or taking the place of a male family member. See Beatrice Medicine, "'Warrior Women'—Sex Role Alternatives for Plains Indian Women," in *The Hidden Half: Studies of Plains Indian Women*, edited by Patricia Albers and Beatrice Medicine (Lanham, Md.: University Press of America, 1983), 267–80; and John C. Ewers, "Women's Roles in Plains Indian Warfare," *Plains Indian History and Culture: Essays on Continuity and Change* (Norman: University of Oklahoma Press, 1997), 191–204.
5. Densmore, *Teton Sioux Music*, 178.
6. Wooden Leg, quoted in Thomas B. Marquis, *Wooden Leg: A Warrior Who Fought Custer*, reprint (Lincoln: University of Nebraska Press, 1957), 118; originally published as *A Warrior Who Fought Custer* (Minneapolis, Minn.: Midwest, 1931).
7. Iron Teeth, quoted in Thomas B. Marquis, "Iron Teeth, a Cheyenne Old Woman," in *Cheyenne and Sioux: The Reminiscences of Four Indians and a White Soldier*, compiled by Thomas B. Marquis and edited by Ronald H. Limbaugh (Stockton, Calif.: University of the Pacific, 1973), 5.
8. E. Adamson Hoebel, *The Cheyennes: Indians of the Great Plains* (New York: Holt, Rinehart and Winston, 1960), 70.
9. Plenty Coups, quoted in Frank B. Linderman, *Plenty-coups, Chief of the Crows*, reprint (Lincoln: University of Nebraska Press, 1962), 55; originally published as *American: The Life Story of a Great Indian, Plenty-coups, Chief of the Crows* (Rahway, N.J.: John Day, 1930).
10. Linderman, *Plenty-coups*, 55–56.
11. Joseph Medicine Crow, *From the Heart of the Crow Country: The Crow Indians' Own Stories* (New York: Orion Books, 1992), 42.
12. Ibid., 45.
13. Loretta Fowler, *Tribal Sovereignty and the Historical Imagination: Cheyenne-Arapaho Politics* (Lincoln: University of Nebraska Press, 2002), 8–12.
14. Wooden Leg, quoted in Marquis, *Wooden Leg*, 56–58.
15. Ibid., 58–59.
16. George Bird Grinnell, *The Cheyenne Indians: Their History and Ways of Life* (Lincoln: University of Nebraska Press, 1972), 2:48.
17. Stan Hoig, *The Peace Chiefs of the Cheyennes* (Norman: University of Oklahoma Press, 1980), 85–87.

18. Arthur Amiotte, author interview, May 2013.
19. Clark Wissler, *Societies of the Plains Indians, Anthropological Papers of the American Museum of Natural History*, Vol. 11, Pt. 1 (New York: American Museum of Natural History, 1916), 41–48; Densmore, *Teton Sioux Music*, 326–32.
20. Alfred L. Kroeber, "The Arapaho," *Bulletin of the American Museum of Natural History* 18 (1907; reprinted, Lincoln: University of Nebraska Press, 1983): 153–59; Loretta Fowler, "Arapaho," in *Handbook of North American Indians*, Vol. 13, Pt. 2, *Plains*, edited by Raymond J. DeMallie (Washington, D.C.: Smithsonian Institution, 2001), 844–46; Loretta Fowler, *Arapahoe Politics, 1851–1978: Symbols in Crises of Authority* (Lincoln: University of Nebraska Press, 1982), 9.
21. Kroeber, "The Arapaho," 207–8; Fowler, "Arapaho," 846; Fowler, *Arapahoe Politics*, 77.
22. Kroeber, "The Arapaho, 153–59; Fowler, "Arapaho," 844–46; Fowler, *Arapahoe Politics*, 9.
23. Alfred Kroeber, quoted in Jeffrey D. Anderson, *The Four Hills of Life: Northern Arapaho Knowledge and Life Movement* (Lincoln: University of Nebraska, 2001), 158.
24. Gloria A. Young, "Intertribal Religious Movements," in *Handbook of North American Indians*, Vol. 13, Pt. 2, *Plains*, edited by Raymond J. DeMallie (Washington, D.C.: Smithsonian Institution, 2001), 996.
25. Jean Afton, David Fridtjof Halaas, and Andrew E. Masich, *Cheyenne Dog Soldiers: A Ledgerbook History of Coups and Combat* (Denver: Colorado Historical Society, 1996), xxxvii; Mari Sandoz, *The Story Catcher* (Lincoln: University of Nebraska Press, 1963), 157.
26. Grinnell, *The Cheyenne Indians*, 187–88; Paul Dyck, "The Plains Indian Shield," *American Indian Art Magazine* 1, no. 1 (1975): 38.
27. Dyck, "The Plains Indian Shield," 34.
28. Ibid.
29. Robert H. Lowie, "The Religion of the Crow Indians," *Anthropological Papers of the American Museum of Natural History*, Vol. 25, Pt. 2 (New York: American Museum of Natural History, 1922), 409–10.
30. Ibid., 410.
31. Ibid., 418–19.
32. See Evan Maurer, *Visions of the People: A Pictorial History of Plains Indian Life* (Minneapolis, Minn.: Minneapolis Institute of Art, 1992), 125; and William Wildschut, *Crow Indian Medicine Bundles*, edited by John C. Ewers (New York: Museum of the American Indian and Heye Foundation, 1975), 67–68.
33. Medicine Crow and Viola, *Counting Coup*, 14.
34. Ibid., 15–16.
35. Hansen, *Memory and Vision*, 266–69.
36. See "Crow Tribe Welcomes Soldier Back from Her Tour in Iraq," *Billings Gazette*, August 11, 2004.
37. Curly Bear Wagner, author interview, June 26, 2006, Plains Indian Museum, Cody, Wyoming.

CHAPTER 3 WHITE SWAN

1. White Man Runs Him, quoted in "The Day of Death," in *Little Bighorn Remembered: The Untold Indian Story of Custer's Last Stand*, edited by Herman J. Viola (New York: Times Books, 1999), 23.
2. Medicine Crow noted that White Man Runs Him's name more accurately translates as "Chased by a White Man." White Man Runs Him received the name in recognition of his clan uncle, who "was once chased by a white trapper, apparently as a joke, much to the amusement of some Crow men." Joseph Medicine Crow, "The Crow Scouts after Little Bighorn," in Viola, *Little Bighorn Remembered*, 125, 128.
3. James Welch with Paul Stekler, *Killing Custer: The Battle of the Little Bighorn and the Fate of the Plains Indians* (New York: W. W. Norton, 1994), 285.
4. Several photographs of the scouts are in Edward S. Curtis, "The Apsaroke, or Crows," in *The North American Indian* (Cambridge, Mass.: The University Press, 1909), 4:1–128. Also see James S. Hutchins, *The Papers of Edward S. Curtis Relating to Custer's Last Battle* (El Segundo, Calif.: Upton and Sons, 2000); and James S. Hutchins, "Edward S. Curtis and Custer's Crow Scouts," in Viola, *Little Bighorn Remembered*, 154–69.
5. Elbridge A. Burbank, as told by Ernest Royce, *Burbank among the Indians* (Caldwell, Idaho: Caxton Printers, 1944), 154–61; Ernest Thompson Seton, *Sign Talk of the Cheyenne Indians and Other Cultures* (Mineola, N.Y.: Dover, 1918), v; Caroline Reynolds Riebeth, *J. H. Sharp among the Crow Indians, 1902–1910* (El Segundo, Calif.: Upton and Sons, 1985), 153; Forest Fenn, *The Beat of the Drum and the Whoop of the Dance: A Study of the Life and Work of Joseph Henry Sharp* (Santa Fe, N.M.: Fenn, 1983), 83.
6. Medicine Crow, "The Crow Scouts after Little Bighorn," 125.
7. Crow tribal member Alden Big Man wrote a brief biography of White Swan in association with a tomahawk attributed to the warrior. Acquired by William Wildschut in 1924, the tomahawk is currently in the collections of the National Museum of the American Indian. Alden Big Man, in Cécile R. Ganteaume, *Infinity of Nations: Art and History in the Collections of the National Museum of the American Indian* (Washington, D.C.: Smithsonian, 2010), 159.
8. Hansen, *Memory and Vision*, 162–64; Linderman, *Plenty-coups*, 100.
9. For a discussion of the motivations for Native American men to enlist as U.S. Army Scouts, see Thomas W. Dunlay, *Wolves for the Blue Soldiers: Indian Scouts and Auxiliaries with the United*

States Army, 1860–90 (Lincoln: University of Nebraska Press, 1982), 122–24.

10. White Swan was also identified by two different names. His name was sometimes translated as "White Goose," and according to Arikara scout Young Hawk, he was also called "Strikes Enemy." Orin G. Libby, *The Arikara Narrative of Custer's Campaign and the Battle of the Little Bighorn* (Norman: University of Oklahoma Press, 1998), 99.
11. Joseph Medicine Crow, "Custer and His Crow Scouts," in Viola, *Little Bighorn Remembered*, 117.
12. Libby, *The Arikara Narrative*, 113–15.
13. Frank B. Linderman, *Pretty-shield: Medicine Woman of the Crows*, reprint (Lincoln: University of Nebraska Press, 1974), 140. Originally published as *Red Mother: The Life Story of Pretty-shield, Medicine Woman of the Crows* (Rahway, N.J.: John Day, 1932).
14. Medicine Crow, "The Crow Scouts after Little Bighorn," 125.
15. Burbank and Royce, *Burbank among the Indians*, 154–61.
16. Publications on other paintings and drawings attributed to White Swan include Douglas E. Bradley, *White Swan: Crow Indian Warrior and Painter* (Notre Dame, Ind.: Snite Museum of Art, University of Notre Dame, 1991); David C. Cowles, "White Swan, Crow Artist at the Little Big Horn," *American Indian Art Magazine* 7, no. 4 (1982): 522–61; Candace S. Greene, "The White Swan Muslin: Deeds of Honor," in *Father Lindesmith's Collection: History into Art and Anthropology* (Notre Dame, Ind.: Snite Museum of Art, University of Notre Dame, 2012), 54–64; Kevin Smith, "The Native American Collection," in *Treasures of Gilcrease: Selections from the Permanent Collection*, edited by Anne Morand, Daniel C. Swan, Kevin Smith, and Sarah Ervin (Norman: University of Oklahoma Press, 2003), 101–200.
17. This incident is described in David Humphrey Miller, *Custer's Fall: The Indian Side of the Story* (Lincoln: University of Nebraska Press, 1985), 101.
18. Medicine Crow, "Custer and His Crow Scouts," 116–17.
19. Medicine Crow, "Crow Scouts after Little Bighorn," 127.

CHAPTER 4 ARTISTRY OF WOMEN

1. Beatrice Medicine, "Women's Roles," in *Memory and Vision: Arts, Cultures, and Lives of Plains Indian People*, by Emma I. Hansen (Seattle: University of Washington Press, 2007), 94.
2. Ibid., 94.
3. Katherine Weist, "Beasts of Burden and Menial Slaves: Nineteenth Century Observation of Northern Plains Indian Women," in *The Hidden Half: Studies of Plains Indian Women*, edited by Patricia Albers and Beatrice Medicine (Washington, D.C.: University Press of America, 1983), 38–41.
4. John Dunbar and Samuel Allis, "Letters Concerning the Presbyterian Mission in the Pawnee Country, Near Bellevue, Nebraska, 1831–1849," *Collections of the Kansas State Historical Society* 14 (1915–1918): 610–11.
5. Ella Deloria, *Speaking of Indians* (New York: Friendship Press, 1944). 40.
6. Alma Hogan Snell, author interview, January 22, 2000, Plains Indian Museum, Cody, Wyoming.
7. Ibid.
8. Medicine Crow, *From the Heart of the Crow Country*, 120.
9. For a conversation about traditional Crow tipis and their use at Crow Fair, see Heywood and Mary Lou Big Day, "*Ashta'ahile* (Crow Tipis)," in *Tipi: Heritage of the Great Plains*, edited by Nancy B. Rosoff and Susan Kennedy Zeller (Seattle: University of Washington Press, 2011), 69–75.
10. Mary Helen Medicine Horse, *A Dictionary of Everyday Crow: Crow-English/English-Crow* (Crow Agency, Mont.: Bilingual Materials Development Center, 1987), 42, 126.
11. Dale D. Old Horn and Timothy P. McCleary, *Apsáalooke Social and Family Structure* (Crow Agency, Mont.: Little Big Horn College, 1995), 51.
12. Ibid., 54; Timothy P. McCleary, *The Stars We Know: Crow Indian Astronomy and Lifeways* (Prospect Heights, Ill.: Waveland Press, 1997), 64.
13. Weltfish, *The Lost Universe*, 144–45, 379–81.
14. Just as the number of poles used in tipis varied, so did the number of hides and, consequently, the overall size of the lodges. Once horses became available to Plains tribes by the eighteenth century, women were able to construct larger lodges to be carried on horse-drawn travois. According to Lowie, Crow tipi covers required fourteen to eighteen buffalo hides. Robert H. Lowie, *The Crow Indians*, reprint (Lincoln: University of Nebraska Press, 1983), 87. According to Hassrick, the size of a Lakota tipi depended as much on the man's ability to provide hides as on the woman's ability to prepare them. Royal B. Hassrick, *The Sioux: Life and Customs of a Warrior Society*, reprint (Norman: University of Oklahoma Press, 1969), 215.
15. Weltfish, *The Lost Universe*, 144.
16. Ewers, *The Blackfeet*, 114–16.
17. Kroeber, "The Arapaho," 60–65; Hassrick, *The Sioux*, 214.
18. Ewers, *The Blackfeet*, 116.
19. Carl Sweezy, quoted in *The Arapaho Way: A Memoir of an Indian Boyhood*, edited by Althea Bass (New York: Clarkson N. Potter, 1966), 12.
20. Ibid., 11.
21. Ibid., 8.
22. Ibid., 10.

23. Deloria, *Speaking of Indians*, 56.
24. Ibid., 56–57.
25. Amiotte, author interview, January 20, 2000.
26. Linderman, *Pretty-shield*, 32–33.
27. Ibid., 34.
28. Snell, author interview, January 22, 2000.
29. Mardell Hogan Plainfeather, quoted in Peggy Albright, *Crow Indian Photographer: The Work of Richard Throssel* (Albuquerque: University of New Mexico Press, 1997), 150.
30. Emil Her Many Horses, "Woman's Dress," in *The Plains Indians: Artists of Earth and Sky*, edited by Gaylord Torrence (Paris: Skira Rizzoli, 2014), 182; and Evan M. Maurer, *The Native American Heritage: A Survey of North American Indian Art* (Chicago: Art Institute of Chicago, 1977), 45–46.
31. Arthur Amiotte, "Ritual Footsteps: Lakota Moccasins for Ceremonial Use," in *Plains Indian Art of the Early Reservation Era*, edited by Jill Ahlberg Yohe, with Janet Catherine Berlo (St. Louis: St. Louis Art Museum, 2016), 158–61.
32. Arthur Amiotte, cited in Yohe, *Plains Indian Art*, 161.
33. N. Scott Momaday, introduction to *Gifts of Pride and Love: Kiowa and Comanche Cradles*, edited by Barbara A. Hail (Providence, R.I.: Haffenrefer Museum of Anthropology, Brown University, 2000), 15.
34. Marquis, "Iron Teeth," 56.
35. Linda Poolaw, quoted in Barbara A. Hail, "A House for the Beginning of Life," in *Gifts of Pride and Love: Kiowa and Comanche Cradles*, edited by Barbara A. Hail (Providence, R.I.: Haffenrefer Museum of Anthropology, Brown University, 2000), 17.
36. Hail, "A House for the Beginning of Life," 23.
37. Ibid.
38. Vanessa Paukeigope Jennings, "Why I Make Cradles," in Hail, *Gifts of Pride and Love*, 95.

CHAPTER 5 LEADERSHIP, RESEPECT, AND CEREMONY

1. Joseph Medicine Crow, "Crow Tribal Leaders," in *Memory and Vision: Arts, Cultures, and Lives of Plains Indian People*, by Emma I. Hansen (Seattle: University of Washington Press, 2007), 198.
2. Ibid., 198.
3. Linderman, *Plenty-coups*, 57.
4. Hassrick, *The Sioux*, 16–17; James R. Walker, *Lakota Society*, edited by Raymond J. Demallie (Lincoln: University of Nebraska Press, 1992), 28–29; William K. Powers, *Oglala Religion* (Lincoln: University of Nebraska Press, 1982), 41; Marla N. Powers, *Oglala Women: Myth, Ritual, and Reality* (Chicago: University of Chicago Press, 1986), 26–27.
5. John G. Neihardt, *Black Elk Speaks: Being the Life Story of a Holy Man of the Oglala Sioux* (Lincoln: University of Nebraska Press, 1979), 56.
6. William K. Powers, *Oglala Religion*, 40–41; Marla N. Powers, *Oglala Women*, 26–27; Hassrick, *The Sioux*, 8, 27–28, 90.
7. Barbara A. Hail, *Hau, Kóla! The Plains Indian Collection of the Haffenreffer Museum of Anthropology* (Bristol, R.I.: Haffenreffer Museum of Anthropology, Brown University, 1980), 68.
8. Grinnell, *The Cheyenne Indians*, 336–340; Hoebel, *The Cheyennes*, 37–39.
9. Linderman, *Plenty-coups*, 63–64.
10. Ted J. Brasser, "Teton Sioux Man's Shirt, ca. 1860," in *Splendid Heritage: Perspectives on American Indian Art*, edited by John Warnock and Marva Warnock (Salt Lake City: University of Utah Press, 2009), 180.
11. Herbert J. Spinden, "The Nez Perce Indians," *Memoirs of the American Anthropological Association*, Vol. 2, Pt. 3 (Lancaster, Pa.: New Era, 1908), 217; Samuel Black, *Faithful to Their Tribe and Friends: Samuel Black's 1829 Fort Nez Perces Report*, edited by Dennis Baird (Moscow: University of Idaho Library, 2000), 22.
12. Marquis, *Wooden Leg*, 256.
13. Ibid., 85.
14. David W. Penney, *Art of the American Indian Frontier: The Chandler-Pohrt Collection* (Seattle: University of Washington Press, 1992), 107.
15. James R. Murie, "Ceremonies of the Pawnee, Part I: The Skiri," edited by Douglas R. Parks, *Smithsonian Contributions to Anthropology* 27 (Washington, D.C.: Smithsonian Institution, 1981), 45.
16. Murie, "Ceremonies of the Pawnee, Part I: The Skiri," 45; George Bird Grinnell, "Pawnee Mythology," *Journal of American Folklore* 6 (1893): 116; Mark van de Logt, *War Party in Blue: Pawnee Scouts in the U.S. Army* (Norman: University of Oklahoma Press, 2010), 20; Waldo R. Wedel, *The Dunbar-Allis Letters on the Pawnee* (New York: Garland Publishing, 1985), 707–8.
17. James R. Murie, "Ceremonies of the Pawnee, Part II: The South Bands," edited by Douglas R. Parks, *Smithsonian Contributions to Anthropology* 27 (Washington, D.C.: Smithsonian Institution, 1981), 335.
18. For a full description of the ceremony, see ibid., 385–94.
19. Beatrice Medicine, "Indian Women and the Renaissance of Traditional Religion," in *Sioux Indian Religion*, edited by Raymond J. DeMallie and Douglas R. Parks (Norman: University of Oklahoma Press, 1987), 170.
20. According to Frances Merle Haas, a fundamental value of the Arapaho people is *ni'iihi,'* "in a good way." The term refers to "living in accordance with the laws of protecting and caring for the earth."

It can also be translated as "in a sacred way." Frances Merle Haas, foreword to Sara Wiles, *Arapaho Journeys: Photographs and Stories from the Wind River Reservation* (Norman: University of Oklahoma Press, 2011), ix.

21. Scholars continue to research museum and private collections in order to connect works of art to specific artists. In her book on Kiowa and Comanche cradles, Barbara Hail was able to connect cradles in museum collections with known cradle makers through consultations with the descendants of the artists. It may still be possible to identify additional artists represented in museum collections by consulting with families and other community members. See Hail, *Gifts of Pride and Love.*
22. Grinnell, *The Cheyenne Indians*, 159.
23. Ibid., 161.
24. Ibid., 159–60.
25. Ibid., 160–64; Hoebel, *The Cheyennes*, 63–64.
26. Hoebel, *The Cheyennes*, 160–63. Grinnell attributed the description of the quilling society ceremony, in this publication, to a woman he identified as Picking Bones Woman. She achieved the highest honor for a quiller: the completion of thirty buffalo robes.
27. Kroeber, "The Arapaho," 30.
28. Barbara A. Hail, "To Honor Her Kindred: Women's Arts Centered in the Tipi," in *Tipi: Heritage of the Great Plains*, edited by Nancy B. Rosoff and Susan Kennedy Zeller (Seattle: University of Washington Press, 2011), 229.
29. Fowler, *Arapahoe Politics*, 112.
30. Hassrick, *The Sioux*, 223. W. K. Powers, *Oglala Religion*, 58–59. M. N. Powers, *Oglala Women*, 73–74.
31. Ewers, *The Blackfeet*, 119–20.
32. Hail, "To Honor Her Kindred," 124.
33. Ibid., 138.
34. Curly Bear Wagner, author interview, January 20, 2000, Plains Indian Museum, Cody, Wyoming.

CHAPTER 6 PLAINS INDIAN PEOPLE AND THEIR HORSES

1. Densmore, *Teton Sioux Music*, 302.
2. Although several historical concepts revolve around when and how Native people of the Plains first obtained horses, it is generally accepted that horses were distributed from the Southwest after the Pueblo Revolt of 1680, when the Spanish were driven out of the region. John C. Ewers provides detailed information based on historical documentation concerning the diffusion of the horse among the Blackfoot and other Plains peoples. See John C. Ewers. "The Horse in Blackfoot Indian Culture: With Comparative Material from Other Western Tribes," *Bureau of American Ethnology Bulletin* 159 (Washington, D.C.: Smithsonian Institution, 1955), 3–19; Herman J. Viola, *After Columbus: The Smithsonian Chronicle of the North American Indians* (Washington, D.C.: Smithsonian Institution, 1990), 60–61.
3. Preston Holder, *Hoe and the Horse on the Plains: A Study of Cultural Development among North American Indians* (Lincoln: University of Nebraska Press, 1970), 90–107.
4. N. Scott Momaday, *The Names: A Memoir* (Tucson: Sun Tracks/University of Arizona Press, 1987), 28.
5. Momaday, *The Names*, 28.
6. Quoted in Ewers, "The Horse in Blackfoot Indian Culture," 16.
7. Medicine Crow, *From the Heart of the Crow Country*, 101.
8. Baillargeon and Tepper, *Legends of Our Time*, 25.
9. Ibid., 48.
10. Marquis, *Wooden Leg*, 5.
11. Peter Nabokov, *Two Leggings: The Making of a Crow Warrior* (New York: Thomas I. Crowell, 1967), 191–92.
12. Densmore, *Teton Sioux Music*, 391.
13. Ibid., 388.
14. Linderman, *Plenty-coups*, 100.
15. Ewers, "The Horse in Blackfoot Indian Culture," 29.
16. Marquis, "Iron Teeth," 58.
17. Frederick E. Hoxie, *Parading through History: The Making of the Crow Nation in America, 1805–1933* (Cambridge: Cambridge University Press, 1995), 211–12.
18. Jaw also illustrated his war experiences in muslin paintings that displayed his body paint as well as that of his horse. See ibid., 388; Emma I. Hansen, "Cultural Expressions of Plains Native Arts," in *Splendid Heritage: Perspectives on American Indian Art*, edited by John Warnock and Marva Warnock (Salt Lake City: University of Utah Press, 2009), 11–12.
19. Medicine Crow, *From the Heart of the Crow Country*, 103.
20. Ibid., 103.
21. Densmore, *Teton Sioux Music*, 237.

CHAPTER 7 ENDURING LEGACIES OF THE PAUL DYCK COLLECTION

1. Arthur Amiotte, "A New and Different Life on a Small Part of a Very Old Place: Traditional Arts in the Early Reservation Period in the Dakotas, 1870–1920," in *Memory and Vision: Arts, Cultures, and Lives of Plains Indian People*, by Emma I. Hansen (Seattle: University of Washington Press, 2007), 246.
2. Andrew C. Isenberg, *The Destruction of the Bison: An Environmental History, 1750–1920* (Cambridge: Cambridge University Press, 2000), 93, 106.
3. Ibid., 131–32.

4. Valerius Geist, *Buffalo Nation: History and Legend of the North American Bison* (Stillwater, Minn.: Voyageur Press, 1996), 91.
5. Linderman, *Pretty-shield*, 250.
6. J. S. Clark, "A Pawnee Buffalo Hunt," *Chronicles of Oklahoma* 20, no. 4 (1942): 387–95.
7. Although oral histories documenting the increasing scarcity of buffalo and final hunting expeditions are significant events in tribal histories, Jeffrey Ostler argues that publications about Plains Indians' "last buffalo hunts" reflect "the standard trope of the 'Vanishing Indian'" and support the concept of history following the inevitable laws of "progress." See Jeffrey Ostler, "'The Last Buffalo Hunt' and Beyond Plains Sioux Economic Strategies in the Early Reservation Period," *Great Plains Quarterly* 21, no. 2 (2001): 115; and Brian W. Dippie, *The Vanishing American: White Attitudes and U.S. Indian Policy* (Lawrence: University Press of Kansas, 1991).
8. Plenty Coups, quoted in Linderman, *Plenty-coups*, 311.
9. David J. Wishart, *An Unspeakable Sadness: The Dispossession of the Nebraska Indians* (Lincoln: University of Nebraska Press, 1994), 160; George E. Hyde, *The Pawnee Indians* (Denver, Colo.: University of Denver Press, 1951; reprint, Norman: University of Oklahoma Press, 1974), 365.
10. Russell Thornton, *American Indian Holocaust and Survival: A Population History since 1492*, reprint (Norman: University of Oklahoma Press, 1990), 91.
11. Ibid., 94.
12. Ibid., 96–99.
13. Ibid., 95.
14. Ibid.
15. Mike Bruised Head, "The Impact and Effects of the Lewis and Clark Expedition from the Eyes of the Blackfoot," paper presented at the Plains Indian Museum Seminar "Native Perspectives on the Lewis and Clark Expedition," Buffalo Bill Center of the West, October 4, 2003.
16. Thornton, *American Indian Holocaust and Survival*, 101–2.
17. Amiotte, "Artists of Earth and Sky," 40.
18. Ostler, "'The Last Buffalo Hunt,'" 115–30.
19. Colin G. Calloway, "Change and Survival on the Great Plains," in *The Plains Indians: Artists of Earth and Sky*, edited by Gaylord Torrence (Paris: Skira Rizzoli, 2014), 33.
20. Jordan Dresser, *What Was Ours*, Mat Hames, director; Beth Hames, executive producer; film produced by Wyoming PBS, 2016.
21. Beatrice Medicine, "The Anthropologist as the Indian's Image Maker," *Indian Historian* 4, no. 1 (1971): 25–26.
22. Dresser, *What Was Ours.*
23. Hunter Old Elk, e-mail to author, October 26, 2016.

BIBLIOGRAPHY

ARCHIVAL SOURCES

Dyck, Paul. "A Passion for the Indian." Attachment C to *Plains Indian Buffalo Culture Collection Feasibility Study*, C4–C10. Rimrock, Ariz.: The Paul Dyck Foundation, 1994. Paul Dyck Papers, McCracken Research Library, Buffalo Bill Center of the West. Reprinted from Abe Chanin and Mildred Chanin, *This Land, These Voices: A Different View of Arizona History in the Words of Those Who Lived It* (Flagstaff, Ariz.: Northland Press, 1977), 246–53.

———. Transcript of interview with the *Tucson Arizona Daily Star*, September 1975. McCracken Research Papers, Buffalo Bill Center of the West, Cody, Wyoming.

Paul Dyck Foundation Research Institution of American Indian Culture. "News Release," June 25, 1987. Paul Dyck Papers, McCracken Research Library, Buffalo Bill Center of the West, Cody, Wyoming.

Paul Dyck Papers. McCracken Research Library, Buffalo Bill Center of the West, Cody, Wyoming.

BOOKS, ARTICLES, PAPERS, AND THESES

Afton, Jean, David Fridtjof Halaas, and Andrew E. Masich. *Cheyenne Dog Soldiers: A Ledgerbook History of Coups and Combat*. Denver: University Press of Colorado, 1998.

Albers, Patricia, and Beatrice Medicine. "The Role of Sioux Women in the Production of Ceremonial Objects: The Case of the Star Quilt." In *The Hidden Half: Studies of Plains Indian Women*, edited by Patricia Albers and Beatrice Medicine, 123–42. Washington, D.C.: University Press of America, 1983.

Albright, Peggy. *Crow Indian Photographer: The Work of Richard Throssel*. Albuquerque: University of New Mexico Press, 1997.

Amiotte, Arthur. "Artists of Earth and Sky." In *The Plains Indians: Artists of Earth and Sky*, edited by Gaylord Torrence, 35–45. Paris: Skira Rizzoli, 2014.

———. "The Lakota Sun Dance: Historical and Contemporary Perspectives." In *Sioux Indian Religion: Tradition and Innovation*, edited by Raymond J. DeMallie and Douglas R. Parks, 75–90. Norman: University of Oklahoma Press, 1987.

———. "A New and Different Life on a Small Part of a Very Old Place: Traditional Arts in the Early Reservation Period in the Dakotas, 1870–1920." In *Memory and Vision: Arts, Cultures, and Lives of Plains Indian People*, by Emma I. Hansen, 246–251. Seattle: University of Washington Press, 2007.

———. "Ritual Footsteps: Lakota Moccasins for Ceremonial Use." In *Plains Indian Art of the Early Reservation Era*, edited by Jill Ahlberg Yohe, with Janet Catherine Berlo, 158–61. St. Louis, Mo.: St. Louis Art Museum, 2016.

———. "The Sun Dance." In *Native American Dance: Ceremonies and Social Traditions*, edited by Charlotte Heth, 135–37. Washington, D.C.: National Museum of the American Indian, Smithsonian Institution, 1992.

Anderson, Jeffrey D. *The Four Hills of Life: Northern Arapaho Knowledge and Life Movement*. Lincoln: University of Nebraska Press, 2001.

Archambault, JoAllyn. "Sun Dance." In *Handbook of North American Indians*. Vol. 13, Pt. 2, *Plains*, edited by Raymond J. DeMallie, 983–95. Washington, D.C.: Smithsonian Institution, 2001.

Baillargeon, Morgan, and Leslie Tepper. *Legends of Our Times: Native Cowboy Life*. Vancouver: UBC Press and University of Washington Press, 1998.

Baker, Gerard. "The Buffalo as Part of the Mandan-Hidatsa Way of Life." In *Memory and Vision: Arts, Cultures, and Lives of Plains Indian People*, by Emma I. Hansen, 146–47. Cody, Wyo.: Buffalo Bill Historical Center; in association with Seattle: University of Washington Press, 2007.

Bass, Althea. *The Arapaho Way: A Memoir of an Indian Boyhood*. New York: Clarkson N. Potter, 1966.

Basso, Keith H. "Wisdom Sits in Places: Notes on a Western Apache Landscape." In *Senses of Place*, edited by Steven Feld and Keith H. Basso, 53–90. Santa Fe: School of American Research Press, 1996.

Berlo, Janet Catherine, ed. *Plains Indian Drawings 1865–1935: Pages from a Visual History*. New York: Harry N. Abrams, 1996.

Berthong, Donald J. *The Southern Cheyennes*. Norman: University of Oklahoma Press, 1963.

Big Day, Heywood. Foreword to *Sun Dance: The 50th Anniversary Crow Indian Sun Dance,* by Michael Crummett, vii. Helena, Mont.: Falcon Press, 1993.

Big Day, Heywood, and Mary Lou Big Day. *"Ashta'ahile* (Crow Tipis)." In *Tipi: Heritage of the Great Plains,* edited by Nancy B. Rosoff and Susan Kennedy Zeller, 69–75. Seattle: University of Washington Press, 2011.

Big Man, Alden. "Tomahawk Associated with Mee-nah-tsee-us (White Swan, Apsáalooke [Crow] ca. 1851–1904)." In *Infinity of Nations: Art and History in the Collections of the National Museum of the American Indian,* edited by Cécile R. Ganteaume, 158–59. Washington, D.C.: Smithsonian Institution, 2010.

Black, Samuel Black, and Dennis Baird, eds. *Faithful to Their Tribe and Friends: Samuel Black's 1829 Fort Nez Perces Report.* Moscow: University of Idaho Library, 2000.

Black Elk. *The Sixth Grandfather: Black Elk's Teachings Given to John C. Neihardt,* edited by Raymond J. DeMallie. Lincoln: University of Nebraska Press, 1984.

Bostwick, Todd W., Charles E. Rozaire, and George Kritzman. "The 1962–1972 Excavations of the Dyck Rockshelter along Wet Beaver Creek, Central Arizona: An Archival Reconstruction." *Verde Valley Archaeology Center Occasional Papers* No. 2. Camp Verde, Ariz., 2015.

Bowers, Alfred W. *Hidatsa Social and Ceremonial Organization. Smithsonian Institution Bureau of American Ethnology Bulletin* 194. Washington, D.C.: U.S. Government Printing Office, 1965. Reprint, Lincoln: University of Nebraska Press, 1992.

———. *Mandan Social and Ceremonial Organization.* Chicago: University of Chicago Press, 1950. Reprint, Moscow: University of Idaho Press, 1991.

Bradley, Douglas E. *White Swan: Crow Indian Warrior and Painter.* Notre Dame, Ind.: Snite Museum of Art, University of Notre Dame, 1991.

Brasser, Ted J. "Teton Sioux Man's Shirt, ca. 1860." In *Splendid Heritage: Perspectives on American Indian Art,* edited by John Warnock and Marva Warnock, 180. Salt Lake City: University of Utah Press, 2009.

Bruised Head, Mike. "The Impact and Effects of the Lewis and Clark Expedition from the Eyes of the Blackfoot." Paper presented at the Plains Indian Museum Seminar "Native Perspectives on the Lewis and Clark Expedition," Buffalo Bill Center of the West, Cody, Wyo., October 4, 2003.

Burbank, Elbridge A., as told by Ernest Royce. *Burbank among the Indians.* Caldwell, Idaho: Caxton Printers, 1944.

Calloway, Colin G. "Change and Survival on the Great Plains," In *The Plains Indians: Artists of Earth and Sky,* edited by Gaylord Torrence, 25–34. Paris: Skira Rizzoli, 2014.

Catlin, George. *Indian Art in Pipestone: George Catlin's Portfolio in the British Museum,* edited by John C. Ewers. Washington, D.C.: Smithsonian Institution Press, 1979.

———. *Letters and Notes on the Manners, Customs, and Condition of the North American Indians: Written During Eight Years' Travel (1832–1839) Amongst the Wildest Tribes of Indians in North America.* 2 vols. New York: Wiley and Putnam, 1844. Reprint, New York: Dover Publications, 1973.

———. *O-kee-pa, a Religious Ceremony, and Other Customs of the Mandans.* London: Trubner, 1867. Reprint, New Haven, Conn.: Yale University Press, 1967.

Chardon, Francis A. *Chardon's Journal at Fort Clark, 1834–39.* Pierre: State of South Dakota, 1932.

Clark, J. S. "A Pawnee Buffalo Hunt." *Chronicles of Oklahoma* 20, no. 4 (1942): 387–95.

Coe, Ralph T. *Sacred Circles: Two Thousand Years of North American Indian Art.* Kansas City, Mo.: Nelson Gallery Foundation, 1977.

Conn, Richard. *Circles of the World: Traditional Art of the Plains Indians.* Denver, Colo.: Denver Art Museum, 1982.

———. *Native American Art in the Denver Art Museum.* Denver, Colo.: Denver Art Museum, 1979.

Cowles, David C. "White Swan, Crow Artist at the Little Big Horn." *American Indian Art Magazine* 7, no. 4 (1982): 52–61.

Curtis, Edward S. "The Apsaroke, or Crows." In *The North American Indian,* 4:1–126. Cambridge, Mass.: The University Press, 1909.

Deloria, Ella C. *Speaking of Indians.* New York: Friendship Press, 1944. Reprint, Vermillion, S. Dak.: Dakota Books, 1992.

DeMallie, Raymond J., and John C. Ewers. "History of Ethnological and Ethnohistorical Research." In *Handbook of North American Indians.* Vol. 13, Pt. 1, *Plains,* edited by Raymond J. DeMallie, 23–43. Washington, D.C.: Smithsonian Institution, 2001.

Dempsey, Hugh A. "Blackfoot." In *Handbook of North American Indians.* Vol. 13, Pt. 1, *Plains,* edited by Raymond J. DeMallie, 604–28. Washington, D.C.: Smithsonian Institution, U.S. Government Printing Office, 2001.

Densmore, Frances. *Pawnee Music. Smithsonian Institution Bureau of American Ethnology Bulletin* 93. Washington, D.C.: U.S. Government Printing Office, 1929.

———. *Teton Sioux Music. Smithsonian Institution Bureau of American Ethnology Bulletin* 61. Washington, D.C.: U.S. Government Printing Office, 1918.

Dippie, Brian W. *The Vanishing American: White Attitudes and U.S. Indian Policy.* Lawrence: University Press of Kansas, 1991.

Dresser, Jordan. *What Was Ours.* Directed by Mat Hames. Beth Hames, Executive Producer. Film produced by Wyoming PBS, 2016.

Dunbar, John, and Samuel Allis. "Letters Concerning the Presbyterian Mission in the Pawnee Country, Near Bellevue, Nebraska, 1821–1849." *Collections of the Kansas State Historical Society* 14 (1915–1918): 570–741.

Dunlay, Thomas W. *Wolves for the Blue Soldiers: Indian Scouts and Auxiliaries with the United States Army, 1860–90*. Lincoln: University of Nebraska Press, 1982.

Dyck, Paul. *Brulé: The Sioux People of the Rosebud*. Flagstaff, Ariz.: Northland Press, 1971.

———. "The Plains Indian Shield." *American Indian Art Magazine* 1, no. 1 (1975): 34–41.

Ewers, John C. *The Blackfeet: Raiders on the Northwestern Plains*. Norman: University of Oklahoma Press, 1958.

———. *The Horse in Blackfoot Indian Culture: With Comparative Material from Other Western Tribes. Smithsonian Institution Bureau of American Ethnology Bulletin* 159. Washington, D.C.: U.S. Government Printing Office, 1955.

———. "The Humble Digging Stick: Symbol of Women's Contributions to Plains Indian Culture." Paper presented at the Plains Indian Museum Seminar, Buffalo Bill Center of the West, Cody, Wyo., September 28, 1996.

———. *Plains Indian History and Culture: Essays on Continuity and Change*. Norman: University of Oklahoma Press, 1997.

———. *Plains Indian Sculpture: A Traditional Art from America's Heartland*. Washington, D.C.: Smithsonian Institution Press, 1986.

Feest, Christian F. "American Indians and Ethnographic Collecting in Europe." *Museum Anthropology* 16, no. 1 (1992): 7–11.

Fenn, Forrest. *The Beat of the Drum and the Whoop of the Dance: A Study of the Life and Work of Joseph Henry Sharp*. Santa Fe, N.Mex.: Fenn, 1983.

Fish, Paul R., and Suzanne K. Fish. *Verde Valley Archaeology: Review and Perspective*, Research Paper No. 8. Flagstaff, Ariz.: Museum of Northern Arizona, 1977.

Fletcher, Alice C., assisted by James R. Murie. "The Hako: Song, Pipe, and Unity in a Pawnee Calumet Ceremony." In *Twenty-Second Annual Report of the Bureau of American Ethnology*. Washington, D.C.: U.S. Government Printing Office, 1904. Reprint, Lincoln: University of Nebraska Press, 1996.

Fowler, Loretta. "Arapaho." In *Handbook of North American Indians*. Vol. 13, Pt. 2, *Plains*, edited by Raymond J. DeMallie, 840–72. Washington, D.C.: Smithsonian Institution, 2001.

———. *Arapahoe Politics, 1851–1978: Symbols in Crises of Authority*. Lincoln: University of Nebraska Press, 1982.

Geist, Valerius. *Buffalo Nation: History and Legend of the North American Bison*. Stillwater, Minn.: Voyageur Press, 1996.

Gilman, Carolyn. *Lewis and Clark: Across the Divide*. Washington, D.C.: Smithsonian Books, 2003.

Gilman, Carolyn, and Mary Jane Schneider. *The Way to Independence: Memories of a Hidatsa Indian Family, 1840–1920*. St. Paul: Minnesota Historical Society, 1987.

Greene, Candace S. "The White Swan Muslin: Deeds of Honor." In *Father Lindesmith's Collection: History into Art and Anthropology*, edited by Joanne M. Mack, 54–64. Notre Dame, Ind.: Snite Museum of Art, University of Notre Dame, 2012.

Grinnell, Calvin. "The Oral Tradition of the Mandan and Hidatsa on Lewis and Clark." Paper presented at the Plains Indian Museum Seminar, Buffalo Bill Center of the West, Cody, Wyo., October 3, 2003.

Grinnell, George Bird. *The Cheyenne Indians: Their History and Ways of Life*, Vols. 1–2. New Haven: Yale University Press, 1923.

———. "Pawnee Mythology." *Journal of American Folklore* 6 (1893): 113–30.

Haas, Frances Merle. Foreword to *Arapaho Journeys: Photographs and Stories from the Wind River Indian Reservation*, by Sara Wiles, ix–x. Norman: University of Oklahoma Press, 2011.

Hail, Barbara A., ed. *Gifts of Pride and Love: Kiowa and Comanche Cradles*. Bristol, R.I.: Haffenreffer Museum of Anthropology, Brown University, 2000.

———. *Hau, Kóla! The Plains Indian Collection of the Haffenreffer Museum of Anthropology*. Bristol, R.I.: Haffenreffer Museum of Anthropology, Brown University, 1980.

———. "A House for the Beginning of Life." In *Gifts of Pride and Love: Kiowa and Comanche Cradles*, edited by Barbara A. Hail, 17–39. Bristol, R.I.: Haffenreffer Museum of Anthropology, Brown University, 2000.

———. "To Honor Her Kindred: Women's Arts Centered in the Tipi." In *Tipi: Heritage of the Great Plains*, edited by Nancy B. Rosoff and Susan Kennedy Zeller, 119–40. Seattle: University of Washington Press, 2011.

Hansen, Emma I. "The Art of Tipi Living." In *Tipi: Heritage of the Great Plains*, edited by Nancy B. Rosoff and Susan Kennedy Zeller, 69–75. Seattle: University of Washington Press, 2011.

———. "Crow Rawhide Cases, ca. 1850"; "Lakota Sioux Saddle Blanket, ca. 1850"; "Nez Perce Shirt, ca. 1850." In *Splendid Heritage: Perspectives on American Indian Art*, edited by John Warnock and Marva Warnock, 120–121; 142–143; 182–183. Salt Lake City: University of Utah Press, 2009.

———. "Cultural Expressions of Plains Native Arts." In *Splendid Heritage: Perspectives on American Indian Art*, edited by John Warnock and Marva Warnock, 11–13. Salt Lake City: University of Utah Press, 2009.

———. *Memory and Vision: Arts, Cultures, and Lives of Plains Indian People*. Buffalo Bill Historical Center, in association with Seattle: University of Washington Press, 2007.

———. "Powerful Images: Art of the Plains and Southwest." In *Powerful Images: Portrayals of Native America*, by Sarah Boehme, Gerald T. Conaty, Clifford Crane Bear, Emma I. Hansen, Mike Leslie, and James H. Nottage, 3–34. Seattle: University of Washington Press, 1998.

———. "Quirt"; "Ghost Dance Dress"; "Ghost Dance Drum." In *The Plains Indians: Artists of Earth and Sky*, edited by Gaylord Torrence, 174–75; 232–33; 238–39. Paris: Skira Rizzoli, 2014.

———. "Thread the Needle: Beauty in Utility." In *American Indian: Celebrating the Voices, Traditions, and Wisdom of Native Americans*, edited by Mariah Bear, 217–20. San Francisco: Weldon Owen, 2008.

Hansen, Emma I., with contributions by Rebecca T. Menlove, Anne Marie Shriver, and Rebecca S. West. *Plains Indian Museum Curator's Notes*. Cody, Wyo.: Buffalo Bill Historical Center, 2004.

Hassrick, Royal B. *The Sioux: Life and Customs of a Warrior Society*. Reprint, Norman: University of Oklahoma, 1988. Originally published 1969.

Her Many Horses, Emil. "Woman's Dress." In *The Plains Indians: Artists of Earth and Sky*, edited by Gaylord Torrence, 182. Paris: Skira Rizzoli, 2014.

Hoebel, E. Adamson. *The Cheyennes: Indians of the Great Plains*. New York: Holt, Rinehart and Winston, 1960.

Hoig, Stan. *The Peace Chiefs of the Cheyennes*. Norman: University of Oklahoma Press, 1980.

Holder, Preston. *The Hoe and the Horse on the Plains: A Study of Cultural Development among North American Indians*. Lincoln: University of Nebraska Press, 1970.

Hoxie, Frederick E. *Parading through History: The Making of the Crow Nation in America 1805–1935*. Cambridge: Cambridge University Press, 1995.

Hudson, Marilyn. "'We Are Not Here to Sell Our Land': The Mandan, Hidatsa, and Arikara People and the Flood Control Act of 1944." Paper presented at the Plains Indian Museum Seminar, Buffalo Bill Center of the West, Cody, Wyo., October 1, 2005.

Hutchins, James. "Edward S. Curtis and Custer's Crow Scouts." In *Little Bighorn Remembered*, edited by Herman J. Viola, 154–64. New York: Times Books, 1999.

———. *Papers of Edward S. Curtis Relating to Custer's Last Battle*. El Segundo, Calif.: Upton and Sons, 2000.

Hyde, George E. *The Pawnee Indians*. Denver, Colo.: University of Denver Press, 1951. Reprint, Norman: University of Oklahoma Press, 1974.

Irving, Washington. *The Adventures of Captain Bonneville, U.S.A., in the Rocky Mountains and the Far West*. 1837. Reprint, Norman: University of Oklahoma Press, 1961.

Isenberg, Andrew C. *The Destruction of the Bison: An Environmental History, 1750–1920*. Cambridge: Cambridge University Press, 2000.

James, Edwin. "Account of an Expedition from Pittsburgh to the Rocky Mountains, Performed in the Years 1829, 1820, under the Command of Major S. H. Long." In *Early Western Travels, 1748–1846*, Vol. 17, edited by Reuben Gold Thwaites. Cleveland, Ohio: Arthur H. Clark, 1905.

Jennings, Vanessa Paukeigope. "Why I Make Cradles." In *Gifts of Pride and Love: Kiowa and Comanche Cradles*, edited by Barbara Hail, 95–102. Bristol, R.I.: Haffenreffer Museum of Anthropology, Brown University, 2000.

Kroeber, Alfred L. "The Arapaho." *Bulletin of the American Museum of Natural History* 18. Reprint, Lincoln: University of Nebraska Press, 1983. Originally published 1902, 1904, 1907.

Lame Deer, John (Fire), and Richard Erdoes. *Lame Deer, Seeker of Visions: The Life of a Sioux Medicine Man*. New York: Simon and Schuster, 1972.

Libby, Orin G., ed. *The Arikara Narrative of Custer's Campaign and the Battle of Little Bighorn*. Norman: University of Oklahoma Press, 1998.

Liberty, Margo W., Raymond Wood, and Lee Irwin. "Omaha." In *Handbook of North American Indians*. Vol. 13, Pt.1, *Plains*, edited by Raymond J. DeMallie, 399–415. Washington, D.C.: Smithsonian Institution, 2001.

Linderman, Frank B. *Plenty-coups, Chief of the Crows*. Reprint, Lincoln: University of Nebraska Press, 1962. Originally published as *American: The Life Story of a Great Indian, Plenty-coups, Chief of the Crows*. Rahway, N.J.: John Day, 1930.

———. *Pretty-shield: Medicine Woman of the Crows*. Reprint, Lincoln: University of Nebraska Press, 1974. Originally published as *Red Mother: The Life Story of Pretty-shield, Medicine Woman of the Crows*. Rahway, N.J.: John Day, 1932.

Logt, Mark van de. *War Party in Blue: Pawnee Scouts in the U.S. Army*. Norman: University of Oklahoma Press, 2010.

Lowie, Robert H. *The Crow Indians*. New York: Farrar and Rinehart, 1935. Reprint, Lincoln: University of Nebraska Press, 1983.

———. "The Religion of the Crow Indians." *Anthropological Papers of the American Museum of Natural History*, Vol. 25, Pt. 2. New York: American Museum of Natural History, 1922.

———. "Societies of the Crow, Hidatsa and Mandan Indians." *Anthropological Papers of the American Museum of Natural History*, Vol. 11, Pt. 3. New York: American Museum of Natural History, 1913.

Mallery, Garrick. "A Calendar of the Dakota Nation." *Bulletin of the United States Geological and Geographical Survey of the Territories* 3, no. 1 (1877): 3–25. Washington, D.C.: U.S. Government Printing Office.

———. "Picture Writing of the American Indians." In *10th Annual Report of the Bureau of Ethnology for 1888–89*. Reprint, New York: Dover Publications, 1972. Originally published 1893.

Marquis, Thomas B. "Iron Teeth, a Cheyenne Old Woman." In *Cheyenne and Sioux: The Reminiscences of Four Indians and a White Soldier*, compiled by Thomas B. Marquis and edited by Ronald H. Limbaugh, 4–26. Pacific Center for Western Historical

Studies Monograph 3. Stockton, Calif.: University of the Pacific, Center for Western Historical Studies, 1973.

———. *Wooden Leg: A Warrior Who Fought Custer.* Reprint, Lincoln: University of Nebraska Press, 1957. Originally published as *A Warrior Who Fought Custer.* Minneapolis, Minn.: Midwest, 1931.

Marriott, Alice Lee, and Carol K. Rachlin. *American Indian Mythology.* New York: New American Library, 1968.

Maurer, Evan M. *The Native American Heritage: A Survey of North American Indian Art.* Chicago: Art Institute of Chicago, 1977.

———. *Visions of the People: A Pictorial History of Plains Indian Life.* Minneapolis, Minn.: Minneapolis Institute of Art, 1992.

McCleary, Timothy P. *The Stars We Know: Crow Indian Astronomy and Lifeways.* Prospect Heights, Ill.: Waveland Press, 1997.

Medicine, Beatrice. "The Anthropologist as the Indian's Image Maker." *Indian Historian* 4, no. 3 (1971): 25–29.

———. "Indian Women and the Renaissance of Traditional Religion." In *Sioux Indian Religion*, edited by Raymond J. DeMallie and Douglas R. Parks, 159–72. Norman: University of Oklahoma Press, 1987.

———. "'Warrior Women'—Sex Role Alternatives for Plains Indian Women." In *The Hidden Half: Studies of Plains Indian Women*, edited by Patricia Albers and Beatrice Medicine, 267–78. Washington, D.C.: University Press of America, 1983.

———. "Women's Roles." In *Memory and Vision: Arts, Cultures, and Lives of Plains Indian People*, by Emma I. Hansen, 94–96. Seattle: University of Washington Press, 2007.

Medicine Crow, Joseph. "The Crow Scouts after Little Bighorn." In *Little Bighorn Remembered*, edited by Herman J. Viola, 125–32. New York: Times Books, 1999.

———. "Crow Tribal Leaders." In *Memory and Vision: Arts, Cultures, and Lives of Plains Indian People*, by Emma I. Hansen, 198–201. Seattle: University of Washington Press, 2007.

———. "Custer and His Crow Scouts." In *Little Bighorn Remembered*, edited by Herman J. Viola, 105–22. New York: Times Books, 1999.

———. *From the Heart of the Crow Country: The Crow Indians' Own Stories.* New York: Orion Books, 1992.

Medicine Crow, Joseph, and Herman J. Viola. *Counting Coup: Becoming a Crow Chief on the Reservation and Beyond.* Washington, D.C.: National Geographic Society, 2006.

Medicine Horse, Mary Helen. *A Dictionary of Everyday Crow: Crow-English/English-Crow.* Crow Agency, Mont.: Bilingual Materials Development Center, 1987.

Miller, David Humphrey. *Custer's Fall: The Indian Side of the Story.* Lincoln: University of Nebraska Press, 1985.

Momaday, N. Scott. Introduction to *Gifts of Pride and Love: Kiowa and Comanche Cradles*, edited by Barbara A. Hail, 13–16. Bristol, R.I.: Haffenreffer Museum of Anthropology, Brown University, 2000.

———. *The Names: A Memoir.* Reprint, Tucson: University of Arizona Press, 1987. Originally published 1976.

Mooney, James. "The Ghost-Dance Religion and the Sioux Outbreak of 1890." In *Fourteenth Annual Report of the Bureau of Ethnology, 1892–93*, Part 2, 653–1136. Washington, D.C.: U.S. Government Printing Office, 1896. Reprint, Lincoln: University of Nebraska Press, 1991.

Moore, John H. *The Cheyenne Nation: A Social and Demographic History.* Lincoln: University of Nebraska Press, 1987.

Murie, James R. "Ceremonies of the Pawnee, Part I: The Skiri." Edited by Douglas R. Parks. *Smithsonian Contributions to Anthropology* 27. Washington, D.C.: Smithsonian Institution, 1981.

———. "Ceremonies of the Pawnee. Part II: The South Bands." Edited by Douglas R. Parks. *Smithsonian Contributions to Anthropology* 27. Washington, D.C.: Smithsonian Institution, 1981.

———. "Pawnee Indian Societies." *Anthropological Papers of the American Museum of Natural History*, Vol. 11, Pt. 7 (1914): 543–644.

Nabokov, Peter, ed. *Native American Testimony: A Chronicle of Indian-White Relations From Prophecy to the Present, 1492–1992.* 1978. Reprint, New York: Penguin Books, 1992.

——— *Two Leggings: The Making of a Crow Warrior.* New York: Thomas Y. Crowell, 1964.

Nabokov, Peter, and Lawrence Loendorf. *American Indians and Yellowstone National Park: A Documentary Overview.* Yellowstone National Park, Wyo.: National Park Service, 2002.

———. *Restoring a Presence: American Indians and Yellowstone National Park.* Norman: University of Oklahoma Press, 2004.

Neihardt, John G. *Black Elk Speaks: Being the Life Story of a Holy Man of the Oglala Sioux.* Reprint, Lincoln: University of Nebraska Press, 1979. Originally published 1932.

Old Horn, Dale D., and Timothy P. McCleary. *Apsáalooke Social and Family Structure.* Crow Agency, Mont.: Little Big Horn College, 1995.

Ostler, Jeffrey. "'The Last Buffalo Hunt' and Beyond Plains Sioux Economic Strategies in the Early Reservation Period." *Great Plains Quarterly* 21, no. 2 (2001): 115–130.

Parks, Douglas R., ed. *Traditional Narratives of the Arikara Indians.* 4 vols. Lincoln: University of Nebraska Press, 1991.

Parks, Douglas R., and Waldo R. Wedel. "Pawnee Geography: Historical and Sacred." *Great Plains Quarterly* 5, no. 3 (1985): 143–76.

Penney, David W. *Art of the American Indian Frontier: The Chandler-Pohrt Collection.* Seattle: University of Washington Press, 1992.

Peters, Virginia Bergman. *Women of the Earth Lodges: Tribal Life on the Plains.* New Haven, Conn.: Archon Books, 1995.

Petersen, Karen Daniels. *Plains Indian Art from Fort Marion.* Norman: University of Oklahoma Press, 1971.

Pike, Zebulon Montgomery. *The Expeditions of Zebulon Montgomery Pike to Headwaters of the Mississippi River, through Louisiana*

Territory, and in New Spain, during the Years 1805–1807. Minneapolis, Minn.: Ross and Haines, 1965.

Powers, Marla N. *Oglala Women: Myth, Ritual, and Power.* Chicago: University of Chicago Press, 1986.

Powers, William K. *Oglala Religion.* Lincoln: University of Nebraska Press, 1977.

Reid, Gordon. *Head-Smashed-In Buffalo Jump.* Calgary, AB: Fifth House Press, 2002.

Riebeth, Caroline Reynolds. *J.H. Sharp among the Crow Indians, 1902–1910.* El Segundo, Calif.: Upton and Sons, 1985.

Rosoff, Nancy B., and Susan Kennedy Zeller, eds. *Tipi: Heritage of the Great Plains.* Seattle: University of Washington Press, 2011.

Sandoz, Mari. *The Story Catcher.* Lincoln: University of Nebraska Press, 1963.

Schneider, Mary Jane. "Three Affiliated Tribes." In *Handbook of North American Indians.* Vol. 13, Pt. 1, *Plains*, edited by Raymond J. DeMallie, 391–98. Washington, D.C.: Smithsonian Institution, 2001.

———. "Women's Work: An Examination of Women's Roles in Plains Indian Arts and Crafts." In *The Hidden Half: Studies of Plains Indian Women*, edited by Patricia Albers and Beatrice Medicine, 101–22. Washington, D.C.: University Press of America, 1983.

Seton, Ernest Thompson. *Sign Talk of the Cheyenne Indians and Other Cultures.* Minneola, N.Y.: Dover Publications, 1918.

Smith, Kevin. "The Native American Collection." In *Treasures of Gilcrease: Selections from the Permanent Collection*, edited by Anne Morand, Kevin Smith, Daniel C. Swan, and Sarah Erwin, 95–122. Norman: University of Oklahoma Press, 2003.

Snell, Alma Hogan. *Grandmother's Grandchild: My Crow Indian Life.* Edited by Becky Matthews. Lincoln: University of Nebraska Press, 2000.

Spinden, Herbert J. "The Nez Percé Indians." *Memoirs of the American Anthropological Association* 2, no. 3 (1908): 217. Lancaster, Pa.: New Era Printing.

Stamm, Henry E., IV. *People of the Wind River: The Eastern Shoshones, 1825–1900.* Norman: University of Oklahoma Press, 1999.

Standing Bear, Luther. *My Indian Boyhood.* Boston: Houghton Mifflin, 1931. Reprint, Lincoln: University of Nebraska Press, 1988.

———. *My People the Sioux.* Edited by E. A. Brininstool. New York: Houghton Mifflin, 1928. Reprint, Lincoln: University of Nebraska Press, 1975.

Stands In Timber, John, and Margot Liberty, with the assistance of Robert M. Utley. *Cheyenne Memories.* New Haven, Conn.: Yale University, 1967. Reprint, Lincoln: University of Nebraska Press, 1972.

Thornton, Russell. *American Indian Holocaust and Survival: A Population History since 1492.* Reprint, Norman: University of Oklahoma Press, 1990. Originally published 1987.

Torrence, Gaylord. *The American Indian Parfleche: A Tradition of Abstract Painting.* Seattle: University of Washington Press in association with the Des Moines Art Center, 1994.

———, ed. *The Plains Indians: Artists of Earth and Sky.* Paris: Skira Rizzoli, 2014.

Utley, Robert M. *The Last Days of the Sioux Nation.* New Haven, Conn.: Yale University Press, 1963.

VanDevelder, Paul. *Coyote Warrior: One Man, Three Tribes, and the Trial That Forged a Nation.* Boston: Little, Brown, 2004.

Viola, Herman J. *After Columbus: The Smithsonian Chronicle of the North American Indians.* Washington, D.C.: Smithsonian Institution, 1990.

———. "The Day of Death." In *Little Bighorn Remembered: The Untold Indian Story of Custer's Last Stand*, edited by Herman J. Viola, 23–32. New York: Times Books, 1999.

———. *Diplomats in Buckskins: A History of Indian Delegations in Washington City.* Bluffton, S.C.: Rivilo Books, 1995.

Voget, Fred W. *The Shoshoni-Crow Sun Dance.* Norman: University of Oklahoma Press, 1984.

Voget, Fred W., assisted by Mary K. Mee. *They Call Me Agnes: A Crow Narrative Based on the Life of Agnes Yellowtail Deernose.* Norman: University of Oklahoma Press, 1995.

Walker, James R. *Lakota Society.* Edited by Raymond J. Demallie. Lincoln: University of Nebraska Press, 1992.

Warnock, John, and Marva Warnock, eds. *Splendid Heritage: Perspectives on American Indian Art.* Salt Lake City: University of Utah Press, 2009.

Wedel, Waldo R. *The Dunbar-Allis Letters on the Pawnee.* New York: Garland, 1985.

Weist, Katherine. "Beasts of Burden and Menial Slaves: Nineteenth Century Observation of Northern Plains Indian Women." In *The Hidden Half: Studies of Plains Indian Women*, edited by Patricia Albers and Beatrice Medicine, 29–62. Washington, D.C.: University Press of America, 1983.

Welch, James, with Paul Stekler. *Killing Custer: The Battle of the Little Bighorn and the Fate of the Plains Indians.* New York: W. W. Norton, 1994.

Weltfish, Gene. *The Lost Universe: Pawnee Life and Culture.* Lincoln: University of Nebraska Press, 1965.

Wildschut, William. *Crow Indian Medicine Bundles.* Edited by John C. Ewers. New York: Museum of the American Indian Museum, Heye Foundation, 1975.

Wiles, Sara. *Arapaho Journeys: Photographs and Stories from the Wind River Reservation.* Norman: University of Oklahoma Press, 2011.

Will, George F., and George E. Hyde. *Corn among the Indians of the Upper Missouri.* Lincoln: University of Nebraska Press, 1964.

Wilson, Gilbert L. "Agriculture of the Hidatsa Indians: An Indian Interpretation." University of Minnesota Studies in the Social Sciences No. 9. Reprinted as *Buffalo Bird Woman's Garden: Agriculture of the Hidatsa Indians*. St. Paul: Minnesota Historical Society Press, 2009. Originally published 1917.

———. *Waheenee: An Indian Girl's Story: Told by Herself to Gilbert L. Wilson*. St. Paul, Minn.: Webb, 1927. Reprint, Lincoln: University of Nebraska Press, 1981.

Winship, George Parker. "The Coronado Expedition, 1540–1542." In *Fourteenth Annual Report of the Bureau of American Ethnology to the Secretary of the Smithsonian Institution, 1892–1893*. Pt. 1. Washington, D.C.: Smithsonian Institution, 1896.

Wishart, David J. *An Unspeakable Sadness: The Dispossession of the Nebraska Indians*. Lincoln: University of Nebraska Press, 1994.

Wissler, Clark. "Societies and Dance Associations of the Blackfoot Indians." *Anthropological Papers of the American Museum of Natural History*, Vol. 11, Pt. 4 (New York: American Museum of Natural History, 1913), 359–460.

———, ed. *Societies of the Plains Indians. Anthropological Papers of the American Museum of Natural History*, Vol. 11, Pt. 1 (New York: American Museum of Natural History, 1916).

Wood, Raymond J., and Lee Irwin. "Mandan." In *Handbook of North American Indians*. Vol. 13, Pt. 1, *Plains*, edited by Raymond J. DeMallie, 349–64. Washington, D.C.: Smithsonian Institution, 2001.

Yellowman, Gordon L. Sr. "Noaha-Vose—Hoxehe?Eohe?E." Paper presented at the Plains Indian Museum Seminar, Buffalo Bill Historical Center, Cody, Wyoming, September 15, 2000.

Yellowtail, Thomas. *Yellowtail, Crow Medicine Man and Sun Dance Chief: An Autobiography as Told to Michael Oren Fitzgerald*. Norman: University of Oklahoma Press, 1991.

Young, Gloria A. "Intertribal Religious Movements." In *Handbook of North American Indians*. Vol. 13, Pt. 2, *Plains*, edited by Raymond J. DeMallie, 996–1010. Washington, D.C.: Smithsonian Institution, 2001.

Young, Gloria A., and Erik D. Gooding. "Celebrations and Giveaways." In *Handbook of North American Indians*. Vol. 13, Pt. 2, *Plains*, edited by Raymond J. DeMallie, 1011–25. Washington, D.C.: Smithsonian Institution, 2001.

INDEX

Page numbers in *italics* indicate illustrations.

Copyedited by Nancy L. Warrington
Indexed by Sherry L. Smith
Book design and composition by Julie Rushing
Set in Warnock Pro and Scala Sans Pro
Jacket design by Julie Rushing
Image prepress by University of Oklahoma Printing Services
Manufactured by Four Colour Print Group, China
Printed on 157 gsm Sun matte
Bound in JHT cloth